THE REBIRTH OF TERRITORY

The concept of territory is central in international law, but a detailed analysis of how the concept is used in both discourse and practice has been lacking until now. Rather than reproducing the established understanding of territoriality within the international legal order, this study suggests that the discipline of international law relies on an outmoded spatial paradigm. Gail Lythgoe argues for a complete overhaul of our understanding of territory, to engage more effectively with key processes, structures, and actors relevant to contemporary global law and governance. In this new theoretical account of an essential aspect of public international law, she argues that territory is a dynamic social reality created by the exercise of power. Territories are constituted by the practices of a more diverse array of actors than is acknowledged. Mapping the reassembling of functions, Lythgoe argues these new spaces are being constituted by state and non-state actors alike.

GAIL LYTHGOE is a lecturer in Global Law at the University of Edinburgh. Her research has appeared in *International Organizations Law Review*, *Canadian Yearbook of International Law*, and *European Journal of International Law*.

CAMBRIDGE STUDIES IN INTERNATIONAL AND COMPARATIVE LAW: 186

Established in 1946, this series produces high-quality, reflective and innovative scholarship in the field of public international law. It publishes works on international law that are of a theoretical, historical, cross-disciplinary or doctrinal nature. The series also welcomes books providing insights from private international law, comparative law and transnational studies which inform international legal thought and practice more generally.

The series seeks to publish views from diverse legal traditions and perspectives, and of any geographical origin. In this respect it invites studies offering regional perspectives on core *problématiques* of international law, and, in the same vein, it appreciates contrasts and debates between diverging approaches. Accordingly, books offering new or less orthodox perspectives are very much welcome. Works of a generalist character are greatly valued and the series is also open to studies on specific areas, institutions or problems. Translations of the most outstanding works published in other languages are also considered.

After seventy years, Cambridge Studies in International and Comparative Law sets the standard for international legal scholarship and will continue to define the discipline as it evolves in the years to come.

A list of books in the series can be found at the end of this volume.

THE REBIRTH OF TERRITORY

GAIL LYTHGOE
University of Edinburgh

CAMBRIDGE
UNIVERSITY PRESS

CAMBRIDGE
UNIVERSITY PRESS

Shaftesbury Road, Cambridge CB2 8EA, United Kingdom

One Liberty Plaza, 20th Floor, New York, NY 10006, USA

477 Williamstown Road, Port Melbourne, VIC 3207, Australia

314–321, 3rd Floor, Plot 3, Splendor Forum, Jasola District Centre, New Delhi – 110025, India

103 Penang Road, #05-06/07, Visioncrest Commercial, Singapore 238467

Cambridge University Press is part of Cambridge University Press & Assessment,
a department of the University of Cambridge.

We share the University's mission to contribute to society through the pursuit of
education, learning and research at the highest international levels of excellence.

www.cambridge.org
Information on this title: www.cambridge.org/9781009377911

DOI: 10.1017/9781009377874

First published 2024

A catalogue record for this publication is available from the British Library

Library of Congress Cataloging-in-Publication Data
Names: Lythgoe, Gail, author.
Title: The rebirth of territory / Gail Lythgoe, University of Edinburgh.
Description: Cambridge, United Kingdom ; New York , NY : Cambridge University Press, 2024. |
Series: Cambridge studies in international and comparative law |
Includes bibliographical references and index.
Identifiers: LCCN 2023040239 (print) | LCCN 2023040240 (ebook) | ISBN 9781009377911
(hardback) | ISBN 9781009377898 (paperback) | ISBN 9781009377874 (epub)
Subjects: LCSH: Territory, National. | Jurisdiction (International law) | Jurisdiction, Territorial.
Classification: LCC KZ3675 .L98 2024 (print) | LCC KZ3675 (ebook) | DDC 341.4/2–dc23/eng/
20231003
LC record available at https://lccn.loc.gov/2023040239
LC ebook record available at https://lccn.loc.gov/2023040240

ISBN 978-1-009-37791-1 Hardback

CONTENTS

ACKNOWLEDGEMENTS

It is traditional to end with the most important people for a book's acknowledgements, but I have rarely read to the end of these. If you are one of those readers, then you should know this book would not have happened without Akbar Rasulov. He has been my chief sounding board, inspiration, and support.

The book effort has benefited from the institutional, intellectual, and personal support and advice I have received over the years. I want to thank everyone who has helped me during this journey. There are too many to name, and no doubt I will accidentally miss very important people, but I want to particularly thank the following.

First, I want to thank my PhD supervisors Professor Christian Tams and Dr Charlie Peevers. Both were and continue to be incredibly supportive, engaging, and empowering. I am very much indebted to Christian Tams, whose comments and advice have been invaluable in shaping first the PhD project, then the book, but also me. I am tremendously grateful for his patience, guidance, and support, and for the many opportunities over the years. He has taught me much about brevity and the art of being succinct, but I may have ways to go yet. I am so grateful for Charlie Peevers' input and advice on this project, her continual advice on many things, and friendship. Thank you both, immensely.

To those who have read and commented on, or even examined, drafts, I want to thank Jean d'Aspremont, Eleni Methymaki, and George Pavlakos. Your comments and advice have shaped this argument and my writing. Many of the ideas in this book have been tried and tested over the years at conferences and workshops and pushed further in discussions during those special social moments that in-person events afford us. Thank you to Andrea Bianchi, Catherine Brölmann, Phil Burton, Pat Capps, Richard Collins, Eliana Cusato, Dan Danielsen, Deval Desai, Beshara Doumani, Lorenzo Gasbarri, John Haskell, Isabelle Haßfurther, Devika Hovell, David Kennedy, Jan Klabbers,

Martti Koskenniemi, Hans Lindahl, Euan MacDonald, Scott Newton, Kalypso Nicolaïdis, Sarah Nouwen, Anne Orford, Paul O'Connell, Umut Özsu, Sundhya Pahuja, Keisha-Khan Perry, Nik Rajkovic, Guy Fiti Sinclair, Thomas Skouteris, Cait Storr, Wiebke Staff, Gavin Sullivan, Jens Theilen, and Joseph Weiler, who have given me opportunities, posed questions, and offered feedback and thoughts at various points. The European Society of International Law, with its interest groups and annual conferences, has been an invaluable forum over the years. Thank you to all the organising and programme committees.

For all their support and banter, I want to thank many at the Glasgow Centre for International Law and Security and the friends in and outside Glasgow I have made along the way. There are too many to name, but special thanks go to Jeanne Gillet, Eleni Methymaki, Asli Olcay, Athene Richford, Jessica Schechinger, and Joanna Wilson.

I would be remiss if I did not blame and thank Antonios Tzanakopoulos, without whose very early advice I would never have started this journey – thanks, I think. I also want to dearly thank Rebecca Mignot-Mahdavi for her friendship, inspiration, and light. Thank you to everyone at the Manchester Law School, but especially Jean d'Aspremont, Luke Graham, John Haskell, and Yenkong Hodu, who were not only excellent colleagues but also dear friends.

There are many who have enabled this project in different ways over the years. I want to thank everyone at the Max Planck Institute for the Study of Religious and Ethnic Diversity for my time there, especially Elisabeth Badenhoop, Mareike Riedel, Stefan Salomon, and Ayelet Schachar. The intellectually stimulating research environments in Glasgow, St Andrews, Göttingen, Manchester and more recently Edinburgh have contributed greatly to my research, and I warmly thank the researchers and staff in all institutions for this. I want to thank the OUP, OXIO, EJIL, ESIL Interest Group on International Organisations, ESIL DAB, and EJIL:Talk! teams for making it easy for me to focus on my research when necessary over the years.

Back to the traditional order of things. Above all, I could not be where I am today without my family. The biggest acknowledgement of course went already to Akbar Rasulov – no words will do justice summing up how grateful I am for you and the support and advice you have given me. Thank you to my parents for their support and counsel. I am here today because of your unending support and belief in me, and everything you have equipped me with. Thank you to all my family, especially my sister,

Karen, for your unwavering support, and most of all for the time we have sacrificed that we could and should have spent together – time which I am glad we can start to make up now.

Note Regarding Chapter 5

Parts of this chapter appear in:

Gail Lythgoe, 'Distinct Persons; Distinct Territories: Rethinking the Spaces of International Organisations' (2022) 19 International Organisations Law Review; and

Gail Lythgoe, 'The Changing "Landscape" of Sovereignty Viewed through the Lens of International Tax: Reterritorializing the Offshore' (2022) 59 Canadian Yearbook of International Law/Annuaire canadien de droit international 171.

TABLE OF CASES

Al-Skeini and Others v The United Kingdom [2011] Grand Chamber, European Court of Human Rights Application no. 55721/07

Application Instituting Proceedings, Aerial Incident of 10 August 1999, Pakistan v India (ICJ)

Award of the Arbitral Tribunal in the First Stage of the Proceedings between Eritrea and Yemen (Territorial Sovereignty and Scope of the Dispute), Eritrea and Yemen Award [1998] Permanent Court of Arbitration (PCA) 1996-04, 1 Vol XXII pp. 209–332, 17

Case Concerning Delimitation of the Maritime Boundary in the Gulf of Maine Area (Canada–United States of America), Judgment (1984) ICJ Reports 246 (International Court of Justice)

Case Concerning the Frontier Dispute (Burkino Faso/Republic of Mali), Judgment [1986] ICJ Reports 554 (International Court of Justice)

Case Concerning Kasikili/Sedudu Island (Botswana/Namibia), Judgment [1999] ICJ Reports 1999, p. 1045

Case Concerning Maritime Delimitation and Territorial Questions between Qatar and Bahrain (Qatar v Bahrain), Merits [2001] ICJ Reports 2001, p. 40 (International Court of Justice)

Case Concerning Military and Paramilitary Activities in and against Nicaragua (Nicaragua v United States of America), Judgment (Merits) [1986] ICJ Reports 1986 14 (International Court of Justice)

Case Concerning Right of Passage over Indian Territory (Portugal v India), Judgment [1960] ICJ Reports 1960 6 (International Court of Justice)

Case Concerning Sovereignty over Pedra Branca/Pulau Batu Puteh, Middle Rocks and South Ledge (Malaysia/Singapore), Judgment [2008] ICJ Reports 2008 12 (International Court of Justice)

Corfu Channel (United Kingdom of Great Britain and Northern Ireland v Albania), Judgment [1949] ICJ Reports 1949 4 (International Court of Justice)

Dispute Concerning Coastal State Rights in the Black Sea, Sea of Azov, and Kerch Strait, Ukraine and the Russian Federation [2020] Annex VII Arbitral Tribunal PCA Case No. 2017-06

Fisheries Case (United Kingdom v Norway), Judgment 116 (International Court of Justice)

Georgia v Russia (II) (Application no 38263/08), Judgment Merits [2021] European Court of Human Rights, Grand Chamber 38263/08

Government of the Cayman Islands v Commission, Case T-85/03 (Court of Justice of the European Union)

In the Matter of the Chagos Marine Protected Area Arbitration between the Republic of Mauritius and The United Kingdom of Great Britain and Northern Ireland, Award (Annex VII Arbitral Tribunal, UNCLOS)

In the Matter of the South China Sea Arbitration, The Republic of the Philippines and the People's Republic of China, Award [2016]

Island of Palmas Case (Netherlands/USA) (1928) Volume II Reports of International Arbitral Awards 829 (Permanent Court of Arbitration)

Jaloud v The Netherlands [2014] Grand Chamber, European Court of Human Rights Application no. 47708/08

Land, Island and Maritime Frontier Dispute (El Salvador v Honduras: Nicaragua intervening), Judgment [1992] ICJ Reports 1992 351 (International Court of Justice)

Legal Status of Eastern Greenland (Norway v Denmark) [1933] PCIJ Ser. A/B, No. 53 (Permanent Court of International Justice)

Legality of the Threat or Use of Nuclear Weapons, Advisory Opinion [1996] 1 ICJ Reports 1996, p. 226 (International Court of Justice)

Maritime Delimitation in the Black Sea, Romania v Ukraine, Judgment [2009] ICJ Reports 2009, p. 61 (International Court of Justice)

Maritime Delimitation in the Caribbean Sea and the Pacific Ocean (Costa Rica v Nicaragua) and Land Boundary in the Northern Part of Isla Portillos (Costa Rica v Nicaragua), Judgment [2018] ICJ Reports 2018, p. 139 (International Court of Justice)

Nationality Decrees Issued in Tunis and Morocco (French Zone) on November 8th, 1921, Great Britain v France, Advisory Opinion (1923) no. 4 (1923) PCIJ Series B no. 4 (Permanent Court of International Justice)

North Sea Continental Shelf Cases (Federal Republic of Germany/Denmark; Federal Republic of Germany/Netherlands), Judgment 3 (International Court of Justice)

Pretty v United Kingdom [2002] European Court of Human Rights Application no. 2346/02

Reparation for Injuries Suffered in the Service of the United Nations, Advisory Opinion [1949] ICJ Reports 1949, p. 174 (International Court of Justice)

The Government of the State of Eritrea and The Government of the Republic of Yemen, Award on Territorial Sovereignty and Scope of the Dispute [1996] (1998) XXII RIAA 211 (Permanent Court of Arbitration)

TABLE OF TREATIES, RESOLUTIONS, AND ACTS OF INTERNATIONAL ORGANISATIONS

Treaties

Covenant of the League of Nations 1919 (108 LNTS 188)

Convention on the Rights and Duties of States 1933 (165 LNTS 19) ('Montevideo Convention')

Convention on International Civil Aviation 1944 (15 UNTS 295) ('ICAO Convention')

Charter of the United Nations 1945 (1 UNTS XVI) ('UNC')

Statute of the International Court of Justice 1946 (33 UNTS 993) ('ICJ Statute')

Vienna Convention on the Law of Treaties 1969 (1155 UNTS 331) ('VCLT')

United Nations Convention on the Law of the Sea 1982 (1833 UNTS 3, UN Reg No I-31363) ('UNCLOS')

Agreement relating to the Implementation of Part XI of the United Nations Convention on the Law of the Sea of 10 December 1982 (1836 UNTS 3) ('1994 Implementing Agreement')

Marrakesh Agreement Establishing the World Trade Organization 1994 (1867 UNTS 3) ('WTO Agreement')

Treaty of Amsterdam amending the Treaty on European Union, the Treaties Establishing the European Communities and Certain Related Acts 1997 (OJ C340/1) ('Treaty of Amsterdam')

Consolidated versions of the Treaty on European Union and the Treaty on the Functioning of the European Union 2012 (2012/C 326/01) ('TEU' and 'TFEU')

Treaty on the Prohibition of Nuclear Weapons 2017 (A/CONF.229/2017/8) ('TPNW')

Protocol to the Treaty Establishing the African Economic Community Relating to the Free Movement of Persons, Right of Residence and Right of Establishment 2018 ('AEC Protocol')

UN Resolutions and Documents

United Nations General Assembly Resolution 1514 (XV): Declaration on the granting of independence to colonial countries and peoples (1960) (UN Doc A/RES/1514 (XV)) ('UNGAR 1514 (XV)')

United Nations General Assembly Resolution 2625 (XXV): Declaration on Principles of International Law concerning Friendly Relations and Cooperation among States in accordance with the Charter of the United Nations (1970) (UN Doc A/RES/2625 (XXV)) ('UNGAR 2625 (XXV)')

United Nations General Assembly Resolution 48/263: Agreement relating to the Implementation of Part XI of the United Nations Convention on the Law of the Sea of 10 December 1982 (1994) (UN Doc A/RES/48/263) ('UNGAR 48/263')

United Nations Security Council Resolution 1031 (1995) on implementation of the Peace Agreement for Bosnia and Herzegovina and transfer of authority from the UN Protection Force to the multinational Implementation Force 1995 (UN Doc S/RES/1031(1995)) ('UNSCR 1031')

United Nations Security Council Resolution 1244 (1999) on the deployment of international civil and security presences in Kosovo 1999 (UN Doc S/RES/1244(1999)) ('UNSCR 1244')

Regulation No 1999/1 on the Authority of the Interim Administration in Kosovo 1999 (UNMIK/REG/1999/1)

Draft Articles on the Responsibility of International Organisations 2011 (UN Doc A/RES/66/100, Annex) ('DARIO')

United Nations General Assembly Resolution 67/19. Status of Palestine in the United Nations 2012 (UN Doc A/RES/67/19) ('UNGAR 67/19')

EU Law

Commission Regulation (EC) No 2257/94 of 16 September 1994 laying down quality standards for bananas [1994] OJ L245/6 ('Commission Regulation No. 2257/94 (1994)')

Directive 98/70/EC of the European Parliament and of the Council of 13 October 1998 relating to the quality of petrol and diesel fuels and amending Council Directive 93/12/EEC, [1998] OJ L350/58 ('Directive 98/70/EC (1998)')

Directive 2003/88/EC of the European Parliament and of the Council of 4 November 2003 concerning certain aspects of the organisation of working time 2003 ([2003] OJ L299/9)

Council Regulation (EC) No 2007/2004 of 26 October 2004 establishing a European Agency for the Management of Operational Cooperation at the External Borders of the Member States of the European Union [2004] OJ L349/1 ('Council Regulation 2007/2004 (2004)')

Regulation (EU) No 995/2010 of the European Parliament and of the Council of 20 October 2010 laying down the obligations of operators who place timber and timber products on the market [2010] OJ L295/23 ('Regulation 995/2010 (2010)')

Regulation (EU) No 2015/757 of the European Parliament and of the Council of 29 April 2015 on the monitoring, reporting and verification of carbon dioxide emissions from maritime transport, and amending Directive 2009/16/EC [2015] OJ L123/55 ('Regulation 2015/757 (2015)')

Commission Implementing Decision (EU) 2015/789 of 18 May 2015 as regards measures to prevent the introduction into and the spread within the Union of Xylella fastidiosa (C(2015) 3415)

Regulation (EU) No 2016/399 of the European Parliament and of the Council of 9 March 2016 on a Union Code on the rules governing the movement of persons across borders ([2016] OJ L77/1) ('EU Regulation 2016/399')

Directive (EU) 2016/1164 of 12 July 2016 laying down rules against tax avoidance practices that directly affect the functioning of the internal market ([2016] OJ L193/1)

Regulation (EU) 2016/1624 of the European Parliament and of the Council of 14 September 2016 on the European Border and Coast Guard and amending Regulation (EU) 2016/399 of the European Parliament and of the Council and repealing Regulation (EC) No 863/2007 of the European Parliament and of the Council, Council Regulation (EC) No 2007/2004 and Council Decision 2005/267/EC ([2016] OJ L251/1) ('EU Regulation 2016/1624')

Other

Global Charter-Agenda for Human Rights in the City, United Cities and Local Governments, Committee for Social Inclusion, Participatory Democracy and Human Rights 2011

The Nantes Declaration of Mayors and Subnational Leaders on Climate Change 2013

ABBREVIATIONS

AEC	African Economic Community
ALR	American legal realism
AO	Advisory Opinion
ASEAN	Association of Southeast Asian Nations
AU	African Union
BIT	bilateral investment treaty
CHM	common heritage of mankind
CIL	customary international law
CIS	Commonwealth of Independent States
CLS	critical legal studies
ea	emphasis added
ECJ	European Court of Justice
ECtHR	European Court of Human Rights
EEA	European Economic Area
EEZ	exclusive economic zone
EIB	European Investment Bank
EPZ	export processing zone
EU	European Union
FAO	Food and Agriculture Organization
FATF	Financial Action Task Force
IAEA	International Atomic Energy Agency
ICANN	Internet Corporation for Assigned Names and Numbers
ICC	International Chamber of Commerce
ICJ	International Court of Justice
ILC	International Law Commission
IMF	International Monetary Fund
IR	international relations
ISA	International Seabed Authority
ISO	International Organization for Standardization
ITU	International Telecommunication Union
LoN	League of Nations
NATO	North Atlantic Treaty Organization

NGO	non-governmental organisation
OAS	Organization of American States
OECD	Organisation for Economic Co-operation and Development
OPCW	Organisation for the Prohibition of Chemical Weapons
PCIJ	Permanent Court of International Justice
SDG	sustainable development goal
SEZ	special economic zone
SOFA	status of forces agreement
TEU	Treaty on European Union
TPNW	Treaty on the Prohibition of Nuclear Weapons
UN	United Nations
UNCLOS	United Nations Convention on the Law of the Sea
UNESCO	United Nations Educational, Scientific and Cultural Organization
UNFCC	United Nations Framework Convention on Climate Change
UNGA	United Nations General Assembly
UNHCR	United Nations High Commissioner for Refugees
UNMIK	United Nations Interim Administration Mission in Kosovo
UNSC	United Nations Security Council
UNSG	United Nations Secretary General
UNTAC	United Nations Transitional Authority in Cambodia
UNTAET	United Nations Transitional Administration in East Timor
WFP	World Food Programme
WHO	World Health Organization
WTO	World Trade Organization

1

Introduction

> I've been thinking about 'space' for a long time. But usually I've come at it indirectly, through some other kind of engagement. The battles over globalisation, the politics of place, the question of regional inequality, the engagements with 'nature' as I walk the hills, the complexities of cities. Picking away at things that don't seem quite right. Losing political arguments because the terms don't fit what it is you're struggling to say. Finding myself in quandaries of apparently contradictory feelings. It is through these persistent ruminations – that sometimes don't seem to go anywhere and then sometimes do – that I have become convinced both that the implicit assumptions we make about space are important and that, maybe, it could be productive to think about space differently.
>
> Doreen Massey, *For Space*[1]

In recent decades, international lawyers have sought to make sense of the development and entrenchment of the many processes and phenomena associated with globalisation and global law and governance and their effects on the role and importance of everything from the likes of the concept of sovereignty, the role of the state, and the place of domestic and international law. This surge of interest has sparked many interesting debates. In the scholarship emerging from these, globalisation and global governance is typically seen to present a problem for international law – a legal order which 'articulate[s] around the system of sovereign and independent states'[2] and its operative concepts, such as sovereignty and territory – because it signals the displacement of competences, powers, and functions away from their typical assembly inside territorial states.

Lying underneath the surface of much of these discourses is a conceptual and theoretical indeterminacy deriving from the, often unperceived, conflicting nature of the spaces of globalisation and the space of state

[1] Massey (2005) at 1.
[2] Hinojosa-Martínez (2019).

sovereignty. Globalisation is often understood as having changed the 'importance and meaning of space, place, distances and borders' since it is 'not hindered or prevented by territorial or jurisdictional boundaries'[3] of states. Globalisation and global governance are habitually imagined as taking place in a smooth global space of continual movement, a space that never settles, a space that is often imprecise and taken as a totality. This is fundamentally at odds with state space, understood as a static phenomenon, which is of vital importance to international law's implicit geography. This radical contrast between state space and the spaces of globalisation, between territorial space and the spaces of flow, between the spaces of modernity and spaces of, dare I say, postmodernity, is more or less present at the surface of much of contemporary international law writing. Yet, little attention seems to have been given to many of the basic background assumptions driving this way of thinking. What is the relationship between space, law, and power? What constitutes state territorial practice and thought? What is the concept of territory's spatial characteristics? What sort of spatial logic informs the exercise of governance by non-state actors? This failure to undertake a sustained in-depth critical examination of international law's implicit theory of space and the role it plays in constituting its theory of power and of law has resulted in a persistent tendency, even among those international law scholars whose capacity for critical reflection in other contexts remains unprecedented, to prejudge the nature of territory and unintentionally prioritise the importance of state space.

Space is a factor of law that is often assumed in international legal discourse and legal reasoning, and the question 'what is the relationship between law and space?' is taken for granted. Yet concepts such as statehood, jurisdiction, and sovereignty are deeply spatialised theoretical categories – in the sense that they are mediated and informed by a very specific set of spatial assumptions. Not only this, but their inherent spatial outlook directly structures the discipline's broader theoretical framework and engagement with all manner of political and economic phenomena and processes, from war and refugee flows to capital and markets. Indeed, assumptions about the space and time of international law, what I call international law's spatial imaginary, are fundamental to international law's constitution and operationalisation. If the structure of the international legal system is indeed undergoing such a radical

[3] Hudson (1998) 89, 90.

transformation due to global governance and globalisation, as is often asserted, it seems all the more crucial then that the geographies and spatial frameworks implied and produced by the various processes of globalisation are subjected to critical scrutiny, as orthodox concepts must be too. But while the subject of globalisation – and concerns about whether this means the end of sovereignty or the state as we know it – has been addressed in the discipline of international law, the question of its geographic and spatial constitution has received less study. Where space is discussed, state territory tends to be the space in focus; the old statocentric conceptions of legal spatiality provide the governing model. This is reflective of a wider issue as, generally, where the subject of space is raised in any international law context, the course of theoretical discussions typically turns either to a surface-level analysis of the concept of state territory or to spaces whose construction is a direct reference to the concept of state territory, such as, for example, the High Seas, *terra nullius*, cities, or the common heritage of mankind (CHM).

The continuing theoretical hegemony of the concept of state territory prevents the discipline from being able to make sense of the new territories created by globalisation and global governance, resulting in an enduring sense of confusion and disorientation. The limited spatial imaginary of international law misdirects attention and prompts the proliferation of questions such as: 'are borders still relevant?' or 'has territory been replaced by other logics of organising governance?' If global governance processes no longer rely on a legal geography centred around state territories, does that mean that states are declining in significance?[4] One does not need to go far to find evidence of such inquiries in international law scholarship.[5]

The discipline of international law is not alone in grappling with questions about the decline or continuing relevance of the state, territory, and borders. The same inquiries are also present in other disciplines and in the broader arena of public discourse.[6] Indeed, according to some

4 Sassen (2000) 109, 109.

5 Schachter (1997) 7, 7; Krieger and Nolte (2016); Ryngaert and Zoetekouw (2014); Bethlehem (2014) 9; Koller (2014) 25; Douglas (1997) 165; Kwiecień [2012] 45; Buzan and Little (1999) 89; 'Spaces beyond Sovereignty' (2019).

6 Syal (2016); Dalrymple (2012); Hanson (2016); Davis (2008); Setser (2008). Indeed, Massey highlights that 'If once it was "time" that framed the privileged angle of vision, today, so it is often said, that role has been taken over by space . . . One of the moving forces in social science thinking in recent years has been an urge to respond positively: to "spatialise". For reasons which range from a deeply political desire to challenge old

theoretical traditions, many of these questions have been with us for some time. Already in 1848 Marx and Engels, for example, wrote that the 'expanding market … chases the bourgeoisie over the entire *surface* of the globe' and observed that 'all fixed, fast-frozen relations … are swept away, all new-formed ones become antiquated before they can ossify. All that is solid melts into air.'[7] Underlying this narrative, although never explicitly acknowledged, is the idea of a fundamental clash between the spatial logics of the market contained within state territory – with its presumed centralised framework of state control and state law-making processes – and global markets with their supposedly uncontainable, dynamic, and unpredictable political and economic flows. The static state territory versus spaces of flow assumption is clear here. This thinking, however, is also structured by the same geographic imaginary of the world that operates in international law; it is a geography that can only observe state territories and the globe at large.

One response seeking to make sense of the changes and challenges globalisation and global law and governance have supposedly brought to the territorial paradigm is Teubner and Fischer-Lescano's influential idea of the move from territoriality to functionality. They argue that the organising logic of legal regimes is changing such that they now 'define [] the external reach of their jurisdiction along issue-specific rather than territorial lines'.[8] As part of this, they suggest there has now emerged a model of a 'global society without an apex or centre'.[9] Teubner and Fischer-Lescano's account has been taken up in different disciplines including political science, international relations, and geography.[10] In international law discourse, a good example of its adoption can be found in the writings of Brölmann,[11] Arcuri and Violi,[12] Milano,[13]

formulations, through a characterisation of "postmodern" times as "spatial rather than temporal" … much serious attention has been devoted to what has been called "the spatialisation of social theory" … for a number of authors "globalisation" has been the prime form taken by this effort to spatialise sociological thinking' (Massey (2005) at 62). The 'spatial turn' more broadly therefore seems related to this 'postmodern shift'.

7 Emphasis added, from Marx and Engels (2010) at 16.

8 Teubner and Fischer-Lescano (2004) 999, 1009.

9 ibid at 1017; quote originally in Luhmann (1981) at 22.

10 Palan (1998) 625; Helmig and Kessler (2007) 240; Sassen (2013) 21; Mezzadra and Neilson (2013).

11 Brölmann (2007).

12 Arcuri and Violi in Kuijer and Werner (2017) at 175–216.

13 Milano (2013).

Pistor,[14] and others, who apply the functionalist hypothesis to study various aspects of the contemporary international legal system. The term 'deterritorialisation' is often used to capture the idea of this movement away from territoriality towards functionality.

There is much to be gained from these perspectives. However, the spatiality on which they all rely – that the system of global governance has moved from the logic of territoriality to functionality – has always seemed to me to reproduce the same underlying spatiality of the present understanding of spaces in international law. This was something, like Massey, I wanted to keep picking at. It seemed to me that state space dominates the landscape to such an extent that scholars often struggle to see past or through it. As a result, several issues arise. In presenting the global society as a political system without apex or centre, this narrative portrays the corresponding political spaces as smooth, wild, and abstract, which fundamentally misrepresents, indeed fails to notice, their spatial logics.

Drawing such a stark contrast between a territoriality model centred around the concept of state territory and a functionality model centred around the concept of 'no territory' also leaves little room for the notion that the logic of global governance in this age of globalisation can ever be reconciled with the enduring relevance of state territory. Witness the repeated objections and assertions that one might call the 'territory still matters' counter-narratives produced as frequently by international lawyers as by scholars from other disciplinary backgrounds.[15] For example:

> The State remains central to modern-day public international law and contemporary international relations, and territoriality is one of the most characteristic features, if not the most characteristic feature, of the State. *Territoriality still significantly shapes our contemporary legal system.* Most treaties still take State territory as the spatial application, but more importantly in the absence of a centralised international authority the functioning and enforcement of international law is largely dependent on effective territorial control to avoid a situation in which no entity responds to infringements of rules of international law.[16]

[14] Pistor (2017) 491.

[15] This may appear in different words, but the underlying idea is still the same, see: Kuijer and Werner, 'The Paradoxical Place of Territory in International Law', Bílková, 'A State Without Territory?', and Arcuri and Violi, 'Reconfiguring Territoriality in International Economic Law' in Kuijer and Werner (2017).

[16] Emphasis added, from Kuijer and Werner (2017) at 4.

The phrasing is not always as direct as this. Sometimes the argument is cloaked in more indirect language – for example, 'the global legal order is still significantly shaped along territorial lines'[17] – but it comes down to the same basic idea that 'territory still matters'. Scholars have found analyses claiming the 'end of geography',[18] or the advent of full deterritorialisation[19] problematic, drawing attention to the many ways in which (state-)territory is still relevant. Many highlight how territorial reasoning remains central: 'while it might be more difficult for States to defend their territory in the era of globalization, the territory of the State clearly remains the main unit of security . . . in times of crisis people turn back to territory'.[20] Others have emphasised its continuing role in the broader operationalisation of the legal system,[21] or in the context of jurisdictional practices.[22]

However, it would be more accurate to think of both Teubner and Fischer-Lescano's hypothesis, as well other scholars', as being less a claim about full deterritorialisation, or the wholesale replacement of territory with functionality, and more of an attempt to acknowledge the advent of a process where territory matters *alongside* the move to functional ordering; where territory is not fully displaced or wholly irrelevant. Moreover, it is conceivable, on this view of things, that practices creating deterritorialisation are uneven among the different fields of law: perhaps territory matters 'more' for international refugee law than, say, for international economic law.

But this nuanced hypothesis only partly addresses the problem. There is a further, more important, reason why the functionalist and deterritorialisation responses are incomplete, beyond the idea that evidently state territory still seems to matter. However, the argument requires an analysis of the spaces assumed in functionalists' accounts

[17] Arcuri and Violi in Kuijer and Werner (2017) at 180.

[18] Bethlehem (2014); Koller (2014); Landauer (2014) 31.

[19] Brölmann (2007); Elden (2005) 8.

[20] Bílková in Kuijer and Werner (2017) at 38–39. This was a theme in the recent pandemic. Many felt they saw the apparatus of the state more clearly than ever. The return to the local was prominent in our everyday lives, especially during 'lockdowns'. Rather than 'the nation state striking back', Christian Tams and I proposed 'viewing the response to Covid-19 as a multi-layered regime of governing public health in operation. This regime integrates different levels of decision-making, from the global to the local', but our experience was of the local delivery of this, not the global coordination; Lythgoe and Tams (2020) 3.

[21] Arcuri and Violi in Kuijer and Werner (2017) at 180.

[22] Bílková in Kuijer and Werner (2017) at 39.

which has not yet been made. Indeed, one of the objectives of this book is to make that argument. The starting point of this argument, in a nutshell, is this: the functionalist hypothesis loses sight of, and fails to account for, the spatial character of global governance and its political and legal realities. Functionalist theories propose that there has been a move away from a territorial logic to one of functions. The ordering of the international legal and political systems is conceived without an account of the corresponding space in which these systems exist and operate as if the corresponding processes, competences, and functions are not now exercised with regard to any specific territorial framework. Put simply, there is a move from theories of an international system with an overly determined spatial logic, to one without any account of space. I do not share this view. These competences and functions continue to exist and are exercised *somewhere*. Once we understand this, we have two further insights: first, that many deterritorialisation theories lose sight of the 'spatial' – offering an aspatial and certainly an aterritorial narrative; and second, that they do so because they think of territory only as state territory. Territory is associated only with the spaces of states.

It could, of course, be argued that the 'new' space presumed by the functionalist narrative is the space of the 'global'. But such a solution creates more problems than it seems to resolve. Firstly, it implies that the different functionally ordered regimes operate equally and simultaneously in a single, smooth, uniform space. Secondly, it implies that calling this space 'global' automatically settles the question of its spatial structure and configuration. Both of these suggestions are inaccurate, and one only needs to consider the actual exercise of governance functions traditionally associated with the concept of sovereignty by non-state actors, such as the European Union (EU), African Union (AU), Organisation for Economic Co-operation and Development (OECD), World Bank, or the International Seabed Authority (ISA), to name but a few, to see why. None of these organisations, strictly speaking, has a global reach, nor are their legal spaces uniform and equivalent.

This point leads me to a further observation regarding the shift to deterritorialised functionalist ordering: this account of contemporary global governance is essentially incomplete. For the most part, the accounts tend to focus only on *the move away from* territory to functions. In my view, this only presents the beginning of the story. No account is given of the ongoing spatial dynamics of functions within the new legal and political regimes. There is little to no discussion about *where* functions go nor of the spatial logics of the new spaces in which they are exercised. In short, the spaces of relocation or reterritorialisation are missing. As a result, functions and powers now exercised 'outside', 'beyond', or 'between' state territories appear to be 'floating free' of the highly specific territorialised legal order that is international law. This leads me to another claim I make in this book: such theories cannot account for reterritorialisation because the territories of non-state actors are invisible to international legal thought *because* its orthodox spatial imaginary only makes visible state territories.

The debates regarding what is happening to 'territory' and 'sovereignty' or 'states' in the face of globalisation and increasing global governance are intriguing, as is the counter-narrative 'territory still matters'. The discourse seeking to make sense of and respond to the effects of globalisation on the international legal order caused me to question how we think about the concepts of territory and sovereignty in this age. Clearly, territory still matters and yet acknowledging this fact does not undo any of the challenges recent trends in global governance have raised to international law's arrangement of space as a framework built around stable, fixed units of state territory 'over which' sovereignty is exercised.

The answer to many of these questions, I suggest, begins with the recognition that the discipline of international law, by and large, operates on the basis of an outdated spatial paradigm. The discipline's understanding of territory is objectified or 'thingified', and much of the knowledge developed in other social sciences to apprehend space, including the space of territory, as relational and constructed is absent. The concept of territory is unproblematised, both in international legal theory and in mainstream international law discourse. Territory is understood as simply existing as a fact of life. Further, concepts like subjecthood, sovereignty, territorial sovereignty, and jurisdiction are themselves fundamentally structured by this outdated conceptualisation of territory. The very role of territory in structuring the operationalisation of these concepts is also significantly underappreciated in international law discourse. As a result of this outdated spatial paradigm, the discipline becomes incapable of recognising the possibility of the emergence of any new territories. Where the state is the only referent for territory in orthodox international legal theory, and all international legal spaces – such as those designated as *terra nullius* – are understood and constituted only in relation to state territory (the fact that they *are not state territory*), other legal spaces and territories are unknowable.

Solving this problem requires a systematic deconstruction and rethinking of this overly determined conception of territory. One way to achieve this goal is to examine how the concept has developed in other disciplines. By doing so, we can undetermine international law's conception, reconstitute its understanding of spatiality more generally, and as a result make visible the spaces and territories currently unfamiliar to international legal thought. To do this, however, we need to re-examine not only the concept of territory but also those fundamental building blocks of international law which are spatially mediated: concepts such as subjecthood, sovereignty and territorial sovereignty, and jurisdiction. By so doing, because of this study and rethink, I propose that it is possible to 'territorialise' that which is thought to have floated 'free' into abstract global space.

1.1 Terminology

Before explaining the structure of the argument in this book, let me first outline some considerations relating to terminology.

1.1.1 Territory

By far the most troublesome term is 'territory'. It is problematic because 'territory' refers both to a certain specific concept, understood and imagined in many ways, and it will also be the name of a certain kind of space. The interpretation I advocate uses territory to refer to *a space created for and by the exercise of power*, without prejudging which actor or institution exercises that power. This is not how most international lawyers tend to understand the concept. In Chapter 3, I evidence that international lawyers tend to use territory to indicate an object. But while 'territory' is a noun, there is a tendency in many disciplines 'of overemphasising its apparent "thingness" and . . . neglect [] its relations to a range of social phenomena, most especially the social activities, practices, and processes that are implicated in its production and transformation.'[23]

To recognise this distinction, at times I use the phrase 'territory as understood by international lawyers'; most of my discussion of 'territory' throughout Chapters 2 and 3 uses territory in this sense. As I show in Chapter 3, the traditional concept of territory assumed by most international lawyers has a dominant meaning and configuration: when international lawyers use territory, by and large, it stands for *state*

[23] Delaney (2005) at 13.

territory, even if territory is also sometimes used to discuss territorial administration by international organisations. I therefore often use the term '(state-)territory' to represent this.

The concept of territory I propose is based on a rethinking of space that was carried out in philosophy and geography in the 1970s onwards, but which does not yet seem to have impacted the discipline of international law greatly. I propose this concept in some detail in Chapter 4, which is written in a way to hopefully enable those working with international law to start recognising the existence of an entirely different concept of space. This conceptualisation understands territory as neither container nor object but as something that does not exist without the social relations which provide the conditions for its constitution. It is a space created because of control and also the space in relation to which control is exercised.

To avoid terminological overlap, I might have called this 'second' concept something else, currently invisible in the eyes of international law, avoiding the vocabulary of territory and territoriality altogether. But alternatives were problematic. No other term 'fits'. Territory 2.0 might have implied a more advanced territory, and yet, in a way, I advocate a more basic, less normative, less statocentric, and 'de-reified' understanding. Distinguishing the concept of territory proposed here from the traditional understanding used in the discipline by, for example, capitalising one as 'Territory' and the other simply 'territory', seemed unusable in practice and to have negative ramifications if picked up and used on an ongoing basis. I do not want to think of one as more important than the other, which is usually implied by capitalisation. I might have given the legal and political spaces produced and inhabited by international organisations an entirely new name altogether, but that would be inventing a term for the sake of it – not least because there is an entirely suitable word with a matching definition already available. Such duplication was nonsensical to me when there is a perfectly good definition of territory applicable to the territories of all institutions, state and otherwise. One could, of course, just call them *the spaces* of international organisations, but I want to give these spaces an equal footing to the spaces of states since they really deserve to be understood thus. These territories are produced in much the same way as state territory and are used to structure the exercise of control – consisting in the assertion or performance of *some kind of governance function* – in relation to a specific geolocatable space. They are therefore rightly named territories rather than simply referred to as the spaces of international organisations.

Finally, the decision to retain the term 'territory' also made sense because it helps differentiate between spaces which are created as a result of the exercise of political and economic control from other kinds of spaces. Not all spaces are territories. A territory in this view of things is 'a bounded social space that inscribes a certain sort of meaning onto . . . the material world.'[24] A space in comparison is a much broader concept. In contrast to earlier 'absolutist' concepts of space, Leibniz transformed the understanding of space and posited it as 'fundamentally relational, that space in and of itself does not really exist at all.'[25] Space is social according to Lefebvre and '(social) space is a (social) product'.[26] A territory is a kind of space *created for and by the exercise of power.* Therefore, I retain the term 'territory' as the name given to this category of spaces, acknowledging at the same time that not all spaces will necessarily be territories.

1.1.2 Sovereignty and Territorial Sovereignty

I wish I could avoid these terms. Unfortunately, the very inquiry of this study requires wrestling with them. If it is not already well established, it will become evident in Chapter 3 that there is a real ambiguity that exists in how these concepts are used in international law discourse. Crawford, for example, observed that there are often two meanings of sovereignty: 'sovereignty may refer to the title to territory or the rights accruing from the exercise of title'.[27] Shaw indicated that 'territorial sovereignty is . . . centered upon the rights and power coincident upon territory in the geographical sense'[28] but also that '[t]he essence of territorial sovereignty is contained in the notion of title. This term relates to both the factual and legal conditions under which territory is deemed to belong to one particular authority or another.'[29] In yet more instances, territorial sovereignty refers to a particular regime: '[s]overeignty in regard to a territory is known as territorial sovereignty.'[30] There seems in much international law discourse to be a blurring of the distinction between these two concepts.

24 ibid at 14.
25 Tally (2012) at 28.
26 Lefebvre (1991) at 26.
27 Crawford (2012) at 448.
28 Shaw (1982) 61, 73.
29 Shaw (2017) at 354.
30 Güzel (2020) at 143.

As a result of this lack of clarity, in Chapter 5 I outline how I propose such terms could be used going forward to understand the reterritorialisation of competences once associated with (state-)sovereignty. This clarifies both how I think about and use these terms and also serves the purpose of providing a proposed route to the understanding of the reterritorialisation of sovereignty. Going forward, the concept of sovereignty that is applied in the rethink is one developed using a legal realist account of law and legal relations. Sovereignty is understood as divisible bundles of legal relations (rights, duties, privileges, immunities) that may be distributed between different actors (state and non-state alike) who exercise them in relation to their own territories. Indeed, it is through the very exercise of these sovereign bundles that territories of different actors are produced and continually reproduced. And I propose 'burying'[31] the concepts of title and territorial sovereignty entirely. They become superfluous to purpose and their continued usage will only cause confusion.

1.1.3 Globalisation and Global Governance

Globalisation is neither an exact nor precise term. Broadly understood, it is meant to describe all 'social, political and economic activities stretch[ing] across communities, regions and continents'[32] and 'the widening, deepening and speeding up of worldwide interconnectedness',[33] which at times can seem like a rather unhelpful construct considering how many different phenomena are caught under this definition. The concept is overly broad and at times does not help explain any of the specific processes it is meant to cover. It also often contains many ideological undertones and is not, in this sense, at all politically neutral. It does, on a pragmatic view of things, however, help convey the idea of a certain 'stretching of social relations across space and time' and of 'processes which are not hindered or prevented by territorial or jurisdictional boundaries.'[34] In so doing it projects an expressly aterritorial and spatially unspecific picture of the world, which both captures the main challenge perceived by international lawyers to the territorial ordering of legal, cultural, economic, and political relations and helps diagnose the key problems of this perception, namely, that it is abstract and

[31] Gathii (2020).
[32] Held (2004) at 1.
[33] Held and McGrew (2007) at 1.
[34] Newman (2013) at 90.

despatialised at the same time. The same is true of global governance. It is too broad and insufficient. The spatiality of the global is particularly imprecise and unhelpful, but it is the recognised term for both a discipline and ontological reality.

Perhaps the person who most helped me understand the spatial assumptions of globalisation discourses is Doreen Massey. She has argued that 'globalisation is not a single all-embracing movement (nor should it be imagined as some outward spread from the West and other centres of economic power across a passive surface of "space"). It is a making of space(s), an active reconfiguration and meeting-up through practices and relations of a multitude of trajectories.'[35] What this conveys is the time–space of globalisation and that all space making is constituted through practices; there is no a priori space that exists outside this social realm. Massey also captured the politics of the time–space of globalisation's spatial imaginaries:

> Clearly, the world is not totally globalised (whatever that might mean); the very fact that some are striving so hard to make it so is evidence of the project's incompletion. But this is more than a question of incompletion – more than a question of waiting for the laggards to catch up. There are multiple trajectories/ temporalities here. Once again, as in the case of modernity, this is a geographical imagination which ignores the structured divides, the necessary ruptures and inequalities, the exclusions, on which the successful prosecution of the project itself depends. A further effect of the temporal convening of spatial difference here again becomes evident. So long as inequality is read in terms of stages of advance and backwardness not only are alternative stories disallowed but also the fact of the production of poverty and polarisation within and through 'globalisation' itself can be erased from view. This is – - again - – a geographical imagination which ignores its own real spatiality.[36]

What is at stake in understanding time–space better, and the territories of all actors associated with globalisation and global law and governance is enormous.

1.1.4 Geographical and Physical Geography

Geography can refer to both the discipline and the brute physical facts. I try to use the term geography to refer to the discipline and the term

[35] Massey (2005) at 83.
[36] ibid at 84.

physical geography to refer to the 'features of the earth and its atmosphere'.[37] Physical geography can be more than just land and can include water. I use the term physical geography to refer to physical facts, given that the concept of territory is often confusingly used to indicate land, sea, and air – the natural or 'brute' reality – and I want to avoid perpetuating this confusion.

1.1.5 Essentialised or Essentialising

Essentialising means the attribution of fixed characteristics or elements, that is, the tendency to present a certain phenomenon as necessarily having those particular features and qualities. A concept becomes essentialised whenever it is assumed that the exact same set of fixed characteristics will be shared by all its referents, no matter what the particular circumstances are, such that the individual characteristics are often overlooked or the idea that these characteristics can be differently configured is neglected. A relationship (between concepts or legal principles) can also be essentialised, for example, by projecting an assumption that there exists an inherent arrangement or function to the relationship.

1.1.6 Naturalising

I adopt the term in the following way: 'naturalisation is a significant mode of the circulation of knowledge during which the relation between knowledge and power becomes fixed in such a way that is appears to be given by nature and thus an unchangeable face and determinant of human actions.'[38] A concept becomes naturalised when its content or meaning is presented as the product of some objective brute fact (e.g., the physical reality), rather than a historically contingent, social construction. It is closely linked to essentialisation but here I want to highlight explicitly the 'naturalness' that is associated with territory – the relationship between the natural world and the political, legal, social world being essentialised.

1.2 Situating the Argument

This thesis contributes to the ongoing discussion about the politics, epistemology, and ontology of territory, sovereignty, globalisation, and

[37] 'Geography, n.' (2020).
[38] Liste (2016) 199.

global governance taking place in and across many different disciplines.[39] As I engage with those who write on this issue from an transdisciplinary perspective, this book may be of interest not only to international lawyers but to anyone seeking to understand current institutional and legal arrangements. In the pages ahead, I argue for a fundamental reconceptualisation of the concepts of territory and sovereignty as they are used in the context of international law. The analysis I propose seeks to remove the narrow confines into which these concepts have been traditionally forced, to problematise and deconstruct their content, and to uncover the implicit assumptions concerning their spatial characteristics.

Many of these assumptions – such as, for example, the idea of territory as a static and container-like space closely associated with statehood or the notion of globalisation as a fluid, spatially imprecise process – exist in many disciplines. The problems I pursue in this book, thus, are not unique to international law, nor is international law, in this sense, cut off from other disciplines or, for that matter, from broader mainstream discourses. The argument I develop in these pages is intended, ideally, to stimulate a wide-ranging reappraisal of international spatial structures that go beyond a specific disciplinary context.

Originally, my project had a slightly different orientation. I had intended to examine the extent to which the process of deterritorialisation had taken place in the arena of international law, to what extent the international legal order, in other words, could be said to have been deterritorialised, and what implications this might have for the relevance of territory to various international law structures and processes. I had already assumed territory was less relevant. Such an examination predictably required an immediate clarification of the concept of 'deterritorialisation'. Acquainting myself with the relevant literature, I found considerable overlap between the deterritorialisation debate and the aforementioned 'shift to functionality' narrative. I also found that this debate often reflected a pervasive anxiety about the changing role of the state, and that many contributors to this debate were unable to approach the subject of globalisation/global governance other than through the prism of this underlying anxiety. In doing so they also unfailingly ended up replicating the traditional positivist bias of normatively prioritising the Westphalian institutional form. In particular, many

[39] Lindahl (2013); Lindahl (2010) 30; Sassen (2008); Massey (2005); Massey (1992); Sokol (2011); Bartelson (2010) 219; Elden (2005); Elden (2006) 47; Held and McGrew (2007); Sloterdijk (2009) 29; Strandsbjerg (2010).

of these contributions continued assuming and applying without question the same underlying conception of territory. Prompted by my reading of this deterritorialisation literature from the discipline of international law, I decided at this point to go 'back to basics' to understand the concept of territory and how tools from different disciplines, such as geography, might differently inform our thinking about spaces and spatial concepts, especially the concept of territory.

Influenced by the suggestions made by scholars in other disciplines that borders were not disappearing but proliferating and becoming more heterogeneous,[40] I asked what if, rather than territory disappearing or becoming less relevant, territories are actually proliferating and doing so as increasingly heterogeneous spaces? If borders can be understood as more complex, could the same be true of territory? Borders, after all, delineate *something* and, more often than not, bound a territory. Did this approach help explain what I thought was missing in accounts of territory, deterritorialisation, and globalisation? Could this help me understand what I thought legal theory is struggling to understand? This approach reflects a similar shift from debates asking, 'is the nation state dead/in decline?' to more fruitful questions of 'how is statehood changing?'[41] The same applies to the idea of territory. Rather than ask whether territory is still relevant, whether it is dead, or whether it is the 'end of geography', we can instead ask how territory can be thought of as changing.

This idea became central to my research. Of course, the number of territories at the international plane proliferated as a result of decolonisation, as well as other secessionist movements. However, this only increased the number of *state* territories in international law. So, while proliferating, territories did not become more heterogeneous – these new territories were constituted and configured in habitually the same way. Territories were increasing in number but not in diversity. What if, instead, territories are being refashioned? If so, we – international lawyers, as I see myself as belonging to this community of international lawyers – need to redefine and re-imagine the concept of territory. Rather than deterritorialisation being a one-way process, implying territory is being replaced by functionality, what if those functions are

[40] Mezzadra and Neilson (2013); Reece Jones and others (2017) 1, 1.

[41] Schachter (1997); Horsman and Marshall (1994); Kwiecień [2012]; MacCormick (1999); Jackson and James (1993); Sørensen (2001); Cutler (2016) 95; Biswas (2002) 175; Sur (1997) 421; Homann in Miller and Bratspies (2008).

reterritorialising into differently configured (non-state) territories? How can these territories become visible? Or rather, what makes these territories invisible? I began to explore and question the underlying assumptions about territory in international law, and why there is a spatial hegemony. Thus, 'territory does not cease to be important, rather it is no longer bound within a single state'[42] or tied to a certain category of actor. As a result, I propose reconceptualising territory, and, as a result, the contingent concept of sovereignty, in a manner that makes the legal spaces of reterritorialised functions and competences visible.

1.2.1 Overview

In the following chapter, I examine how the phenomena associated with globalisation and global governance are understood and trace the reliance on the orthodox spatial imaginary of international law as both positive enactment of law and discourse. Discussing the main theories offered by scholars to make sense of the major societal, political, and legal shifts because of globalisation and global governance, I address what I call the deterritorialisation narrative present in much of these discourses. I identify three main threads to these theories and examine them in turn: first, are those which describe a shift in the organising logic of international law and politics from territoriality to functionality; second, are those theories that relocate power without concretely knowing what to call these spaces of relocation; and third, are theories concerning the porosity of borders. Yet, as I conclude, what is common to all these theories is an incomplete spatial account; they show deterritorialisation without reterritorialisation. I identify several reasons for this, including an analytical conflation between functions and spaces, and that the spaces of reterritorialisation are invisible and unknown. These spaces are made invisible because of the hegemonic concept of territory and analytical prioritisation of (state-)territory. As a result, these theories reproduce the same spatial imaginary of international law, in particular the same assumptions about the concept of territory, which, as a result, forces a non-territorial or aterritorial account.

Chapter 3 begins a deep dive into the content of the concept of territory that underpins and informs the deterritorialisation narratives, and the related body of discourse about the end of territory, geography,

[42] Elden (2005) 16.

sovereignty and/or the state, producing this identified aterritorial response. The conceptualisations of territory that are unpicked invariably tend to be reified, physical, 'flat', and statocentric. Much of international law (and its reasoning and operative concepts, such as of sovereignty, territorial sovereignty, and jurisdiction) is built on an implicit geography that uncritically accepts the cartographic imaginary that prioritises state space, while entirely disregarding the space created and inhabited by other categories of actors. As a result, when legal competences move from states to other actors, this way of thinking is inevitably drawn to generating the kind of narratives explored in the previous chapter. The excavation exercise in this chapter looks at the artefacts and features of this traditional concept of territory and problematises many of its outdated spatial assumptions. For it is as a result, that international legal thought finds it impossible to comprehend as territories the spaces of non-state actors, territories which will and do overlap with the territories of states. In other words, there can be no reterritorialisation because the spaces of reterritorialisation are illegible to international lawyers.

In Chapters 4 and 5, I take the spaces of reterritorialisation seriously and propose how international lawyers might rethink the spatiality of international law in order to recognise the territories that are created by non-state actors. I demonstrate that it is possible to account for the 'new' or once-exceptional spaces by questioning and removing the imposed limitations and assumptions about territory. I propose two main phases to reconceptualise territory and consequently sovereignty and jurisdiction, dedicating a chapter to each.

Chapter 4 outlines how territory is being conceptualised differently. This alternative understanding builds on insights drawn from various disciplines, especially critical geography and the work of spatial theorists like Henri Lefebvre and Doreen Massey who would understand territory as socially produced space. The chapter rethinks the basic building blocks of the concept of territory, producing as a result a new appreciation about territory as a space produced by actors exercising control. I discuss how spaces are understood by the likes of Elden, Lefebvre, and Massey who in their own way have revolutionised the understanding of space for many disciplines; from an objectified and container understanding of space to one that is socially constructed, dynamic, multiple, and relational. I then explain the relationship between territory and the material world (or as I call it the physical geography or brute fact): a territory understood within this spatial paradigm becomes understood as 'a bounded social *space that inscribes a certain sort of meaning onto* defined segments of the *material* world', that is, the physical geography.[43] It is not physical but is produced and exists in the realm of social relations.[44] I suggest that it might be useful to think of there being a central characteristic to the concept of territory – a characteristic that distinguishes this type of space from other spaces. I propose understanding that defining characteristic in terms of the notion of control. I also suggest re-imagining the concept of territory as consisting of a bundle of different characteristics. In this view of things, that bundle can be differently arranged, some characteristics changed, and others removed but there is still a space recognisable as territory where control and power are exercised. Social practices and relations of control then become the central definition and 'test' of the presence of a territory. I then turn to other considerations, first problematising the 'time of territory', including the assumption that territories are static, and more or less permanent, before thinking about the boundaries of territories and how territories are mappable. Where we end up, if we adopt this concept of territory as constituted through practices of control, is that any space constituted through social practices meeting those criteria is a territory. Therefore, if the spaces of other actors are similarly constituted but configured differently, these too could be considered as their territories. Without this step, we are forced to adopt the aterritorial responses diagnosed in Chapter 2; the spaces of other actors become conflated with unstructured and unfocused global space.

However, what is problematic about redefining territory in this way is that orthodox international legal theories conceptualise territory as an object and the orthodox understanding of sovereignty is something that is exercised 'over' and structured by discrete state territories. Therefore, this new concept needs to be worked out in practice. Following this rethink concerning solely the concept of territory, Chapter 5 returns to the level of broader narratives about the contemporary global legal order. Utilising legal realist and social constructivist lenses, I implement this 'new' geography for international law. Applying the idea of territorial pluralism and departing from a 2-D cartographic imaginary, the chapter proposes how the idea that territories are not diminishing but are instead proliferating might be reinserted into international legal theories. As part of the final steps of rethinking the conceptual and theoretical

[43] Delaney (2005) at 14, emphasis added.

[44] Massey argued that space is relational in its construction, its production is realised 'through practices of material engagement. If time unfolds as change then space unfolds as interaction. In that sense space is the social dimension.' Massey (2005) at 61.

frameworks, aided by insights developed by legal realists, I argue that the concept of sovereignty can be understood as bundles of legal relations. This insight helps explain the continual redistribution of the bundle of sovereign powers, competences, rights, and duties to different actors with their own spaces. In this chapter, I also argue that title is not a useful operative legal concept any longer. This is because conceptualising territory as an object or possession of the state is integral to the concept of title *and given territory is a space, not an object*, the discipline of international law can do away entirely with the concept of title. This chapter also deals with the notion of exclusivity. A legal realist approach, combined with the insights from earlier chapters, helps show that what exclusivity describes is actually a relationship between actors, not the relationship between the state/sovereign rights holder and territory. Finally, a social constructivist perspective helps free the sovereignty bundle from the state, by removing the normative positivist 'view from nowhere' that states are the only actors capable of exercising power, rights, duties, etc. in relation to their territories. This is a vital chapter in the story re-imagining territory because it explains the legal relationship between actors who exercise powers in relation to their own territories, and who indeed actually constitute their own territories by exercising different parts of the legal bundle of sovereignty. Taking the idea of reterritorialising seriously, I propose a legal account of the relationship between actors and their spaces and think through the implications of this argument for the spatially mediated legal concepts of sovereignty and jurisdiction. In short, I propose a 'rebirth' of the concept of territory for international law.

1.3 Methodology

Methods are central to this project. Here I broadly sketch out the approaches and insights I have found most useful in developing my ideas. The very first consideration is that this is a transdisciplinary project. Individuals may disagree generally with trans- or interdisciplinary approaches, but the nature of the issues addressed – geography, the spatial, legal rights, 'global society', global governance, global law, globalisation, etc. – prompts a transdisciplinary response. Originally the discipline of international law adopted ideas about territory from geography,[45] therefore, it is important to understand how this discipline

[45] Jennings (1963) at 74.

and its discourse developed. It is entirely commonplace for disciplines to create their own meaning for words. Territory is a prime example of a concept borrowed from the discipline of geography, but debate and discourse have moved on in that discipline and the two disciplines have not been in discourse with each other. Such developments are to be expected. Often the purpose of inter- or trans-disciplinary research is to understand how far apart the conceptualisations have become. Further, although I study the structure and operation of a legal system, globalisation as a subject, and its ontology, are challenging, and being challenged in, many disciplines besides international law, making it sensible to explore how they have framed their debates and responses to it. Further still, law is a social practice that exists in and creates legal spaces, making a study of how other social sciences relate to the spatial and its productive effects necessary.

Second, I adopt a 'legal geography' approach which seeks to understand 'the where of law' as practised, as opposed to relying on legal positivist accounts of where territories ought to be. Legal geography is not a subdiscipline of human geography, or of law, but a specialised area of scholarship where 'space is foreground and serves as an organising principle'.[46] This approach offers a way to understand the 'unacknowledged assumptions about the space[s] that work to stabilise . . . the very meaning of "law"'.[47] Legal geography helps us comprehend the diversity of spaces of law, how these spaces are configured, and how this affects the operationalisation of the legal system itself. By reading legal geography's insights, we gain more clarity regarding the false binary that exists in the functionality versus territoriality discourse outlined in Chapter 2, showing that instead what has taken place is a shift from the organisation of competences in the territory of one actor to a redistribution of these competences to the territories of other actors. More than this, there is a critical sensibility, in the sense of critical (legal) geography, and there is a huge debt to Doreen Massey's and Stuart Elden's work for my thinking about space and in understanding many of the philosophical and political theory debates concerning concepts such as space, time, deterritorialisation, globalisation, place, local, and global.

As such, it is also a critical methodology – not critical in the sense of disapproving or fault finding – but in the sense of interpreting, commenting on, and analysing how international lawyers think about

[46] Braverman and others (2015) at 2.

[47] Blomley, Delaney, and Ford (2001) at xv.

territory and its role in mediating other concepts. I feel I must acknowledge this because 'critical' work is often off-putting to those who approach law through more doctrinal or positivist sensibilities, and I would like these ideas to be read, used, discussed, critiqued, worked on further, by both 'camps'. There is always a fundamental and ongoing role for questioning accepted meanings and the assumptions creating them. The ultimate aim of Chapter 3 is deconstructing how the concept of territory[48] is understood and applied in practice from someone who also 'gets' international law from an internal perspective. The aim of such deconstruction exercises can be to question the hegemony of thought and 'does not reject the need for law and institutions, but rather seeks to work within those structures to reveal new possibilities.'[49] Being critically aware is an emancipatory process.[50] More focused and sharper thinking can result from continually questioning whether blindspots exist in orthodox theories. Critical methods create opportunities to better understand the structure and ideology of the legal system and offer a different intellectual framework for understanding of the likes of the concept of territory. Deconstruction as a tool can offer insights that may produce conceptual clarity in a discourse that has become burdened with exceptions and conceptual slippages. This book is an invitation to engage in the possibilities rather than to command or find fault or create strawmen to knock down.[51] It aims to find the 'enrichment of a multi-dimensional understanding of, on the one hand, drivers, backgrounds, influences, power relations and, on the other hand, consequences, effects and feedback loops of legal endeavors in social contexts (reality and realities) [which] offers a much wider horizon of intellectual and scholarly mutual enrichment.'[52] The book in many ways is broadly written in an arc that deconstructs and then reconstructs the concept of territory and the legal categories such as sovereignty mediated by it. The reconstruction I offer in Chapters 4 and 5 is not the objective truth or 'correct' understanding of territory.[53] It is an alternative that allows us to entertain a different

[48] A very difficult task, because there is no single understanding of territory in international law discourse, but instead a lot of conceptual ambiguity and imprecision, but with certain identifiable key or commonly occurring characteristics.

[49] Turner (2016).

[50] Korhonen (2017) 625, 632.

[51] ibid at 633.

[52] ibid at 637.

[53] Litowitz (2000) 41, 57. I am also quite aware that I knock down one totalising way of thinking and could be critiqued as proposing another. Such totalising moves can often be

understanding of contemporary legal orders; 'territorialising' that which has been deterritorialised by our dominant way of thinking. By examining insights from different disciplines, as I do in these two chapters, we may receive new ways of thinking and new skills that can lead to disciplinary change. Lawyers cannot remain frozen[54] in our understanding of territory because legal realities are changing; while traditionally understood as a stable base associated with one actor, territories too are dynamic. That essentialism can be unlearned.[55]

1.3.1 *International Lawyers and the Enchanted Heartland Concept of Territory*

The task confronting this research project is so much greater and all the more challenging because territory is a central concept of international law. This book contributes to rethinking some foundational concepts of law that are often treated and used self-evidently and uncritically, with assumptions about the concepts being uncritically reproduced. Therefore, I have found it useful to understand these as *heartland* concepts which have *enchanted* international lawyers. Given I have just introduced two new concepts – enchantment and heartland – developed by different scholars, I feel I must first explain what I mean by these terms and describe their use.

unpopular in critical scholarship. I could have written this book in a way that only deconstructed how international law discourse misdiagnoses issues by excavating its conceptualisations of territory. This would have in many ways have been easier and kept my powder dry, so to speak. I decided to take the step of suggesting an alternative way of thinking. On totality, I have found Milton Santos instructive, especially since he writes about the timidity of geography 'in its approach to totality', Santos (2021) at 69. I entirely appreciate critiques of world systems theory or Hegelian Marxist accounts of capitalism, for example, for their totalising moves. What I offer in these pages is not a theory of how power or international law works, or ought to work. I have found that concentrating on the 'control' element of territory as a concept has been a very useful diagnostic tool. This will make more sense in Chapter 4 where I explain it in more detail. Throughout, I emphasise that I think concepts are only in use for as long as they are useful, and that I think the concept of territory's meaning can and will change. In this book I am trying to dissect this control element, as it is an especially useful way of understanding territory, at this precise moment in time and in how I understand the constitution of its space. In 500 or 1,000 years, if the planet survives that long, the concept may have shifted in terms of content considerably or fallen into disuse entirely.

54 Schlag (1986) 917, 917.

55 Koskenniemi (2004) 229, 240.

I use the idea of enchanted concepts to describe concepts that are used and invoked by international lawyers so frequently such that they are treated uncritically; these concepts are credited with functions and explanatory power that logic and critical reasoning suggest should not be ascribed to them. This understanding of enchantment is reflected in, for example, the following passage from Koskenniemi's interview with Schult: 'lawyers are enchanted by the law that is familiar to them and the institutions and practices they are involved with; that makes them often unable to find a good solution to the problem they are faced with. International lawyers are enchanted by international law.'[56] Notice the emphasis on the disabling impact that enchantment has on reasoning faculties: being enchanted by familiar law and institutions, Koskenniemi argues, or at least in how I have interpreted him, makes lawyers often unable to resolve problems confronting them effectively and with clarity. This characterisation also holds true regarding how international lawyers think of, and apply, many key concepts. The concept of enchantment can also be understood in relation to its opposite, the concept of disenchantment. Here is how, for example, Kennedy, drawing on Weber, defines the latter: '[d]isenchantment is an existential or phenomenological category. It means loss of belief that … events are part of a system of [pre-established, self-evident] meaning,'[57] that is miraculously immune to any logical contradictions and, often, rational explanations. It is 'the attempt to find a rational answer [that] sets us down a path of "disenchantment"'.[58]

The idea of heartland concepts as I use it comes from Jenkins, for whom: '[t]hese are concepts such as time, evidence, empathy, cause and effect, continuity and change'.[59] In his discussion of the general conceptual framework of modern history, Jenkins explains that certain concepts, such as time and space, tend to be used by historians in a fundamentally 'unproblematic' manner[60] – because 'the impression is strongly given' within the discipline that their meaning is somehow 'obvious and timeless'.[61] The discipline of international law shares many of the same heartland concepts, such as time and space. In addition, it also has

[56] Koskenniemi and Schult (2018).
[57] Kennedy (2004) 1031, 1057.
[58] ibid.
[59] Jenkins (2003) at 19.
[60] ibid at 61.
[61] ibid at 19.

numerous heartland concepts of its own. Those of territory, sovereignty, territorial sovereignty, and jurisdiction could be included among them.

Concepts like territory and sovereignty, in this sense, can be understood as the essential 'building blocks' of international lawyers' understanding of the legal system they work with and study. Yet, these are historically and socially produced constructs and their use should not forever be continued unproblematically. Their content is not static. It is, therefore, important to study them historically and critically, to understand their potential application, and justify their content and application when faced with new legal and political challenges.

The idea that sovereignty and territory are core concepts in international legal thought, of course, is not novel. Thus, for example, Shaw observes that 'international law is based on the concept of the state. The state in turn lies upon the foundation of sovereignty [which is] founded upon the fact of territory. Without territory a legal person cannot be a state. It is undoubtedly the basic characteristic of a state.' He continues: 'fundamental legal concepts such as sovereignty and jurisdiction can only be comprehended in relation to territory.'[62] This means, he concludes, that, inevitably, 'territory becomes a vital part in any study of international law.'[63] In a similar vein, Simpson describes sovereignty and territory as 'the classic legal principles'[64] 'that structure international politics';[65] Tomuschat remarks that '[t]raditionally, international law rested on the principle of territoriality';[66] Bilkovà observes that 'States possess[ing] and control[ling] territory is [] one of the most important assumptions that international law stems from';[67] and Brierly comments that '[a]t the basis of [all] international law lies the notion that a state occupies a definite part of the surface of the earth, within which it normally exercises . . . jurisdiction over persons and things to the exclusion of the jurisdiction of other states.'[68] According to O'Connell, the fact that 'the exercise of sovereignty is predicated upon territory' is why territory 'is perhaps the fundamental concept of international law.'[69] The ICJ in the *Corfu Channel* case indicated that 'respect for territorial

62 Shaw (2017) at 361.
63 ibid.
64 Simpson in Crawford and Koskenniemi (2012) at 40.
65 Simpson in ibid at 45.
66 Tomuschat (1993) 195, 210.
67 Bílková in Kuijer and Werner (2017) at 43.
68 Brierly (1949) at 142.
69 O'Connell (1971) at 181.

sovereignty is an essential foundation of international relations,'[70] and in his lectures, Jennings, who later would become ICJ President, declared '[t]he whole course of modern history testifies to the central place of State territory in international relations'.[71] In short, 'territory [has become] "perhaps the fundamental concept of international law"'.[72]

The enchantment referred to by Koskenniemi is, I contend, more likely to arise with heartland concepts. The reproduction of assumptions is more likely to arise with concepts that are core to a discipline. Concepts, such as territory, are used and invoked by international lawyers so commonly and frequently, they are treated as self-evident and, as a result, may become essentialised and naturalised. As Elden argues:

> However central the notion of territory is to definitions of the state, it generally tends to be assumed as unproblematic. Theorists have largely neglected to define the term, taking it as obvious and not worthy of further investigation ... it is unhistorically accepted, conceptually assumed and philosophically unexamined. Its meaning is taken to be obvious and self-evident and can therefore be assumed in political analysis.[73]

And yet, as we will see, there are deep inconsistencies which go unnoticed. Territory is sometimes an area, sometimes a space, sometimes a portion of the surface of the earth, sometimes airspace, sometimes primarily land and sometimes it is air, land, and water equally. Each of these descriptions is a result of different assumptions about the reality of territory that create different legal and political orders as a result. The same applies with territorial sovereignty and the understanding of territory underlying the particular theory adopted (if one is indeed explicitly adopted).

Further, when enchanted by a concept, or so the argument goes, those applying it are also unable to see past it or be prepared to adopt different understandings of it. Added to this, international law as a discipline, indeed most legal disciplines, are in their nature doctrinal, tending to stick with the known doctrine. But such doctrinal approaches may mean, recalling Koskenniemi, that many international lawyers are unable 'to

[70] *Corfu Channel (United Kingdom of Great Britain and Northern Ireland v Albania) Judgment* [1949] ICJ Reports 1949 4 (International Court of Justice) 35.
[71] Jennings (1963) at 1.
[72] Shaw (2017) at 361.
[73] Elden (2005) 10.

find a good solution to the problem they are faced with'.[74] One such important and pressing problem is the changing legal and political realties wrought by globalisation. What is common to many international law accounts of globalisation is they reproduce this heartland concept of territory. And given their enchantment, the concept is thought to have relatively *static content*.[75] The key element that is common to most international law conceptions of territory is that territory 'belongs' only to states (something that itself is unquestioned).

There is a broader pattern whereby lawyers tend to treat their basic tools as objects; this includes territory. Schlag identified this pattern, calling it an instance of the *objectivist aesthetic*: '[l]egal actors and thinkers come to believe that when they talk about rules, principles, doctrines and the like – they are talking about things that are incontestable . . . [they] treat rules, principles, doctrines and the like as if they were physical objects.'[76] This creates a stable identity for these rules, principles, concepts, doctrines, etc. – if these objects are incontestably real they are increasingly unproblematically used and essentialised. Bring into the picture territory, a concept that is associated with the 'real world', 'tangible'[77] and material physical geography, the likelihood of this transformation into the physical object is greater. Almost then as a direct result of enchantment, territory has been reified in discourse – reification describing the process of making an abstract space more concrete and real.[78] In other words, the enchantment has influenced international lawyers' ontological understanding of this concept.

Territory is a deeply rooted concept – both in the sense that it is core to the understanding of international law and that is has been an important concept for a long period of time. The meaning of territory however has changed over time and yet it is common to unconsciously overlay historical thinking with the meaning held by scholars today or allow the assumptions of the historical text to slip into today's application. When reading a historical text or legal provision, scholars may

[74] Koskenniemi and Schult (2018). And here I am, someone who thinks of herself as also belonging to this community, telling international lawyers 'what to think', but I hope that this is not taken as an insult. We can sometimes stand too close to the object of study, and I was fortunate to have the time and space for several years to ponder this question.

[75] I discuss this further in Chapter 3 in which I deconstruct the content of the concept of territory.

[76] Schlag (1998) at 98.

[77] Wallace (1986) at 81.

[78] Also, objectification has taken place. See Chapter 3, Section 3.4 for an explanation on this.

(unconsciously) attach to the concepts of territory and territorial sovereignty a contemporary understanding, and vice versa. It is not possible to assume the term has been used uniformly.

These are all issues affecting the use of heartland concepts, contributing to the reification and essentialisation of territory in discourse. These considerations are all important to bear in mind when using the concepts of territory and sovereignty in modern practice, as well as justification for the proposed rethinking.

—

This contribution is intended to be an intervention in, and a continuation of, an important debate concerning territory to further thinking on the issue. It is not the final answer, nor does it claim to be the 'right' answer – if we can believe there is such a thing. Although prompted by the need to respond to debates about sovereignty, globalisation, or global governance, and of moves away from territoriality toward functionality, what emerges is a project offering a fundamental rethink of territory and touching on the way this will affect the operationalisation and structure of other international law concepts. I therefore hope it is of use to the wider discipline, as well as to those in international relations and politics who also use the concepts of territory and state as building blocks to their analysis. It explores my original hypothesis that territory is proliferating and that where deterritorialisation occurs, so too does reterritorialisation. But *where* powers and competences have been reterritorialised to must be identified because these territories are not visible to legal theory. The book is an effort to outline my thinking on the spaces and territories of international law. The task ahead is best captured in the following terms:

> Perhaps one of the most difficult lessons for anyone to learn is the way in which their own worlds are geographically coded; to understand the relationship between the visible and the invisible, the proximate and the distant, and to recognize the complex folds of past and present that constitute place and experience as we know it. The modern world-view has been so lodged upon naturalist notions of experience that people are very reluctant to question their belief in the stability and reality of their visual world. How could it be otherwise? Isn't the world clearly apparent to us? Isn't sight the purest of all our senses, the one least affected by social values and cultural practices? Well, it turns out that it isn't so clear or so stable.[79]

[79] Pickles (2004) at 81.

Reconceptualising territory in the way I propose, impacts many topics of international law from drone warfare to international organisations, from refugee journeys and camps to the law of treaties. With further development and wider input, it could have, I appreciate, widespread consequences for how international law is operationalised, its spatial logic, and how legal relations and regimes are structured. But 'the world is changing. Our conventional legal picture of the patterns of power is no longer adequate. We need new thinking' while remembering at the same time that international law is also a 'project[] of reinvention', requiring 're-imagining' and remaking.[80] It is possible to uncover and recreate, through different narratives, the legal order itself and by reinterpreting legal spaces, perhaps a different spatial constitution of the world emerges.

[80] Kennedy (2008) 827, 835.

2

Deterritorialisation Discourse in International Law

> Space is fundamental in any form of communal life; space is fundamental in any exercise of power
>
> Michel Foucault, 'Space, Knowledge and Power'[1]

Although the form taken in recent years by discourse about international law's deterritorialisation may draw on more modern theories, the broader attempt to theorise law 'beyond the state' is not new. One of the most well-known research agendas is the project of *transnational* legal studies. In the almost sixty-five years since American international law scholar and later International Court of Justice (ICJ) judge Philip Jessup first published his account of transnational law, more questions have been raised than answered. In 1957, Jessup submitted that the term 'international law' 'suggests that one is concerned only with the relations [of states]' which is 'inadequate to describe' 'transnational situations [that] may involve individuals, corporations, states, organizations of states, or other groups.'[2] Since such situations are now central to understanding the realities of international politics and economics, it seems at times that the traditional vision of international law as a discipline is being progressively critiqued and even set aside in favour of new approaches.[3]

The red thread running through transnational law literature is the fundamental connection between traditional international law's inveterate stato-centricity and its preoccupation with territoriality. The 'tremendous transformations' occurring in the contemporary 'world power process', declared Myres McDougal in his 1953 Hague Academy lectures, have put

[1] Foucault (1984) at 239–56.

[2] Jessup (1956) at 1–2.

[3] Schmidt (2018); Zumbansen (2011); Benvenisti (2014); The IGLP Law and Global Production Working Group (2016) 57; Kingsbury, Krisch, and Stewart (2005) 15; Krisch (2021).

an end to the dominance of '[t]he traditional, territorially organized bodies politic, known as "nation-states" [that have been] dwarfed by the ... regional groupings and ... host of new and powerful functional organizations – including international governmental organizations, transnational political parties, transnational pressure groups and transnational private associations.'[4] McDougal also suggested that all 'governmental forms of territorial organization, so exalted in importance by traditional theory, are frequently but channels for the expression of decisions in fact made in some one or more of [these] functional groupings.'[5] Despite gaining numerous supporters and advocates, the transnational law project has never quite succeeded in entirely displacing the traditional discipline of international law. To this day, it is still largely regarded by many as more of a sub-discipline, and by a fewer number as something entirely distinct, and the project of transnational law is still spoken of as an emerging field.[6]

In many ways, what is most significant about the project of transnational law is its framing. Notwithstanding the purported attempt to move away from the discipline's preoccupation with states, they continue to serve as a central anchor for most transnational law thinking and an integral structure to accounts of law. The concepts of state territory and state borders continue to operate as 'crucial reference points',[7] a function they can only perform if they remain the stable background against which transnational (and indeed international) law exists. A certain degree of reliance seems inevitable: after all, without states, there would be nothing 'trans-' about transnational law. Yet, the extent of international and transnational law's dependence on stato-centricity goes beyond just providing the backdrop for further theorisation and reasoning. These theories continue to project and reproduce the spatial imaginary inherent to this backdrop, which limits their attempts to understand the phenomena they study. Specifically, they reproduce an overly essentialised (state-)concept of territory. In otherwise seeking to transcend the state and its space, much of these discourses end up reinforcing traditional international law ideas of statehood and its associated model of legal and political spatiality.

Though the phenomena studied today are more intense perhaps than those appearing in the fifties and sixties, and captured by Jessup, and

[4] McDougal (1953) 137, 161.
[5] ibid 162.
[6] Zumbansen (2021) at 5.
[7] ibid at 23.

there has been much development in legal thought,[8] the basic intellectual construction of the concept of territory that underpins much of the discourse of international and transnational law's deterritorialisation continues to be no different from mid-twentieth century thinking about transnational law. State territory continues to serve as the anchor from which the narrative about deterritorialisation begins. It is the assumed starting point of all analysis. It is also, as I argue, the only model of space that the discourses taking place within international law and its subdisciplines really 'know' or can 'see'; the only model the disciplines can grasp and identify as concrete reality. The spaces created by the processes of deterritorialisation are, by contrast, unknown, abstract, and insubstantial. As such, rather than decentring state territory, in much of the analysis state territories play an extraordinary centring role.

To compound the lack of clarity this brings, the state and territory, more often than not, are also constructed as essentially synonymous and interchangeable concepts. The deeply spatialised language used to describe phenomena 'beyond the state' is predicated on the idea that 'beyond the state' is basically '*beyond state territory*'. Yet, the realm of the spatial has receded, is never acknowledged, because territory could only ever refer to that of a state and the spaces beyond are not nearly as well understood. Further, the standard operating assumption in the discipline of international law is that 'territory' refers to 'state territory' only. The resulting absence in awareness and scrutiny of the spatial is, as this chapter argues, deeply problematic in that it not only fails to make sense of the broader legal realities of global governance, but actively distorts and obscures them.

The first stop in this systematic and critical exploration of the concept of territory and its proposed rebirth is the different theories offered by scholars trying to make sense of the major societal, political, and legal shifts resulting from the processes associated with globalisation and global governance. Over the course of the last twenty years there has been a crystallisation in these theories, many of which include accounts of a shift to functionally arranged legal and political orders, as opposed to territorially arranged orders, or explanations of the transformations arising as a result of the porosity of borders. These accounts can all be

[8] There has also been a growth in vocabulary, even outright fields, to describe this changing legal order. As Zumbansen has elaborated there is also: '"regulatory governance," "transnational private regulation," "global governance," "global administrative law," or "global law,"' see discussion by Zumbansen (2021) at 19.

said to contain an element of 'deterritorialisation' – by which is often meant the weakening of ties with, detachment from, or a movement away from a particular territory or system of territoriality (read: stato-centric territorial organisation).

This chapter provides an overview of this deterritorialisation discourse, before identifying its limitations. The first sections identify and sketch out the three main strands to this discourse. The first strand contains those accounts that suggest there has been a fundamental transition in the organising logic of international law. Theories falling into this category all agree that there has been a shift from ordering competences on the basis of territory to sectoral ordering instead. This move may be understood as a deterritorialisation of functions and competences; a functions-focused approach to organising the processes of global governance, according to this narrative, has superseded a territorial approach which, in turn, has led to a progressive deterritorialisation of the international legal system. The second strand, by contrast, groups together those accounts that address the relocation of power. The common assumption here is that at some point in the recent past there has been a systematic transfer of power from states to non-state actors, such as regional organisations or cities. A defining feature of this strand is that it often results in an imprecise, unexplained, or undertheorised understanding of the spaces of these actors, and as a result power too has stopped having an identifiable territorial basis. The third strand of deterritorialisation discourse includes those accounts which concern the porosity of state borders. A central theme here is the constantly expanding and intensifying flows of goods, services, people, and capital that stream relatively easily through these borders, also decreasing the importance of state territoriality to international law. As I show in the discussion below, each of these discursive strands assumes something different is being deterritorialised – functions, organising logics, power, material goods, etc. And yet, each appear to be applying a very similar legal-spatial imaginary, and in so doing more often than not entirely omit the resulting account of the spaces produced by this deterritorialisation.

The final pages of this chapter turn to what is problematic about these discourses. Despite each strand being anchored by a different object, what is common to all is that they continue to apply a particular and unproblematised concept of territory, which will always limit their theoretical insights. The first consequence of reproducing the same concept of (state-)territory is that these theories consistently produce deterritorialisation without reterritorialisation. This, in turn, results in the production of an aterritorial and at times entirely despatialised theory or framework – where power, authority, and control are exercised in relation to an unidentified spatial framework. For example, in many accounts about the porosity of state borders, the state clearly remains the prime focus and there is a lack of insight about the 'external' agents or 'forces' that are penetrating state space and the fact that each of these agents and forces has its own spatial logic, including in the context of 'penetrating' the state space.

Another important consequence of the uncritical reproduction of the old spatial paradigm is analytical confusion. Lurking not far beneath the surface of many of these theories is a conflation at an analytical level between actors, spaces, and functions. This 'conceptual lumping' as I inelegantly call it, occurs particularly often with regard to actors and spaces, as well as between spaces and functions. The reason for this conceptual lumping again lies in the continuing – and continuously unacknowledged – prioritisation and dominance of the stato-centric approach to thinking about territory within international law's implicit geography. In essence, the spatial assumptions – or the imagined geography – of international law[9] remain consistent and are unconsciously reapplied in even the very best efforts to explain the rise of, and subsequent role played by, international organisations and other non-state public and private actors in global lawmaking and governance.

2.1 Introducing Deterritorialisation

Before elaborating upon the three strands of deterritorialisation discourse I have identified, I must first address as an essential preliminary inquiry what deterritorialisation involves and why it is a useful frame through which to examine this big question of our time. The term itself stems from Deleuze and Guattari's work in two volumes on *Capitalism and Schizophrenia*.[10] Much has been written about these two and the influence of their ideas,[11] the impact of which can perhaps be seen most clearly in the disciplines of cultural studies and geography. However, international law has had its fair use of the term and, more importantly, the ideas that deterritorialisation seeks to convey.

[9] This account will also be familiar with much of mainstream international relations discourse and theory where many of the same ideas and theories are percolating.
[10] Deleuze and Guattari (1983); Deleuze and Guattari (1987).
[11] Holland (1991) 55; Elden (2005) 8; Massumi (1992).

The term deterritorialisation is most often used to describe the undoing of fixed social structures. It is most commonly associated with globalisation, where deterritorialisation is used to describe when 'the bonds that [once] tied economics, politics, and culture to fixed spatial configurations such as national territories are loosened under globalization pressures.'[12] It should be noted that the concept is not always used in a literal sense involving 'territory' and 'territorialisation' as we know it in international law: Deleuze and Guattari, particularly in their second volume, use deterritorialisation to describe processes taking place in everything from geology and biology to botany where the term is used to describe how wasps pollinate orchids.[13] However, it is in relation to territories and political and legal spaces that the term is used in this book.

The value of the framework given by the concept of deterritorialisation to the analysis contained herein, specifically in this chapter, manifests in two key ways. The first consideration is that Deleuze and Guattari's deterritorialisation is nearly always accompanied by reterritorialisation. Yet notably deterritorialisation in legal discourse is most often used in a way that is entirely cut off from its 'relative' concept of reterritorialisation and the insights this relationship offers. In my research into this discourse, use is made almost entirely of the concept of deterritorialisation alone. But for Deleuze and Guattari deterritorialisation and reterritorialisation are 'always connected [and] caught up in one another' and that 'each [process] brings about the deterritorialisation of one term and the reterritorialisation of the other.'[14] There is a 'continual process of de- and reterritorialisation', writes Stuart Elden, and a '*reconfiguration of spatial relations rather than their end*'[15] (emphasis added). Thus, where deterritorialisation is used in isolation in legal discourse, to describe social change as unidirectional, the concept's real insightfulness and analytical power is diminished. It is most valuable because it informs a broader method involving both de- and reterritorialisation. This insight, Elden argues, 'is often missed: deterritorialisation is part of a process ... deterritorialisation "always occurs in relation to a complementary reterritorialisation."'[16]

The second contribution of this framework is that deterritorialisation and reterritorialisation describe a *process* or even a series of *processes*.

[12] Popescu (2010) at 723.
[13] Deleuze and Guattari (1987) at 10.
[14] ibid at 31.
[15] Elden (2006) 47, 50.
[16] ibid.

Deterritorialisation is not about the end of some element of social life, often the conclusion reached by much of the broader discourse.[17] The term as used by Deleuze and Guattari does not describe the end of, decline, or failure of a system or structure, but instead signifies a story of continuity and open-endedness.[18] Moreover, de- and reterritorialisation describe a complex and *simultaneous* process or set of processes. With deterritorialisation, there is almost always an instantaneous and interconnected reterritorialisation.

In the following sections, the chapter outlines three strands of discourse that use deterritorialisation explicitly or give effect to many of its ideas. Each strand adopts a slightly different anchor for its analysis of the changes to contemporary global order. Often all three strands are used in conjunction, but this frequently does little to help clarify the discourse. It is therefore productive to identify the different prisms of analysis. For one, doing so demonstrates that each strand often unwittingly creates a distinctive legal space as a result of its analysis. But with space having receded, everything from the space of the global or the space of the city are neither properly interrogated nor deemed relevant. The overarching ideas come preloaded with their own, usually unconscious, spatialities which are assumed and untested. Each discursive strand also assumes that something different is being deterritorialised, as I go on to identify in the following section, but these different objects are rarely distinguished in what can sometimes be a rather murky and muddled discourse.

2.2 Diagnosing Deterritorialisation: Territoriality to Functionality as an Organising Logic of Authority

This first strand includes those theories that might be said to describe a process of deterritorialisation in the organising logic of international law and politics, from territorial orders to sectoral orders. The classic theory was advanced first by Luhmann,[19] then Teubner in many of his works on global legal pluralism, and then in Teubner's joint work with Fischer-Lescano. It is well articulated in their 2004 article 'Regime Collisions' where they explore the sectoral fragmentation that arises when legal and

[17] Bethlehem (2014) 9; Ryngaert and Zoetekouw (2014); We might also trace some of this thinking in discourse using 'decline', such as Schachter (1997).

[18] Holland (1991) 55.

[19] Luhmann (1971) 21, reprinted in Soziologische Aufklärung (1986).

political regimes are functionally orientated and organised. Indeed, discussions about fragmentation of international law, a topic which has occupied the minds of many international lawyers,[20] as far as it assumes the 'turn to' functionality narrative, may be further refined or rethought as a result of the analysis set out in the following pages.

The idea that there has been a turn away from territoriality to functionality as an organising logic has influenced many scholars from a variety of disciplines including international law.[21] What is common to all these thinkers is an argument that certain powers or competences which were located within the territorial state, and therefore arranged on the basis of the ordering of state territories, have moved to international organisations or private actors that are defined by, and organised around, the functions performed, that is, 'the field of activity or the area of competence'.[22] Importantly, these organisations and actors are assumed not to be territorially ordered, nor to 'have' a territory. These theories continue to assume it is primarily states that 'have' territories and are territorially defined and located.

In 'Regime Collisions', Fischer-Lescano and Teubner argue that fragmentation is widespread, reflective of a 'fundamental, multidimensional fragmentation of global society itself', and here to stay.[23] They posit that international lawyers should give up on certain 'social legal conceptions and replace[] them'[24] in order to understand the changes taking place in the global legal order and what is at stake from legal fragmentation, including the increasing influence of private actors and their private legal regimes. Of primary relevance for the purposes of this project is their assessment of global political and legal society. Noting the creation of different regimes for the economy, science, culture, technology, health, the military, transport, tourism, sport, politics, and welfare, they argue there has been a shift to a 'global society without an apex or centre':[25]

[20] 'Fragmentation of International Law: Difficulties Arising from the Diversification and Expansion of International Law. Report of the Study Group of the International Law Commission – Finalized by Martti Koskenniemi' (International Law Commission, UN General Assembly 2006) A/CN.4/L.682.

[21] Brölmann (2007); Arcuri and Violi in Kuijer and Werner (2016); Pistor (2017) 491; Berman (2002) 311; Berman (2005) 1819; Dinwoodie (2000) 469.

[22] *Legality of the Threat or Use of Nuclear Weapons, Advisory Opinion* [1996] 1 ICJ Reports 1996, p 226 (International Court of Justice) [19].

[23] Fischer-Lescano and Teubner (2004) 4, 999–1046x.

[24] ibid at 1005.

[25] ibid at 1017.

> For centuries law had followed the political logic of nation-states and was manifest in the multitude of national legal orders, each with their own territorial jurisdiction. Even international law, which viewed itself as the contract law of Nation-States, did not depart from this model. The final break with such conceptions was only signalled in the last century with the rapidly accelerating expansion of international organisations and regulatory regimes, which, in sharp contrast to their genesis within international treaties, established themselves as autonomous legal orders. The national differentiation of law is now overlain by sectorial [sic] fragmentation . . . the traditional differentiation in line with the political principle of territoriality into relatively autonomous national legal orders is thus overlain by a sectorial differentiation principle: the differentiation of global law into transnational legal regimes, which defined the external teach of their jurisdiction along issue-specific rather than territorial lines, and which claim a global validity for themselves.[26]

According to Fischer-Lescano and Teubner, this sectoral fragmentation along issue-specific rather than territorial lines does not entirely displace state-territorial structures; instead, there is an *overlaying* of these sectoral regimes. This is a vital point, overlooked in some of the more exaggerated or misunderstood claims of deterritorialisation interpreting 'the end of geography' in theories of this nature. It should be made be clear that most theorists applying Fischer-Lescano and Teubner's insights would not understand there to be a total displacement of state territory taking place. It is being 'overlain' by sectoral competences. This in turn gives pause to note that *overlaying* is a spatial concept. There is an implicit spatial imaginary operating in this explanation. What is more, Fischer-Lescano and Teubner appear to have a spatial imaginary that is 'global' in scale, or the multitude of all state territories taken together. The shift is from a striated pattern of state territorial jurisdiction to a smooth space of sectoral competences. These sectors are often not spatially differentiated and instead overlay the totality of state spaces at a global scale.

Within this shift to sectoral ordering, it is possible to detect an incoherent and fragmented change occurring within different functional areas, including the rate at which they are being reorganised from territorial to sectoral organisation. The pace of change, it is claimed, may differ, as well as the type and mode of change and mix of actors involved. For many functions, the state dominates as lawmaker and political actor, yet it is not so in all sectors. Fischer-Lescano and Teubner identify different trends in the functional areas of copyright,

[26] ibid at 1008–9.

health, and trade regimes,[27] but it is possible to see differing trends in relation to many traditional fields of international law. The law of armed conflict has a different arrangement of powers, rights and duties, and mix of relevant actors, than, for example, internet governance or international criminal law. For the field of internet governance, private actors and transnational private regulation are significant. In the field of international criminal law, there are very different patterns of power and competences between state and international actors, as well as the development of a public, global criminal law.

This move from territoriality to functionality has been identified by many international lawyers. 'Deterritorialisation' occurs for Brölmann, for example, when there is a 'detachment of regulatory authority from a specific territory.'[28] Brölmann studies the move away from the traditional divide between national and international law because this divide presumes a territorial conception of law that separate these legal spheres, one being state territory and the other being, presumably, global space. Instead 'the role of territory as a parameter in international law has come to be in decline ... [and] other normative regimes have come into existence.'[29] Brölmann's inquiry focuses on regulatory authority, sites of 'law-making', and the relevant norm-setting non-state actors, all of which are increasingly non-territorial.[30] The study explores transnational private networks, specifically those regulating the internet, and international institutional regimes, such as WHO monitoring of health concerns. The point is not just that transnational private networks (such as ICANN, ISOC, World Wide Web Consortium, the Internet Engineering Task Force, etc.) are, according to Brölmann '"non-statal" (in the way of a confederative structure) but are also "nonterritorial" (in the way of a regime tied to a specific functional area).'[31] Accordingly, territories are, in this analysis, being displaced as the organising logic by *nonterritorial* normative regimes.

Arcuri and Violi likewise note a shift to functionality, but with a more diverse spatial imaginary than state space and, or even opposable to, global space. They also observe that '[t]he emphasis on deterritorialisation has shift[ed] the attention of scholars on functionality as an

[27] For a full discussion, see ibid 1017–40.
[28] Brölmann in Nijman and Nollkaemper (2007) at 92.
[29] ibid at 84.
[30] ibid at 100–1.
[31] ibid at 87.

alternative analytical grid to better understand the dynamics of global law.'[32] For these two scholars, deterritorialisation is a phenomenon 'in which authority is removed from specific territories (but notably, state territories).'[33] Arcuri and Violi argue the two concepts of territory and functionality 'impart meaning to each other', observing that rather than territory being less relevant, there is instead often a territorial fightback.[34] They consider a number of examples where deterritorialisation might be said to be taking place, in particular '[t]he contractual provisions contributing most significantly to the phenomenon of deterritorialisation are choice of law and stabilization clauses included in State contracts.'[35] They identify 'choice of law' clauses in contracts and take as an example one specific contract between a Norwegian company and Senegal. They argue that by selecting French Law as the law applicable to the contract and the ICC in Paris as the dispute settlement forum 'the selected law is deprived of any nexus with the spatial ambit'.[36] Yet to Arcuri and Violi the principle of territoriality is resilient because, in this example, there are *other measures* relevant to the implementation of the contract in question including and especially the host state's laws on working conditions, environmental issues, and fiscal arrangements.[37]

Arcuri and Violi's argument regarding stabilisation clauses in contracts is similar. These 'petrification' clauses typically provide either compensation or an exemption in favour of the investor, where the legislative framework governing the investment activities covered by the contract is amended by the host state. A legal enclave might be thought of as being created as a result of this contract. In many instances, the production of this enclave ends up in effect alienating natural resources from states – as deterritorialisation – given the state can no longer affect law and policy as a result of the stabilisation contract. However, the introduction of a human rights exception to such clauses, so Arcuri and Violi argue, has the effect of 'circumscribing the effects of petrification provisions, so that they cannot be extended to the point of jeopardising the realization of the human rights involved.'[38] There it is

[32] Arcuri and Violi in Kuijer and Werner (2016) at 2.
[33] ibid at 9.
[34] ibid at 3–4.
[35] ibid at 25.
[36] ibid at 27.
[37] ibid at 29.
[38] ibid at 31.

framed as a 'territorial resistance' or fight back, at least as far as human rights are concerned, dismantling this legal enclave.

There is, however, an alternative way of viewing both of these examples. In the first, elements of dispute resolution in Arcuri and Violi's choice of law remain 'deterritorialised' *even if* other measures relevant to the contract (working conditions and environmental protection) are provided for by the host state. Contracts can be thought of as a number of different rights and duties rather than a monolithic entity that is either territorialised or deterritorialised as a whole. It is possible to separate out individual elements of a contract to examine individual rights, privileges, or activities and understand the organising logic and spaces of each. The same is true in the second case of stabilisation clauses. There is some element of deterritorialisation taking place even if the state continues to a role in ensuring human rights protection. In their petrification example, there are instead two applicable legal regimes, overlapping but equally applicable in relation to the same physical geography: human rights law and the law found in the 'legal enclave'. Thus, the competences located in the legal enclave can still be thought of as deterritorialised but competences in relation to, say, human rights remain territorialised in the state.

The deterritorialisation of (state) sovereignty is a recurring theme in several recent studies. Chimni, for example, frames 'functional processes' as 'aggregating . . . at a global level' but importantly 'without displaying the territorial state'.[39] The global imperial state is characterised explicitly as a '*non-territorial* Global State'.[40] Chimni explains that 'contemporary modes of divisibility of sovereignty are more complex. The slice of sovereignty that is parted with today finds a non-territorial home.'[41] Similarly, Pistor, in her article 'From Territorial to Monetary Sovereignty', argues that sovereignty has transformed, as it is now 'not limited to control over territory and people'. Here, it is the competences associated with sovereignty that are the focus of the work, but it still broadly traces the same theme of deterritorialising sovereignty from a territorial basis to a sectoral one. Pistor argues that 'control over monetary affairs is a critical part of *genuine sovereignty*' (emphasis added) and in this 'age of globalization . . . the relevance and importance of territorial

39 Chimni (2006) 17, 20.
40 ibid at 18. Emphasis added.
41 ibid.

versus monetary sovereignty has shifted in favour of the latter.'[42] This argument then notes a shift from a territorial logic for sovereignty to one driven by money (a competence or sector) and globalisation; whereas control over territory *was* the most essential element or organising logic of sovereignty, it is increasingly ordered by control over money instead. Although Pistor says 'territorial sovereignty still matters',[43] this idea is not really dealt with. How territory still matters while being thus challenged is never reconciled.

Pistor ties '*actual*' sovereignty to control over money and 'given the central importance of finance for the operation of states, this raises the question of how sovereign most states truly are.'[44] Her test of 'control' in relation to sovereignty is never spelled out. According to Pistor:

> only some countries that issue their own currencies retain control over their monetary policies, a precondition for "monetary" sovereignty. Countries that adopt a foreign currency (by dollarizing their economies) or join forces with others to adopt a new, common currency (the euro) give up more than control over interest rate policy. They also relinquish their ability to address financial crises.[45]

In Pistor's account 'private money' and regional currencies, such as the Euro, challenge the monetary sovereignty of states. The patterns of control over money indicates there is a challenge to the authority of some states by other states, by international organisations, but especially worryingly by private entities, given their ability to influence and even collapse economies.[46]

Crucial to Pistor's argument, is the claim that territorial sovereignty is flat[47] whereas money and monetary sovereignty are hierarchical: '[t]he flatness of territorial sovereignty stands in marked contrast to the "inherently" hierarchical nature of money and, by implication, of monetary sovereignty.'[48] Territorial sovereignty, as

[42] Pistor (2017) 1.
[43] ibid at 10.
[44] ibid at 2.
[45] ibid.
[46] ibid at 20–22.
[47] ibid 15. In full: 'Territorial sovereignty is based on control over land and the people residing on it. How exactly control is organized is irrelevant for the recognition of territorial sovereignty. It may vary internally, but in the external relation to other states sovereignty is flat.'
[48] Pistor (2017) 23.

presently conceived by the discipline of international law, as I demonstrate in the following chapter, often is conceived of as a flat, one layer, system, as well as supposedly non-hierarchical (and here we must critique the role space plays in constituting the imagining of the sovereign equality of states doctrine).[49] Pistor, here, thinks of territory as an *object* of sovereignty, in the same way that money is. Conceiving of territory as a space, not an object, and thus not even slightly comparable with money in this way, would result in a different analysis of legal relations.[50] Indeed, as I highlight below, I find this to be an example of a confusion of registers between space, actors, and functions.

In a similar vein, Milano, in his reflection on *The Deterritorialisation of International Law*, examines the 'extent to which international law has been affected by and has contributed to new forms of power exercise *detached from territory*: in other words, whether international law itself is in a process of deterritorialisation'.[51] Milano points to the 'evolution of the notion of jurisdiction in international human rights regimes' as an example of deterritorialisation as it shows a 'shift from territorially-defined legal competence to functional competence.'[52] Not only this, but, according to Milano, there is a 'crisis' for 'territory as a central concept in international law' which has 'gone hand in hand with the phenomenon of globalization and with the displacement of the State, as a territorially bound political organization, as the protagonist of international law as we knew it, mainly induced by a factual lack of sovereignty, especially in the economic field.'[53] This is similar to Pistor who also seeks to examine where *factual* or *actual* sovereignty lies. Milano posits that territory is less of a central concept in international law because:

[49] For more on this see Lythgoe (2024) at 14.

[50] This topic, and the alternative way of understanding territory and how that space is constituted, is addressed further in Chapter 4. It is, I contend in this book, overly simplistic to think of space as an *object* of governance (and an error to think of it as a material object of governance); it is instead the 'complex' of populations, groups, individuals, things, and activities that are the object of governance. Space is what is created by those social relations. For more on this, see Elden and Crampton (2016) at 7. See also Massey on space as the realm of social interactions: Massey (2005) at 61.

[51] Milano (2013) 6.

[52] ibid at 3–4.

[53] ibid at 2.

> territory is no more up for grabs in contemporary international law due to the emergence of peremptory norms, such as the prohibition to use force to acquire territory and the principle of self-determination. The *uti possidetis juris* principle is nowadays considered a principle of general international law and the territorial configuration of the earth is determined by borders established mainly by colonial powers in the 19th century and by multinational States in the course of the 20th century.[54]

He argues 'international law's diminished concern for territory, is matched by an increasing preoccupation with the governance of people.'[55] It is not clear why the fact that territory is no longer 'up for grabs' in turn produces the cross-border globalisation and 'the differentiation of global law into transnational legal regimes.'[56] It appears to be *non sequitur* argument. States could have continued to operate only within their borders once there was no more physical geography to 'acquire'. This narrative can never account for why states created international organisations nor why states made it so easy for multinational corporations to operate transnationally. States never had to create the many processes that then created globalisation.

Putting aside the unilinear historical narrative, Milano appears to assume territory is *the same as* physical geography when he maintains that it was because territory stopped being up for grabs, once all physical geography was 'assigned' to states, that transnational legal developments appear. He explicitly says this in summing up: 'despite the fact that the earth is not up for grabs as it was 200 years ago . . .'.[57] Territories, it is assumed, are parcels of physical geography. On this, Milano seems to miss the point by Quadri that he quotes. Quadri had said: 'territory neither has an object, nor as an essential attribute of state sovereignty, but as one of the (spatial) ambits in which sovereignty displays its functions and it is hence protected by international law.'[58] Territory is understood by Quadri not as an object but a space, and spaces could overlap the same physical geography. More on this later. For now, we can conclude by saying that Milano, it appears, uses the

[54] ibid at 3.
[55] ibid.
[56] ibid at 2.
[57] ibid at 4.
[58] Rolando Quadri, *Diritto internazionale pubblico* (Liguori 1968), as quoted in Milano (2013) 3.

concept of territory in a different sense. As with many of the examples in this strand, territory is assumed to be fixed, flat, and often confused with the physical world. Further, we can note in concluding here that the body of discourse appearing in this first theme is likely to construct the field of global governance and 'law beyond the state' as unspecific global, transnational, or international legal space (usually without apex or centre). Even work purporting to 'define the space of transnational law' fails to define this space any more precisely than the globe: there is only disembedding without re-embedding.[59] Global space is often assumed to be flat, homogeneous, and unbound. The following two chapters examine these individual spatial characteristics in more detail. For the time being, what is also emerging at this point in the above accounts is they each reproduce a common understanding of the territory that is being deterritorialised from.

2.3 Diagnosing Deterritorialisation: The Relocation of Competences and Power

The second strand of deterritorialisation discourse involves theories that more explicitly discuss the *relocation* of competences and powers to different actors. These theories might be thought of as telling a story of the deterritorialisation of control over particular competences from states and reterritorialisation to other actors, but, as will be seen, the spaces of these actors are under-theorised. This differs from the previous strand where it appears that it is the organising logic of power and authority that drives the theoretical framing, that assumes the globe at large or 'transnational space',[60] imprecisely defined as the deterritorialised space. In the following analysis, while it is true that many of the supra-state projects explored might be made to also fit in to the above strand, it is the focus on the *specific place of relocation* that sets them apart and not their functional competence ordering. The European Union (EU) for example is generally conceived of as more than a functional organisation. Moreover, the relocation of competences at a sub-state level would not have the same logic of sectoral organisation and would not fit in the above strand for that reason.

[59] Zumbansen (2011) 10, 19.

[60] Schmidt (2018) at 50.

Two broad research projects are highlighted in relation to this category. The first are projects which might be classed as supra-state: the relocation of competences to the EU and customs territories, for example. The second are projects that consider sub-state actors and spaces: the relocation of power to cities as global actors. It should be noted that even adopting the labels 'supra-' and 'sub-'state reproduces a particular geography, where the state territory is the starting point of analysis. The forthcoming analysis continues to perform this division because that is how it is conceived of in the discourse being examined. Moreover, it is as a result of the state-orientated implicit geography that international legal theory differs in its explanations of why the relocation of competences or power is taking place at sub- and supra-state levels. As such, international law adopts different explanations of the ability of supra- and sub-state entities to make, and impact the making of, international law. In other words, the legal reasoning is something that is itself produced by the prioritisation of state space.

2.3.1 Supra-state Entities: EU and Customs Unions

There are some studies, such as those undertaken of customs unions and the EU, where there are identifiable actors exercising competences once performed by states. Arcuri and Violi in their research also feature examples fitting into this second strand. Their research demonstrates that:

> customs territories possessing "full autonomy in the conduct of [their] external commercial relations and of ... other matters" ... were/are eligible to become Contracting Parties/Members under GATT 1947 and the WTO Agreements ... [this provision] attests to the formal recognition of customs unions *as equal to States*. Accepting customs territories as WTO ... Members is an interesting manifestation of the encounter between functionality and territoriality. The criterion to multiply the legally relevant territorial units is manifestly functional: what is required to become a WTO Member is the full autonomy in the conduct of external commercial relations. Yet the criterion remains bitingly territorial: the *customs territory is the unit to be eligible.*
>
> (emphasis added)[61]

[61] Arcuri and Violi in Kuijer and Werner (2016) at 11–12.

The EU is an interesting case in point: while all EU member states have World Trade Organization (WTO) membership in their own right, the Commission speaks for EU member states at many meetings and often settles disputes. According to Arcuri and Violi, there is *territoriality* 'because the EU, as a political entity, is encased in a precise geography and authority is exercised only within these boundaries.'[62] However, they never exactly define the conceptual relationship between territoriality and territory, as they stop short of referring explicitly to EU territory. The WTO Appellate Body does explicitly use the language of territory. In *Customs Classification of Certain Computer Equipment*, the report states 'the [EU] constitutes a customs union, and as such, once goods are imported into any Member State, they circulate freely within *the territory of the entire customs union*. The export market, therefore, is the [EU] not an individual Member State'[63] (emphasis added). Thus, the relevant unit of space in this dispute was the territory of the customs union, the EU, not individual member states due to the rules for the circulation of goods across the entirety of the space being those of the EU.

It could be observed at this point that the WTO also uses the term 'territory' as a subject, which is a usage distinct from the idea of a territory of states or customs unions. For WTO purposes *customs territories* are equivalent to states: 'The WTO currently has 164 members, of which 117 are developing countries or separate customs territories.'[64] The WTO Agreement provides that: 'Any State or separate customs territory possessing full autonomy in the conduct of its external commercial relations and of the other matters provided for in this Agreement and the Multilateral Trade Agreements may accede to this Agreement, on terms to be agreed between it and the WTO.'[65] The WTO only has two customs territories however: the EU and Separate Customs Territory of Taiwan, Penghu, Kinmen, and Matsu (Chinese Taipei). The latter Separate Customs Territory is a political compromise regarding a controversy surrounding a particular instance of statehood and political status. As such, all territories have a territory.

62 ibid at 12.

63 *European Communities – Customs Classification of Certain Computer Equipment*, Report of the Appellate Body [1998] WTO AB-1998-2, para 96.

64 WTO, 'Overview' <www.wto.org/english/thewto_e/whatis_e/wto_dg_stat_e.htm>.

65 Article XII, Agreement Establishing the World Trade Organization 1994 (1867 UNTS 3).

Of course, the EU is more than a customs union, even if that is the reason for its inclusion as a WTO member. The EU also speaks for member states on issues related to law of the sea and appears as a party in related dispute settlement, having signed the United Nations Convention on the Law of the Sea (UNCLOS) in 1984. Thus, it is the non-state organisation that is the relevant entity for many law of the sea purposes. The EU is recognised as an interested party to any negotiations and disputes arising under UNCLOS and affecting EU law. This is because EU treaties, in accordance with Article 52 TEU, apply to the same space as member states territories and EU law applies 'directly' to inland, coastal and territorial waters, the EEZ, the continental shelf,[66] and to vessels flying the flag of member states.[67]

The study of EU space is more advanced and yet still underdeveloped. The reason for its underdevelopment is that while the EU has been difficult to ignore because there has been a persistent and widespread movement of competences from states to the EU, orthodox theory about legal territoriality is overwhelmingly associated with the specific instance of state space. As a result, the EU often appears on an ad hoc list of *sui generis* territorial actors.[68] Yet, its space is more advanced than other regional organisations which have not received the same degree of exploration. The EU is the main organisation consistently explicitly identified as belonging to this *sui generis* category of actors having their own territoriality. However, I do not think we must limit this category to the EU. The African Union (AU), African, Caribbean and Pacific Group of States, Arab Maghreb Union, Central African Economic and Monetary Community, Andean Community of Nations, etc. are also 'encased in a precise geography' and there is a (re)location of varying degrees of authority from states. This raises several questions, unresolvable in this project, that include the following: does the lack of research arise because western scholars pay little attention to these regional organisations? Is this because deterritorialisation discourse is taking place primarily within western academia? Or, is there something qualitatively different

[66] Confirmed in: Case C-6/04 *Commission of the European Communities v United Kingdom of Great Britain and Northern Ireland* [2005] ECR I-9017 ('Case C-6/04 *EC v UK*'), para 117; Case C-347/10, *A Salemink v Raad van bestuur van het Uitvoeringsinstituut werknemersverzeeringen* [2012] ILEC 079 ('Case C-347/10 *Salemink v Raad*'), para 35.

[67] For further discussion on this see: Paasivirta (2015).

[68] Shaw (2014) at 162–83. However, I submit that *sui generis* space is an unresolved category. I argue this further in Lythgoe (2023).

in the way the EU has been transferred powers and competences, in comparison to other regional organisations? On the last question, given the African Economic Community (AEC), for example, is developing an African passport, this regional organisation is taking on an institutional form similar to the EU. The AU Commission facilitates the issuing of the passport and provides technical support to member states.[69]

What emerges from this strand of supra-state discourse is usually a focus on regional organisations as opposed to other international public or private institutions, where there is usually a familiar and readily identifiable geographic story to tell. In other words, there is a space of relocation, even if that space is unresolved. Where these regional organisations are admitted to having a territory, this is usually achieved by consigning them into the status of *sui generis*. But I find this *sui generis* category is left thoroughly unresolved in international legal discourse. Besides, the presence of this exceptional category dialectically proves that there is a general rule about the concept of territory being state-orientated. Moreover, it tends to concern 'public' actors. It does not often, for example, include the ISO, ICANN, or the many other more private actors. Nor would these theories usually address and include those actors with a supposedly global reach such as the UN or the Organisation for Economic Co-operation and Development (OECD).

2.3.2 Sub-state: Cities

The second notable body of discourse that fits within this strand is that which looks at the role of sub-state actors as global actors, notably cities.[70] The logic of these actors and the theorisation in relation to the redistribution of power operates slightly differently to the EU and customs unions. In these latter two examples, there is a pattern of redistributing competences once located in the state to non-state supra-state actors. The rise or 'renaissance' of cities is less about an explicit transfer of competences once residing in states being relocated to cities, and more about a *redistribution of power* in relation to particular

[69] Protocol to the Treaty Establishing the African Economic Community Relating to the Free Movement of Persons, Right of Residence and Right of Establishment 2018, Article 10.

[70] Nijman (2016); Curtis (2011) 1923; 'UN Forum' (2018).

functional or sectoral areas by cities which has the effect of *reconstituting a city and its competences*. In this view of things, competences could generally be understood as having been created *ex nihilo*.[71]

Cities increasingly have a voice in matters directly relevant to international law and politics, leading some to claim there is an 'inversion of the hierarchy of power'[72] – notably also a spatialised framing. For example, in July 2018, New York became the first city to 'report directly to the international community on its efforts to reach global benchmarks in addressing poverty, inequality and climate change.'[73] Although this reporting is entirely voluntary, this event represents a wider shift in how the idea of what constitutes the international community has come to be conceptualised in recent years. Of course, New York is not obligated in international law, to report on its SDG (sustainable development goal)-promoting activities. It is difficult to see cities, no matter how big or wealthy, as holding any real power for the moment, from an international law point of view, to effect or prevent (or be held responsible for) the kind of changes the SDG programme envisages. However, when one considers that even for states SDGs are but political aspirations, the pursuit of which entails no legal responsibility, the point seems somewhat moot. The same trend for the greater involvement of 'sub-national' political units can also be seen in further examples both within and outside the UN institutional framework, in areas such as disarmament and environmental protection. A considerable push, for example, in favour of the 2017 Treaty on the Prohibition of Nuclear Weapons (TPNW) comes from municipal authorities and city councils, claiming: 'Nuclear Weapons put all … cities at risk. Now cities all over the world

[71] However, this creation of *ex nihilo* competences can, I think, take place with international organisations and other non-state actors too. Prior to the UN Charter, there was no right for an actor to determine the existence of a threat or breach of the peace and as a result decide to take measures to maintain or to restore peace and security; nor was there a prior duty to make available to the UN Security Council armed forces, assistance, facilities, rights of passage, etc. These are 'new', even if the broad *area* of peace and security, until the creation of the UN, resided with states for much of the nineteenth and early twentieth century. Ferguson and Gupta agree: 'Institutions of global governance are not simply replicating on a bigger scale the functions and tasks of the nation-state, as both proponents and opponents of transnational governmentality often assume', Ferguson and Gupta (2002) 981, 996. Moreover, we can of course remember that the creation of *ex nihilo* rights and duties also took place with nation-states, something normative legal positivism does not internally account for.

[72] Katz and Bradley (2014) at 5.

[73] 'UN Forum' (2018).

are fighting back.'[74] Mayors and subnational leaders also made a significant intervention urging states to undertake a number of steps, including 'to commit, to take and implement all required actions now to limit any further increase in global warming, to approve a climate regime at the UN Climate Conference in Paris 2015 that will ensure the implementation of this goal' and 'request national governments, supranational organizations such as the EU and intergovernmental bodies to create multilateral/bilateral partnerships or initiatives through existing or new mechanisms to enhance and support local, low-carbon, resource-efficient, climate-resilient action.'[75]

Scholars have turned their attention to this changing relationship between states and cities. 'Globalization, urbanization, and decentralization can' according to Nijman 'be said to reshape the state's power structure and to reconfigure its structure of authority and responsibility. Specifically, they empower the city to confront urban issues more independently on a global level.'[76] Nijman adopts a 'social constructivist approach to actorhood' as it makes more visible and accessible 'how the city actually constitutes itself as a global actor by developing foreign policy practices and specifically by connecting to international law and international institutions.'[77] The core argument being that cities are coming to regard international norms as relevant to them, are increasingly participating in international law practices and processes affairs, and are 'imitating foreign policy and international law practices of the state'.[78]

Cities have pretty well-defined spaces, much like the state, although these spaces are mostly visible at a domestic level. Their spaces typically require a 'piercing of the state veil' to observe, despite being increasingly relevant for international politics and legal norm cultivation. As such, the territories of cities are not at all relevant for international law discourse about the concept of territory or its theories of territorial sovereignty. This body of discourse tends to leave the broad underlying territorial framework of international law untouched and the space of cities vis-à-vis these spaces also unresolved. Yet, this is an important point for further exploration. The spatial imaginary held by cities will continue

[74] 'ICAN Cities Appeal'.

[75] The Nantes Declaration of Mayors and Subnational Leaders on Climate Change 2013.

[76] Nijman (2016) at 221.

[77] ibid at 221–22.

[78] ibid at 226–27, 231–32.

to conflict with the imaginary of international law. An interesting example is the Global Charter-Agenda for Human Rights in the City (2011) – an example often cited of cities seeing themselves as global actors. In the Charter cities agree to create action plans for human rights within their cities. Interestingly, the Global Charter explicitly refers to the question of its spaces: 'A "territory" is a managed area which falls directly or indirectly under the jurisdiction of the city.'[79]

While leaving the territorial framing of international law untouched, the spaces of cities tend to be seen through the prism of the spaces of flow, of postmodernity, highlighted in the introduction. Their spaces are fundamentally different to, and often perceived as a challenge to, state territory. And yet, their construction and identification, at least as in the Global Charter above, is broadly similar to (state-)territory, which makes the turn to flow explanation curious. Global cities are, according to Curtis, 'essential to processes of globalization, providing a material and infrastructural backbone for global *flows*, and a set *of physical sites that facilitate command and control functions* for a decentralised global economy'[80] (emphasis added). The rise of cities, Curtis continues, 'poses important questions about a discipline conditioned to examine a world of territorial nation-states. It signals a fundamental challenge to some of the core logics of the modern international system.'[81] The logic of state-centric conceptions of territories are as internally homogeneous, contiguous, smooth, and abstract space.[82] Yet, the spatial form of global cities is understood, as Curtis outlines, as one of 'nodes, regions and networks'.[83] So while these sub-state spaces are locatable, the where of power being deterritorialised from the state to the city is knowable in much of this body of discourse, they continue to be thought of as opposable to the space of territories (despite there being at least one example of cities thinking of themselves as having territories in a remarkable similar to way states.).

Taking supra- and sub- together, what emerges is that while this discursive strand focuses on the point of relocation from one actor to

[79] Global Charter-Agenda for Human Rights in the City, United Cities and Local Governments, Committee for Social Inclusion, Participatory Democracy and Human Rights 2011.

[80] Curtis (2011) 1923.

[81] ibid.

[82] These characteristics are discussed in further detail in the following chapter. I also speak of them in more detail in Lythgoe (2024).

[83] Curtis (2011) 1925.

another – from state to EU, from state to customs territories, from state to cities – the spaces in relation to which these non-state actors are exercising power are either undertheorised or explicitly not territories, indeed often opposable to territories. In other words, these discourses also tend to reproduce the same concept of (state-)territory, resulting in one tending to be understood as a *sui generis territorial entity* and the other as opposable to territory because they are involved in spaces of flow. The spaces of the sub-state actor, as with the supra state entity, do not fit the concept of territory understood in international law nor does the discourse try to confront this long-established concept. With the sure rise of sub-state actors with, I argue, their very own territories and the redistribution of power to global actors, also with their own (*sui generis*) territories, international legal theory and the discipline overall cannot continue to operate with its orthodox conception of territory that is limited to the state. The *sui generis* category of non-state territorial entities continues to be stretched.[84] Before examining this orthodox concept of territory that produces this *sui generis* structure in legal thought in more detail in the following chapter, I address the final category of deterritorialisation discourses.

2.4 Diagnosing Deterritorialisation: Across Borders

The third strand that emerges in deterritorialisation discourse involves theories that address cross-border phenomena. Such discourse usually posits that one of the major developments wrought by globalisation has been the increasing porosity of state borders. It differs from the previous two strands as it tends to focus on the cross-border element of activities, for example, tracing the movements of materials, goods, people, and services, making the border the primary unit of analysis. Yet, it can still be seen as a theory trying to make sense of global governance and globalisation and it is also one which responds with a deterritorialising account, for state territory is, in this way of thinking, seen either as 'less relevant' and thus less able to mitigate against and fight back against these phenomena or as states allowing their territorial decision making to matter less by allowing in these 'external' forces.

This explanation of the processes and effects of globalisation is relatively popular and widespread. Theories concerning the porosity of

[84] See further the argument made in Lythgoe (2023).

borders tend to also focus on what allows for and creates the conditions for the mobility of people, goods, and services as well as its effects. What often allows for this mobility is a change in the way people, goods, and services interact with borders, those 'immobile infrastructures that organise the intermittent flow of people, information, and image, as well as the borders or 'gates' that limit, channel, and regulate movement or anticipated movement.'[85] A handful of examples will suffice to understand the observations made by this approach:

> [t]he borders of nations and regions have become increasingly porous to goods, services and, above all, information.[86]
>
> Contemporary globalization has irrevocably made borders porous to capital, services, goods, and persons.[87]
>
> Under globalization, the goal is to harden the border for some, while making it more elastic and porous for others.[88]

The general idea is that (state) borders are, through a variety of legal and political measures and technological changes, letting more things – goods, services, information, people – pass through them and into state territory. One of the most evocative descriptions of this can be found in the work of Bethlehem who said:

> While the geography of statehood is likely to remain at the root of the international system, it is becoming increasingly less important as people, goods, services, and funds flow across borders; as individuals and corporations engage directly with one another without the intermediation of states or of their paraphernalia . . . as international and non-governmental organizations proliferate and operate transnationally on the basis of technical mandates that transcend, or endeavour to transcend, narrow sovereign interests. On this vision of international society, sovereignty and boundaries are like rocks in a river. They may impede the flow, and even perhaps, on occasion, dam up the water. More usually, however, they simply act as an impediment to the directionality of the flow of the water, which eventually finds a new pathway on its free-flowing gravitational course.[89]

This third strand is also often conceived of as a 'post-territoriality' thesis, whereby 'in a globalised and digitalised world, territoriality is in fact

[85] Sheller and Urry (2006) 207, 212.
[86] Aoki (2000) 913, 915.
[87] Dagron (2014) 949, 949.
[88] Wonders (2007) 33, 34.
[89] Bethlehem (2014) 15.

often perceived as an obstacle to the effective exercise of those tasks.'[90] While this third strand has been framed by some as 'post-territorial', it is also in many ways not as radical as its sounds. It often continues to analytically centre and prioritise state territories and their bounding, noting that it is *their* borders that are increasingly permeable to goods, services, and information. In other words, state territories continue to matter and continue to serve as a backdrop for this 'post-territorial world'. Or put again in another way, continues to reproduce the same concept of (state-territory). Implicit within some of this discourse is the idea that state territories and their borders are more tangible than these external forces. They are also more permanent, with borders being described as 'rocks in a river' while these external forces are like flowing water. But all this flowing water imagery does is show that the spaces of these external forces are unknown and undertheorised.[91] State borders are also hard, immoveable, *physical* objects, unlike water, it is just that they are becoming more accessible to spatially incongruent goods, services, and classes of people.

It must be noted that this analysis contains the potential to powerfully critique developments from the point of view of class and race. It makes visible the power of certain categories of people to be mobile, as well as the hard, or less porous, borders faced by the poor or refugees. For example, Kapur argues that studying the movement of people, 'legitimate and illegitimate, across national and international borders' can 'expos[e] the porosity of borders, the transnational reality of subaltern existence, and the contingent foundations of international law.'[92] Porosity also has important explanatory power to understand the movement of capital, goods, and services in and out of states, as well as how uneven this is, especially when compared with the mobility of people: '[borders] may be highly porous for some things (e.g. capital) but relatively impervious to others (e.g. labour immigration).'[93] But it must be matched with a spatial understanding of those external forces, which is more often than not incomplete because of the limited spatial imaginary of international law as a discipline.

[90] Schmidt (2018) at 11.

[91] There is an attempt to better understand these spaces, usually in adjacent disciplines, by the likes of: Khalili (2020); Easterling (2014); The IGLP Law and Global Production Working Group (2016) 57.

[92] Kapur (2003) 6.

[93] Anderson and O'Dowd (1999) 593, 596.

2.5 Producing Aterritoriality: Problems, Insights, and Stakes

These examples are reflective of the discourse noting a shift in the organising logic of power and authority in the contemporary global order, the relocation of competences to non-state actors, and the performance of borders. There is much to be taken from these accounts, including the plurality of relevant actors and polycentricity of the global legal and political order. There is also much to be fine-tuned about these accounts.

Despite the differences explored above there are some commonalities between these three strands, and the resulting aterritoriality. One thing they share is that the starting point for the analysis is always state territory. State territories are the static backdrop from which their analysis begins. Second, they each reproduce assumptions about the concept of (state-)territory, such that it is often perceived of as flat or as static. The third thing they share is a broad predisposition towards constructing territory in an ontological sense as an object. The following chapter will outline this concept of territory in more detail by excavating that concept's content. The remainder of this chapter will show there are significant consequences as a result of these shared traits. Each strand of deterritorialisation discourse operates within the same set of imaginational constraints and is limited by the reproduction of a particular concept of territory. These blind spots create two key problems: deterritorialisation without reterritorialisation, because the territory of reterritorialisation cannot be imagined and as a result of the state and its territory often being treated as synonymous, there is a lack of analytical clarity. The final section assesses the stakes of (re)thinking deterritorialisation with reterritorialisation.

2.5.1 Deterritorialisation without Reterritorialisation

Reproducing the orthodox concept of territory results in assuming deterritorialisation is a one-way and straightforward process; as a move away from territory, in the sense of functions moving away from (state-) territory, or a move away from (state-)territory as a central relevant organising idea. The discourses outlined above, as I claim a direct result of reproducing the concept of (state-) territory, entirely prevents the recognition that *deterritorialised processes result in reterritorialisation.* Such accounts fail to see the reterritorialisation that was so vital to and instructive in Deleuze and Guattari's thesis. They are instead often acknowledging, even implicitly, a move from the territorial to the non- or aterritorial.

If we remember, Deleuze and Guattari thought of deterritorialisation and reterritorialisation as 'always connected' and that 'the deterritorialisation of one' brings about 'the reterritorialisation of the other.'[94] As a result, a 'continual process of de- and reterritorialisation' means that there is a 'reconfiguration of spatial relations rather than their end.'[95] Too often the shift to functional ordering is understood entirely aspatially – as an end of geography or the end of spatial ordering. The competences and functions in each particular analysis are rarely acknowledged by scholars as being reassembled in new territories and legal spaces – indeed it is nigh on impossible for this to take place because the concept of territory refers in the main only to state territory. The territory of reterritorialisation is unimaginable.

In some instances, there is an assumed or latent, but incomplete and abstract space of reterritorialisation. Fischer-Lescano and Teubner argue there is an overlaying of sectoral functions over the territories of states. This theory assumes some kind of spatial overlapping. What is the space that is overlapping? For these two, the sectoral functions are assumed to now operate in global space, as their repeated references to 'global sphere', 'global level', and 'global society' indicate. Pistor also latently adopts the global level, arguing that 'capital can and does roam the globe'[96] This spatiality is also assumed by Pistor in another recently published work *The Code of Capital*:

> we can see the makings of an even more impressive empire of law, which stretches far beyond the territory of a single state and encompasses the globe: the legal empire that sustains global trade, commerce, and finance, the most lucrative of them all for lawyers as well as for their clients.[97]

Money and monetary sovereignty also have legal spaces of operation, but these are not acknowledged. I argue instead that money does not float or roam at random around the global financial system. Currencies have their own spaces.[98] Capital is reterritorialised. Yet, if we only reproduce

94 Deleuze and Guattari (1987) at 31.
95 Elden (2006) 50.
96 Pistor (2017) 3.
97 Pistor (2019) at 159.
98 This is already well established by many who own on the geographies of money. See: Leyshon and Thrift (2005); Corbridge, Martin, and Thrift (1994).

the orthodox concept of territory, which tends to be understood as 'one layer deep' or 'flat', the specific sites of reterritorialisation are invisible to the analysis. Instead, the analysis often operates at a scale which imagines global space as smooth, continuous, and homogeneous space and, as a result, loses crucial insight as to how capital, trade, human rights, and internet governance actually operate. Capital does not roam the globe freely; it depends on several structures and actors operating with different legal regimes and each with their own legal-political space.[99]

Functions are not understood to reterritorialise because the relevant spaces are not (yet) recognisable as legal spaces in the onto-theoretical lexicon of scholars. While never explicit, these contributions assume states are the only actors to 'have' territory. This is the logical deduction from theories positing a move from territory (of states) to functionality, that there has been a shift from the 'political logic of nation-states ... manifest[ed] in the multitude of national legal orders, each with their own territorial jurisdiction'[100] to 'transnational legal regimes which define the external reach of their jurisdiction along issue-specific rather than territorial lines.'[101] The issue-specific regimes are non- or a-territorially defined because the actors are assumed to be non-territorial. Even the second strand identified above, which often does acknowledge that there are spaces of relocation, cannot adequately explain whether or how these spaces relate to the concept of territory. They create either a *sui generis* category of territory as the space of reterritorialisation because territory is assumed in orthodox discourse to 'belong' only to states or oppose those spaces to territory, as in the case of spaces of flows.[102] So, the third limitation in reproducing the orthodox concept of territory is that it limits the actors 'having' a territory to states and the systems 'having' territoriality to state-based systems.

Moreover, analysis that concentrates on deterritorialisation over or entirely without reterritorialisation is often ahistorical. The natural

[99] I am choosing here to keep this reference at the generic level of space for now. I do argue in Chapter 4 that these can be understood as territories and outline how we can think of them as so, but I want to keep readers with me for now.

[100] Fischer-Lescano and Teubner (2004) 1008.

[101] ibid 1009.

[102] Spaces of flows are assumed not to be territorial because of the assumption that this space is static, so it would be incongruent to think of these as reterritorialising. This exemplifies a classic characteristic of territory: it is assumed to be static.

referent or starting point for analysis is state territory. The deterritorialisation is always from the state to supra (global, regional, transnational general space) or sub-state levels. This may be created by an underlying normative belief that these powers 'naturally' reside in state territory or simply from an ahistorical view of things. It ignores, or fails to tell the story in full, that many of these competences were earlier reterritorialised into the state, deterritorialised from monarchies, city states, leagues, feudal lords, the church, and private individuals.[103] Yet more competences were constituted at the moment of the constitution of states and the international legal system or at various points throughout the life of this system.[104]

2.5.2 Analytical Clarity: Functions, Actors and Spaces

The second implication of the imaginational constraints outlined above is a lack of analytical clarity. This way of thinking very frequently results in 'conceptual lumping', whereby actors, their spaces, and the functions they exercise are conflated. They are conflated for two reasons. The first and key reason is that the terms state and territory are often used or thought of synonymously; one commonly infers the other. This is because the concept of territory primarily used refers to state territory only, which allows the easy slide into equivalence between the two concepts. The second and related reason is the domination of state-territory as the relevant space for international law. This 'draws the eye' and makes less visible the spaces of other actors.

At this point, I advocate taking a step back from the current approaches and implementing a structural analysis of the spatial distribution of functions and the spaces of the respective actors separately, with a view to more clearly identifying the pattern of (re)location of functions. If we were to undertake a spatial analysis of competences – without allowing state territory to dominate and predetermine – we might describe competences as having shifted from one actor's space to another. On this view of things, what is happening could be understood

[103] See for a small sample: Spruyt (1994); Osiander (2001a) 251; Osiander (2001b) 119; Osiander (2007); Sassen (2006); Larkins (2009); Branch (2014); Kratochwil (1986) 27; White (2004).

[104] I explore this theme further in Chapter 5.

as a fundamental shift in the spatial organisation of competences, whereby the distribution of competences and broad functional areas shift from a default position of concentration and synchronisation, where the entire bundle of competences is typically retained by one actor (the state), to an increasingly default position of dispersal, where the same competences are exercised by different actors. In this understanding, competences are seen as being redistributed from one category of subjects (states) with highly particular spaces (state territories) to a wide range of different categories of subjects (such as international organisations or even private actors as in the case of transnational private networks) each of which has its own spatial logic. The proposed reconceptualisation would result in separating the bundle of competences associated with sovereignty into its different constituent parts and tracing the patterns of their redistribution across differently configured spaces.

The advantage of this reconceptualisation is that it prevents the analytical conflation between functions and spaces. The understanding that sectoral regimes overlay territorial regimes is one gigantic analytical conflation. It also constitutes a faux binary between functionality and territoriality. This conflation is a common theme within much of the discourse discussed above. Within these accounts, the description quickly moves from a contemplation of the territorial dimension of global legal, political, and economic processes (a space) to a contemplation of their functional dimension (a non-spatial focus). What this indicates is a certain confusion of registers: the focal point of the analysis appears to shift from a consideration of the spatial organisation of one actor (territory of a state) to a consideration of the objective organisation of functions in the global political space. What this means then, is that sectoral regimes overlay territorial regimes. That is to confuse the registers. The story that governs the first strand of deterritorialisation discourse might instead be retold as sovereign competences (*functions*) that were once consolidated within one actor's, that is, states' (*actor*), territories (*space*), are instead (according to this explanation) being exercised by non-state actors (*actor*) operating in a global or transnational space (*space*). Yet, this retelling continues understanding global space as imprecise, abstract, and incapable of representing the real spatial logics of, for example, capital or the exercise of power by non-state actors. In Arcuri and Violi's examples, they argue there has been a multiplication of territorial units which are legally relevant for the regime of international trade.[105] This multiplication of territorial units fits into their overall thesis of the move to a functional ordering because they argue 'territoriality is meaningful vis-à-vis functionality.'[106] The EU is a trading system (function) with its own territorial unit (NB it is never explicitly referred to as 'EU territory'), that is, the 'precise geography' the EU is 'encased in'.[107] However, the phrase, 'territoriality being meaningful vis-à-vis functionality', is not, in my view, satisfactory as an explanation of what is happening. What does it mean in practice? It appears with the greatest respect, to me at least, to lack conceptual and analytical clarity. While I continue pondering what Arcuri and Violi are trying to communicate with this, I cannot help but wonder whether this 'formula' of words arises because the discipline offers few tools to analyse and discuss plainly the patterns of functions and competences reterritorialising into the *territories* of actors other than states.[108] To say this so explicitly would prompt more questions and inquiries, given that it challenges international law's foundational concepts: that of territory, and its mediation of the concepts of sovereignty and jurisdiction. At many times, legal discourse can be quite explicit in saying international organisations do not have territory.[109] An explicit account of de- and reterritorialisation challenges the theory of territorial sovereignty, as Arcuri and Violi themselves point out,[110] which is perhaps why the formula of words 'territoriality being meaningful vis-à-vis functionality' was fashioned. Moreover, it demonstrates why in this book I have felt it necessary to also address the concepts mediated by territory and the impact this rebirth of territory would have on the operationalisation of much of international legal theory in Chapter 5; we cannot, in other words, rethink territory without also questioning the orthodox understanding of sovereignty and territorial sovereignty which are structured by the concept of (state-)territory.

A similar but simpler move to understand functionalism took place in UK constitutional law with lessons I have found for developments at the

105 Arcuri and Violi in Kuijer and Werner (2016) at 10.

106 ibid at 12.

107 ibid at 12.

108 I think it important to acknowledge that Arcuri and Violi's article, more so than many others, highlighted what was wrong with current thinking. They do some incredibly interesting work in pushing the debate along. This article was one of the most self-aware contributions and it went further in probing what is going on in a concrete manner and gave some thought to what frameworks and models underpin current thinking.

109 See for example: Menon (1992) 21, 88.

110 Arcuri and Violi in Kuijer and Werner (2016) at 2.

'international or global level'. The default position for UK judicial review had been that courts could only review actions by public authorities. However, a gap was developing with the increasing privatisation of public functions, as well as the blurring of the line between what could be considered public and private. In England and Wales, a series of cases developed that became known as the 'public functions' test.[111] The result of this test meant that the logic for the purposes of judicial review instead focused on the *function* being carried out 'not the institutional nature of the defendant itself'.[112] In other words, the reasoning of the courts tracked the redistribution of powers; they 'followed' the functions. As a result, powers that were in a public body, but which had relocated to a different institution, could still be judicially reviewable.

This UK legal development tells us that it is possible to trace the functions between different subjects without conflating the actor and the functions, or their nature as public or private. Evidently, the spaces of actors were not at issue in this case as such.[113] For that reason, this domestic example is perhaps simpler than the present examination of shifts at the international level because the spatialities of actors did not dominate the intellectual engagement. Indeed, it is why I maintain that it is because the state and its territory are often used synonymously in international legal discourse that this analytical slippage can take place. The spaces of states should not dominate this analysis either, but state territories do. It throws into sharp relief just how much state territory unconsciously directs the analysis. Yet the episode, I have found, helps demonstrate the analytical separateness of actors and functions and does this by its tracing of the relocation of functions from one actor to another. It is a useful example for understanding what has happened in international law and politics as it highlights the analytical conflation that has taken place when spaces are misdiagnosed, conflated, or ignored. This conceptual lumping that otherwise takes place, I argue, constitutes a

[111] *R v Panel on Take-Overs and Mergers, ex parte Datafin plc* [1987] QB 815 ('*ex parte Datafin*'); *R (Beer) v Hampshire Farmers Markets Ltd* [2004] UKHRR 727.

[112] Williams (2017) 15, 15.

[113] This is not to say that an analysis of legal geography is not relevant to either UK judicial review example. The decision about which places are determined to have predominantly private relations and thus out of the reach of the public is an important one. If more and more functions and thus places are deemed private, it reduces the space of the state. The ideologies behind differently imagined legal geographies of the UK are thus vital to dissect.

binary between functionality and territoriality, and in stepping back to observe this, I hope to offer some analytical clarity about functions, subjects, and spaces.

A similar 'follow the' exercise, distinguishing analytical functions, actors, and spaces, might be undertaken for understanding the borders that bound state territory. These also reproduce assumptions about the physical location of the (state) border and assume it is fixed and permanent. To note, for example, that states are 'set[ting] up border controls *away* from the border'[114] continues to assume that borders refer to the cartographic or physical border and it is the power, functions, controls, etc. that can be detached from the border rather than the border coming into existence where these controls themselves are located. It is a problematic assumption for, as Balibar argues, borders are not immobile but moveable and heterogeneous:

> *some borders are not situated at the borders at all*, in the geographical-politico-administrative sense of the term. They are in fact elsewhere, wherever selective controls are to be found, such as, for example, *health* or *security* checks ... The concentration of all these functions (for example, the control of goods and people ...) at a single point ... was a dominant tendency during a particular period, the period of the nation-state ...'[115]

Instead, what we are witnessing is the redistribution of functions associated with bordering to different physical locations and into an increasingly heterogeneous set of processes that are also undertaken by diverse actors, which might include university staff being asked to act as a border agent for their students[116] and carrier sanctions requiring airline staff to act as border agents.[117]

Here again, I advocate a need to take a step back and rethink the methods that are engaged in modern bordering practices. The first reason to step back is to deprioritise the 'old' concept of state territory, removing the assumption that state borders and state territories are the starting

114 Emphasis added. Hemme Battjes, 'Territoriality and Asylum Law: The Use of Territorial Jurisdiction to Circumvent Legal Obligations and Human Rights Law Responses' in Kuijer and Werner (2016) at 263.

115 Balibar (2002) at 84.

116 Topping (2014). I always feel distinctly uncomfortable when asked to report on meetings with students for the purposes of immigration control.

117 Rodenhauser (2014) 223, 223.

point from which analysis commences, and instead view state territories and their borders as one of many relevant categories of legal and political spaces. One of the key reasons for this is that it makes it possible to observe the legal and political spaces in relation to which non-state actors exercise control. The space the EU constitutes through Frontex is a prime example here, but so is the African passport facilitated by the AU Commission mentioned above.[118] The second reason for taking a step back is to rethink the monolithic concept of borders. And instead think of the border as being constituted by bordering *practices*; in other words, to decentre and reassemble our analysis of borders. This understanding splits up the functions undertaken 'at the border', the different legal rights and duties relevant to bordering practices, identifies who is responsible for which bordering practices, and establishes *where* these borders are and how they relate to other legal and political spaces. Consequently, we might see that the borders of the EU as distinct from the borders of its member states or the state borders that exist inside refugee camps.[119]

2.5.3 *Knowing Our Reality: Spatialising Legal Orders*

Lastly, why does any of this matter? What are the stakes of this critical spatial thinking exercise? Why complicate what seems an already complicated debate about law and global governance that has been developing over the last twenty years? The answer offered in this book is, perhaps surprisingly, to simplify our understanding of the concept of territory in international law by questioning and exposing some core assumptions that will otherwise continue to muddle analysis and allow for conceptual slippages. Moreover, there are two additional reasons why any attempt to spatialise legal orders is a vital undertaking.

The first reason is one of theoretical demystification: without gaining a clearer purchase on the spatialities of global law and governance and the correspondingly territorial frameworks that are produced through the

118 I work this more fully in Chapter 5.

119 Reynolds and Muggeridge (2008) 4–5, 17–18. This is also known as 'upstreaming' migration control to stop migrants reaching the UK in the first place. See also 'New Government Proposals a Wrecking Ball to the Right to Claim Asylum in the UK' (2021). This describes how only those refugees that come via 'official' routes, which is often the refugee processing in camps in Lebanon or Syria, that will be given the right to settle in the state. This is another example of upstreaming bordering practices.

exercise of power, most of our debates and understanding of law – governing, capital, refugees, flow – risk resolving into a jumble of observations, a proliferation of paradoxes (state territory matters less, but state territory still matters) and *sui generis* cases. Understanding the spatiality of legal orders and social relations helps to make the understanding of our reality more concrete and knowable. Without maps, and the images they produce, and that each of us can reproduce in our imagination, we would struggle to know, even at a basic level, our globe given it is unlikely any of us will visit every square metre. Knowing the space of the community is key to the story that Benedict Anderson tells of how one imagines communities.[120]

This is also true for international law as a discipline. Global space, or rather representations of it,[121] is one of the most common images associated with international law and this is no accident. These representations are used on everything from conference posters, society and institutional logos, or books, to Twitter (now 'X') profile pictures. The 'globe' (as representation, not as actual space) is helpful to some extent; it can help us know and imagine our own discipline better. Maps, while predominantly only offering a 2-D and timeless representation of space, play a major role in the practice and interpretation of many areas of international law.[122] Without maps, many international lawyers would struggle to do their jobs. Without making the spaces of the legal order concrete, through representation, they are abstract and intangible; it is difficult to know with any certainty (but it is important not to reduce space to that representation). Yet, our maps, mental and material, more often than not reproduce and entrench the stato-centric concept of territory present in international law discourse. They can also be what contributes to the production of non-territorial and at times aspatial analysis. What is not mapped are these other spaces. Those unmapped spaces are, because of a lack of representation, more abstract and less concrete. We have less ways of knowing it and being sure of their existence.

We must find ways of making what currently seems aterritorial and aspatial more concrete, to spatialise, reterritorialise, and inevitably

120 Anderson (2006) at 6, 122.

121 Massey has greatly influenced my thinking of representation as spatialisation. See Massey (2005).

122 Brownlie (1998) at 156–61. For more on the role maps play as evidence in international law, see Worster (2018) 570.

perhaps find ways of representing those spaces. Otherwise, we will continue to think in terms of the produced binaries: there is territoriality or aterritorialty, 'territorial and de-territorial',[123] state governance or global governance, and so on. This can also be a highly politicised binary, where (state-)territory becomes a floating signifier for political and ideological positions. For example, Pistor exercises alarm about the deterritorialised monetary system, where the alternative, it seems, safeguarding against this, is to 'practice monetary autarchy, an isolationist stance that is [also] not very attractive.'[124] Milano noticeably understands the deterritorialised human rights system as a good thing, in contrast to Pistor's judgement of a deterritorialised monetary system. What is at stake here then is that these political and ideological driven arguments are too often hidden because of one side of the binary being spatially unidentifiable and unknown.[125]

Moreover, where accounts are entirely *aspatial* (where there is no consideration given to the spatialities of where functions go), there is often no capacity to consider and critique the spaces of the actors exercising these competences. International law's concept of territory is unable to make these territories legible in the first place. This might also be referred to, as Brölmann does, a process of 'despatialisation'.[126] In such accounts, functions appear to just float free of territory; they are spatially unbound and untethered. This is a typical understanding of the global arena and specifically of globalisation. As Massey observes 'the imagination of globalization [is] in terms of unbounded free space' and she points to the language and spatial imagining of 'free trade' to evidence this.[127] There is a failure, she argues, 'to recognise the multiplicities of the spatial' and instead of understanding globalisation as 'a single all-embracing movement' she advocates understanding it as 'a making of space(s), an active reconfiguration . . . through practices and relations of a multitude of trajectories'.[128] It is only then that we can politicise all spaces and their construction, but also, through knowing the where of the exercise of functions, politicise the power exercised in relation to these functions.

[123] Zumbansen (2011) 34.
[124] Pistor (2017) 24.
[125] For more on the politics of binaries created by spatial assumptions, see Lythgoe (2024).
[126] Brölmann (2007) at 88.
[127] Massey (2005) 83.
[128] ibid.

This problem is not limited to the rather fuzzy global space associated with the shift from a territorial order of competences to a functional one. Much of the legal discourse about the permeability of borders also entirely fails to conceptualise and explain the external forces working against and in the state, specifically the nature of the legal spaces of these 'external' or non-state ordered forces. The thing external to the state tends to lack detailed definition – it is just trade, capital, international, information, refugees, or technology – without seeking to conceptualise the diverse and dynamics patterns of refugees, trade, or capital in their own right.[129] It is just some institution or some process, perhaps functionally organised, that is penetrating the state's territory but what that is, is not fully rationalised. The analysis in such descriptions fails to comprehend the spaces of capital, people, goods, services, and information which may overlap with state space, how these spaces are produced by specific actors, and the relationship of power to these spaces. In other words, state territory, and the state exercise of power, dominates the intellectual framework. In operating with a far too often-underexplored background geography, the analysis will never be able to account for the territories overlapping state territory in relation to the same physical geography. Perhaps we might instead think of goods and labour as directed and disciplined according to the laws and logic of another territory, like the OECD's, EU's, or a free trade territory, each of which overlap the same physical geography as the state.

The second reason is a critically practical one. I advocate for a drastic expansion in international lawyers' capacity for understanding the politics of space, law, and governance and to respond to these politics systematically. Without an accurate picture of the proverbial lie of the land, the ability to prosecute political projects and promote alternative economic and political interests will be limited to the global elite, who are also those who encode the spatial logic of contemporary global governance. Politics and power are key to making and remaking many spaces;

[129] There are numerous studies that are undertaken outwith the discipline of international law. See for a small sample: Khalili (2020); Leyshon and Thrift (2005); Martin (1999); Easterling (2014). What tends to be missing from most of these accounts is the law that constitutes and affects activities in these spaces. Both international law and domestic law are important to these 'external' phenomena. However, there is an increasing number of critical voices in international law that are reflecting on the legal geography of trade and capital in particular. See The IGLP Law and Global Production Working Group (2016).

and territory is a key product of the exercise of power. Therefore, it is imperative that legal scholars can understand these spaces and the role of power, and especially legally sanctioned power, in constituting them. As Massey in particular has argued, the spatial imagination of contemporary discourse is one which is 'dominantly produced' in the global North and it directly 'enables the imposition of programmes of structural adjustment' in the 'unbounded global trading space', or at least this is how its space is typically conceived, of the global South.[130] Fundamentally, the spatial is central to how we relate to, and make sense of, the social world. The central ordering role played by 'the spatial imagination . . . in the legal construction of social life'[131] can never be underestimated. Where theories fail to account for the spaces of activities, they also make less concrete the systems, orders, actors, or regimes in question. This, in turn, affects the ability to comprehend or observe these. This is a crucial reason why globalisation and global governance often appear quite fuzzy and abstracted. Quite simply, the more accurate the 'map' of global governance, the more effectively the way forward can be charted.

2.6 Conclusion

This chapter presented an overview of the theories adopted and offered by international lawyers that seek to make sense of and explain the changes to the global legal order as a result of globalisation, global governance, and transnational (private) regulation. The analysis sought to identify the different discursive anchors that are used and to categorise the theories narrating the transformations based on these anchors. The first sections identified three main strands to this discourse: first came the shift to functionality, second, the relocation of competences to different actors, and third, the increasing porosity and permeability of state borders. Inherent to each is a slightly different spatial logic that is overlooked when the deterritorialisation or transnationalisation of law is discussed at a general level. Yet, in problematising the assumptions underpinning these theories, what becomes obvious is that regardless of what is being deterritorialised, common to all is a reproduction of the orthodox concept of territory and the orthodox spatial imaginary of international law.

130 Massey (2005) at 83.
131 Haskell ('The Spatial Dimensions of Extraterritoriality', nd).

There are many limitations created by operating using an outdated and under-critiqued legal geography. For example, it has created a binary in much of the discourse between functionality and territoriality, between state territory and global space, or between processes of globalisation and state processes. Upon deconstructing these binaries, they can be understood as having been constituted partly because of a conflation of functions and spaces in analytical terms – something I have rather inelegantly called 'conceptual lumping'. As a result of this jumble, and without realising it, many of these accounts have tracked the shift of functions or power without (re)spatialising them. Functionalism and territoriality might appear in the way they are posed in the discourses explored above as opposites. But analytically they are not. This chapter strongly advocates taking a step back and assigning the correct analytical category to them.

Although I concur a great deal with these theories' broad observations relating to the changing patterns of functions and competences, there are several issues with the current discourses on the move to functionality or the porosity of borders. These might be summarised as the absence of a concrete respatialisation of competences and functions and of the actors exercising them. Indeed, using the de- and reterritorialisation explanation by Deleuze and Guattari, it becomes apparent that reterritorialisation will never be possible where international legal theory continues to apply the orthodox concept of territory, referring only to state spaces, and the traditional model of legal space. Attempts to make sense of contemporary global governance are continually limited by this act of reproduction.

In the foregoing analysis, I have suggested framing the distribution of power differently and in a way that more accurately reflects the exercise of power globally today. Accordingly, the changing patterns of global law and governance may be understood as follows: every competence deterritorialised from the space of one actor is reterritorialised into the space of another. At an analytical level this is much cleaner. Nor does this explanation start with the state or prioritise state space. Moreover, it can be also help situate current developments historically rather than the often-ahistorical account inherent to those international legal theories which are always centred by the state. Yet, much ground must be covered before international law can begin reconstructing and coming to terms with this proposed account of global governance. Chapters 3 and 4 help cover that ground ahead of Chapter 5.

For now, it has been demonstrated that assuming all territory is state territory, as well as the domination of this model of legal space, limits the ability of contemporary theories to make sense of the multiplication and heterogenisation of territories and the redistribution of competences and functions and their constitution of and exercise in non-state spaces. The model of traditional territoriality needs to be further exposed to understand its pervasiveness, as well as its distinguishing constituent features so as to identify its usage and reproduction. The following chapter offers a deep excavation of what this orthodox concept of territory is and how it constitutes the implicit geography of international law. This excavation deconstructs the content of international law's concept of territory, and then its application in and mediation of thinking about legal concepts such as sovereignty.

3

Excavating the Territory of International Law

> What understanding of space was necessary for the idea of territory to be possible?
>
> Stuart Elden, 'Land, Terrain, Territory' [1]

This chapter gets to the heart of why the disciplinary imagination of international law is predominantly only able to see deterritorialisation without reterritorialisation. In it, I excavate the content of the orthodox concept(s) of territory.[2] It scrutinises the spatial assumptions about the concept that underlies such theories about a shift from territoriality to functionalism and the decline of territory. For it is in the very way that we think about territory that forces the production of functionalism as a theory in the first place. It is also in the reproduction of a stato-centric concept, visible throughout the analysis, that precludes the recognition of non-state actor territories that could constitute international law's 'new' legal geography, and which would present a different ontological understanding of the spaces relevant to international law and global governance today.

The first part of this chapter sets out how I go about deconstructing this concept. There is no single correct way of going about this deconstructing exercise nor even of understanding concepts themselves. The method adopted here – thinking about concepts as constituted by different ideas and assumptions and diagnosing these from positive law and scholarly discourse[3] – offers insights relevant to this study of understanding how territory is used in international law discourse and theory.

[1] Elden (2010) 799, 810.

[2] It would be neater to say there is one concept, but as I go on to show, there is conceptual instability in international lawyers' and international law practised by states' understanding of territory. These concepts are however similar in the essentials, especially the physicalised stato-centrism.

[3] I adopt here something similar to the 'componential approach' to concepts, that understands them as having an internal structure and that 'they are made up of smaller elements

Concepts are only in use so long as they are useful. Thus, territory is thought of as being 'replaced' in international law by functions because the orthodox understanding of the concept is not useful to describe the transformations taking place to global legal and political structures. This includes the rise of private actors and international organisations that Jessup's transnational legal theory was already diagnosing in 1957. To understand why the role of territory is in 'decline',[4] it is helpful, I argue, to deconstruct the discipline's understanding of territory, to diagnose what it is about the concept that is causing perceptions of decline.

The second part of this chapter offers an account of the standard definition(s) of territory that will be recognisable as belonging to the mainstream of international law.[5] As is explored in this chapter, there are really multiple concepts of territory, many of which differ only marginally from each other. Yet, while there may be conceptual instability at the margins, there remain recognisable commonalities that allow international lawyers to say 'look, that is a territory' and find agreement with their colleagues. It is many of these common elements and assumptions that contribute to the perception of a declining of territory as a central concept of international law – and at the same time, it is as a result of the slight conceptual instability that analysis of the challenges wrought by global law and governance can become unclear.[6] This part of the chapter goes below the surface level definitions of territory and deconstructs the assumptions and qualities informing the concept of territory that rarely make it to the conscious level of international law discourse. Using insights from the discipline of geography, these qualities and assumptions can be said to include: the idea that territory is that only of states';[7] that territory is imagined in a two-dimensional, flat, jigsaw-like form; that the physical referents tend to be analytically prioritised over the social; that territory tends to be imagined as homogeneous, uniform, and contiguous space; that territory is bound by a particular technology and representation of borders; and that territories are relatively stable and static. It is because of these assumptions, in particular that territory is the

of meaning, variously referred to as properties, features or attributes'. For more on this way of understanding the internal content of a concept see Moss, Tyler, and Taylor (2007).

4 Brölmann (2007) at 84.

5 It is also likely a familiar concept to mainstream positivist international relations and political theory discourses, as well as to contemporary public discourse.

6 Milano (2013) at 2.

7 And indeed, is the property only of states in so far as doctrinal debate assume that territory is an object that may be the target of ownership.

domain of states alone, flat, and physicalised, that the conditions arise to think of the state as 'above' territory and territory as 'subject to' the state. These assumptions in turn create the conditions for assuming that territory exists a priori, as opposed to constituted by the institution of the state itself. This stato-centricity in turn entirely prevents imagining of territories in addition to, or overlapping with, state territories.

In the third section, I delve deeper into the signification of 'territory' and outline five different uses for territory in international law discourse: one, where territory is intended to refer to an object; the second, where territory is intended to refer to a subject of international law; the third, where territory is intended to refer to a framework; fourth, where territory is used as an organising logic; and fifth, where territory is understood as a space proper. I then show that there is considerable potential for conceptual slippage between these different meanings in international law discourse and outline the implications of this. The final part of this chapter explores how the traditional conceptualisation of territory has mediated our understanding of sovereignty in international law, creating the assemblage of competences in a spatially organised centralised pattern 'within' state territory.

Together these assumptions about the spatial characteristic informing the concept of territory build an imaginary and understanding of territory that produces the non- or aterritorial responses in international law and related discourses to the phenomena associated with globalisation and global governance demonstrated in the previous chapter. These discourses, when reproducing these orthodox ways of imagining territory, lack vital spatial insights and tools to make sense of contemporary global legal and political orders.

3.1 Deconstructing Concepts

While it might seem a trite point, deconstructing an idea or concept is not the same as annihilating or destroying it.[8] Nevertheless, this is often the association made of deconstruction by many legal scholars, mostly it could be said because of the destabilising quality of the deconstructing

[8] Derrida (1985) at 1. The deconstruction exercise, according to many poststructuralists, will never fully end (there are also some that would dispute this is a 'method' – and I would agree if we were to think of a method as having precise steps and insights and reasoning protocols, because deconstruction can take many forms). In years to come I will continue to deconstruct my thinking about space.

move.[9] One of the more common 'deconstructing' moves, is to deconstruct binaries. Obviously, there is the binary between territorial / a- or non-territorial. By now this is a fairly rudimentary insight that the deconstruction of the concept of territory might offer.[10] In many ways, the focus in this chapter is to 'uncover' how the concept of territory is understood in international law discourse, such that the spaces of other processes and actors are perceived to be aterritorial. The process of deconstructing a concept such as territory may bring to the surface inconsistencies already present in the discourse, as this chapter finds, while also being a process by which it is possible to 'uncover' the framing of underpinning concepts.[11] This process seeks to 'uncover the unconscious'[12] and 'make the not-seen accessible to sight'.[13] Problematising these framing ideas and assumptions underpinning territory shows just how naturalised and physicalised the international law conceptualisation of territory is, impacting our disiplinary response to different spatially organised orders and actors and rendering these others invisible. Ultimately, the task is to 'deconstruct and make visible the ideological, implicitly accepted assumptions of our spatial categories.'[14]

There is also no right or wrong way to understand the anatomy of a concept. What I mean by a concept's anatomy, is how we understand the ideas, assumptions, and background framing that inform our conceptualisation. Here I adopt a pragmatic heuristic way of explaining the anatomy of the concept of territory that helps structure the analysis and its

[9] David Kennedy recalls the story of Abe Chayes bursting into his office proclaiming that given international law is not yet constructed, it is not yet time to deconstruct it. See: Kennedy (2002) 397, 426; Kennedy [1997] 545, 562.

[10] Derrida (1998) deals in detail on oppositions in western thought. This is not at all rudimentary and worth a read.

[11] According to Eagleton, 'to 'deconstruct', then, is to 'reinscribe and resituate meanings, events and objects within broader movements and structures; it is, so to speak, to reverse the imposing tapestry in order to expose in all its unglamorously disheveled tangle the threads constituting the well-heeled image it presents to the world.' Eagleton (1986) at 80. See all Turner (2016). Many of the characteristics, when 'uncovered, can, at the same time with reflection and critique, also help direct the mind to look for alternative interpretations.

[12] Barry (2002) at 71.

[13] Derrida (1998) at 168. Sassen attempts a similar project with her effort to 'understand aspects of territory that came to be buried, operationally and formally, with the ascendance of the territorial nation-state.' Sassen (2013) at 21.

[14] van Houtum (2004) at 22.

insights.[15] My proposal of how to think of the structure of the concept of territory is as follows: there are several ideas, characteristics, and elements that combine to configure the concept of territory. These can be thought of as a bundle of characteristics that can be changed, altered, or potentially removed altogether. For example, the space could be seen as uneven or as homogeneous, such that law applies uniformly across the whole space or it could apply unevenly. Borders may be differently practised depending on the laws and technologies in place,[16] 'bounding' territory in different ways as a result. Each of these ideas, elements, and characteristics to greater or lesser degrees give form to how we imagine territory.

Given that there is whole bundle of ideas constituting the concept of territory, they are regularly and consistently (re)applied and assumed. In other words, there is much about the content of the concept of territory that can become essentialised. This makes having a shared discourse easier in some ways. It means international lawyers do not have to continue tracing our thoughts back to first principles just to have a simple conversation. And yet in so doing, and especially over longer periods of time, many of these separate ideas are analytically flattened; the individual elements are no longer visible in the concept, nor the individual practices constituting them recognisable. It is for this reason that international law as a discipline cannot make visible the application of the concept to instances of the spaces of other institutions that could also be understood as territories. As such, these other instances of territory are unrecognisable in international law because they are not spatially configured in the same manner as (state-)territory – or at least this is where the argument will end up by Chapter 4. For the purposes of this chapter, the approach adopted understands a concept as structured by many other concepts, ideas, and even values. As a result, I also understand the concept of territory as a bundle of ideas, characteristics, and qualities, many of which I explore in turn below to excavate how the discipline of international law, broadly, arranges this bundle.

15 This approach is not uncontroversial for those well versed in this discourse. I will not go into detail regarding the ins and outs of classical versus prototype theory, the issues with radical atomism, or the promises of a pluralist understanding of concepts (although this is the most persuasive). The approach I adopt here is most akin to that developed by Rorty (1991).

16 Mezzadra and Neilson (2013). Borders are themselves concepts that might be understood as a bundle of characteristics.

3.2 Finding Territory in International Law

The concept of territory is used every day in international law discourse and pedagogy. As has been quoted many times before 'amazingly little has been published about the concept of territory, although much speech, ink, and blood have been spilled over territorial disputes.'[17] Saying that little has been published about the concept of territory, is not to say that a lot has not been written about territory, including attempts to define it, teach it, and identify it in a dispute, and writings about that dispute. Yet, upon closer inspection, even the very definition of territory is far from straightforward in legal discourse. Given territory is such a core concept of international law, that difficulty establishing a coherent definition was quite surprising. Territory is rarely defined in the positive legal regime. Instead, in law and in discourse about the law, the definition and concept of territory is assumed to be obvious. As a result, its intended definition must be deconstructed from discourse and context.[18] What was also noticeable from my reading, is that the concept of territory is very rarely defined in its own right without reference to concepts such as the state, sovereignty, and jurisdiction. Moreover, where there is a given definition of territory, very rarely will the text refer to the constitutive elements important to our imagining of territory.[19] Thus, an inquiry that looks beyond the surface-level definition to the conceptual level, which deconstructs the assumptions and background knowledge that shape the concept, is sorely needed.

Finally, before making this deep dive into the content of the concept, I want to address a question of sources as an important methodological consideration. Given the sheer volume of text mentioning territory in international law discourse – incidences of its definition, and its usage in explaining other legal concepts, principles, and doctrines, and the regularity with which territory appears in positive law – it is impossible to include everything ever written about territory or account for its every usage. This would be futile and impossible. Therefore, I use sources

[17] Gottmann (1973) at ix.

[18] Jean d'Aspremont has written with great insight into the postponement of meaning in international law. See d'Aspremont (2021). The same analysis might be performed for the 'meaning' of territory in law and legal discourse – there is a constant deferral of meaning, often because we assume it is so obvious, so why bother.

[19] There are exceptions of course. Outside the discourse of international law, this is fairly common: see Sassen (2008); Spruyt (1994); Elden (2013); Branch (2014); Osiander (2007); Mezzadra and Neilson (2013). In international law, the most detailed accounts include: Shaw (1982); Kuijer and Werner (2017).

representative of both the positive legal regime in force, state practice, and the scholarly discourse about these legal regimes. My understanding of the regime of international law is grounded in this study in the traditional doctrine of sources: treaties, arbitration awards, case law, pleadings before courts and tribunals, and resolutions of international organisations as evidence of customary international law. Each of these either directly inform or offer use clues as to how international lawyers and states as lawmakers think about the concept of territory. My approach to understand how the concept of territory is understood in scholarly discourse is informed by the major English language[20] textbooks, books, chapters, and articles dealing specifically with territory, jurisdiction, and sovereignty or with territorial disputes. Textbooks are an essential part of international law pedagogy and thus provide invaluable indications of orthodox thinking and mainstream approaches.

3.3 The Content of the Concept of Territory

The classic reference to territory, and perhaps the most obvious place to start, is the one made by Max Huber in the *Island of Palmas* arbitral award. Huber observed: 'sovereignty in relation to a portion of the surface of the globe is the legal condition necessary for the inclusion of such portion in the territory of any particular State. Sovereignty in relation to territory is in the present award called "territorial sovereignty".'[21] The quote has been used widely since[22] and can be seen virtually unchanged in variations such as 'territory ... refers to ... any portion of the surface of the earth.'[23] Many have taken this to mean that 'territory' *is* 'a portion of the surface of the globe'. However, perhaps this explanation does not so much offer a *definition* of territory, as instead refer to how territory can be *identified* – that is, where sovereignty is

[20] A major limitation of course, but my limited skills of translation and attempts to 'think' to the level required to fully understand the discourse concerning territory in any other language would render any further inquiry a disaster. It would be eminently useful to understand how territory is imagined in other languages and other legal discourses. I have benefited greatly from translations of Milton Santos and Henri Lefebvre for my thinking on space. This is an issue that was raised by Davies (2022).

[21] *Island of Palmas Case (Netherlands, USA)* (1928) Volume II Reports of International Arbitral Awards 829 (Permanent Court of Arbitration) 838.

[22] See a handful of examples: Verzijl, Heere, and Offerhaus (1968) at 263; Fassbender in Walker (2003); Akehurst (1972) 145; Jensen (2015) 275; Emmenegger (2016) 33, 31; Wong (2013).

[23] Kohen (2016) at xii.

exercised in relation to a portion of the globe, that portion of the globe is included in the territory of the state. This might seem a minor difference. But one approach reduces territory to the portion of the globe; the other helps identify a territory but does not analytically flatten it to the same extent. This is important: the reduction of territory to being the portion of the globe, not only analytically flattens the concept, but flattens our imagining of the ontological reality of territory, which, as a result, *also* determines the imagined physicality of territory as will be seen below.

3.3.1 Area or Space: Two or Three Dimensions

Starting with the basics then: is territory an area or a space? Or is it both? What is the distinction between these two, and what are the implications of one or the other? While seemingly insignificant, there are different imaginings involved with and implications attached to imagining territory as area or space. While it must be admitted here that it is highly likely that international lawyers have not always chosen one or the other term in an informed or active way, the use of one term over the other can however indicate the unconscious spatial imaginings informing the use of either area or space.

There is much literature that does indeed define territory as an area, as in the following examples: 'the territory of the State . . . is an area';[24] '[t]erritory is . . . a geographical conception relating to physical areas of the globe';[25] 'it means any area of the earth's surface which is the subject of sovereign rights and interests';[26] 'the whole territory of the state, i.e. to all areas of the Earth's landmass over which it has title'[27] and 'the concept of territory is defined by geographical areas separated by borderlines from other areas'.[28] There are three things to note about defining territory as an area. First, imagining an area arises from and creates different assumptions compared to the abovementioned 'territory as a portion of the earth'. A portion takes as its starting assumption that there is a whole space being apportioned, whereas an area looks at the shape in question without implying apportionment of some larger whole.[29] However, and

[24] Lowe (2007) at 137.
[25] Shaw (1982) 61.
[26] O'Connell (1971) at 181.
[27] Milanovic (2014) at 2.
[28] Malanczuk (1997) at 76.
[29] Bartelsen has written extensively on how this approach to understanding of space has created the conditions for the modern practice of territoriality and nation states. An area

second, what both 'areas' and 'portions' have in common is that they often involve and project a two-dimensional understanding of the thing in question. It is common in international legal discourse to imagine territory as relating to the 'surface' of the earth only. A surface is usually understood as flat, as a level surface, or at the very least with only one 'layer' – I think here of the surface of a table, or the surface of the grass or soil (which are not strictly flat, but there is only one layer on the surface). The two-dimensional aspect of (state-)territory, and its implications, can also be traced in critiques invoked by those concerned by the cartographical disciplining of modern territoriality.[30] The third issue to note for now, is the prominence of physical or geographical terms – 'a geographical conception', 'the earth's surface' – in how international lawyers understand the area in question. The physical geography is a topic I return to again below.

In yet other definitions, territory is a space, as in the following examples: 'territory determines the space … subject to the sovereignty of a concrete state';[31] '[t]erritory is a portion of geographical space that coincides with the spatial extent of a government's jurisdiction';[32] '[a] space in which human activity is displayed';[33] and 'territory is politically and legally defined space'.[34] 'Areas' and 'spaces' are different spatial concepts with particular implications. While an area is two-dimensional (i.e., the '*surface* area'), a space may be three- (or even four-) dimensional. More dimensions allow for depth or volume.[35] The implication being that a three- or four-dimensional understanding of territory, might allow, for example, airspace to be included in the territory of a state, as opposed to thinking in terms of surface, which could exclude airspace – but this is not to say that all international lawyers have necessarily engaged fully with why they employ one term or another, or that they are even consistent in this regard.

Finally, it might be observed that while an area tends to draw the imagination only to the physical geography, spaces *can be* associated with more than just the physical features of the globe. We can notice there is

does not carry the same connotations. An area does not imagine the same whole – the global – that a portion does. See, in particular, Bartelson (2010) and (2011).

[30] Branch (2014); Rajkovic (2018) 267; Strandsbjerg (2010). I return to cartography and mapping territory in Chapter 4.

[31] Bílková in Kuijer and Werner (2017) at 26.

[32] Gottmann (1973) at 29.

[33] Kohen (2016) at xii.

[34] Brölmann (2007) at 88.

[35] See reflections on volume in 'Dynamic Territories (S. Elden)' (2014).

the possibility, as above, to use the term to think of a more abstract construct, that is, space as 'political' or 'legal' as well as geographical. The term space opens up different constructs to the potential of territoriality, such as two obvious examples of non-geographical spaces – cyberspace and outer space - which would otherwise be excluded from being conceptualised as territory where the concept is understood geographically or as surface area only.[36] Thus, imagining territory as a space produces a more multidimensionally applicable concept. Yet, the literature is inconsistent in this regard. There remains an obvious and dominant trend in international law literature to physicalise the space of territory, which is examined in the following section. What all this points to, is a lack of serious engagement with the onto-theoretical lexicon that is being employed in the discourse and the spatial imaginings are not fully interrogated; instead, they are taken for granted.

3.3.2 The Role of the Physical

The second feature is the role and position of physical reality in how international lawyers conceptualise territory. It is a feature that dominates the classical concept(s). Most definitions and references to territory cannot but mention 'the physical parts of the globe'[37] that territory is thought to 'include'. Here too, international lawyers have divergent understandings, specifically of the relationship between territory and physical geography and *which parts* of the physical world 'are' territory.

This following analysis makes several significant observations. First, many international lawyers conceptualise territory as something physical; they 'physicalise'[38] territory, reducing the concept to the physical world. There is a distinction to be drawn between conceptualisations reducing territory to the physical geography – where territory *is* the physical geography – and those where territory refers to physical geography in some way that is more abstracted, where the concept is something more than the physical geography. This distinction is subtle and much of the literature is ambiguous on this question. It emerges most clearly in the application of the concept of territory in a legal problem.

[36] See Shaw (2017) at 364.

[37] Shaw (1982) at 61.

[38] This phrasing might be a little awkward, but I find it helpful to think of physicalising as a process, rather than the concept actually as something physical. It also helps convey slippage in reasoning and varying and inconsistent tendencies to physicalise.

A second, related, observation is that many international lawyers think of territory as 'primarily' physical, such that land territory is 'principal'. When territory is understood *only* as the physical geography, it obviously excludes the concept of territory from applying to the likes of cyberspace. Yet, this physicalising move also impacts whether the likes of airspace is understood to be part of a territory. What emerges from the discourse is that international lawyers have very different ideas concerning land, water, and atmosphere, their connection to each other, and their relationship with territory. For example, some will understand territory as just land; others as *primarily* land; still more as land and sea *equally*; and others as land, sea, *and* air. Why does this matter? The consequence is that without land, for the vast majority of conceptualisations, there can be no territory. Yet it will also affect legal rights and obligations: whether we understand airspace as being part of a state's territory or not, will affect, for example, at what point the territorial inviolability of a state has been violated.

This pattern of 'assimilation' between the concept of territory and the referent physical geography has also been noted by Szigeti who remarks that 'the physical counterparts are [thereby] projected onto the abstract concept' which as a result is 'reified [and] treated as a fact of nature, an unquestionable given.'[39] Typical examples of this physicalising reductionism are found in discussions of territory as a 'tangible'[40] or a 'material'[41] phenomenon, a 'physical base'[42] or a 'physical foundation'.[43] Territory *is* the land or maritime waters, seabed, subsoil, etc. A further example of the physicalising move can be found in Gottmann's observation that 'territory *consists* ... of material components ordered within geographical space according to certain laws of nature',[44] a clear reference to territory as effectively synonymous with physical geography. While Gottmann acknowledges that territory is *more than* just a 'purely physical phenomenon,'[45] his argument appears to presume the concept of territory is essentially just a representation of the underlying physical reality, rather than a socially constructed abstraction that may or may not be anchored in physical facts.

39 Szigeti (2009) 311, 314.
40 Wallace (1986) at 81.
41 Gottmann (1975) 29, 29.
42 Crawford (2012) at 204.
43 Lachs (1984) at 36.
44 Gottmann (1975) at 29, emphasis added.
45 ibid.

An understanding of how this physicalising can operate in legal practice can be gleaned from various territorial and boundary disputes, where political and legal controversies concerning the delimitation of territorial competences are routinely reformulated as 'simple' exercises in fact finding. For example, in the *Gulf of Maine* case, charged with the task of dividing up rights relating to fisheries and oil and gas exploration, the ICJ recast the whole dispute as an inquiry into the 'natural' configuration of the underlying 'bathymetric' and 'geomorphological features',[46] observing in the process that the resolution of this type of dispute is essentially a function of the presence or absence of a sufficiently 'abrupt' 'natural separation' in the 'geological continuity' of the respective part of the continental shelf.[47] The tendency to reduce legal disputes about the delimitation of territorial competences to examinations of physical geography can also be seen in the *Black Sea* case, where an important part of the Court's reasoning ultimately came down to the inspection of the 'encroach[ments] on the natural prolongation' of each party.[48] There is a point to this rehearsal of ICJ reasoning: if territory is naturally informed, there is a strong tendency to think that territory *is* the physical geography. It becomes all too easy to equate the conceptual with the physical when factors like natural features so strongly determine the creation of territory or reason a judgment that a particular space *ought* to be part of the territory of one state. This logic identifies particular physical geography, landmarks, coasts, rocks, or even coordinates as *being* the territory of one state or another. And as a consequence of this process, a naturalising and physicalising of territory occurs: naturalising because the natural features and physical geography start to determine where a territory – a socially constructed territory – begins and ends; physicalising because territory comes not to be represented by the physical world, but the physical world becomes the territory – that is, that the *coast is now the territory* of Costa Rica.

The aspiration to ground legal analysis in objective facts, is not limited to international law and the law of territorial disputes in particular. What bears noting here, however, is how bluntly 'physicalist' the construction

[46] *Case Concerning Delimitation of the Maritime Boundary in the Gulf of Maine Area (Canada – United States of America) Judgment* (1984) ICJ Reports 246 (International Court of Justice) [45].

[47] ibid [47].

[48] *Maritime Delimitation in the Black Sea, Romania v Ukraine, Judgment* [2009] ICJ Reports 2009, p 61 (International Court of Justice) [199].

of the facts in question are. There is no acknowledgement that as a concept territory is an essentially abstract construction; that it is, furthermore, socially constructed.

Where practice leads, scholarly discourse often follows. There are numerous examples of this physicalising move in legal discourse. But it is a large and sprawling discourse. Therefore, I have found it helpful to sort it into different strands of thought, depending on how the categories of physical geography (land, water, air) are prioritised and ordered.

One strand of thinking involves conceptualisations of territory as *only* or *primarily* land – the implication being that without land there can be no territory. One instance in which this strand is manifested is in the 'appurtenance' approach to (state-)territory. An appurtenance is 'an incidental right (such as a right-of-way) attached to a principal property right and passing in possession with it',[49] making land the principal element of territory with airspace and sea as 'accessories' that are incidental to it. This approach clearly suggests that without land, there could be no territory. This approach is common to both scholarly discourse and legal practice. For instance, Crawford suggests state territory is land which has 'its *appurtenances* (airspace and territorial sea)'.[50] Rosenne, too, adopts the term appurtenant to describe the relationship of 'air space' to 'State territory', which is defined as 'all the land within its frontiers, together with a belt of sea adjacent to its coast known as the territorial sea, and the airspace above its land territory and territorial sea.'[51] It could be observed that an appurtenance approach is incompatible with a conceptualisation of territory that refers to physical areas of the globe without any land. The implication of the approach is that it excludes spaces without any land at

[49] 'Definition of Appurtenance' <www.merriam-webster.com/dictionary/appurtenance> accessed 3 December 2018. The second definition given, which is how appurtenance is used in law, is also the oldest known usage of the term (from the fourteenth century). The definition in law is as follows: 'an incidental right (such as a right-of-way) attached to a principal property right and passing in possession with it'.

[50] The full quote reads: '[s]tate territory and its appurtenances (airspace and territorial sea), together with the government and population within its boundaries, constitute the physical and social base for the state (emphasis added); Crawford (2012) at 204. The physical base of the state could be said to be land, airspace, and territorial sea and the social base of the state could be said to be the government and population, which can be contrasted with the approach adopted by Arendt: '[territory] relates not so much . . . to a piece of land as to the space between individuals in a group whose members are bound to . . . each other by all kinds of relationships, based on a common language, religion, a common history, customs, and laws' in Arendt and McCaddon (2011) at 262–63.

[51] Rosenne (2002) at 266.

all from being territories, such of offshore platforms like the Principality of Sealand, but also diverging from definitions of territory that include high seas and outer space but 'belong to no one'.[52]

Closely related to the appurtenance approach is the 'primarily land' approach. It has the same pattern of prioritising physical land and is sometimes interchangeable. Kohen proposes that:

> the concept of territory in international law primarily, although not exclusively, refers to land, that is, any portion of the surface of the earth that is permanently above water. Subsoil is also part of territory. Land includes watercourses (rivers, lakes, groundwater). The territory of the State also includes maritime areas such as internal waters and the territorial sea.[53]

Whereas Crawford's approach views air and sea as appurtenances to land, Kohen considers territory as *primarily* land with maritime areas (but not rivers, lakes, etc. which are 'land'), by implication, as secondary. Notably, Kohen does not consider airspace. In a similar vein, 'land territory' for Simma and Müller 'forms the *core* space of the territorial state'[54] and Lauterpacht observes that '[t]he territory of a State consists *in the first place* of the land within its boundaries. To this must be added . . . certain waters.'[55] In a later paragraph, Lauterpacht refers to territorial waters as '*appurtenant* to the territory of the State',[56] suggesting that 'in the first place' has an appurtenant logic to it.

Contrast these examples with Klabbers, for whom '[t]he notion of territory encompasses internal waters and the territorial sea.'[57] Klabbers does not appear to make a similar assumption that land is 'primary', nor that appurtenances are distinguishable. In a similar vein, O'Connell observes that '[i]n law territory is a much wider conception than that of mere land. It means any area of the earth's surface which is the subject of sovereign rights and interests.'[58] Presumably, given O'Connell refers to

52 Shaw (2017) at 364.
53 Kohen (2016) at xii.
54 Simma and Müller in Crawford and Koskenniemi (2012) at 138, emphasis added.
55 Lauterpacht (1955) at 172, emphasis added.
56 ibid 173.
57 Jan Klabbers (2017) at 76.
58 O'Connell (1971) at 181. It should be noted that 'any area of the earth's surface which is the subject of sovereign rights and interests' would probably include the continental shelf within the concept of territory. O'Connell's text was published in 1971, before the 1973–1982 UNCLOS negotiations, and its entry into force in 1994 which gave a different meaning to sovereign rights. Yet, the continental shelf offers further illuminating

the earth's surface, this definition of territory, like Klabbers', would not include airspace. Lowe refers to the state as having 'jurisdiction' to the 'airspace above its territory'[59] which seems to fall into the same strand as Klabbers and O'Connell, because airspace is 'above' the territory not part of the territory in a plain interpretation of the phrase. Later, land and airspace are also kept separate when Lowe refers to rights of passage.[60]

There are many definitions that **do** include airspace in the concept in some way. Malanczuk's definition of territory 'includes the air space above the land ... and the earth beneath it, in theory, reaching to the centre of the globe. It also includes up to twelve miles of the territorial sea adjacent to the coast.'[61] Noticeably in this excerpt, land, sea, and air have equal status – they are not imagined as primary/secondary or appurtenances. It appears that Shaw's concept is similar to Malanczuk's with regard to all three (water, air, and land) equally: '[i]t clearly includes land areas, subterranean areas, waters, rivers, lakes, the airspace above the land etc. and the territorial sea.'[62] However, in a different text Shaw

discussion. Whether or not the continental shelf is part of territory could even create some disagreement between international law scholars today. There are those who might say the very idea of there being a territorial sea which exists up to twelve nautical miles possibly indicates that beyond twelve nautical miles is non-territorial (Art 3 United Nations Convention on the Law of the Sea 1982 (1833 UNTS 3, UN Reg No I-31363 (Signed 10 December 1982, Entered into Force 16 November 1994)). However, we could also disaggregate water and land and Article 76 of UNCLOS does explicitly say that the 'continental shelf ... comprises the seabed and subsoil ... that extend beyond its territorial sea throughout the natural prolongation of its land territory'. I will get to the remarkable issue of this being understood as 'natural' later in this chapter. What an 'extension' 'throughout' of the natural prolongation of the land territory means has been subject to some discussion. The wording came from the ICJ's *North Sea Continental Shelf* case and has proven to be rather unhelpful – *North Sea Continental Shelf Cases (Federal Republic of Germany/Denmark; Federal Republic of Germany/Netherlands), Judgment* 3 (International Court of Justice) [39]. See some interpretation in Pinto (2013) 215, in particular 225–26. See also Cavnar (2009); Suarez (2008) 241–42; Oude Elferink (2008). The general position is that the continental shelf is not part of territory but that a state has rights to it because it is connected to the land territory (above water) – which simply reinforces this point about the primacy of the physical, and, in particular, the physicality of land, to our understanding of territory. This is also the position because territory is usually understood to be where *all* sovereign rights are exercised, not just some as in the case of the continental shelf to which the state only has sovereign rights for the 'purpose of exploring it and exploiting its natural resources', Article 77 UNCLOS.

59 Lowe (2007) at 41.

60 ibid at 152.

61 Malanczuk (1997) at 76.

62 Shaw (1982) 66.

later states: 'the territorial sea appertains to the territorial sovereignty of the coastal state and thus belongs to it automatically.'[63] We can also note that Lowe elsewhere defines territory as 'includ[ing] both [a state's] territorial sea ... and the airspace above its land and sea territory.'[64] There is sufficient evidence in the discourse of all three positions being taken – appurtenance, primary/secondary, and equal status –, often by the same thinker, and very little to reconcile these.

State practice and positive law is also important to consider here, not least because this is where the definition of territory requires most clarity. However, state practice tends to be mixed and the concepts confused. There may be several reasons for this, not least that states will adopt conceptualisations that suit their positions in a dispute.

There are instances suggesting the concept of territory, while divisible into identifiable separate elements of airspace, waters, and landmass, does not prioritise any one category. As a result, violation of any of these equates to the violation of territory. For example, Iranian officials, after shooting down a US drone in Iranian airspace said: 'The drone was certainly in Iranian territory by 4 miles or 7 kilometers.'[65] The implication of this is that territory includes airspace because the drone was in Iranian territory by being in its airspace at the moment of it being shot down. At the same time, and in contrast, there are examples of the concept of territory not including airspace. One such pertinent example is the International Civil Aviation Organization (ICAO) Convention.[66] According to Article 2, 'For the purposes of this Convention the *territory* of a State shall be deemed to be *the land areas and territorial waters* adjacent thereto under the sovereignty, suzerainty, protection or mandate of such State' (emphasis added). The ICAO also provides that the 'state has complete and exclusive sovereignty over the airspace above its territory';[67] explicitly, airspace is not territory.[68] That is not to say that

[63] Shaw (2017) at 422.
[64] Lowe in Evans (2003) at 336.
[65] 'Iran Files Complaint against U.S. over Violating Its Airspace' (2019).
[66] Convention on International Civil Aviation (ICAO Convention) 1944.
[67] ibid, Article 1. Emphasis added.
[68] This is the same understanding of the relationship between natural features and the concept of territory as in the Paris Convention of 1919: 'Article 1. The High Contracting Parties recognise that every Power has complete and exclusive sovereignty over the *air space above its territory*. For the purpose of the present Convention, *the territory of a State shall be understood as including the national territory, both that of the mother country and of the colonies, and the territorial waters adjacent thereto*. Article 2. Each contracting State undertakes in time of peace to accord freedom of *innocent passage above its territory to*

being in another state's airspace would not violate its sovereign rights relating to the airspace. A reading of 'territory-as-land', distinguishing airspace from 'territorial' space, but where the intrusion into airspace would still violate a state's legal rights pertaining to sovereignty, can be found in Pakistan's ICJ application holding India responsible for the shooting down of an unarmed naval aircraft in 1999. In their application, Pakistan claimed:

> The wreckage of the plane was about 2 km inside Pakistan territory which is a clear proof that when the aircraft was shot it was well within Pakistan's air space ... The Indian helicopters, knowing the actual position of the shooting down of Pakistan's aircraft, sneaked into Pakistan's territory to pick up a few items from the debris. By this criminal act India once again *violated Pakistan's air space and territorial sovereignty*, by sending helicopters into Pakistan territory to remove parts of the wreckage.[69]

A straightforward reading of this suggests that territory and airspace are not the same. For if territorial sovereignty applies to territory, and airspace were part of territory, there would be no reason to mention each separately.[70] The wreckage itself was claimed to be found inside the

the aircraft of the other contracting States, provided that the conditions laid down in the present Convention are observed. Regulations made by a contracting State as to the admission *over its territory of the aircraft* of the other contracting States shall be applied without distinction of nationality' (emphasis added). Convention Relating to the Regulation of Aerial Navigation Signed at Paris, October 13, 1919.

69 *Application Instituting Proceedings, Aerial Incident of 10 August 1999, Pakistan v India* (ICJ) 2. *Aerial Incident Proceedings* (1999) 2. Emphasis added.

70 This can also be found in, for example: 'This dispute arises from the destruction of an Iranian aircraft, Iran Air Air-bus A-300B, flight 655, and the killing of its 290 passengers and crew by two surface-to-air missiles launched from the USS Vincennes. a guided-missile cruiser on duty with the United States Persian Gulf/Middle East Force in the Iranian *airspace over the Islamic Republic's territorial waters* in the Persian Gulf on 3 July 1988.' Application Instituting Proceedings filed in the Registry of the Court on 17 May 1989 *Aerial Incident of 3 July 1988 (Islamic Republic of Iran v United States of America)*, 4. In this case it is the territorial waters and the airspace that are distinguishable and notably it is not phrased 'territorial airspace'. Also, in *Aerial Herbicide Spraying (Ecuador v Colombia)*: 'In addition, on some occasions aircrafts participating in Colombia's fumigation operations have, without authorization, crossed into Ecuadorian airspace and sprayed within the territory of Ecuador', Application Instituting Proceedings, filed in the Registry of the Court on 31 March 2007, para 3, 4. Here the spraying seems to land on something, that is, the territory, which is separate from the airspace which was also accused of being violated. An exception to this is *Aerial Incident of 7 November 1954 (United States of America v Union of Soviet Socialist Republics)*, wherein the US does refer to 'Japanese territorial air space' repeatedly, see, e.g., at 10, in

territory, that is, on the ground, whereas the airspace in which the aircraft was shot down was mentioned separately.[71] And yet, it must be observed that later in the application Pakistan claimed 'India's unprovoked and blatant use of force against an unarmed Pakistani aircraft over Pakistani *territorial airspace* contravenes the basic purpose of the United Nations'[72] which muddies the conceptual distinctions made earlier. It is unclear whether Pakistan assumed that territorial airspace is different from territory or was just conceptually inconsistent and slipped between two different imaginings of territory. This conceptual instability is, by now, a regularly occurring theme in international law and its discourse.[73]

Understanding whether the concept of territory includes air is vital in contemporary legal analysis of, for example, the law relating to the use of drones. Already in social sciences more generally, there is much critical scholarship on drones and their contribution to the ongoing 'contemporary entanglements of natural and technological environments'.[74] Drones are fundamentally changing the modern battlefield and espionage, not just in terms of potential weaponry and terror on the ground from the purveillance[75] of drones, but in terms of our very episteme of how we relate to the world around us. Yet to understand these debates fully, it is important to comprehend that how we understand the relationship of the physical features of land and airspace affects our analysis – especially our legal analysis. The former UN Special Rapporteur on Counter-Terrorism and Human Rights, Ben Emmerson, questioned in which circumstances 'the deployment of remote targeting technology [would] amount to a violation of the sovereignty of the State on whose territory it is used.'[76] Unfortunately it is not clear how territory is defined

their Application Instituting Proceedings ICJ Pleadings, Aerial Incident of 7 November 1954, June 8 1959.

71 Pakistan also seems to take this approach regarding US drones. According to a UN Report, Pakistan passed a resolution clarifying 'the process by which consent may lawfully be given in Pakistan for the deployment of another State's military assets on its *territory* or in its *airspace*' (emphasis added). Emmerson (2012) para 54.

72 *Aerial Incident Proceedings* (n 69) 2.

73 More on this below in Section 3.5.

74 Vehlken (2018) 107, 110.

75 ibid. Vehlken argues that perveillance is more successful as communicating the activities and practices of drones as opposed to surveillance because of the 'live', dynamic, real time and searching nature or behaviour of the drone: 'with a set of behaviors or "instincts" simulating predatory birds or bats – like lurking in hideouts or perching from lookouts – they could be enabled to autonomously "pervey" a given area for long periods', 110.

76 Emmerson (2012) para 4.

by Emmerson. Clearly, *strikes* would violate territorial integrity but it is unclear whether the presence of the drones in the airspace/territory equally violates territorial integrity. Perhaps the use of the preposition 'on' is an indication of how territory is being imagined in this particular instance; one is 'in' airspace, never 'on' it.[77] There is a similar lack of clarity in a 2020 report by a UN Special Rapporteur on extrajudicial, summary, or arbitrary executions which, in looking at the drone strike against the Iranian major general Qassem Soleimani, found 'that the strike and those before it took place on the territory of a third State.'[78] Further hints that it is the strike taking place on or in territory, as opposed to the presence of armed drones in the airspace, that is key for the purposes of international law[79] as is evident in the following discussion:

> It is understood that IHL may be applied to an act rather than spatially. Nevertheless, when the "first strike" theory is operationalized, its result may be the existence of an IAC limited to the vehicle in which General Soleimani was travelling and inevitably the asphalt within its immediate proximity. But as limited as these are spatially, they nevertheless are located on Iraq's sovereign territory.[80]

What is notable is the separate mention of asphalt. This seems to be important to the reasoning. Territory has an ambivalent air in much of this discourse. Is it the output of the strike, that is, the consequence that takes place on the landmass, that violates the territorial integrity of a state, or is it the presence of drones in the airspace that violates this right? Depending on the conception of territory adopted, the position will change. Applying the ICAO Convention, it would appear the former

[77] The role of prepositions in spatialising international law has never been explored until this point. They are key in diagnosing the 'where' international law is imagined as existing in and as. The role of prepositions has been explored in other disciplines. According to Gorji, 'spatial imagining is registered in the deep grammar of [] writing in and through prepositions—those small, often overlooked words like "by," "at," "where," "to" and "from" that tend to be used to anchor or locate the speaker in space and place, and to register how spaces are encountered and experienced'. Gorji (2019) 9, 10. Prepositions in law are important, as this little reflection on 'no smoking in these premises' shows: Wordsworth (2008) 62. Prepositions are also important for understanding the temporality of spaces, on which see Kranjec and others (2010) 111.

[78] Callamard (2020).

[79] While this might appear insignificant, it may one day happen that time and space are split to such as extent that it becomes much more necessary to understand when and where the violation of territorial integrity or a 'first strike' occurs, or that an event/incident takes place entirely in airspace and does not impact land territory at all.

[80] Callamard (2020) para 28.

would be the correct position to take, whereas Iran's reasoning above follows the latter logic.

Turning from the air to the sea, the role of the physical in determining the content of the concept of territory is equally as prevalent. We can point here to two examples: the first relates to the idea of whether 'low-tide elevations' can be 'appropriated' and thus form part of the 'land territory', and the second is the idea of land territory determining the rights of coastal states. First, the very idea that only land territory can be appropriated relies on a physicalist notion of territory – that there is an ability to occupy, *physically in a way that sustains life* continually, the physical rocks that may be in question. This was the finding of the Arbitral Tribunal in the South China Sea Award.[81] The dominance of the physical reality in determining the concept of land territory is plain to see. The territorial sea, that contains these submerged landmasses, may also be included in many conceptions of territory, but it is only included because of the land territory in the first place. It recentres the importance of land territory to the definition of territory. Without land territory, there can be no territorial sea (which is conceived of as somehow less physical and thus less capable of appropriation in the specific way imagined – of course many 'resources', as they are often referred to, of the sea can be and are appropriated but there is a very particular idea about what appropriation is in a way that sustains life for the idea of territoriality in this discourse). Second, that it is land territory that determines rights in the sea, and indeed the territorial sea, points to the idea that land territory is 'primary' in the conceptual ordering. The territorial sea is appurtenant to land territory. It is sown into the very fabric of this regime. As a result, UNCLOS Annex VII Tribunals may have no option but to find they lack jurisdiction 'in cases where sovereignty over the land territory fronting a coast is disputed'[82] or where the

[81] *Award, In the Matter of the South China Sea Arbitration, The Republic of the Philippines and the People's Republic of China* [2016]. Here the Tribunal found: 'low-tide elevations, as distinct from land territory, cannot be appropriated. As the Tribunal has now found, Mischief Reef is a low-tide elevation; it follows from this that it is incapable of appropriation, by occupation or otherwise' (para 1040). See also para 309.

[82] *In the Matter of the Chagos Marine Protected Area Arbitration between the Republic of Mauritius and The United Kingdom of Great Britain and Northern Ireland, Award* (Annex VII Arbitral Tribunal, UNCLOS) [203]. This was also a key part of the dispute between the parties in *Dispute Concerning Coastal State Rights in the Black Sea, Sea of Azov, and Kerch Strait, Ukraine and the Russian Federation* [2020] Annex VII Arbitral Tribunal, PCA Case No. 2017-06. In this Award, the Tribunal upheld Russia's objection 'that the Arbitral Tribunal has no jurisdiction over Ukraine's claims, to the extent that a

land territory is framed as the 'core' of the dispute, with the sea territory[83] being of a second order importance.

**

There are two takeaways from this discussion on the dominance of the physical geography to the concept of territory. First, concerns the categories of physical geography constituting the imagining of territory: landmass, which is *always, and must be, present*; water, which is often present in the concept but with differing relations to land; and airspace, which is present in some conceptualisations of territory and not in others. Second, is the ordering and underlying logic concerning how the different features relate to each other – as appurtenances, as primary/secondary, or as equal. The different ordering is important: one arrangement may assume territory is physical and related to the surface of the earth, whereas another would broaden the spatial application of international legal rules to more than just the physical surface of the earth. Underlying values may play a role in determining the ordering. Where the concept of territory includes the column of air 'above' land territory, this may arise out of necessity in order to maintain and protect the 'primary' territory of landmass. This reprioritises and recentres land in the conceptualisation. And while the appurtenance approach seems to adopt a broadly similar logic to the primary/secondary approach, the conception of territory is more physicalised and naturalised in its underlying reasoning. Understanding territory as primarily land, although not excluding water and/or airspace, tends to prioritise the landmasses of

ruling of the Arbitral Tribunal on the merits of Ukraine's claims necessarily requires it to decide, directly or implicitly, on the sovereignty of either Party over Crimea' (para 492).

83 This arguably also points to the idea that land territory is the core of territory if it is the core of the territorial dispute. This is certainly the implications of Russia's argument in *Dispute Concerning Coastal State Rights in the Black Sea, Sea of Azov, and Kerch Strait, Ukraine and the Russian Federation* (n 82). Especially in this discussion of 'sovereignty': 'The Russian Federation points out that Ukraine has sought declarations that the Russian Federation "is violating Ukraine's sovereignty and sovereign rights" and "has interfered with Ukraine's sovereignty" on the basis that Ukraine is the coastal State in Crimea and has also sought to "vindicate Ukraine's national sovereignty." Accordingly, in the Russian Federation's view, the question of who is sovereign over the land territory is again central' (para 134).

physical geography. While the distinction appears subtle, the underlying logic of the appurtenance approach shows naturalised reasoning concerning the relationship between land, sea, and air; natural appurtenances or prolongation, as in the example of the continental shelf, sees 'scientific' reasoning and physical reality dominating the conceptualisation of territory. Science and fact are deemed, in the eyes of the court or tribunal, or during negotiations of treaties, in relation to for example UNCLOS, to be naturally occurring – there is supposedly nothing anyone can do about this – and where this informs the concept of territory, the concept too is naturalised and physicalised.

What hopefully is emerging is a story that different spatial imaginaries inform the diverse approaches to conceptualising territory. Common to these approaches is the dominance of physical geography which often dictates the practice of the concept of territory. The *physicalising* of the concept arises when there is a strong association of territory with physical geography. This excludes non-geographical spaces, such as, cyberspace. The hegemonic nature of this assumption permits international lawyers to lose sight of anything but the physical geography. This is especially true where airspace is excluded, as it tends to demonstrate that there is an underlying two-dimensional, surface-level, physical understanding of territory. The appurtenance approach may even be based on another very particular assumption; it seems to be guided by a 'naturalising' impulse, as I now explore.

3.3.3 Naturalising Territory

There are two ways that the concept of territory can be understood as naturalised in international law discourse. The first is related to the underlying natural physical geography, as previewed above, and the second is naturalisation as an organising idea. I look first at the idea of the natural that is closely related to the physicalising move: the natural physical geography. The adoption of the appurtenances approach is contingent on a particular understanding of the relationship between the concept of territory and the physical world; that relationship is often quite simply a flattening of the conceptual into the natural – territory *is* the physical world. It is possible to see this reasoning most clearly in several ICJ cases. For example, the ICJ considers 'territorial waters as [an] appurtenant to the land territory.'[84] The same goes for the sea: it is an appurtenance of the continental shelf to coastal states[85] – a fact supposedly existing 'inherently' because the appurtenance in question was a '*natural* prolongation of the land mass'.[86] The Court determined in El Salvador's and Honduras' territorial dispute that: 'as always, the entitlement to these rights [to the seas and seabed and subsoil off a coast] depends upon and reflects the territorial position of the coast to which the rights are appurtenant.'[87]

The 'natural prolongation' reasoning prompts an important reflection: do international lawyers consider territory to be naturally or socially constructed? At the very least, territory, even if recognised by many scholars as *created* by law, is often naturally *informed*. What I mean by this is that the reasoning which determines whether a delimitation is correct or fair, is informed by naturally occurring physical geography. This, in turn, offers an insight into the disciplinary understanding of territory: the natural prolongation and 'facts of the geography' reasoning verbalises assumptions made about territory pertaining to it actually being a natural feature, with 'natural extensions'. In the *North Sea Continental Shelf Cases*, the Court stated that:

> the rights of the coastal State in respect of the area of continental shelf that constitutes a natural prolongation of its land territory into and under the sea exist *ipso facto* and *ab initio*, by virtue of its sovereignty over the land, and as an extension of it in an exercise of sovereign rights for the purpose of exploring the seabed and exploiting its natural resources. In short, there is here an inherent right.[88]

Note here how the inherent quality of the right stems from this natural prolongation, tying legal rights very closely to natural features and facts; the rights are resulting from these natural features; the natural features

84 *Fisheries Case (United Kingdom v Norway), Judgment*, 116 (International Court of Justice) [128].

85 *North Sea Continental Shelf Cases* (n 58) paras 95 and 96. See also claims re the appurtenances of 'Middle Rocks and South Ledge' in *Case Concerning Sovereignty over Pedra Branca/Pulau Batu Puteh, Middle Rocks and South Ledge (Malaysia/Singapore), Judgment* [2008] ICJ Reports 2008 12 (International Court of Justice) [31, 171, 285]. See also *Land, Island and Maritime Frontier Dispute (El Salvador v Honduras: Nicaragua intervening), Judgment* [1992] ICJ Reports 1992 351 (International Court of Justice) [81, 88, 256, 333, 346, 347, 420].

86 *North Sea Continental Shelf Cases* (n 58) para 19. Emphasis added.

87 *El Salvador v Honduras* (n 85) para 420.

88 *North Sea Continental Shelf Cases* (n 58) para 19.

determine the legal rights. It flattens the legal into the natural. Also note that it is by virtue of sovereignty over land that this arises, which also implies that the justification is due to the natural features of the physical geography. This 'natural prolongation' thinking also underlies Article 76 of UNCLOS which provides that '[t]he continental shelf of a coastal State comprises the seabed and subsoil of the submarine areas that extend . . . throughout the natural prolongation of its land territory.'[89]

More generally than just natural prolongation, the 'facts of geography' are given a major role in international legal reasoning. In the *Gulf of Maine* case, the ICJ recalled 'that *the facts of geography* are not the product of human action amenable to positive or negative judgment, but the result of natural phenomena, so that they can only be taken as they are',[90] which not only offers an ahistorical account of the physical facts,[91] but these physical facts heavily influenced what the Court imagined it could determine in the delimitation of territories.[92] Indeed, the Court found this delimitation tricky because '[t]he situation in the present case as regards the sea-bed of the delimitation area is therefore different from the situation that may prevail in areas where a *natural*

[89] UNCLOS 1982. See discussion of this in n 58.

[90] *Gulf of Maine* (n 46) para 37. Emphasis added.

[91] The very idea of the 'facts of geography' assumes geography does not change, unless through human intervention such as the creation of false islands (in the South China Sea). Yet geography does change, both because of naturally occurring reasons (volcanic eruptions, earthquakes, erosion (some of which may also be human induced)) and as a result of anthropocentric developments (climate change). The ICJ assumes that were it naturally informed, it is acceptable to base the decision settling the territory on these facts. Increasingly however, it is becoming more and more well known that facts of natural geography have already been altered by humans. This is indeed the idea behind the Anthropocene 'the proposed new geological unit that says that humans are altering the planet, including long-term geological processes, at an increasing rate, and that we have already changed the Earth system sufficient to produce a distinct stratigraphic signature in sediments and ice', Gordon (2021) at 232. The questions may then become for the Court to assess whether humans have indeed changed the physical world in the particular instance before them and what instances of human involvement are problematic for the dispute.

[92] The Court said: 'the Parties have repeatedly charged each other with trying to refashion nature or geography in the case of this or that feature of the area. It is not possible to accept the US claim that the south-westward protrusion of the Nova Scotian peninsula from the Chignectou isthmus is an anomaly, a geographical distortion to be treated as such, and to be considered an irregular derogation from the general south-south-west/north-north-east trend of the eastern seaboard of the North American Continent. It is likewise not possible to accept Canada's claim that the existence of so substantial a peninsula as Cape Cod may be ignored because it forms a salient on the Massachusetts coast on the western side of the Gulf of Maine.' *Gulf of Maine* (n 46) para 37.

separation does exist.'[93] The presence of a natural separation would presumably determine the territorial delimitation. The word 'natural' for reasoning is used time and time again. For example, it also used to determine whether the proposed maritime boundary in the *Black Sea* case cut off entitlements to the continental shelf and EEZ of Romania and Ukraine.[94] Also, in determining the maritime delimitation in *Costa Rica v Nicaragua*, the ICJ indicated that 'the length of the relevant coasts should preferably be measured on the basis of their natural configuration.'[95]

Allowing the facts of geography to speak for themselves, not only unduly elevates the natural or physical world, naturalising the concept of territory through reliance on the physical geography as determinant, but it is also through this naturalising of the physical geography, that the Court allows itself to think of its role as a technical and scientific one. On the one hand, it is reassuring that the Court has not gone down a 'Blut und Boden' (blood and soil) avenue in its reasoning over territorial disputes – thinking that some people or peoples naturally belong to a particular landscape. That approach has been roundly discredited. And yet, the decision to go down a technical and scientific route, to avoid judgement on political situations, is a political and ideological move. This is something Gathii has also addressed: he argued in relation to the *Case Concerning Kasikili/Sedudu Island* that the Court placed 'more probative value on physical, geographic, scientific and economic evidence at the expense of evidence of the use and occupation of the disputed island by the Masubia, an African community, over the disputed island.'[96] We see the appearance of the natural world determining legal reasoning in this case too. For example, the court found it could not 'rely on one single criterion in order to identify the main channel of the Chobe around Kasikili/Sedudu Island, because the natural features of a river may vary markedly along its course and from one case to another'[97] and that after looking at maps and photographs was 'unable to conclude that, from its

[93] *Gulf of Maine* (n 46) para 47. Emphasis added.

[94] *Black Sea Delimitation* (n 48) para 199.

[95] *Maritime Delimitation in the Caribbean Sea and the Pacific Ocean (Costa Rica v Nicaragua) and Land Boundary in the Northern Part of Isla Portillos (Costa Rica v Nicaragua), Judgment* [2018] ICJ Reports 2018, p 139 (International Court of Justice) [114].

[96] Gathii (2002) 581, 582.

[97] *Case Concerning Kasikili/Sedudu Island (Botswana/Namibia), Judgment* [1999] ICJ Reports 1999, p 1045 (International Court of Justice) [30].

bed configuration, the southern channel constitutes the principal and natural prolongation of the course of the Chobe before the bifurcation.'[98] It has made me wonder what the Court is doing taking it upon itself to determine what is natural or not, and why this even matters, if not, firstly, because the physical geography is a major determinant of what a territory is and secondly, that this in some way should determine the outcome of a legal and political dispute. Allowing the physical geography to play such a role also allows the pretension that practices by non-western-recognised political institutions and technologies are not being overlooked, as Gathii highlights.[99] The landscape was 'empty' of authority, empty other than the natural geography which imperial powers then interpreted (badly in this case it seems – they did not have the right 'knowledge' of the channel')[100] and it was this interpretation of the physical that dominated the determination of the dispute before the ICJ. Thus, territory was treated by the Court 'as an inert geographical space over which transactions between Europeans take place without regard to the presence of non-European peoples',[101] but in so doing the Court continued treating the contemporary situation also as inert physical geography that had a more or less accurate story to tell them about territory compared to the colonisers' interpretation – and still ignoring the practices of the Masubia.

The second naturalising of the concept of territory that takes place, is the idea that territory is the natural starting point of analysis and the natural end point of processes such as decolonisation. A good example of the former is the idea that EU 'territory' is supra-state and local government space is sub-state. I addressed some of this thinking in the previous chapter, but here I want to draw attention to the fact that implicitly it is the space of the state that is the referent point. It is commonplace to think of regional, supranational and global orders as existing or operating 'above the state' – and local governments, provinces, and cities as existing or operating 'below the state' or at the 'sub-state'. Fischer-Lescano and Teubner speak of 'relatively autonomous national legal orders' being 'overlain' by the sectoral fragmentation[102] – that is, these global legal

[98] ibid [39].

[99] Gathii (2002) 584.

[100] *Case Concerning Kasikili/Sedudu Island (Botswana/Namibia), Judgment* (n 97) para 43; See also Gathii's discussion on this Gathii (2002) 593–95.

[101] Gathii (2002) 613.

[102] Fischer-Lescano and Teubner (2004) 1008–9.

functionalist orders, they suggest, *lie atop* state territory. And Nijman observes '[t]he growing practice of intercity agreements seems to fit a broader practice of sub-state actors concluding transnational agreements'.[103] Important to note however, is that these legal orders are always understood *in relation to state space*. Such spatially hierarchical informed analysis always starts and ends with state territory. Storr provides examples of the latter with her work examining 'the normalisation of the territorial sovereign state as the endpoint of decolonisation' and how this has 'entrenched Eurocentric constructions of territory as a 'natural' human, and thus universal, mode of relation with earth.'[104] This is a process that has allowed for the commodification, 'objectification and domination'[105] of the physical world.

These naturalising tendencies in legal thought is partly what has contributed to the domination of state territory as the implicit geography of international law. Thinking territory *is* the physical world is, as Storr similarly argues, what has allowed territory to become a 'natural rather than legal fact'[106] and produces the dearth of scholarship in international law examining territory as a concept in and of itself, without quick descent into the murky overlapping concepts of sovereignty, statehood, and jurisdiction.

This second naturalising move is also then related to the tendency to physicalise the concept of territory explored above, that is, to reduce the construct of territory to the respective physical geography, as it is only a short step away from understanding territory as an objective feature of the natural world. For one of the implications of the physicalising move is to create the impression that territory constitutes a feature of the 'natural world', such that they 'exist[] in nature; not made or caused by humans.'[107] This in turn enables the presentation of the concept of territory in a way that obscures its artificial character.[108] Moreover, these two naturalising moves can be thought of as related. If territory is thought to simply be there – because it *is* the physical natural world – it

103 Nijman (2016) at 228.
104 Storr (2022) at 22.
105 ibid at 3.
106 ibid at 4.
107 'Natural' in Oxford Learner's Dictionary.
108 I understand the concept of artificiality here in the same way as Unger does in the following passage: '[m]odern social thought was born proclaiming that society is made and unmade, that it is a human artefact rather than the expression of an underlying natural order.' Unger (1987) at 1.

can lead to the assumption that it is impartial as well as natural to order international law upon territory because states are territorial actors and territory is a physical fact. This has not only resulted in the idea that 'the state has come to be viewed almost geographically or spatially'[109] but is has created 'an understanding of [international law as] divided into territorially organized states.'[110] Territory is ultimately a social construct, but this is obscured. Space is socially produced. Territory is space, and yet much of the legal discourse is underpinned by assumptions pertaining to the naturalisation of territory.

3.3.4 Homogeneous and Contiguous Space

These physicalising and naturalising tendencies produce the idea in international law discourse that the concept of territory is de facto constructed as a spatially exclusive legal regime, in the sense that its operation is essentially presumed to preclude the possibility of overlapping territories; such there cannot simultaneously exist more than one territory with regard to any given piece of physical geography. The legal order created by the assemblage of these spatially configured legal regimes can be analogised to a one-level-deep (flat) structure lacking any 'vertical' dimension. That one level at which the concept of territory is understood as existing, is *only* at the level of the state. While so much of contemporary international law discourse examines the multiple interpenetrating legal orders and institutions that exist in addition to (or 'atop') the state, these spaces are invisible to international law's cartographically disciplined gaze.[111] What I mean by this, and what this

[109] Walker (1984) 529, 534.

[110] Helmig and Kessler (2007) 240.

[111] The mapping of state space has *encoded* rather than decoded the world for international lawyers. As a result, cartography has *overdetermined* the territorial state within our discipline and essentialised the idea of political geography. Cartographic depictions of territory result in and create the understanding of territory as flat, homogeneous, and uniform space; projecting and shaping the image of territory as a container for state, sovereignty, and jurisdiction. Cartography transformed the relationship between the state and territory (this might be called the 'cartographisation of sovereign jurisdiction' (see Kritsiotis (2009) 21, 547). The cartographic gaze has over-determined how international lawyers imagine the world, conceive of the concept of territory and consequently what territories are visible and relevant to international law. The very design of cartographic maps contributes to the flattening of territory identified above. Most maps illustrate state space as a flat space (indeed, most only depict state space in this dimension). This cartographical imagination of space has disciplined the legal

gaze is disciplined to see, as the default assumption seems to be that any particular physical geography can be subsumed only within one homogeneous territorial regime and there cannot be more than one subject of international law exercising 'territorial' control in regard to it. This speaks to Anderson's observation that '[i]n the modern conception, state sovereignty is fully, flatly and evenly operative over each square centimeter of legally demarcated territory'[112] and to Pistor's reach for monetary sovereignty as an alternative to the 'flat' territorial sovereignty.

In this section, picking up on many of the definitions given above (specifically Shaw and Crawford's observations that in respect of physical geography there is only one territorial regime (state territory, *terra nullius*, or *res communis*)[113] and on the natural prolongation and 'physical features' of territory), I do the following: demonstrate that the flattening and physicalising moves rely on spatial characteristics such as homogeneity/uniformity (and their constitutive opposites, striated puzzle-like pieces) and contiguity; review the enabling assumptions behind each move; and detail their implications for the international legal imagination, namely, that flattening utterly prevents the idea of overlapping territories into which functions deterritorialised from state space are reterritorialised into.

First, there is the tendency to present the arrangement of the legal space of international law as an assemblage of adjacent but never overlapping territories parcelled out on a horizontal plane. That classic 'portions of the globe' definition is a prime example. Territories in this

imagination of territory. Consequently, territory exists only on a single plane in legal discourse. Fundamentally, because of this cartographic gaze, the exercise of political authority is directed to, and connected to, the physical geography thought to be 'occupied' by states, which are cartographically represented to the exclusion of other political structures. States are assumed to not just 'look like' the depictions on maps but to actually be, or exist, in reality as represented. Maps have produced the *assumed synchronicity of the spaces* of territory, jurisdiction, and sovereignty. In other words, territory and the territoriality of international law are based on a presumption of spatial divisions corresponding to the traditional cartographic representation of states, with jurisdiction and sovereignty synchronised over the same space. This synchronicity makes invisible the activities of states that are exercised outside their territory. There are many already who have written on the cartographic gaze of international law, in particular see: Rajkovic (2018); Jones (2016) 307; Worster [2017]; Hill (2021) 15. There is similar work in international relations. See Strandsbjerg (2010); Branch (2014).

112 Anderson (2006) at 19.

113 This is a major contributor to the inability to account for the *relocation* of sovereignty into the functional regimes sharing the same physical geography as states or *res communis*.

understanding are 'parceled out over a *horizontal plane*'.[114] It bears mentioning that this imaginary occurs in addition to, or perhaps even despite, the many doctrinal definitions of territory which include not only the 'surface' elements of the respective physical geography – land, territorial sea, internal waters – but also the 'above' and 'below' physical geography: the subsoil, the column of airspace, and the entirety of the water mass within the state's borders.

An example of the spatial imaginary that I am referring to can be seen in the following passage: '[p]aradigmatically, territory, people and government coincide in the state to produce international law's map of the world as a jigsaw puzzle of solid colour pieces fitting neatly together.'[115] The metaphor of the jigsaw puzzle here evokes the same motif that Hurd, from a slightly different angle, summarises as the idea that 'the laws and practices of state sovereignty' in international law consistently induce an image of 'the map that delineate[s] physical territory into separate countries.'[116] A similar sensibility is implicitly present in the following from Schwarzenberger:

> Sovereign States have apportioned among themselves practically all land areas of the world, together with the maritime belt bordering on their coastal territories. With the exceptions of portions of Antarctica and bodies in outer-space, scarcely any land territory remains that is free form the jurisdiction of an international person.[117]

Note how Schwarzenberger refers to land areas of the world all being *apportioned* between states, with the result that 'over' each given piece of 'land' territory there now exists the jurisdiction of *one* – and only one – international person.

With examples abound, a final largely analogous impression is left by Khan's discussion of 'Spaces beyond State Territory', a rubric which he constructs as comprising only the High Sea, the Antarctic, and the 'Outer-Space, including the moon and other celestial bodies'. The rest of the globe in this presentation, in the meantime, is understood to have been '(re-)distributed . . . without . . . leaving any blank spots of stateless domain on the world map.'[118]

114 Larkins (2010) at 6.
115 Knop in Crawford and Koskenniemi (2012) at 95.
116 Hurd (2014) at 8. Conceptualising territory as something physical is thus absolutely key to this geographical imaginary.
117 Schwarzenberger and Brown (1976) at 96.
118 Khan (2012) at 247.

Homogeneity: In the eyes of international law, for many purposes, a state's territory has the characteristic of homogeneous and uniform space. The space is uniformly the same; all state spaces are internally homogeneous in the sense that for most purposes, the space all 'belongs' to the state. There are no 'not central or peripheral locations. All locations are equally situated'[119] and understood as state territory. In other words, the container of the state (its territory) is 'filled with' homogeneous and uniform space. This is how international law predominantly 'sees' territory. For example, Article 29 of the VCLT provides that '[u]nless a different intention appears from the treaty or is otherwise established, a treaty is binding upon each party in respect of its entire territory'.[120] Territory is treated as homogeneous in this case: the treaty binds uniformly over all state space as the norm.

Much of the law on the use of force, as another example, is based on homogeneous assumptions of state territory. Thus, any incursion into state territory, whether it be in a city, a rural area, its internal waters, an industrial zone, a nuclear power plant, a farm, a nature reserve, at the centre or at the periphery, could violate a state's territorial integrity and also the law prohibiting the resort to armed force.[121] The implication of this assumed homogeneity is, as others have highlighted, that the law on the use of force is structurally unable to make sense of 'a distributed network on loosely articulated groups supposedly operating in over 40 countries, a network of networks;'[122] the spaces of network do not map on to the understanding of homogeneous state space. Consequently, Afghanistan (as a whole) was identified and substituted for Al-Qaeda so it could be the object of the military campaign and occupation. This was visible in the political discourse taking place in America at the time: 'The terrorists . . . need a territorial base of sovereign protection . . . If bin Laden was behind this, then Afghanistan is our enemy. Any country that

119 Sheppard (2003) at 103.

120 Vienna Convention on the Law of Treaties 1969 (1155 UNTS 331), emphasis added.

121 On the face of it, it could appear like the ICJ would distinguish between spaces near the border or spaces in the centre. This could arise as a result of its finding in the Nicaragua case concerning when states are 'merely' sending armed forces across a border or a 'mere frontier incident'. *Case Concerning Military and Paramilitary Activities in and against Nicaragua (Nicaragua v United States of America) Judgment (Merits)* [1986] ICJ Reports 1986 14 (International Court of Justice) [195]. Yet, this would still be a violation of a state's right to 'territorial integrity'. What this finding actually does is qualify the 'scale and effect' (para 195) of an armed attack, that in turn would then legitimate the use of self-defence.

122 Gregory (2004) at 49–56.

harbors and protects him is our enemy. We must carry their war to them.'[123] Al-Qaeda's 'network of networks'[124] is spatially at odds with how the law in this field operates and how military strategy is, as a result, enacted: '[i]ndeed, the recent events in Afghanistan and Iraq have shown how it became easier for the US to fight a territorially identifiable foe rather than the Al-Qaeda "network of networks."'[125]

Contiguity and Continuity: Another quality present in international law's spatial imaginary is the idea that territory is a 'space structured by principles of contiguity and continuity'.[126] The qualities of contiguity and continuity are related to homogeneity and uniformity but are not necessarily implied by them. By contiguity and continuity, I refer to the idea that physical space is divided into territories that are 'contiguous and nonoverlapping areas, each identified with a sovereign state.'[127] The ICJ observed the two meanings of contiguity in international law:

> Contiguity describes a territory that is all of one piece, in which all parts of the territory are connected to one another and contained within a single, continuous boundary line. The term can also be used to describe the relationship between two or more territories; territories are contiguous if they directly border or touch one another.[128]

The contiguity of territory, it could be said, is more of an ideal practice, honoured in its breach just as much as in its observance, because international law is peppered by different practices. Contiguity is present in the work of boundary delimitation as a guide to the allocation of territory between states but it is also the basis of state claims:[129] '[l]and is claimed because it is contiguous with territory already controlled or because some physical connectivity is perceived to exist.'[130] Contiguity is not sufficient to give title ('the title of contiguity, understood as a basis of territorial sovereignty, has no foundation in international law'[131]), but

123 Krauthammer (2001).
124 Elden (2006) 57.
125 ibid.
126 Michel Lussault, *L'Homme Spatial* (éditions du Seuil 2007) as cited in Painter (2010) 1090, 1102.
127 McCarthy (2007).
128 *Case Concerning Maritime Delimitation and Territorial Questions between Qatar and Bahrain (Qatar v Bahrain) Merits* [2001] ICJ Reports 2001, p 40 (International Court of Justice) [100, 170].
129 Van Dyke (2007) 157, 193.
130 Burghardt (1973) 225, 235.
131 *Island of Palmas Case* (n 21) para 869.

is usually evidentiary or an underlying motive: 'it will never be decisive in resolving a dispute, but it is certainly not irrelevant.'[132] There may be other factors, such as a continual presence of a particular ethnicity or nationality, that would make it 'unjust' to 'assign' physical geography to one state over another on the basis of contiguity to the rest of that state's territory alone. But where contiguity is not applied, there needs to be a good reason, which in turn entrenches the characteristic of contiguity as the norm into the content of the concept territory.

The quality of contiguity of territory is also realised in the concepts of appendage or appurtenance. The very idea that something appends to the rest of a state's territory for reasons of it being contiguous to the state's territory, such as the continental shelf, continues following this ideal of contiguity. For example, in *Eritrea Yemen Arbitration* the Tribunal determined: 'there is some presumption that any islands off one of the coasts may be thought to belong by appurtenance to that coast unless the state on the opposite coast has been able to demonstrate a clearly better title.'[133] Huber also assumed the ideal of contiguity, when he observed: '[a]s regards groups of islands, it is possible that a group may under certain circumstances be regarded as in law a unit, and that the fate of the principal part may involve the rest.'[134] In the *Fonseca Case*, 'Meanguerita [being] an appendage' to Meanguera meant that El Salvador succeeded to Spanish sovereignty over it.[135] Indeed, 'the small size of Meanguerita, its contiguity to the larger island, and the fact that is it uninhabited, allow its characterisation as a "dependency" of Meanguera'.[136] Contiguity is clearly preferred as a rule when it comes to islands; they are *usually* allocated or assigned to the territory of the nearest state. Contiguity is also implicit in the justification for the allocation of sovereign rights over the continental shelf, exclusive economic zones (EEZ)[137] and territorial

132 Van Dyke (2007) 193.

133 *Award of the Arbitral Tribunal in the First Stage of the Proceedings between Eritrea and Yemen (Territorial Sovereignty and Scope of the Dispute), Eritrea and Yemen Award* [1998] Permanent Court of Arbitration (PCA) 1996-04, 1 Vol XXII pp 209–332 17 [458].

134 *Island of Palmas Case* (n 21) para 855.

135 *El Salvador v Honduras* (n 85) para 368.

136 ibid para 356.

137 It should be noticed that others have said 'there is no trace of the criteria of contiguity or natural prolongation in the EEZ concept'; see Barbara Kwiatkowska, 'Judge Shigeru Oda's Opinions in Law-of-the-Sea Cases: Equitable Maritime Boundary Delimitation' [1993] German Yearbook of International Law 225, 235.

sea in the law of the sea[138] (note that there is a '*Contiguous* Zone' within twenty-four nautical miles from baselines where a state may exercise control).[139] The evidentiary weight of contiguity is present in the work of various arbitral tribunals and courts determining the rationale for the continental shelf or boundary delimitations.[140]

However, as Shaw notes, giving the example of Pakistan prior to 1971: 'there is no requirement in international law for state territory to be geographically indivisible and contiguous.'[141] And as much of the colonial practices shows, contiguity can be dispensed with. For example, in 1899, Gardiner argued in defence of acquiring non-contiguous territory by conquest, treaty, or discovery: 'the situs of the territory is immaterial; it may be contiguous or remote, on the American continent or in foreign lands. Our abstract right to acquire and hold is as plenary and sovereign in the Philippines as in Alaska or Arizona.'[142] Gardiner's contention highlights the political nature of these qualities, such as contiguity or homogeneity. These qualities are not naturally occurring but are human interventions and assumptions about the qualities of space.[143] This is true whether we are *applying or disapplying* continuity as a spatial characteristic of territory.

Further, the very idea of contiguity of territories denies the existence of overlap. Overlapping spaces are no longer contiguously arranged. When this spatial quality is assumed as international law's spatial imaginary, territories that do overlap with state territory are invisibilised. At first glance, the idea of condominium might be an exception to this. Condominium can be interpreted as two (or more) state territories overlapping the same physical geography, but is more commonly understood as 'a territory over which two or more States jointly exercise governmental authority.'[144] Notably, it is territory in the singular. This territory will be contiguous with the rest of the territories of the states in question. It does not overlap another state space. Contiguity prevails.

[138] Burghardt (1973) 237; Van Dyke (2007) 194.
[139] Article 33 UNCLOS.
[140] *El Salvador v Honduras* (n 85); *North Sea Continental Shelf Cases* (n 58); *Gulf of Maine* (n 46); *Eritrea v Yemen Award* (n 133).
[141] Shaw (1982) 67.
[142] Gardiner (1899) 161, 166.
[143] Understanding that allows the problematisation of the legal reasoning by courts in their work dealing with facts, for example in delimitation cases, which often purport to do so for reasons of geographical fairness.
[144] Morrison (2006).

Moreover, condominium has other similar spatial characteristics: territory is internally homogeneous and uniform space that these two states exercise power in relation to.

One oft pointed to exception to the contiguous and continuous character of territory relevant to the present characteristic is the phenomena of enclaves and exclaves. Yet, these constructs continue to entrench the idea that there is no overlapping of territories, for these enclaves still fit like jigsaw puzzle pieces on the flat surface of international law's spatial imaginary. Examples of enclaves include: Gaza and the West Bank; former East Pakistan and Pakistan; Prussian territory enclaved in German territory; the papal territories including Avignon (now part of French territory) and Vatican City; Spanish and French enclaves (Llívia or the oddity that is Pheasant Island which is French for half the year and Spanish for the other half[145] – a temporal territory); enclaves in India and Bangladesh (noting their recent territory swap bringing about more homogeneity and contiguity);[146] or, more well known to international lawyers, the *Right of Passage over Indian Territory Case*[147] concerning Portuguese enclaves in India. Enclaves and exclaves have been a subject of fascination for international lawyers – probably *because* they are *sui generis* and disrupt the dominant assumptions about the contiguity of territory, thus also reinforcing the general rule that this is an assumed spatial characteristic of territory. Nevertheless, an enclave is internally homogeneous and uniform, that is, within its limits the space is equal and uniform. There is simply a smaller homogeneous space within, and surrounded by, other homogeneous space.

This spatial imaginary is contained within the implicit geography of international law. Consider the implied formula: physical geography not included in the category of 'spaces beyond state territory' are assumed to have been apportioned already between states in an interlocking jigsaw puzzle-like fashion. No room is left for the possibility of overlapping or interpenetrating territorial frameworks, not least because it is assumed that only the state has a territory in the first place. The spatial imaginary that is presumed here is modelled, in other words, on an understanding of the 'world [as] made up of territorially bounded, sovereign entities',

145 'The Island that Switches Countries Every Six Months' (2018).

146 Van Schendel (2002) 115, 115; 'India and Bangladesh Seal Land Swaps' (2015).

147 *Case Concerning Right of Passage over Indian Territory (Portugal v India) Judgment* [1960] ICJ Reports 1960 6 (International Court of Justice).

where '[t]he whole surface of the earth is ... divided up in political territorially delimited units.'[148]

3.3.5 *The Time of Territory*

Historicising concepts such as territory is important to understanding their complexity and lineage, but it is often the only way the concept of territory is temporally analysed. Thus, while time is present in Agnew's territory trap analysis, he primarily used time to historicise and contextualise territory. Valverde calls this the 'reduction of time to history.'[149] It is not, however, the main reason time is important to this excavation. An alternative way to intersect space and time, is to understand the *time of spaces*, or here, the *time of territories*. The time of territory offers insights into the different values and ideologies of the institutions producing territories, but the temporality of space is rarely made explicit in how international law imagines territory. Understanding the potential for the time of territories to change can transform how the concept of territory in international law is understood and applied.

Studying time is essential to understanding how different spaces exist and are practised. It is through practices that space is produced, and those practices have a time. Therefore, all territories are time and space. Further, if we understand that the time and space of territories are produced, we can also understand that they can be changed; the temporalities of territories are not required to be uniform.[150] Some spaces are only practised at particular times – for example, a marketplace only exists whilst market stalls are present and 'open for business', and laws may change the spaces that are physically off limits using barriers in supermarkets with the timing of alcohol licensing.

State territory has traditionally had a static and permanent quality – changing, for example, when a territory is acquired by one state from another.[151] In the discipline of international law, territory is 'understood as a physical entity, stable and not exposed to time or dynamics.'[152] The territorial ordering of states and of international law is assumed to be the 'static background' against which political and legal processes, activities,

[148] Kuijer and Werner (2017) at 4.
[149] Valverde (2015) at 39.
[150] Helmig and Kessler (2007) 253.
[151] See on this Shaw, *International Law* (2017) at 362–63.
[152] Müller-Mall (2013) at 78.

and struggles take place.[153] There is a tendency to 'implicitly rely on "container" notions of the territorial state [and] from this perspective, space is something static that other things happen in.'[154] Agnew referred to this as an implicit assumption, noting that 'a state is a fixed territorial entity'.[155] It is this idea of fixity and the permanency of territory that I highlight as a characteristic that is important to interrogate further.

The implicitly assumed time of territory can often be gleaned from discussions about stability and order in international law. Early traces of the ideas of stability and order, and the impulse towards static and permanent space, can be seen in early sixteenth-century Italian writer Botero's work, someone who is still considered to be influential upon early ideas of sovereignty. Botero posited that the 'State is a stable dominion [*dominio fermo*/strong, firm rule] over people.'[156] And in contemporary times, this impulse towards permanency is exemplified by: '[t]he legal competence of states and the rules for their protection depend on and assume the existence of this stable, physically identified (and normally legally delimited) base.'[157]

Furthermore, this assumption regarding the fixed and static temporality of territory is key to the creation of *sui generis* situations:

> Ordinarily *the lack of territory has either been treated as a temporary phenomenon* caused by foreign occupation or annexation that should sooner or later end, resulting in the full restoration or creation of statehood (national liberation movements, governments-in-exile). Or it has been *accepted as a permanent phenomenon and then, the entity has changed its status from 'State' to a 'sui generis legal person'* (the Holy See, the Order of Malta). The latter scenario could possibly be applied to disappearing States as a result of the rising sea level.[158]

Thus, it is this particular quality of territory that can determine the categories of actor in international law and used to label subjects as one type of actor or another. The ideal is permanency, if in cases where the 'absence of territory turned out to be permanent, the entity typically cease[s] to be considered a State.'[159] This permanency assumption is

[153] Elden (2013) at 328.
[154] Lambach (2020) 482, 8.
[155] Agnew (1994) 53, 55.
[156] Botero, *Della. Ragione di stato* (1956) quoted in Elden (2013) at 269.
[157] Brownlie (2008) at 204.
[158] Kuijer and Werner (2017) at 23, emphasis added.
[159] ibid at 40.

present in how Guantanamo Bay is understood by international lawyers: it is 'Cuban' territory, even when leased *indefinitely* to the US, which is still somehow assumed to be temporary because the assumption is leasing is less than ownership – the ultimate right, which is permanent unless transferred. If there was a 'permanent' transfer of authority, Guantanamo Bay would become US territory. An interesting example of temporal exceptionalism is Pheasant Island which changes state every six months between Spain and France.[160] However, this situation is also assumed to be permanent – the Island will always 'belong' to either Spain or France. Permanency is still maintained as a characteristic.

The way international law understand islands and low tide elevations is illuminating in this regard. There was for a long time, and some might argue there still is, no agreement on 'whether low tide elevations can be considered to be territory'[161] precisely because of their impermanent nature. The South China Sea arbitration mentioned above may have changed this, given it did find 'low-tide elevations, [to be] distinct from land territory'.[162] Permanency as the ideal is also present and relevant for other law of the sea determined spaces. The UNCLOS provides that '[f]or the purpose of delimiting the territorial sea, the outermost permanent harbour works which form an integral part of the harbour system are regarded as forming part of the coast.'[163]

There are several reasons for this static temporality assumed of the concept of territory. Thinking back to the naturalising and physicalising tendency discussed earlier, one reason may be that the relationship between territory and physical geography, especially where the former is assumed to be the latter, has also influenced the time of territory. Physical geography is understood to be more or less 'permanent' in most instances, while recognising that there are long-term changes and exceptions: ice melts, continents drift, islands 'drown', tides, and land is reclaimed. Where territory and physical geography are conflated, territory also becomes static, or at least temporally durable. Thus, closely associating the concept of territory with physical geography has repercussions limiting our understanding of the potential temporalities of

160 'The Island That Switches Countries Every Six Months' (2018).
161 *Qatar v Bahrain* (n 128) para 205.
162 *Award, In the Matter of the South China Sea Arbitration, The Republic of the Philippines and the People's Republic of China* (n 81) para 1040.
163 Article 11, UNCLOS.

territory. Secondly, we can also examine this time of territory through the more traditional frame of temporalising: the timing of territory as permanent and static has a lineage and is closely related to the cartographical imagination, and may indeed be constituted in many ways by the representation of space in this way. Mapping may have contributed to the creation of this static understanding of time associated with territory. Maps are unable to convey *temporal* scale;[164] the time of maps is homogeneous. Time is not *cartographically* mappable; maps are for 'all time'. Once produced and published, they are difficult to alter and the mapped projections of state territory subsist for a long time in the imagination of users. Thus, it may also be the case that our representation of state space plays a role in our imagining of that space.

3.3.6 *Being Bound*

I discuss borders and boundaries last because it is productive to the following analysis to have already discussed the cartographic disciplining of territory, homogeneity, temporality, and other characteristics of territory; these characteristics are necessary to think of territory as bounded in some way. Thus far, the chapter has attempted to address the concept of territory as a concept in its own right. But that is not to say that boundaries are not an important characteristic of territory. It might be better to say that boundaries are just one characteristic that are important to the concept of territory. Yet, international law discourse often thinks of these as distinct phenomena.[165] Craven and Parfitt have noted this tendency in international law discourse too. Relaying the *North Sea Continental Shelf Cases*, which established that territory can still exist even if the borders are not fully delimited,[166] they observe that:

> this appears to suggest that the border and the territory of the State are effectively two different things ... Borders, on one side, seem to be the consequence rather than the cause of an acknowledgment that the possession of territory by some entity is legitimate. Their delimitation, after all, proceeds on the assumption that there are legitimate entitlements on

[164] This builds on ideas of Valverde and de Sousa Santos; see Valverde (2015) at 50; de Sousa Santos [1987] 279.

[165] I once had a major revision suggested to an article submitted to a journal because I discussed territory and borders together. As I remember it, a reviewer had thought these were two different areas of study and that no article could possibly address both together.

[166] *North Sea Continental Shelf Cases* (n 58) para 46.

> either side. Territory, by contrast, seems to be a pre-condition for the assertion of rights of property in relation to space insofar as it concerns the very existence of the legal subject.[167]

Craven and Parfitt comment that while this is an 'appealing distinction' because it does not call into question the 'identity of the States whose borders are the subject of dispute', they argue that 'radical changes to borders can sometimes have precisely that effect' making too sharp a distinction between borders and territories 'hard to sustain.'[168]

I agree with this, but for slightly different reasons. Borders are essential to contemporary conceptions of territory ('a *bounded* space',[169] 'a *defined* portion of the surface of the globe'[170]). Therefore, while territory and borders are distinct phenomena – often treated in the discourse as distinct *objects* – borders, or more specifically the quality of boundedness, are an important element of territory. In understanding a territory to exist, we understand it in relation to spaces that are not a part of that territory. The discourse and the law instead presume that there *must be* a location where a territory and spaces not part of that territory meet or diffuse into one another, but that the precise *where* is unknown and yet to be established. What is more, the way territorial borders are understood in international law does not allow for overlap. The qualities of contiguity and of surface-level flatness are important to international law's spatial imaginary: remembering the words of the ICJ in *Qatar v Bahrain:* 'territories are contiguous if they directly border or touch one another.'[171]

Boundedness is a characteristic integral to the concept of territory. For as Alliés suggests: 'to define territory, we are told, one delimits borders. Or to think the border, must [] already have the idea of homogen[e]ous space'.[172] Elden argues we need to have *a notion of space* first in order to create boundaries rather than the other way around: 'territory can be re-thought of not as bounded space, but as the political form of conceptualisation of space that makes boundaries possible.'[173] So while borders are important to understand the spatial limit of a state's powers, they are

[167] Craven and Parfitt (2018) at 197–98.
[168] ibid at 198.
[169] Storey (2017).
[170] Lauterpacht (1955) para 451.
[171] *Qatar v Bahrain* (n 128) paras 100, 170.
[172] Alliés (2011).
[173] Elden (2006) 62.

'a consequence' of how we understand territory.[174] The space must be understood firstly as calculatable, homogeneous, and divisible in order to create the conditions for borders as they are understood today.

So far, I have used the terms 'boundary' and 'border' interchangeably because I have been talking about the two as a general category. There is often a distinction made between the two however, as distinguished in the following passage: 'a boundary – the line of the map and its corresponding coordinates on the land or in the sea – and a border, a political and administrative technology used to manage, regulate and police entry to and exit from the territory enclosed by the boundary.'[175] But these are not unproblematic definitions. Many would define boundaries more broadly: they are not just the lines on maps but also 'a real or imaginary line that separates two things'.[176] Others define them by their common features: '[b]orders and boundaries, commonly defined as the lines dividing distinct political, social, or legal territories.'[177] Furthermore, the term 'line' is not always helpful because it tends to conjure up the cartographical depiction of borders; it thus associates borders as thin and solid rather than thick and fuzzy, even as opposed to uneven. Better then, is the following description:

> Boundaries and borders signify limits or discontinuities in space … Typically, there is no distinction between the terms boundary and border in everyday language. Specifically, many authors use border to designate the formal political division line between territorial units, such as states, and boundary to signify the cultural and social group difference that may or may not be marked on the ground by division lines. In a geographical sense, boundary and border making is about marking difference in space …[178]

I too prefer to refer to the limits to space and territories generally as 'boundaries' – to 'signify limits or discontinuities in space'[179] – and use 'borders' to refer to the political and administrative technology forming the boundaries of states. Putting this aside, it is really the quality of boundedness and that it is 'a consequence' of how we understand territory that is important for our purposes here. It is a topic I return

174 Elden (2011).

175 Vradis and others (2019) at 1.

176 'Boundaries and Borders: A Story Map' <www.arcgis.com/apps/MapJournal/index.html?appid=7e4ac025d2b54b2b90b1a597b31526a0> accessed 29 September 2019.

177 Hagan (2018).

178 Popescu (2010) at 293.

179 ibid at 292.

to in the next chapter, for I argue that the particular form and practice of this 'meeting place' between territories can differ enormously from the practices of bordering international law recognises, each touching another, represented as clear lines on the map, imagined like the edges of a jigsaw puzzle piece, that fits with another piece.

***

To conclude this exploration of territory, it is important to tie up some key ideas to move forward. This concept of territory, unstable as it is in its precise definition and with some muddied and muddled issues, is reproduced by the theories and accounts explored in Chapter 2. They replicate, often unconsciously, the traditional spatial imaginary of international law, which is based on a stato-centric, flat and physicalised concept of territory. This is hardly surprising. The usage of this concept primarily developed for international law purposes over the course of the eighteenth, nineteenth and twentieth centuries, such that the orthodox meaning of territory today is based very much on the circumstances of that century – one where the state, state theory, and *raison d'état* were fully realised in international legal theory, even if ironically, the twentieth century also witnessed the end of the state as the dominant actor.[180]

We have already seen that there is some conceptual obscurity (space, area, portion, 2D v 3D, etc.). These different assumptions make both the use of the concept in orthodox discourse problematic, and as we will see below, it produces different accounts of territorial sovereignty but can equally make the discourses examined in Chapter 2 problematic and unstable. Despite inconsistencies, there remains, nevertheless, a strong impulse towards treating territory as naturally informed. This predisposition leads to a reduction of the concept of territory to the physical geography and a flattening of global legal territories into a single layer over the earth's surface – which corresponds to the layer of state space. It is the uncritical reliance on this spatial imaginary that drives the conclusion that any processes or phenomena not conforming to this recognised model must, as a result, be aterritorial and also produces the supposed binary between functionality and territoriality.

[180] For an account of the growth of the state and state development, see Scott (1998). See also Foucault (2009), in particular chapters 10–12; Wight (1977); Sassen (2008); Sassen (2000).

3.4 The Signification of 'Territory': Concerning Conceptual Slippage

In international legal discourse, the term 'territory' is required to do and mean more than just one consistent referent. As already suggested above, international lawyers have often lacked the onto-theoretical lexicon to understand territory and tend to use space, area, portion, and base interchangeably as a result. These terms are all different geographical concepts which have very different implications, such as, for example, whether territory is imagined to be two-dimensional or three and whether territory is conceived as something physical or not.

In the following, I delve deeper into the signification of the term 'territory' and outline five different uses for territory in the discourse: one, where territory is intended to refer to an object; the second, where territory is intended to refer to a subject of international law; the third, where territory is intended to refer to a framework; fourth, where territory is used as an organising logic; and fifth, where territory is understood as a space proper. I address territory as a space proper in some detail in Chapter 4 where I fully explain this usage and its implication, therefore, in the following sections I provide examples outlining these different usages focusing more on the first four usages. The picture that emerges is that there is one dominant usage – territory as an object – while the discourse commonly misunderstands and misuses territory as a space.

The discussion below aims to provide some clarity and open up debate about how the term 'territory' is used. This analysis and classification of territory has, to my knowledge, never been undertaken nor even observed before. After identifying and locating four dominant uses in the discourse, I discuss the potential for a correlated issue of conceptual slippage and the potential problems produced by this slippage.

3.4.1 *Object*

Perhaps unsurprisingly, one of the most common intended referents of the concept of 'territory' is a material reality (object).[181] Territory understood as an object is most likely to result from the tendency to refer to territory as an 'area' or 'portion of the earth'. The intended meaning in such cases describes a particular parcel or portion of land, water

[181] I have established the physicalising conception of territory above.

('territorial sea'), etc. that is capable of being owned, acquired, transferred, possessed, ceded, occupied, and so on.[182] What defines this way of thinking about territory is the tendency to construct the referent behind the concept of territory as an *inanimate entity* to which *an action can be directed*: for example, territory as an object of violation, an object of acquisition, an object of contestation, and so forth.

Typical illustrations of this way of using the concept include depicting territory as 'tangible',[183] 'material',[184] a 'physical base',[185] or a 'physical foundation',[186] as well as the idea explored earlier of territory as essentially equivalent with various features of physical geography, such as land or maritime waters, a rock, a seabed, soil, etc. Statements and comments such as the following: 'territory consist[s] of land or waters',[187] '[i]nside a state's territory, naturally, are its internal waters: its rivers, lakes and canals',[188] or '[f]or the purposes of this Convention the territory of a State shall be deemed to *be* the land areas and territorial waters,'[189] capture this approach well. Another example can be found in Schwarzenberger's discussion of the historical expansion of state control over the globe:

> Sovereign States have apportioned among themselves practically *all the land areas* of the world, together with a maritime belt bordering on their costal territories. With the exception of portions of Antarctica and *bodies* in outer-space, scarcely any *land territory* remains that is free from the jurisdiction of an international person (territorium nullius).[190]

The tendency to reify territory and to physicalise it, usually, go hand-in-hand. As the passage above shows, when territory is conceived of as a passive object (of states' activities), it also often ends up being depicted primarily in terms of its physical expression to which it is then reduced. Sometimes, however, the physicality is not as explicit as references like

182 It is remarkable just how similar the discourse of modes of acquisition of territory, etc. are to the modes of acquiring property in Roman law, where property law is *the law of things*. See, e.g., Nicholas (1962) at 115–16.
183 Wallace (1986) at 81.
184 Gottmann (1975) at 29.
185 Crawford (2012) at 204.
186 Lachs (1984) at 36.
187 Lauterpacht (1970) at 171.
188 Klabbers (2017) at 256. This is perhaps another example of the natural slipping in.
189 Article 1, ICAO Convention (n 66). Emphasis added.
190 Schwarzenberger and Brown (1976) at 96.

'physical territory'[191] and must instead be inferred from the context. Thus, for example:

> The importance of State territory lies in the fact that it is the space within which the State exercises its supreme authority. State territory is an object of the Law of Nations, because the latter recognises the supreme authority of every state within its territory. *Whatever person or thing is on*, or enters into, that territory is ipso facto subjected to the supreme authority of the State ... The supreme authority which a State exercises over its territory would seem to suggest that on one and the same territory there can exist only one full sovereign State only ... The first and perhaps only true exception to that rule is the case of the so-called condominium. In this case a *piece* of territory *consisting of land or waters* is under the joint tenancy of two or more States.[192]

Note the wording: territory is something a person or a thing can be *on*, it is something divisible into pieces, and it is also something *consisting of* land or waters (it is also a space). The reduction of territory to the physical is worth noting only here,[193] I want to instead think about prepositions for they can be terribly useful in revealing how a territory is being imagined, regardless of whether the term space, area, base, etc. is being used 'appropriately' (or especially if they are being used 'imperfectly'). If one is *on* a territory, or entering into something, there is a physical imaginary of an object underpinning the thinking. Being 'in' a territory does not necessarily have the same implications, as one can be 'in' a space, but it can indicate there is an 'enframing' of territory taking place – understanding it as a container – but this is not necessarily always going to be the case.[194] More detective work is needed. Other spatial prepositions can also be helpful in understanding the relationship between power and space, and how space is being conceptualised in the particular instance. It could also be said territory-as-an-object is one of the basic assumptions in understanding the relation between the sovereign and its territory. Indeed, it is the particular spatial imaginary that the flattened and physicalised concept of territory produces which allows a state to be 'above' territory, exercising sovereignty, power, control 'over' territory. Typical examples include observations like: 'the concept of territorial sovereignty is concerned with the nature of the authority

[191] Hurd (2014) at 8.
[192] Lauterpacht (1955) at paras 170–71. Emphasis added.
[193] I have already addressed this previously in some detail.
[194] 'in' for example could also be a preposition of time. I find writing *in* the morning is best.

exercised by the state over its territory. The ideas of territory and sovereignty are closely linked in international law, since the concept is concerned with *those geographical areas over which sovereignty of sovereign rights may be exercised*';[195] 'the [State is] entitled to exercise control over its territory';[196] and 'when a state exercises authority ... over a certain territory it is popularly said to have "sovereignty" over the territory'.[197] The spatial imaginary can also be detected in the discourse depicting territory as subjected to state power, as in: 'territory determines the space that is subject to the sovereignty of a concrete state';[198] or '[i]n spatial terms the law knows four types of regime: territorial sovereignty, territory not subject to the sovereignty of any state'.[199] Pistor uses similarly spatialised language to characterise her problematique: '[t]erritorial sovereignty *is based on control over land and the people residing* ***on*** *it*. How exactly control is organized ... may vary internally, but in the external relation to other states sovereignty is *flat*'.[200] Territory here refers to an object – a physical natural geography that is all surface.

The prepositions are helpful in decoding how territory is being understood. Territory-as-an-object and territory-as-a-space are often used interchangeably. Many scholars may define territory as a space but in descriptions, discussions, or applications of the concept, slip into objectification – hence why I suggest the onto-theoretical lexicon needs developing. A typical example of this can be found in the following passage: '[t]he importance of State territory lies in the fact that it is *the space within which* the State exercises its supreme authority. State territory *is an object* of the Law of Nations ... *Whatever person or thing is on*, or enters into, that territory ... In this case a *piece* of territory *consisting of land or waters*.'[201] This slippage is important to recognize. It highlights that there is an ambiguity to the concept of territory. It is unclear how international lawyers, as a group, but also on the individual level, understand the concept, and there is slippage between different concepts. This was demonstrated already in the first part of this chapter and continues as an enduring theme here. There is often a *duality* in how international lawyers understand and then use concepts, which enables and encourages

[195] Shaw (1982) at 73, emphasis added.
[196] Crawford (2012) at 168.
[197] Clapham (2012) at 168.
[198] Bílková in Kuijer and Werner (2017) at 26.
[199] Crawford (2012) at 203.
[200] Pistor (2017) at 507, emphasis added.
[201] Lauterpacht (1955) 170–71, emphasis added.

the slip into physicalising territory. Lawyers can think intellectually about a concept but at the same time apply it and use it as an object. Schlag calls this duality, '"as if" jurisprudence' – 'law is a kind of "as if" discourse'.[202] He observes that 'while legal thinkers will in their intellectualist or theoretical moments seek to reject the metaphysics of the objectivist ... aesthetic, they will in their normative moment of "doing law" rush to bring this back.'[203] This is present in much of the discourse on territory in the discipline, making it vital to bring to the surface these different conceptual usages and their implications that are otherwise submerged.

3.4.2 Subject

The term 'Territory' or 'territories' can also be used to refer to a subject of international law. Typical illustrations of this usage can be found in phrases and legal constructs such as 'Non-Self-Governing Territories' as referenced in, for example, Chapter XI of the United Nations Charter (UNC);[204] 'dependent territories'[205] as referenced in UNGA Resolution 1514 (XV); 'colonial territories';[206] 'Occupied Palestinian Territory' or 'Palestinian Territories';[207] 'Non-Cooperative Countries and Territories' (NCCT) designated by the Financial Action Task Force (FATF) if legal subjects did not comply with rules to prevent money laundering;[208] and 'overseas territory' or 'overseas territories',[209] or indeed the name of British Indian Ocean Territory (or BIOT). Many multilateral agreements are open to signature by non-state subjects known as territories, including the WTO Agreement discussed in Chapter 2 allowing customs territories to become parties to the treaty and members of the organisation. It also includes, for example, UNCLOS

202 Schlag (1998) at 110.

203 ibid at 100.

204 Charter of the United Nations 1945 (1 UNTS XVI). See also 'The United Nations and Decolonization: Non-Self-Governing Territories' (United Nations) <www.un.org/en/decolonization/nonselfgovterritories.shtml> accessed 10 April 2018; Mbengue (2013).

205 United Nations General Assembly Resolution 1514 (XV): Declaration on the granting of independence to colonial countries and peoples 1960 (UN Doc A/RES/1514(XV)).

206 Crawford (2006) at 603.

207 Dugard and Reynolds (2013).

208 FATF, 'About the Non-Cooperative Countries and Territories (NCCT) Initiative' <www.fatf-gafi.org/publications/fatfgeneral/documents/aboutthenon-cooperativecountriesandterritoriesncctinitiative.html> accessed 4 March 2020.

209 Novak (2013).

which provides that '[t]his Convention shall be open for signature by: (a) all States ... (e) all territories which enjoy full internal self-government.'[210]

However, attempts to *conceptualise* territory as a subject and its origins, noting or distinguishing the object from the subject and attempting to differentiate these two, or offering explanations as to how an object can also be a subject in international law are absent from legal discourse. This is surprising given that using territory to refer to legal subjects is fundamentally a different concept to territory as an object. Using 'territory' or 'territories' as subjects is linked to the idea of 'peoples' in international law. Both are employed to classify the status, rights, and duties of actor that are not states. The usual context in which this understanding of territory is used is in discourse about decolonisation or state succession – both historically in the context of non-self-governing territories and in the last remnants today of overseas territories.

This is notable and worthy of further attention. 'Territories' is also used in instances where there is a de facto recognition of a group but no willingness or ability for whatever reason to recognise a state, for example, the status of Taiwan in the WTO[211] or Palestine. The status of a subject as a territory indicates it is something less than a state, is something less than sovereign – less even than a 'part sovereign' state.[212] This position – using territory as a subject to describe something less than a state – is confirmed by the UNC Commentary on Chapter XI where 'territories' include 'colonies, protectorates, mandate territories, and all other forms by which a territory is subjected to or integrated into another State without the status of equal rights or without free decision.[213] Here 'territory' is used both as a term of art as the label ascribed

210 Article 305, UNCLOS.

211 See discussion in Chapter 2, and also Kennedy (2016).

212 The term 'part-sovereign' is described by those like Baker (1923) as follows: part-sovereign States 'exercise some of the rights of sovereignty and which, in so far as they exercise these rights, are recognised to be persons in international law.' I never really like this idea of 'full' and 'partial' sovereigns or 'full' and 'partial' legal personality. My approach has been to view states as being presupposed as having a 'uniform' legal personality – that is, their legal personality is the same, whereas other actors, such as international organisations, have variegated personality. To claim one is full and the other partial presupposed a normative claim about the state-centrism of international law. What is more, as I go on to explore in Chapter 5, *no actor* has identical rights that might be identified as belonging to the sovereignty bundle of legal rights.

213 Simma and others (2012) at 1830.

to a category of specific subjects – i.e. 'mandate territories' but it also used to designate a subject. My working hypothesis as to why the term 'territories' are used in this way is closely related to the naturalising move described above. To me, at least it seems that reducing a people to its land/territory works in a way that associates them with more 'primitive connotations', as if they do not deserve the label 'state', as advanced and sophisticated an institution as it supposedly is. To reduce a people to their territories, something physical, natural, base, is to tie them to their natural surroundings and fix their very identity to a more elementary idea.

The same UNC Commentary on Article 73 shows a territory (subject) can have a territory (object): 'the territory of a colony is regarded as separate from [the territory] of the colonial power and thus being distinct territory under international law.'[214] Because territory is an object and a subject in international law, often within the same sentence the term refers to both. Another instance of territories having territories appears in UNGAR 2625(XXV), which provides that 'the territory of a colony or other Non-Self-Governing Territory has, under the Charter, a status separate and distinct from the territory of the State administering it'.[215] Here we can distinguish the subject from the object through one being capitalised. However, the UNC commentaries do not address the complexities of the different usage of 'territories' – nor is it understood whether the territory (object) of a Territory (subject) is defined in a similar manner to the territories of states.[216] On this matter, Crawford suggests the UNC is 'imprecisely worded' in its definition of 'non-self-governing territories' and 'the meaning of these terms is not self-evident and left much to be resolved by subsequent practice.'[217] UNGAR 67/19 also distinguishes between object and subject using capitalisation:

> *Reaffirming also* its resolutions . . . which, inter alia, stress the need for the withdrawal of Israel from the *Palestinian territory* occupied since 1967, including East Jerusalem, . . . and the complete cessation of all Israeli settlement activities in the *Occupied Palestinian Territory*, including East Jerusalem.[218]

[214] ibid.

[215] United Nations General Assembly Resolution 2625 (XXV), 'The Declaration on Principles of International Law concerning Friendly Relations and Co-operation among States' 1970.

[216] Simma and others (2012) at 1829–40.

[217] Crawford (2006) at 606.

[218] UNGA Resolution 67/19. Status of Palestine in the United Nations 2012 (UN Doc A/RES/67/19) para 19, emphasis added.

It is more confusing because it would have been equally correct to indicate an object by the 'occupied Palestinian territory', but the adoption of capital letters indicates a subject.

Capitalisation is not adopted in the WTO Agreement, which provides in Article XII that accession is open to a 'State or separate customs territory'. But it is a subject that is intended, as the explanatory notes provide that '[t]he terms "country" or "countries" as used in this Agreement and the Multilateral Trade Agreements are to be understood to include *any separate customs territory Member* of the WTO.'[219] It is pretty usual in discourse for territory as an object and as a subject to be used in the same sentence, as in the following example: '[o]verseas territories do not include distant territories that are regarded as part of a State's metropolitan territory'[220] where the first two instances are subjects but the latter use is an object.

Thus, territories are territorial actors with territories, and are recognised in international law. And while this might sound a bit irreverent, it is also notable that while only states have territories, territories are never states.

3.4.3 Framework

The third way in which territory is sometimes used in the international legal discourse is to describe a framework. A framework can be imagined in two senses: one is as something physical and the second is as a basic conceptional structure[221] which will lack the concreteness of the physical framework. The dominant meaning when territory as a framework is adopted in international law discourse is as a physical framework, especially where the underlying referent is the physical geography. It is thus like the reified object described above. Yet, what is distinct about this usage, is the imagination of territory as enframed; it is productive of imagining of territory as an a priori container for the state/for state power,[222] as opposed to produced by the exercise of that power in the first place. Enframing adds additional texture to the concept of territory.

[219] Explanatory Notes, Marrakesh Agreement Establishing the World Trade Organization 1994, emphasis added.

[220] Kennedy (2016) at 742.

[221] 'Definition of Framework' <www.merriam-webster.com/dictionary/framework> accessed 20 August 2019.

[222] A container is of course what gives rise to the idea that things may 'leak'.

In the following passage, territory as a framework is explicitly understood as something physical:

> Territory is, of course, itself a geographical conception relating to physical areas of the globe, but its centrality in law and international law in particular derives from the fact that it constitutes the tangible framework for the manifestation of power by the accepted authorities of the state in question.[223]

The framework here, although physical (tangible), is separate from the first use of the concept of territory which refers in the singular to physical geography. This sentence therefore applies territory in two ways. First are the individual areas of the globe – which would fall into the object referent. The second usage – 'territory . . . constitutes the tangible framework for the manifestation of power' – uses the word to indicate a territorial framework for the exercise of control. However, notably, this second usage continues to think of territory as something physical. In this understanding of territory, it is already existing 'out there'. The physical framework is for the *manifestation* of power, implying the purpose of the territory–framework is to *embody* – give a body to – something abstract, with both power and states as the abstractions.

Territory as a framework for the exercise of power is still understood in international law discourse primarily in the sense of physicality. Territory-as-a-physical-framework, while also a physical object, may not to the same extent naturalise the concept of territory but may recognise its socially constructed nature. The abovementioned passage identifies the purposes for its social construction, that is, for the manifestation of power.

3.4.4 *Organising Logic*

The fourth way 'territory' is used is to denote the idea that international law is organised 'territorially'. What is meant by territory used in this way is usually the idea that jurisdiction or sovereignty – key operational legal concepts – are organised by reference to territories; in other words, that the legal system is organised by, implemented via, and operationalised on each state territory. Another way to think of this is of the *system* having a (*state*)-territorial ordering. This usage also assumes territory forms a unit or base for each actor to manage their jurisdiction, their sovereignty, the implementation of treaties, etc.

[223] Shaw (1982) at 61.

The difference between a physical framework and an organising logic of the physical world may initially be subtle. A physical framework provides a structure – a physical thing giving a physical structure to both material and abstract things (for example people or the 'state'). In comparison, an organising logic understands territory as a principle for organising usually more abstract notions such as jurisdiction or law (which may then have material consequences).

While it is different from Jennings' primary usage of the concept of territory as an object, in *The Acquisition of Territory* he also uses the concept to explain an organising logic: 'the mission and purpose of traditional international law has been the delimitation of the exercise of sovereign power on a territorial basis.'[224] This passage articulates an understanding that international law does not operate or organise on the basis of subjects or persons, but it is the territories (of states) that provide this logic. Territory as an organising logic is a subtle but important move in the approach and function assigned to the term. Territories do more than simply exist; all together, as a system, territories provide the principles underlying international law's operationalisation.

The following example demonstrates the use of territory as an organising logic *and* a framework for the legal system *and* as an object: '[t]he development of international law upon the basis of the exclusive authority of the state within an accepted territorial framework meant that territory became "perhaps the fundamental concept of international law". Most nations indeed developed through a close relationship with the land they inhabited.'[225] Here, Shaw uses all three referents to describe how international law developed, and from this we can also understand just how essential a concept territory is to international law from the perception of this well-known and widely respected international lawyer.

3.4.5 Conceptual Slippage

In and of itself, having different meanings intended by the same word, and deliberately slipping, or perhaps even fumbling, between the different uses, is not problematic – especially if those using the terms are familiar enough with the discourse to recognise (even unconsciously) how a term is employed in any particular instance. For example, it is possible to make sense of the different conceptions of territory adopted in

[224] Jennings (1963) at 2.
[225] Shaw (2017) at 361.

this passage: '[o]verseas territories do not include distant territories that are regarded as part of a State's metropolitan territory.'[226] The reason for this is that a common theoretical context is shared; there is a shared background knowledge for those working internally to a discipline.

The problem arises when the conscious theoretical image of a particular concept does not reflect the complex reality of its discursive usage, especially in a specialist disciplinary environment. There is also a problem if the narrator does not realise they are slipping from the likes of understanding territory as a space to territory as an object, given the implications and implied imaginaries and textures of different referents. In international law, the concept of territory typically performs a specific function. For example, in the law of statehood and recognition, it operates as one of the defining criteria for establishing whether a state exists, and in the law of jurisdiction, it helps determine where a state's jurisdiction can be exercised. The meaning assigned to the concept of territory in these contexts largely corresponds to the traditional doctrinal definition given to it in the literature: territory as an object. As seen above, however, in many other contexts the concept of territory can also be used to signal other connotations: legal subjecthood, tangible frameworks for power, or organising logics. The fact that these other connotations are rarely reflected in the traditional definition of territory leads to a distorted understanding of its theoretical content, in the sense that it 'misrepresents' the reality of its disciplinary usages, allowing the switching between the different usages to remain undetected or under-recognised.

A different way of putting this would be to say that a consistent disjuncture between the conscious theoretical image of a concept and the complex reality of its discursive usage tends to encourage and entrench the practice of conceptual slippage. There are three problems with the phenomenon of conceptual slippage. Firstly, it impairs the diagnostic usefulness of the concept in question so that it can no longer be employed as reliably for descriptive and representational purposes. Secondly, it hampers the critical interrogation of the epistemological connotations and political and ideological functions of the concept. Thirdly, it also prevents the concept from being used as effectively for policy response and normative purposes. Each of these complicates discourses trying to understand territory is a globalised world.

226 Kennedy (2016) at 742.

Assuming the concept of territory has a stable and singular meaning leaves the discipline unprepared to confront the fact, not only that there may be more than one theoretical meaning associated with this concept in actual discursive practice, but that this practice may also favour constant shifts from one such meaning to another. Leaving these shifts consistently unrecognised problematises the theoretical status of the particular meaning which the mainstream tradition thinks it recognises as existing behind the concept. It also promotes an unjustified confidence about its explanatory value and analytical potential, that is, its usefulness as a theoretical category and a critical heuristic.

And herein lies the problem when it comes to understanding the underpinning of the accounts of the shift to functionality away from territoriality as an organising logic, as well as the impact other processes and phenomena associated with globalisation have upon a state's territory: the use of territory in this discourse, can slip between the more common territory as object meaning and territoriality as an organising logic. For example, Milano, who adopts the most common usage of territory by and large throughout his contributions, argues at the end:

> The debate between constitutionalist visions, pluralist theories and the GAL project has touched upon the significance of territory in contemporary international law, only to stress that the era in which territory was one of the organizing concepts of international law is long gone. Yet the question of the legitimacy of an international law without or with little anchorage to territory remains largely unanswered.[227]

In so doing, Milano uses different meanings of territory.

A further example of territory as an organising logic and then as framework appears here '[b]y consequence also the divide between national and international law ... hinges on territory. The State's territorial boundary delimitates its political and legal power, and vice versa, and constitutes its border with international law.'[228] And similarly Teubner and Fischer-Lescano, who more rarely use territory in the doctrinal sense adopted by international lawyers, shift between territory as a framework ('global law would experience a radical fragmentation, not along territorial, but along social sectoral lines'),[229] territory as an object or a container when they speak of social systems as 'spring[ing

[227] Milano (2013) at 5.
[228] ibid at 85.
[229] Teubner and Fischer-Lescano (2016) at 1000.

their] territorial confines',[230] and as an organising logic ('international copyright law [decisions] have traditionally been taken in line with the territoriality principle')[231] before shifting back to territory as a framework when describing the 'territorial systems' of copyright law'.[232] As already emphasised, this is entirely normal and not problematic per se. However, it also creates a greater potential for scholars to cloud and obscure the analysis and theory, both in received theory and what they author, in their attempts to make sense of these phenomena when territory slips between an object and a space. It is more usual to think of actions as something done to objects, whereas activities, processes, etc. are undertaken in (and productive of) spaces. Legal theories and concepts will also be implicated as a result of choosing to adopt one understanding over the other. It is to such implications that I now turn by examining the role that different conceptions of territory play in informing the major concepts of international law: sovereignty and territorial sovereignty.

3.5 State Territory and the Production of Sovereignty and Territorial Sovereignty

At long last, sovereignty comes into the conversation; for territory plays a vital role in producing the concepts of sovereignty and territorial sovereignty in orthodox discourse and legal thinking. The importance of territory to understanding and operationalising these concepts is unquestionable. For example, O'Connell observes that 'sovereignty is predicated upon territory' and that while '[t]erritory is not the index of sovereignty', or in other words that it is not a sign of sovereignty, 'neither can [territory] be conceived without sovereignty'.[233] In a similar vein, Gottmann says 'it would seem indeed that sovereignty needs territory on which it is to be exercised, and a territory would appear useless for all practical purposes unless it was under some recognised sovereignty.'[234] Yet it has not always been clear exactly what this role and relationship between the two concepts are – not least perhaps because there is also conceptual instability in the concept of sovereignty.

230 ibid at 1006.
231 ibid at 1019.
232 ibid.
233 O'Connell (1971) at 181.
234 Gottmann (1973) at 3.

After first noting the lack of conceptual clarity between sovereignty and territorial sovereignty, in this section, I demonstrate that however they are understood, both are spatially mediated concepts – in other words, they are both informed by and operationalise a concept of (state-) territory. I then turn to an account of the different theories of territorial sovereignty and analyse the concept of territory they each apply. For it would be problematic to rethink territory without rethinking sovereignty, as both concepts have become entwined; indeed, the understanding of all three concepts (territory, sovereignty, and territorial sovereignty) emerged the way they did as a result of, are contingent upon, and their meaning determined by, the legal and political arrangements, institutions, ideology, and intellectual landscape of the late nineteenth and early twentieth century.

3.5.1 *Of Sovereignty and Territorial Sovereignty*

There is a lack of clarity about the concepts of sovereignty and territorial sovereignty. This obscurity occurs when taking the concepts by themselves and in attempting to find the distinction between the two.[235] Both concepts often mean the same thing. It suffices to note a few examples where this has been pointed out. According to Crawford, '[s]overeignty may refer to the title to territory or to the rights accruing from the exercise of title'.[236] Yet, it has also been understood that 'when a state exercises authority . . . over a certain territory it is popularly said to have "sovereignty" over the territory' while at the same time meaning 'the independence of the state' and is 'a convenient way of contrasting the full set of legal rights over territory with the minor territorial rights.'[237] Judge Alvarez has noted '[b]y sovereignty, we understand the whole body of

[235] For many, sovereignty is a 'much-abused word', cf Clapham (2012) at 186. Sovereignty has been accused of 'evad[ing] concrete definition and lack[ing] a stable referent', Koskenniemi and Schult (2018). As result, some want to kill off sovereignty, cf Herzog (2020). Others have avoided using the term because of this lack of conceptual clarity which in turns means that it is a 'beacon of a sloppy discursive practice', cf d'Aspremont (2021) at viii. I entirely agree with this latter assessment. Yet I think the concept of territory has a lot to do with this and the ambivalent slippage between object, space, framework, and logic has a great deal to do with this and therefore, as difficult as this task is, the concept can and should be explored.

[236] Crawford (2012) at 488.

[237] Clapham (2012) at 168.

rights and attributes which a State possesses in its territory, to the exclusion of all other States, and also in its relations with other States.'[238]

Like sovereignty, territorial sovereignty can have several intended meanings. Territorial sovereignty has been explained as: 'the link between the state and its own territory.'[239] But 'a link' is a rather vague description and the nature of the legal relationship of this link is often muddled and ambiguous. In his understanding of the nature of that relationship, Shaw states that:

> the concept of territorial sovereignty is concerned with the nature of the authority exercised by the state over its territory. The ideas of territory and sovereignty are closely linked in international law, since the concepts is concerned with those geographical areas over which sovereignty of sovereign rights may be exercised. *Territorial sovereignty is, therefore, centered upon the rights and power coincident upon territory in the geographical sense.*[240]

Elsewhere, according to Shaw, '[t]he essence of territorial sovereignty is contained in the notion of title. This term relates to both the factual and legal conditions under which territory is deemed to belong to one particular authority or another.'[241] And in the same vein: '[s]overeignty in regard to a territory is known as territorial sovereignty. Territorial Sovereignty is the right of a State to exercise over its own territory, to the exclusion of any other States, the functions of a State.'[242] Thus *territorial sovereignty*, in addition to title designates a particular regime denoting 'the full set of legal rights over territory'.[243]

Territorial sovereignty is also used to refer to a particular legal regime, which can be approximated as an answer to the question of the legal relationship, as in the following:

> In spatial terms the law knows four types of regime: territorial sovereignty, territory not subject to the sovereignty of any state or states and which possesses a status of its own (e.g. trust territories), res nullius, and res communis. Territorial sovereignty extends principally over land territory and the territorial sea, its seabed and subsoil.[244]

[238] Separate Opinion by Judge Alvarez *Corfu Channel Case* (n 65) 43. This is my own personal favourite definition as it is the most 'legal'.
[239] Distefano (2010) at 28.
[240] Shaw (1982) at 73. Emphasis added.
[241] Shaw (2017) at 354.
[242] Güzel (2020) at 143.
[243] Clapham (2012) at 168.
[244] Crawford (2012) at 203.

If you are still with me, you will also conclude that these explanations are roughly in line with the Crawford's observations about the two meanings of sovereignty ('sovereignty may refer to the title to territory or the rights accruing from the exercise of title'[245]). There is a blurring of the analytical separateness of these two concepts.

Importantly for this study, this ambiguity and interchangeability is present in the conceptual slippage found in the discourse about deterritorialisation and the end of geography. For just one example of this, in Bethlehem's well-cited article 'The End of Geography', one explanation of the 'rocks in the river' that globalisation flows through refers to 'territorial sovereignty'[246] but elsewhere it is just 'sovereignty'.[247]

3.5.2 *Territory and Sovereignty*

Let us assume for the purposes of the analysis going forward that the dominant meaning of sovereignty in international law is not title but the rights accruing from the exercise of title as per Crawford. The organising effect of territory on the operationalisation of sovereignty in international law might be thought of in two different ways. (State-)territory informs the boundary between sovereigns and non-sovereigns; territory is that which makes an actor that exercises sovereignty a potential 'sovereign'[248] in the first place. The spatially mediated thinking is key to the creation of oppositional categories such as sovereign/non-sovereign and state/non-state. The imagined spatiality of international law and specifically a particular category of space – that of state territory – plays a foundational role in determining certain actors as either the norm (the state with sovereignty 'over' its territory) and the *sui generis* or exceptional actor. This in turn re-entrenches the norm and proves its existence; it proves sovereignty is a concept mediated by the concept of (state-)territory.[249] But (state-)territory also informs the organisation of sovereignty in international law on a horizontal plane. It determines where one exercise of sovereignty ends, and another exercise of sovereignty begins, in the jigsaw-like imaginary discussed above; as contained by state space. This is

[245] ibid at 448.

[246] Bethlehem (2014) at 20.

[247] ibid at 15.

[248] I use this term loosely and do not intend to refer to sovereigns in the classical indivisible ultimate source of all authority sense.

[249] I expand on this in Lythgoe (2023).

the central idea underlying Bethlehem's understanding that 'sovereignty . . . rests fundamentally on the notion of exclusive authority over discrete parcels of land.'[250] Sovereignty then is mediated by the spatial assumptions of the concept of (state-)territory explored above on more than one level of analysis. I return to the topic of sovereignty and territory in Chapter 5, reconstructing an alternative way of understanding the spatial mediation of the concept of sovereignty considering the reconceptualised concept of territory proposed in Chapter 4.

3.5.3 *Territory and Territorial Sovereignty*

Let us take a closer look at the discourse law on territorial sovereignty to understand that 'link' between the state and territory. One of the most common explanations, as already established, is title akin to Roman law. Territory and property are often compared in the literature, but there are many ways in which territorial sovereignty does not operate in the same way as title does in property law, and much may depend on one's legal training. Property law is differently understood from one legal regime to another, and international law has been constituted by lawyers who have trained in their domestic legal regimes. Shaw observes this, noting that 'sovereignty'[251] and property are distinguishable but related to Roman law's distinction of *imperium* and *dominium*, but that this 'appears to have been subsequently confused with the rise of feudalism'.[252] International law might be 'built upon the Roman distinction' but other legal schools of thought have left their mark. Concepts like *res communis* and the law developed concerning the seabed are problematic because of the influence of Anglo-American lawyers.[253] Some theories of territorial sovereignty are a result of the influence of private law analogies from Roman law and public law analogies developed by German legal thought.[254] This historic lack of conceptual clarity continues to this day. Indeed, any international legal scholar may apply, without realising, a different theory of territorial sovereignty even within the same piece of

[250] Bethlehem (2014) at 13.
[251] Sovereignty is genuinely used rather than territorial sovereignty.
[252] Shaw (1982) at 74.
[253] ibid.
[254] Distefano (2010) at 30–31.

work, an issue compounded by mixing up the concept of territory applied.

Debates about territorial sovereignty suggest there are between three and four different approaches.[255] These approaches can be broadly mapped as follows. Van Kleffens, writing earlier than others, identified three theories, which are: the property, the 'essential element' or biological, and the jurisdictional theories.[256] Shaw and Distefano identify four: the patrimonial, which evolved into the object theory, or property theory, (or *Eigentumstheorie)*; the subjectivist, or space or quality theory (or *Eigenschaftstheorie* or *Raumstheorie* [sic]); the objectivist or competence theory (or *Kompetentztheorie*); and fourth, the 'composite approach' (Shaw) or 'dominant' (Distefano) theory.[257] Still further scholars would distinguish between *Eigenschaftstheorie* or *Raumstheorie.*[258] I outline and discuss each theory and the concept of territory to which it applies in turn.

Property or Object Theory – Eigentumstheorie: van Kleffen's property theory and the property or object theory identified by Shaw and Distefano are broadly similar. For van Kleffens this theory means: '[u]-nder the influence of Roman law, sovereignty with regard to territory was long regarded and interpreted in terms of property' and it helps explain '"servitudes" on behalf of other states, such as the right to let troops pass, or to establish a foreign garrison, or a prohibition to construct fort-resses.'[259] Shaw classifies the property theory as the oldest with 'territory regarded as a piece of property pertaining to the ruler' evolving into the object or property theory such that 'the state was regarded as exercising its power over its territory much as in private law an owner would treat his possessions.'[260] This, according to Lauterpacht, is the 'object' theory of the nature of state territory.[261] How territory is conceptualised thus determines how we understand territorial sovereignty; this particular theory requires an understanding of territory as object – where some act or practice, like owning or leasing, is done to the object. In a similar vein, Distefano explains this theory thus:

255 See, e.g.: Distefano (2010); van Kleffens (1953).
256 van Kleffens (1953) at 95.
257 Shaw (1982) at 75–77; Distefano (2010) at 29–32.
258 Thirlway (2002) at 370.
259 van Kleffens (1953) at 94–95.
260 Shaw (1982) at 76.
261 Lauterpacht (1970) at 367.

> according to the ... minority theory, the relationship between the State and its territory is precisely the same as the one between the individual and a subject of the national legal system. To put it differently, the territorial sovereignty of the State is a kind of property of international law, that is, an exclusive power of disposing of a territory as is the power to dispose of goods within the municipal legal order. Thus, there is no difference between the two juridical relationships, nor there is a difference [sic] in international law between *dominium* and *imperium*.[262]

He also credits this theory with having 'the merit of having reasonably explained the judicial nature of the activities exercised by a State over a territory (for example, the cession, the sell, the purchase and administrative concession).'[263] What is clearly emerging from this discussion is that territory is understood as an object and the theory is contingent upon this understanding. While the property theory could at least feasibly allow for a non-physical property to be owned, such as intellectual property, the scholarship outline above indicates it is a '*piece*' of property,[264] signalling that territory very much is being conceptualised as a physical object.

This theory is not without its critics. Scholars have argued that this account is inconsistent with legal reality. Van Kleffens for example problematises this property theory by questioning: 'if territory is an essential attribute of the state, without which it simply is a state no longer, how can one conceive of territory as something having an existence apart from the state, something it owns, something outside it?'[265] Lauterpacht too related that opponents of this theory 'point out that territory is not owned by the State but that it is the State, just as the individual, far from owning his body, constitutes an inseparable unity with it and is inconceivable without it.'[266] The opponents of this theory that Lauterpacht and van Kleffens identify would seem instead to adopt the essential elements or *Eigenschaftstheorie*. Shaw also finds issue with the object theory but for slightly different reasons:

> While this theory explains the juridical fact that states may dispose of parts of their territory, it faces problems in dealing with the notion of federal states, and it does not appear to answer the question of why a state disappears upon the disposal of all of its territory.[267]

[262] Distefano (2010) at 29–30.
[263] ibid at 30.
[264] Shaw (1982) at 75–76.
[265] van Kleffens (1953) at 95.
[266] Lauterpacht (1970) at 367.
[267] Shaw (1982) at 76.

The property theory is also criticised for not 'dealing with the phenomenon of multiple properties on the same territory, that is to say the State and individuals (or moral entities).'[268] This criticism appears to assume territory *is* the physical geography and that there can only be one territory in relation to any particular physical geography. This however confuses domestic and international legal rights and it is important to distinguish between national law for individual private property regimes and international law for the state's supposed 'property'. Although, perhaps, this discussion could, if pushed further, at least allow for an acknowledgement that in relation to the same physical space states create overlapping legal rights and legal spaces.

Van Kleffens' and Shaw's criticism is more convincing: if territory is an essential attribute of the state (the notion that what distinguishes a state from other subjects of international law, is its 'existence as a state' which 'entails sovereignty over a territory'[269]), how can territory be conceived of as having an existence apart from the state? That is not to say I agree with either interpretation. It is simply to say this criticism is plausible and well grounded.[270]

Essential Element Theory or Space/Quality Theory – Eigenschaftstheorie or Taumstheorie/Raumstheorie:[271] The 'essential element' theory and the space or quality theory (*Eigenschaftstheorie* or *R/Taumstheorie)* are often classified as similar and taken together, although I am not sure they are indeed the same. The German makes it clearer that the first term, *Eigenschaftstheorie*, at least refers to characteristics or features of the state. For van Kleffens this second theory, which he refers to only as the essential element theory, suggests 'territory, an essential element of the state, is merely the state itself in what is called its territorial aspect.'[272] For Shaw these two theories are described as comparable with the 'subjectivist doctrine, or space or quality theory' but according to which 'the territory

[268] Distefano (2010) at 30.

[269] Thirlway (2002) at 370.

[270] In Chapters 4 and 5, I adopt a different interpretation worth previewing here. Territory cannot exist apart from the state because it is constituted by the activities and social practices of the institution. *Physical geography exists apart from the state*, but territory does not exist until it is created and constituted (continually) by the actors involved. It is therefore not that territory is an essential element of the state because it exists outside it (which would physicalise and reify territory) but because that territory is dependent on the social practices of the institution to exist.

[271] Shaw refers to *Taumstheorie*; Shaw (1982) at 76. Thirlway refers to *Raumstheorie*; Thirlway (2002) at 370.

[272] van Kleffens (1953) at 95.

of a state . . . [is] an integral part of the personality of the sate [sic] itself.'[273] According to Shaw, *Eigenschaftstheorie* and *Taumstheorie [sic] both* hold that the 'territory of a state is regarded not as something separate but as an integral part of the personality of the s[t]ate'.[274] They would understand that aggression against a state's territory is 'a violation of the personality of the state'[275] and that 'an attack on the territory of a state is seen, therefore, not as affecting the property or possession of the state but as a violation of the personality of the victim state.'[276]

It should be noted at this juncture that Thirlway separates *Eigenschaftstheorie* and *Raumstheorie*. He says of the former that it is 'the idea of territory as the physical aspect of the state itself' whereas *Raumstheorie* is 'the mere spatial extent of the State'.[277] This accords with my own assessment of there being a distinction, not least because I propose that *Eigenschaftstheorie* and *Raumstheorie* assume entirely different concepts of territory. The former properly understood would conceptualise territory as something physical, the latter as a space. Although when the concept of territory is physicalised and naturalised, it might be easy to slip into thinking they are both the same.

This second theoretical account, has been understood as problematic for a number of reasons, not least because 'if the territory of a state is of its essence, any modification of that territory would result in that state losing its identity'[278] suggests that any change in territorial extent, whether by cession or by acquisition, seriously affects the personality of the state itself. 'If one of its constitutive element [sic] changes, the State's personality should change accordingly.'[279] Notably, this is only a charge against *Eigenschaftstheorie* and its reification of territory. Thus, notions of this theory can also be traced in the debate about whether disputed boundaries calls into question whether an actor has a defined territory in order for qualify as a state. This was part of the debate surrounding whether Albania, without defined frontiers, could be admitted as a state into the League of Nations. It is more the framing of the debate that is of interest here. If not having established boundaries and a defined territory calls into question the very 'identity of the States whose borders are the

[273] Shaw (1982) at 76.
[274] ibid.
[275] van Kleffens (2002) at 96.
[276] Shaw (1982) at 76.
[277] Thirlway (2002) at 370.
[278] van Kleffens (2002) at 96.
[279] Distefano (2010) at 31.

subject of dispute',[280] then clearly territory is assumed to be an essential element of the state.

According to Shaw, *Eigenschaftstheorie* also struggles to explain federal states, condominiums, and leases.[281] Although not further elaborated on, presumably this is because it is assumed that states cannot share the same body in the case of condominiums or that part of the body can be leased to some other state without losing its identity. As van Kleffens quips: '[t]he whole [essential elements] theory seems to belong to biology rather than law.'[282] Although, this is perhaps more true of *Eigenschaftstheorie* than *Raumstheorie*, if those using *Raumstheorie* do indeed understand territory as merely the spatial extent of the state and nothing more.

Lauterpacht rejected this second theory as in his view 'the practice of states contradicts this view. [the practice of states] offers repeated examples of territory being treated as the object of a right external to the State.'[283] Lauterpacht offers historical examples such as when territory was given in marriage settlements or when Denmark sold the West Indies to the US in 1917. He does grant that 'undoubtedly, territory, however small, is essential to the existence of the state' but he says that by adopting the object theory it is not necessary for territory to be 'as external to the State as ownership is to the individual.'[284] He goes on to argue:

> it is not necessary to deny the indefensibility of territory for the State in order to maintain at the same time that it is the object of the proprietary right of the state. It is indispensable in the sense that for a State to exist some territory there must be.[285]

Lauterpacht appeared to have stronger preference for the object theory over the subjectivist theory. He argues '[t]he individuals in their collective capacity as a State, own the territory of the State. The State owns its territory.'[286] It amounts, in some respects, argues Lauterpacht, to nominal ownership. And yet, this theory still underlies some of the thinking in international law discourse.

280 Craven and Parfitt (2018) at 198.
281 Shaw (1982) at 76.
282 van Kleffens (1953) at 96.
283 Lauterpacht (1970) at 367.
284 ibid at 368.
285 ibid.
286 ibid.

If we remember above, the subject theory was preferable to the object theory in the eyes of its proponents because 'if territory is an essential attribute of the state, without which it simply is a state no longer, how can one conceive of territory as something having an existence apart from the state, something it owns, something outside it?'[287] and 'territory is not owned by the State but that it is the State, just as the individual, far from owning his body, constitutes an inseparable unity with it and is inconceivable without it.'[288] This theory adopts a particular understanding of territory too: while also an object, it is an object with a relationship steeped in naturalised and biological thinking, as opposed to a legal relationship property. Both theories (perhaps with the exclusion of *Raumstheorie*) objectify and reify territory (it is evidently possible to objectify a body).

What this discussion so far also shows is that international legal doctrines pivot between different relationships between territorial sovereignty and territory, and different concepts of territory. The Crime of Aggression is a legal regime that is arguably designed in its origins with an understanding of *Eigenschaftstheorie* assuming a reified concept of territory, and it exists in the same legal system as doctrines and principles assuming a different concept of territory theory of territorial sovereignty, such as the law relating to the 'acquisition' of territory. International law as a positive regime of law is inconsistent in its approach to both the relationship between state/sovereign and territory, and the underlying concepts of territory informing these relationships. No wonder there is little consistency in the discourse.

Jurisdictional Theory or Competence Theory – *Kompetenztheorie*: This theory is unlike the first two in that territory is often, but not exclusively, conceptualised as a space rather than an object. According to van Kleffens: '[t]erritory, in this way of thinking, is that space within which in principle one sovereign state only is entitled to exercise its legal power, to the exclusion of all other states'.[289] This can also be found in Kelsen's work, with his concept of territory being 'legally nothing but the territorial space of validity of the national legal order called a State.'[290]

[287] van Kleffens (1953) at 95.

[288] Lauterpacht (1970) at 367.

[289] van Kleffens (1953) at 96. Notably, it is van Kleffens' final theory of territorial sovereignty. Yet he gave his Hague Academy course in 1953 around the same time that Lautperacht created the fourth combined approach, and it is unlikely Lauterpacht's combined approach could have been taught at this time.

[290] Kelsen (1966) at 307.

This theory, also named the *Kompetenztheorie* and objectivist theory by Shaw, 'sees the territory of a state as the *area* of state jurisdiction or the space in which the state exercises its competence'.[291] Shaw too pays tribute to Kelsen, noting that this was the theory adopted by Oppenheim. It appears this theory is an effort by the Vienna School to 'purify' the legal concept of territory and 'demystify' the state.[292]

Perhaps it would be more correct to say that it is *possible* to conceptualise territory as a space in this theory, but the physicalising tenedencies often slide quickly back in. This theory at first glance would seem to accord much more closely with the understanding of *Raumstheorie* given by Thirlway with territory as the 'mere spatial extent of the State' given that one account at least of *Kompetenztheorie* constructs territory as 'the physical sphere within which the competence of the State is manifested'.[293] Yet even these two passages show that the former understands territory as a space, and the second reifies territory. Kelsen and Shaw's definitions of *Kompetenztheorie* appear to apply a concept of territory as space, not as something physical,[294] so there is clearly the same conceptual instability within this theory vis-à-vis the concept of territory assumed by it. A further example of this object/space slippage is from the *Island of Palmas* case, in which territorial sovereignty most closely resembles the jurisdictional theory throughout, such as in this passage: 'territorial sovereignty ... serves to divide between the nations the space upon which activities are employed.'[295] Yet, as the prepositions hint, 'upon which' appears to think of territory as something physical rather than a space. We see again the potential for slippage.

According to van Kleffens this theory is 'undoubtedly the most satisfactory legal theory' as 'sovereignty in respect of a certain territory *is perfectly compatible with private ownership* ... it also is consistent with

291 Shaw (1982) at 76, emphasis added.

292 Distefano (2010) at 32.

293 Thirlway (2002) at 370, emphasis added.

294 There are many inconsistencies, contradictions, and different concepts of territory applied. This is possibly due to a lack of awareness that there *are* different ways to conceptualise territory. I never found much consideration of the concept of territory itself, how it is understood, and the implications of this by any one particular theory in this scholarship. Territory was just an unquestioned given.

295 *Island of Palmas Case* (n 21) 839, emphasis added.

the existence of federal states, the federation and each of the individual states having their own jurisdictional sphere.'[296] Van Kleffens also notes that Kelsen's approach allows:

> territory in the wider (though rather more abstract) sense, where state exercise only part of their authority: the high seas (where states have jurisdiction over vessels sailing under their flag), and "no man's land", where the same holds good until it is acquired by some state as part of its territory in the narrower sense.[297]

While this conception of territory is neither 'wider' nor 'more abstract', it does indicate that international lawyers have struggled to come to grips with what is plainly 'territorial' actions but that are outside their mapped, familiar territory. The assumption of territory-as-container, framed by borders, is active there, disciplining thinking in terms of what is 'narrow' and 'concrete'. Again, it shows the 'reach' for new ideas and concepts that help explain the 'wider' and 'more abstract' sense of territory, but without the theoretical spatial lexicon to make sense of, and let go of, the cartographically disciplined imagining of territory. This quote touches an important theme for Chapters 4 and 5; the idea that competences may be differently spatially arranged and desynchronised from the 'mapped' orthodox territory recognised by international law. For exercising state authority in such a manner is neither 'wider' nor 'more abstract', but entirely normal, and increasingly regular. It is the idea that many international lawyers labour under that territory is something physical which gives a false sense of narrowness and concreteness.

Composite Theory (combined Kompetentztheorie and Eigentumstheorie): Finally, the composite theory is developed by Lauterpacht's attempt to combine the *Kompetentztheorie* and *Eigentumstheorie* (jurisdictional and object theories),[298] apparently preferring this approach because it adopts 'a highly flexible view of the concept of territorial sovereignty' rather than 'adher[ing] strictly to one of the three major doctrines'.[299] Lauterpacht argued that the object theory did not 'exhaust the relationship between the State and its territory'[300] and that:

[296] van Kleffens (1953) at 96, emphasis added.
[297] ibid at 97.
[298] Shaw (1982) at 77.
[299] ibid.
[300] Lauterpacht (1970) at 369.

> In addition to being the object of its proprietary rights, the territory is the basis upon which and the area wherein the State exercises jurisdiction . . . the State exercises its jurisdiction over persons and things upon its territory and within the air space above it. This is the gist of what has been called the 'space' theory. But much of the discussion bearing on this matter has been rendered sterile by the extreme and exclusive assertions of what may be called the 'object' and 'space' theories. The fact is that it is both. The territory is both the object of the State's right and the space within which is sovereignty and jurisdiction are exercised.[301]

According to Shaw, this theory accounts for split sovereignty (an advantage of the object theory), because 'territorial sovereignty is not an absolute element, it may be divided, and property 'is a bundle of rights capable of modification, division and adjustment' but also for understanding territory as 'the basis on which and the area in which a state exercises jurisdiction.'[302]

It is claimed that this is now the dominant theory.[303] Quoting its appearance in the Rome Court of Appeal, Distefano argues that it allows the 'territorial state' to be 'conceived as space and goods at the same time'. He explains that: 'territory is the object of two different types of powers: personal and real at the same time. As a land, the territory is the place "where the imperium is exercised"; whereas, as a good, it can be subject to appropriation and to the exercises of dominium.'[304] In this theory, the state holds a real right – akin to a property right – and territory becomes 'possessed' by the state, while at the same time, territory is a space for the exercise of jurisdiction.

Conceptually, territory is two things in this theory: it is at times an object, and at others a space. This might not be problematic in and of itself. However, how do we know which concept to apply even when reading the orthodox discourse, never mind trying to make sense of new situations, such as the different spaces of globalisation? All four of the theories depend on, and even within the same theory scholars can project, a different concept of territory – referring at times to spaces, objects, bodies, bases, or platforms, each with different implications for how the concept is operationalised in law and used to relate to other spaces. Does it create room for confusion? In short, yes.

[301] ibid.
[302] Shaw (1982) at 77.
[303] Distefano (2010) at 32.
[304] ibid.

Further Conceptual Slippage: The foregoing analysis shows how scholars understand the relationship between territory and sovereignty, and consequently the concept of territory. For example, Crawford's explanation of 'state territory and its appurtenances ... [as] the physical and social base for the state'[305] might demonstrate the subjectivist theory of territorial sovereignty. Thinking of territory as a body or base tends to adopt the subjectivist theory of this relationship. This is not, however, how I would classify Crawford's general approach, which would appear to fall more squarely into the *Kompetentztheorie*.[306] This conceptual slippage arises due to a lack of conceptual clarity about the nature of territory.

By way of another example, Craven appears to adopt territory as both an object and a space: 'the mere factual possession or control over territory ... but rather the ability to rightfully claim the territory as a domain of exclusive authority.'[307] This points to a property-like relationship between the actor and territory *and* the jurisdictional theory. Craven, it seems, adopts the composite approach. However, Craven also says: 'territory, in the context of statehood, however, seems incapable of being framed purely in terms of ownership or possession for the simple reason that it concerns the prior question as to the very existence of the legal person rather than merely its spatial parameters.'[308] In this second excerpt, Craven, in addition to the property theory, also seems to think territory is required for 'the very existence of the legal person' – perhaps exhibiting the *Eigenschaftstheorie*, dismissed by van Kleffens as being too much like biology.

This blending of the different territorial sovereignty theories and concepts of territory becomes quite noticeable and is indeed quite common – although most follow the composite approach (property/ object + jurisdictional). By way of another example, Clapham here adopts the property theory:

> When a state exercises an authority of this kind over a certain territory it is popularly said to have 'sovereignty' over the territory, but that much-abused word is here used in a rather special sense. It refers neither to a relation of one person over another, nor to the independence of the state

305 Crawford (2019) at 204.

306 'The competence of states in respect of their territory ...' and 'The legal competence of states and the rules for their protection depend on and assume the existence of this stable, physically identified (and normally legally delimited) base', ibid.

307 Craven (2014) at 219.

308 ibid at 220.

> itself, but to the nature of rights over territory; and in absence of a better word, sovereignty is a convenient way of contrasting the full set of legal rights over territory with … minor territorial rights[309] (those being leases, servitudes).

The rationale to categorise this as 'property theory' is that Clapham discusses rights over territory (as a property). However, Clapham goes on to affirm the jurisdictional theory too that '[a]t the basis of international law lies the notion that a state occupies a definite part of the surface of the earth, within which is *normally* exercises, subject to the limitations imposed by international law, jurisdiction over persons and things to the exclusion of the jurisdiction of other states'.[310] These two quotes, blending the property and the jurisdictional theories, demonstrate the composite approach attempted by Lauterpacht.

In short, as demonstrated, there is no single agreed understanding regarding the relationship between territory and the state. All three (or four or five) theories continue to exist in legal thought today. There is little wonder that 'territorial sovereignty' and 'territory' are confused concepts. What is noticeable about all these theories is that they theorise territory and sovereignty *only in relation to the state*. This foregoing analysis demonstrates that it is the essentialising of the relationship between state and territory that creates the conditions producing the aspatial response addressed in Chapter 2. All these theories essentialise the state and territory: they may understand territory as an essential (physical) element of the state, as a 'property' only states can possess (object theory) or as with the *Kompetentztheorie* only the space of state competences is taken into account.

This common thread, as well as the lack of conceptual clarity, has important ramifications for trying to explain what is happening when territory and territorial sovereignty seem challenged or displaced by the processes and phenomena associated with globalisation and global governance. The narratives taking the view that powers and competences 'leave' the state and its physical space of the territory assume a physical concept of territory. For without one clear theory, and without clarity about the concept of territory each applies, attempts to understand what is happening by using concepts in the orthodox discourse toolbox will slip between many of these different frameworks. For example, the

309 Clapham (2012) at 168.
310 ibid.

biology theory can still be traced in discourse about territory and our theoretical understanding of it. The inseparability of state and territory as concepts often demonstrates an essentialised relationship, where an almost biological relationship has been assumed. A biological theory can be found in the definitions above considering that states cannot exist without territory, because it is an essential element of the state (territory being a quality that a state must possess). This is also often a background assumption where territory is a physical base for the state; with territory being equated with the physical geography. The result is that state territories seem to occupy all the physical geography, so following this logic, these powers and competences no longer held by the state are no longer tied to a territory – they have been deterritorialised. And, because, as a rule, territories are objects that only states have, the spaces of other actors, the spaces of reterritorialisation, are unintelligible and less concrete.[311]

3.6 Conclusion

So where are we by the end of this chapter? There are two key messages. First is that territory as a space is not terribly well conceptualised and theorised. As a consequence, its use is often ambiguous and ambivalent in its referent. There is a need to develop a more spatially aware onto-theoretical lexicon. More often than not, territory continues to be conceptually compressed into an object, and that object often understood to actually *be* the physical territory. That object has actions done to it that international law regulates: it is violated, it is owned, it is acquired, and so on. This reification of territory informs the concepts of sovereignty and territorial sovereignty in international law, such as the property/object theory or the subject theory of territorial sovereignty. Territory as a space seems to have a role in *Raumstheorie* and *Kompetentztheorie* but this conceptualisation is not consistently applied and fully understood, and scholars working within both theories are certainly capable of assuming a reified object-territory. The second is that this is *always* a relationship that describes an object/space and *the state*. The state is the only actor to

[311] I say 'as a rule' because of the way theory has rationalised territory and territorial sovereignty – having done so in a manner introducing complex exceptions and the narratives around these exceptions may conceivably apply different concepts of territory and accounts of its relationship to an actor. I explore this exceptionalised legal thought in Lythgoe (2023).

have territory, *unless* it is a *sui generis* situation or actor, which are typically understood as being normatively transitory. The very fact they are *sui generis* means, however, that the norm is state-territory; that state-territory is typically imagined as flat, contiguous, and homogeneous; and it is cartographically disciplined.

These theories cause the problems in outlined in the previous chapter. When these theories continue to reproduce orthodox latent assumptions about territory to explain the contemporary global legal and political orders, the absence of territory from the new order is the only option – for all 'territory' or, more accurately, physical space is already assigned amongst states. Where there was territorial state with territorial sovereignty, in its place are aterritorial actors exercising powers haphazardly without a clear legal theoretical account for when, why, and where. There is deterritorialisation without reterritorialisation. The spaces of reterritorialisation are unknown and unfamiliar to international lawyers and their discipline. Territory, and many other international law concepts, will as a result have limited usefulness in understanding global governance and different patterns of law making. Thus, the production of the end of geography/decline of territory narrative.

I propose entirely rethinking the concept of territory with insights from critical geographers and spatial philosophers. In the following chapters, I offer an alternative interpretation of the legal relationship between actor, competences, and territory that suggests a more spatially insightful way of understanding concepts such as sovereignty, jurisdiction, and territory. Rethinking the spatiality of the international legal order(s), I argue, offers an alternative explanation of what is and has been going on. It requires us to let some things, namely title, go entirely and to de-essentialise certain relationships and concepts. It is to the reconstruction of a theory, and its alternative narrative about the relationship between legal rights, space, and actors that I now turn.

4

Re-imagining the Concept of Territory

> We recognise space as always under construction. Precisely because space on this reading is a product of relations-between, relations which are necessarily embedded material practices which have to be carried out, it is always in the process of being made. It is never finished; never closed. Perhaps we could imagine space as a simultaneity of stories-so-far.
>
> Doreen Massey, *For Space*[1]

This chapter turns to how the concept of territory might be re-imagined. Continuing to think at the level of the conceptual, in this chapter I explore how the concept in focus, territory, might be rethought of as *produced*; specifically, territory as the product of social relations. Territory as the product of lived social relations is a radical departure from thinking that has come before in the discipline of international law. But it must be admitted that many of these insights are not 'new'.[2] Spatial theorists have been critically questioning and rethinking many of our basic spatial concepts and indeed our very epistemologies of space and time. Yet much of international law doctrines, reasoning, and thought rely on a largely outdated understanding of space. Therefore, I offer here insights about how international law as a discipline might differently conceptualise territory, drawing on insights from (critical) spatial theorists about space to 'update' the discipline's onto-theoretical approach to conceptualising territory. These insights allow us to rethink the concept of territory and emancipate international law's spatial imaginary. In the following, I offer an overview of these insights that enable the better observation of the relationship between power, law, and space, that in

1 Massey (2005) at 9.

2 Although perhaps this chapter does in a small way contribute to the thinking of spatial theorists, such as Massey and Lefebvre, specifically in adding to the debate about the relations of control and the conceptualisation of territory not as static but as itself dynamic, multiple, thus, rethinking the binary between 'territory' and 'spaces of flow'. The following chapter adds the legal dimension and account of law that is often missing.

turn allows international law as a discipline to differently conceptualise territory, making sense of the competing state and non-state institutions and their territories 'physically' overlapping one another.

This re-imagining starts with a key and basic proposition: that it is the practises of actors that result in the constitution of territory. Territory, then, is not an essential element of the state in a biological sense.[3] Nor can territory exist apart from or a priori to the state[4] because it is constituted by the activities and social practices of the institution. Physical geography exists apart from the state, but territory does not exist until it is created and constituted (continually) by the actors involved. Therefore, territory is not an 'essential element' of the state, which would otherwise exist outside of it (for this would physicalise and reify territory), but territory is dependent on the state of another reason: it is dependent on the social practices of the institution to exist. Applying insights from critical geography, and with a major debt to the likes of Doreen Massey, I propose an alternative understanding of the relationship between the social world and the physical world. One of the key implications is that understanding territory-as-space negates a physical understanding of territory. It is not an inert thing to which things are done; 'in no way is it a surface'.[5] It is this idea which in turn allows the imagining of territories overlapping the same physical geography.

The second step then, is to further examine what practices, activities, and processes are required to constitute the imagined territory, and who are the relevant actors whose practices matter. In this part of the explanation, I first focus on relations and practices of 'control', which I argue plays a constitutive role in the production of territory. Control, as it will be understood, can be exercised by institutions, states and, non-state alike, and is key to the creation of their territory. While this may seem radically different from the current disciplinary perspective, the account of control I give is built upon ideas that will already be familiar to most international lawyers. Where I evidently differ fundamentally in the operationalisation of this concept is that it takes into account the activities of both state and non-state actors, providing a more reflective account of practises of control existing in international law-making and global governance today. Rather than international law's normative understanding of the exercise of

3 See *Eigenschaftstheorie* of the link between territory and state, Section 3.5 above.

4 Necessary to *Eigentumstheorie* approaches (property/object theory) to the relationship between territory and state. Also see Section 3.5 above.

5 Massey (2005) at 107.

authority which implicates state authority alone, the approach adopted here is a social constructivist one. In other words, I am interested in developing a legal theoretical understanding of control and authority that better reflects contemporary governance, law-making, and regulatory practices, rather than one limited to a twentieth-century state-centric normative international legal positivism.

The chapter then turns to other spatial characteristics, as I have come to call them, that are part of conceptualising territory that might also need to be rethought to allow the concept to reflect the dynamic realities of territoriality. These include problematising and then re-imagining the time of territories, dislodging the implicit disciplinary assumption that territories are static and permanent, and instead envisaging the time of territory as dynamic and contingent. I next turn to the question of the bounding of territories, drawing upon the literature that examines bordering practices and the spatiality of these. As others have done before me, I propose understanding territory as being bounded by more than cartographical lines on a map and seeing more practices and technologies as productive of bounding than previously thought. This chapter then revisits the mapping of territories and calls for an understanding of overlapping, multi-dimensional territories as opposed to the two-dimensional cartographic gaze that currently disciplines the international legal gaze. Finally, the chapter turns to the question of why we need a new legal geography for international law. Influenced by Doreen Massey's insights on the potential for politics when space is conceived of as open and dynamic, I argue that it is vital that international lawyers understand the diverse, multiple, and relational territories of actors relevant for international law, transnational law, global law [insert your preferred term or subfield here], and the law of global governance.

4.1 The Production of Territories: Lived Social Space

But first: what does lived social space even mean? What is it? Why is it different? How is it created, both in abstract terms and in practice? In this section, I outline the proposed understanding of territory. Key to it, is an appreciation of territory as a socially produced space, and not as physical geography, that emerged in the 1970s in the work of Lefebvre and others.[6] Their work had a major impact in many fields of knowledge, changing

[6] For further discussion on this see Müller-Mall (2013) at 71.

how these understand space 'as something we produce by way of our social lives, and not social life as something we do *in* space.'[7]

Given that the epistemological shifts concerning space began in the 1970s, it might be expected that legal texts published before and during this period primarily treat territory as an object. This was the dominant paradigm in all social sciences, and for quite a long time. There is, however, a problem now emerging: international lawyers continue applying object-like, flattened, and physicalised understandings of territory and the legal regime and its concepts (like sovereignty) are mediated by this understanding of territory. International law as a discipline is operating with 'old' spatial models and the legal regime is still operationalised based largely on this pre-1970s spatial paradigm. This is another reason, in addition to the lawyer's objectivist aesthetic,[8] that there is a disconnect between the intellectual appreciation of territory as a space, but continued application of territory as an object. This shift requires international lawyers to profoundly rethink their spatial imaginary and examine their prenotions,[9] that reach far into legal theory and much of the positive legal regime.

Territory can be understood as one specific type of spatial framework.[10] In this way, I understand territory to be a particular category of space. Territory here is thought of as a socially constituted space in relation to which control is exercised by states (and, as I argue below, many non-state actors). Just as grammar is regarded as the underlying framework that structures speech, and speech practices also form grammar, territory structures and is structured by the exercise of power. In the same way as speech and grammar are socially based, created and disciplining, so too is territory.

Territory is not understood as something physical here. It does not exist a priori to the state or any other actor that it constitutes. Nor does it 'contain' something. Thinking of territory in these terms allows for that slip into the essential element theory of the relationship between the state and territory, dismissed by van Kleffens and others.[11] In a similar vein, Lefebvre cautioned against assuming a particular a priori form:

[7] ibid at 73.

[8] See discussion on the objectivist aesthetic in the Introduction (Chapter 1) on enchantment and heartland concepts.

[9] See Bourdieu's discussion on Durkheimian prenotions in Bourdieu (2014) at 3.

[10] Lefebvre (1991) at 281.

[11] See Section 3.5 above.

> Vis-à-vis lived experience, space is neither a mere 'frame', after the fashion of the frame of a painting, nor a form or container of a virtually neutral kind, designed simply to receive whatever is poured into it. Space is social morphology: it is to lived experience what form itself is to the living organism, and just as intimately bound up with function and structure. To picture space as a 'frame' or container into which nothing can be put unless it is smaller than the recipient, and to imagine that this container has no other purpose than to preserve what has been put in it – this is probably the initial error.[12]

Rejecting the idea of imagining territory as a container, and instead imagining it as a lived space, I propose understanding territory, not as containing the state, but as a spatial construction for and created by the exercise of power. Consequently, this space exists *wherever* that power might be exercised and experienced, even if it is outside the 'cartographic borders' (the frame), and by whomever is exercising that power.

But what does this entail in practice. It all sounds rather abstract. Again, Lefebvre is helpful here. He explains it in the following terms: '[i]s this [state] space an abstract one? Yes, but it is also "real" in the sense in which concrete abstractions such as commodities and money are real. Is it then concrete? Yes, though not in the sense that an object or product is concrete.'[13] Territory is concrete because it is a sustained institutional fact and produces real world effects. Territory manifests and becomes real through the exercise of power. In a similar vein, Lefebvre also observed that 'territory must be understood not as a fixed container of political action and international relations, but rather as a dynamic and constitutive dimension and space of struggle, one that is currently being reconfigured rather than eroded.'[14] That it is a space of struggle is also what makes it real – the practices of struggle and what is being struggled against. This reflection brings to the fore two more points deserving of further discussion. First is the idea of territory as dynamic and socially constituted; second is of territory being reconfigured rather than eroded.

This understanding of territory as lived, dynamic, and socially constituted is already dominant in the discipline of geography. Delaney, for example, observes that 'territoriality [i]s a social (and political, economic, cultural) *process* that unfolds not only in a place but through time' and that this understanding 'allows us to more easily see territories as social

[12] Lefebvre (1991) at 94.
[13] ibid at 26–27.
[14] Lefebvre (2010) at 36.

products'.[15] I might add to this that territory is *juridically* produced and recognised space. Territories result from how 'human associations – cultures, societies, smaller collectives – and institutions organise themselves in space.'[16] This is not a pre-existing structure. This organisation is a result of social interactions and how space has been socially mediated, constructed, and understood. Thus, territory is a 'product of interrelations' that is 'constituted through interactions, from the immensity of the global to the intimately tiny'.[17]

Not only is territory political, social, juridical, etc. space, but the process of the constitution of territory can be understood itself to be political and ideological. Territory is the result of territorialising actions; such actions are part of a strategy as opposed to a 'biological impulse'.[18] No human spatial relationship is neutral; and territoriality is 'the primary spatial form power takes' – 'people do not just interact with space and move through space like billiard balls';[19] neither do states, the agents of states, or corporations. State territory was created as a result of sustained practices over a long period of time, for it is not natural that states 'have' a territory to begin with. As Lefebvre calls attention to: 'space has been shaped and moulded from historical and natural elements, but this has been a political process. Space is political and ideological.'[20] In a similar vein, Poulantzas made clear his understanding that 'national territory has nothing to do with the natural features of the land. It is rather of an essentially political character, in that the State tends to monopolise the procedures of the organization of space.'[21] Poulantzas went on to say that the 'State materialises this spatial matrix in its various apparatuses (army, school, centralized bureaucracy, prison system:, patterning in turn the subjects over whom is exercises power.'[22] Territories, then, are created as

[15] Delaney (2005) at 2.
[16] ibid at 10.
[17] Massey (2005) at 9.
[18] Sack (2009) at 21.
[19] ibid at 26.
[20] Lefebvre (1976) at 30, 31.
[21] Poulantzas (2000) at 104.
[22] ibid. Incidentally, Poulantzas, I think because of his conception of territory, was able to see reterritorialisation: 'It may be said that the separation of the direct producer from his means of labour and his liberation from personal bonds involve a process of deterritorialisation. But the naturalist image peddled by this term is no more exact in this context than it is elsewhere. The whole process is inscribed in a fresh space, which precisely involved closures and successive segmentations. In this modern space, people change position *ad infinitum* and traversing separations in which each place is defined by its

a result of political processes as well as 'fundamentally constitutive of the social orders whose features they express'.[23] We cannot understand the territories of international law without reference to the legal and political practices constituting territories.

Further, the practices relevant to constituting territory are not one off. There is no single practice that constitutes a territory but many; one could say, there are usually several activities contributing to this 'constitutive moment'. Planting a flag in the physical geography but doing nothing to exercise control on a continuing basis will not make for a territory. Instead, the control must be exercised on a continual basis. This notion will not be unfamiliar to international lawyers. It very much accords with the idea of continuous control in international legal doctrine. As such, in the *Island of Palmas* Award, it was observed that 'practice, as well as doctrine, recognizes ... that the continuous and peaceful display of territorial sovereignty is as good as a title.'[24] Where I would deviate (quite majorly) from this observation, is the idea that it gives title,[25] which would treat territory as an object. Instead, it is in the specific and continuous practices of control that territory is (continually) (re)made.

It is therefore important to establish here that any kind of 'space as always under construction' and it is precisely because of this that spaces are 'a product of relations' that it is 'always in the process of being made. It is never finished; never closed ... space [i]s a simultaneity of stories-so-far.'[26] Space is never a priori category, something that exists outside of us such that we are then doing something in some pre-made space, but something that is continually in the making. This is also how territories are (re)made: actors exercising control over different functions and competences in relation to their spaces change over time. They may

distance from others; they spread out in this space by assimilating and homogenizing new segments in the act of shifting their frontiers.' This is a marvellous passage. It shows the denaturalising territory can open up this proposed way of thinking.

23 Delaney (2005) at 10.

24 *Island of Palmas Case (Netherlands/USA)* (1928) Volume II Reports of International Arbitral Awards 829, 839 (Permanent Court of Arbitration). It was also confirmed in *Legal Status of Eastern Greenland (Norway v Denmark)* [1933] PCIJ Ser. A/B, No. 53, 45–46 (Permanent Court of International Justice), and later applied in *The Government of the State of Eritrea and The Government of the Republic of Yemen, Award on Territorial Sovereignty and Scope of the Dispute* [1996] (1998) XXII RIAA 211 (Permanent Court of Arbitration) [239].

25 I explore this criticism further in Chapter 5.

26 Massey (2005) at 9.

change as a result of treaties and such formal legal arrangements or because of a transformation in the power dynamics between different actors. Recall here that many who argue that cities are increasingly important and relevant to international law and global governance often put this down to an 'inversion of the hierarchy of power',[27] not some formal transfer of powers. And where territories look stable, it is because they are always being continually made by actors respecting, abiding by, and imagining the territory or territories in question.

In addition to the practices of control by states, the practices constituting state territories may well include the decisions of domestic and international courts and tribunals, concerning, for example, land disputes. While these determinations may play important roles in constituting a territory initially, state practices must continually recognise and implement the decision. Moreover, it is not just in the example of a positive finding of territory (such as in cases to do with territorial delimitation) that we can understand this logic in action. Each time a court or tribunal makes a ruling, even where territory is not at stake, they are always settling it in favour of the territorial status quo by determining that they need not consider the territories of each party before them. And even, for example, where a court is being asked to settle a dispute regarding a particular place, for example 'the course of the boundary between the two countries in the sector from the astronomic marker of Tong-Tong (latitude 14° 25′ 04″ N ; longitude 00° 12′ 47″ E) to the beginning of the Botou bend (latitude 12° 36′ 18″ N ; longitude 01° 52′ 07″ E)',[28] the parties, counsel, and the bench may also be implicitly accepting that there is an agreed status quo for the rest of the territories. Although, perhaps the case may be that the states in question have not yet worked out they do not agree on the rest – and once either one or both states establish that another part of their territory is disputed, they will undertake a variety of practices, including submitting the new dispute to an international tribunal, to establish and constitute their territory.

There are many more actors than just state representatives relevant here. Every individual plays a role. This includes even the seemingly unrelated and mundane activity of children learning about maps throughout their school years, because what they are learning is a

[27] Bruce and Jennifer (2014) at 5.

[28] *Case Concerning the Frontier Dispute (Burkino Faso – Republic of Mali) Judgment* [1986] ICJ Reports 554 (International Court of Justice) [2].

particular representation of state space. All of these practices contribute to determining territories into existence. In carrying the map representing state territory in our minds, we each continue to perform and 'obey' the geographical imaginary of a state-based system. Massey gives an excellent smaller-scale example of this idea of continuing to produce space by being a part of it in her reflections of a train journey to work:

> you are not just travelling through space or across it (from one place – London – to another – Milton Keynes). Since space is the product of social relations you are also helping, although in this case in a fairly minor way, to alter space, to participate in its continuing production. You are part of the constant process of the making and breaking of links which is an element in the constitution of you yourself, of London (which will not have the pleasure of your company for the day), of Milton Keynes (which will; and whose existence as an independent node of commuting is reinforced as a result), and thus of space itself. You are not just travelling through space or across it, you are altering it a little. Space and place emerge through active material practices.[29]

Thus, each time courts and tribunals, states, international organisations, NGOs, or individuals act or omit to act, or even just recall their mental map of international law, they are part of the constitution of the territories of international law – even if it is in the continual *remaking* of existing territories, as opposed to a major disruption and constitution of new territories.

There is one interesting occurrence of a closely related conceptualisation of territory in international law. In an oral speech made before the PCIJ, de Lapradelle, acting on behalf of the French Government in the Nationality Decrees Advisory Opinion,[30] explicitly conceptualised territory as not physical, but instead a (presumably spatial) framework, saying:

> In works with which the Court is cognisant, and which have modified the conception of territory in international law, one reads that *territory is neither an object nor a substance*; it is a framework. What sort of framework? *The framework within which the public power is exercised.*[31]

[29] Massey (2005) at 118.

[30] *Nationality Decrees Issued in Tunis and Morocco (French Zone) on November 8th, 1921, Great Britain v France, Advisory Opinion* (1923) no. 4 (1923) PCIJ Series B no 4 (Permanent Court of International Justice).

[31] 'Part II. Speeches Made and Documents Read Before the Court.' 106 *Nationality Decrees, Advisory Opinion*, emphasis added.

In this conceptual framework, de Lapradelle displayed an appreciation of territory as an intangible, abstract framework and associated this framework with the exercise of public power – again confirming that if territory were to have a central distinguishing feature it would be the exercise of control. Putting this conception into practice, de Lapradelle explained:

> [t]here exists, *side by side* with the Tunisian territory of Tunis, a French Tunisian territory, because, under the regime of composite sovereignty constituted by a protectorate in international law, there is in a sense, from a juridical standpoint, a territory which is the territory of the protected State, and another territory which is the territory of the protecting State. It may be said that *the same geographical area, without losing its physical form*, assumes *from the legal standpoint either* the form of a possession of the protected State or of the protecting State according to circumstances.[32]

This French Tunisian territory is 'an extension of French territory'[33] 'with the same legal characteristics as French territory *in so far as nationality questions are concerned*'.[34] Even more interestingly, the doctrine that de Lapradelle is distinguishing the situation in question from is the exercise of extraterritorial jurisdiction, which is often how the exercise of control 'beyond the state' is viewed.[35] He is instead employing a non-contiguous understanding of territory that allows for the separation of the two spaces that were each French territory, with the territory that existed in the same geographical area as Tunisian territory to be 'French' proper as opposed to the extraterritorial exercise of jurisdiction by France in Tunisia. While it might be notable that de Lapradelle explains the territories of France and Tunisia as *side by side*, it is difficult to read anything further into it, for it may just be that he did not have the words to explain the situation. The very idea is that it is the same physical geography that could be a territory of Tunisia for some competences, and the territory of France for other purposes.

[32] ibid at 97–98, emphasis added.

[33] ibid.

[34] ibid at 100, emphasis added.

[35] I review this distinction further and reinterpret extraterritoriality entirely in Chapter 5. Both extraterritoriality and the 'territory proper' outlined here are techniques and narratives that were and are used in colonialism and neocolonialism. Just because I am highlighting this usage by de Lapradelle, I do not in any way condone or apologise for imperialism and colonialism. Indeed, I am showing the way in which spaces are constructed to support such endeavours.

This is a fascinating incidence of territory-as-space, not territory-as-object. Surprisingly little or nothing is written (nothing if I am correct) in English about this important doctrinal reinterpretation about how territory is understood. For, as de Lapradelle said, this understanding 'modifie [s] the conception of territory in international law' and it does so in a significant way.[36] It is difficult to say why this conception of territory, from such a prominent international lawyer, has not been adopted more often. Perhaps its association with colonisation and its appropriation for the purpose of making 'Tunisian' territory 'French' has made the reasoning unpopular – and not incorrectly if we imagine territory to be the physical geography. However, to make 'Tunisian territory' the physical geography is itself falling into the move of physicalising and naturalising territory. It totalises, assuming the physical geography in its totality 'belongs' to Tunisia. Moreover, it is to homogenise the identity of Tunisia, underpinned by wider discourses equating space-culture-nationhood – an 'isomorphism between space/place on the one hand and society/culture on the other'.[37] I think the proposed reconceptualisation outlined in this chapter offers an alternative narrative that has the power to explain the strategic legal geography of colonisation, where indigenous

[36] Nevertheless, there are problems and perhaps even internal contradictions with what de Lapradelle said: although this space becomes 'French territory in so far *as nationality questions are concerned*', de Lapradelle is unable to satisfactorily explain why the territory 'geographically speaking is called Tunis' – there is thus a physicalised understanding of territory creeping in. However, 'as far as nationality questions are concerned' hints at the idea that territories can be formed for a particular competence, given that for other competences Tunisia was thought to exercise power. Secondly, de Lapradelle appears to assume there can be only one sovereign power or dominant public power and it is not clear whether this is in respect of *each territory* or in respect of 'Tunis', 'Part II. Speeches Made and Documents Read Before the Court' (n 32) 106. It is not also clear whether de Lapradelle understands that sovereignty is only exercised by one state vis-à-vis physical geography and is therefore totalising, with the other actor exercising something less than sovereignty in respect of its territory. Contradicting this, or perhaps providing clarity, de Lapradelle does outline that he understands this is a *composite sovereignty* arrangement. Remarkably, this composite sovereignty, in contrast to how condominium is understood by Shaw and others, has two territories, not one.

[37] Massey (2005) at 64. Massey goes on to say: 'The assumption was firmly established that space and society mapped on to each other and that together they were, in some sense "from the beginning", divided up. "Cultures", "societies" and "nations" were all imagined as having an integral relation to bounded spaces, internally coherent and differentiated from each other by separation. "Places" came to be seen as bounded, with their own internally generated authenticities, and defined by their difference from other places which lay outside, beyond their borders.'

practices are unrecognised in favour of practices of western states,[38] and practices today of what are, in essence, imperialist practices exercising of control. What is clear, however, is that this formulation of territory – territory-as-space – helps make sense of situations where two different actors have power over the same space – and this approach 'detotalises the space' that would otherwise happen with territory-as-object.

Thus, in the understanding being put forward, territory is a social or institutional fact; it is not the brute fact (physical geography). A space becomes territory as a result of its 'relationship with society'[39] and its creation by and signification for various actors.[40] This space is not a substance nor a physical object. This notion requires territory to be unreified, unnaturalised, and dephysicalised; the concept cannot be both object and space: space may refer to brute physical facts, but it is not physical.

4.2 The Relationship of the Physical and the Social Worlds

So, if territory 'has nothing to do with the natural features of the land'[41] what is its relationship to land? Territory in this understanding may *refer to* the natural world but it 'should be examined not as an actual state space, [instead understood] as the powerful, metaphysical effect of practices that makes such spaces appear to exist.'[42] A territory is 'a bounded social space that inscribes a certain sort of meaning onto defined segments of the material world', that is, the physical geography.[43] Thus, territory is not the physical geography, but the space created as a result of particular practices (claiming or occupying) and their effect (inscribing meaning onto that physical geography).

Our experience of territory can easily be confused with the bodily experience of physical geography. This can even be what produces the conceptual collapse in a distinction between the space and the physical geography. I have found Descartes helpful to understand this. He noted that 'it is a frequent habit when we discover several resemblances between two things, to attribute to both equally, even on points in which

[38] In particular, I am thinking of the argument made by Gathii (2002) at 305.
[39] As in Klauser (2008) at 25, 34.
[40] For further discussion on this see: Searle (1995) at 26–27, 34–35.
[41] Poulantzas (2000) at 104.
[42] Painter (2010) at 1116.
[43] Delaney (2005) at 14, emphasis added.

they are reality difference, that which we have recognised to be true of only one of them.'[44] If territory and physical geography resemble each other, it is possible to forget there is a difference. This creates and reinforces the flattened and physicalised concept of territory in the discourse. We may realise objectively that geography, like politics and economics, is a 'social constructed body of knowledge'[45] and that territory is a concept, like free trade, democracy, etc. However, territory differs from these disciplines and their respective concepts because it often represents something very real and physical to us – our ability to experience, touch and be *on* physical geography and *in* a territory at the same time. This profoundly affects our understanding of this concept, helping us to collapse or flatten the distinction. This is a problem I think that may be more peculiar to geography, unlike our understanding of concepts associated with politics and economics (free trade, democracy) which may remain abstracted to many more degrees. While democracy may be materialised in ballot boxes, in institutions of government, etc. and while free trade may materialise in goods and currency, these physical realities are more easily recognisable as one step removed from their concepts.

Thinking about the previous two points together – understanding that territory *refers to* rather than actually *is* physical geography and that territory is socially produced and not physical or natural space – where does this leave the concept of territory for international law? An example might help explain this: would 'Mount Everest' exist if there were no humans on earth to name it? To this we can add the question: What is Mount Everest? A collection of atoms exist – that is the only brute fact. Mount Everest – the signifier of those signified atoms – does not actually exist. Society has named it thus, although only in English. In Nepalese it is सगरमाथा and in Tibeten it is *Chomolungma*. Each language also has its own connotations about what is signified. For example, in Tibetan, *Chomolungma* means 'mother of the world' which implies height, and a particular understanding of 'mother', but also a differently imagined relationship to the physical geography. Thus, the same question arises: could *Chomolungma* even exist without humans to name it? Even our understanding of 'Mount Everest' as 'the tallest' mountain is an interpretation. It is based on some value of understanding the height of something, on some need and ability to measure something. Moreover,

[44] Descartes, Œvres philosophiquesm (1963), cited in Foucault (2002) at 56.
[45] Anastasopoulos and others (2013) at 1–2.

its history and its significance for those who have experienced it firsthand will differ from those who have never been there, etc. Thus, Mount Everest, सगरमाथा, and *Chomolungma refer* to brute facts, but those brute facts do not naturally equal Mount Everest, सगरमाथा, and *Chomolungma*.

Why is this important to international law and our understanding of territory? It helps us understand the territory of the 'UK' or 'Nepal' is a signifier too. And rather than physical geography *becoming* territory, it is space that becomes territory as a result of a 'relationship with society'.[46] Territory is 'informed, semiotised' space which is filled with meaning.'[47] The signified are land, sea, inner waters, lochs, airspace (maybe), etc. This helps us understand territory is not the same as the physical geography. The concept of territory is, as Elden argues, 'inherently related to, yet ultimately distinct from . . . land and terrain'.[48] There are practices and meaning which produce territory. Territory in turn then might be thought of as a socially 'significant space that consists of signifiers . . . and [the] signified.'[49]

At this point we have established that territory is space filled with particular meaning and constituted by the practices of actors; that territories are constantly being made. How they are made and remade is the through practices exercising control and it is to this central idea that I now turn.

4.3 Recentring and Relocating Control

In international law, it is said, the concept of the state is 'rooted in the concept of control of territory'.[50] This idea echoes through much of orthodox legal writing. Thus, for example, Malanczuk writes, '[t]he control of territory is the essence of a state'[51] and Shaw comments, '[t]he principle whereby a state is deemed to exercise exclusive power over its territory can be seen as a fundamental axiom of classical international law'.[52] The exercise of power is often understood to manifest as

46 As in Klauser (2008) at 34.
47 Claude Raffestin (1986a), 'Ecogenèse territoriale et territorialité' in Franck Auriac and Roger Brunet (Hg.), *Espaces, jeux et enjeux* (Paris, S. 173–85) as cited in Klauser (2008).
48 Elden (2013) at 22.
49 Raffestin (n 48).
50 Lowe (2007) at 138.
51 Malanczuk (1997) at 75.
52 Shaw (1982) at 61.

a state having jurisdiction. The exercise of power is important to defining both state and territory because territory is often understood as the thing controlled by the state. While there is a vague idea that it is a central notion, the theoretical justifications have not received enough attention in international law discourse concerning territory, especially when compared with the likes of sovereignty, jurisdiction, statehood, etc. The concept of control often appears in discussions about state responsibility, belligerent occupation, international human rights law extra-jurisdictional tests, and international criminal responsibility.[53] What is noticeable is that control is appearing increasingly as a test for jurisdiction outside a state's recognised territory, and the discourse reflects this, but it is less central for discourse on territory alone – likely because it is assumed 'all territory is under the control of the state' and that is that. But to me it is interesting that control in state territory and control to establish extraterritoriality are clearly linked but undertheorised. In this project, I recentre control in theorising any and all territories and take time to reflect on the concept's relationship to space – or more precisely, the relations of control that constitute the spatial.

4.3.1 *Territories as Controlled Disciplined Spaces*

In Chapter 3, I touched on the idea of an anatomy of a concept. To recall, I suggested thinking of the structure of the concept of territory as follows: there are several ideas, characteristics, and elements that combine to configure the concept of territory. These can be thought of as a bundle of characteristics that can be changed, altered, or potentially removed altogether. For example, the space could be seen as uneven or as homogeneous, such that law applies uniformly across the whole space or it could apply unevenly. Borders may be differently practiced depending on the laws and technologies in place.[54] Yet many spaces may be homogeneous or uneven, contiguous or nonadjacent, fleeting or permanent, like supermarket aisles or the space of shade under a tree on a hot day, but not all spaces are territory. As such I argue there are certain ideas that are constitutive of the concept of territory. Not all spaces that are homogeneous are territories, nor all spaces that have some kind of line of demarcation. That feature which transforms a space into a

[53] In particular 'effective control'. For a discussion of this usage, see Milanovic (2008) at 426–29.

[54] Mezzadra and Neilson (2013).

particular type of space that we call territory, that I suggest should be the most helpful determining factoring in understanding when a territory is constituted, is when a community exercises control in relation to that space and uses that space to order their activities. In other words, it is possible to identify a central characteristic of territory, without which the space described is not territory.

When I say there is a 'central characteristic', let me clarify by saying that I do not think that this is some 'magic' transcendental concept[55] that solves all our problems in diagnosing territoriality for all time. I instead would say that the idea of adopting the concept of control as central to the narrative here has more explanatory and diagnostic power – it is more helpful to the task outlined in the introduction, which is to assess and analyse which actors are exercising power, and how, in contemporary law and politics characterised by multiplicity, plurality, heterogeneity, etc.; certainly more useful in terms of explanatory power than using the concepts of sovereignty, jurisdiction and territorial sovereignty to explain these phenomena, not least because of the ambiguity and lack of conceptual stability of these concepts established above. Yet I also see control as relevant to the discussion of these concepts. It is why they are in the first place connected to the concept of territory; the concepts of sovereignty and jurisdiction can be thought of in many ways as boiling down to the concept of control too.

This idea then should not be alien to international lawyers. As outlined at the opening of this section, control is already understood as central to the relationship between territory and the state, as well as to jurisdiction. Control is an important concept for international law generally, underpinning much of its legal reasoning: control is used to establish (individual criminal or state) responsibility[56] and to define jurisdiction ('jurisdiction [as] a consequence of the fact of control'[57]). This conceptualisation should be fairly uncontroversial given that many definitions of territory highlight this characteristic, as in the 'territory of the state is a part of geographic space which is under the control and sovereignty of the state'[58] and '[t]he relationship between territory and power is clear. Power is essentially, although not exclusively, exercised within a given territorial area.'[59]

[55] Here I am influenced greatly by Cohen (1935) at 809.
[56] Orford in Crawford and Koskenniemi (2012) at 275.
[57] Orford (2008) at 981, 990.
[58] Bílková in Kuijer and Werner (2017) at 33.
[59] Kohen (2016) at xi.

The exercise of control 'over' territory is understood as an essential element of statehood to the point where 'one of the factors taken into account when granting or denying recognition of statehood to Western Sahara and Palestine is the presence or absence of a territory under the effective control of the movement.'[60] This is confirmed by Orford who notes that '[i]nternational law has long treated effective control over territory as an important criterion of statehood.'[61] It is also present in the following:

> A State in international law only exists if its governmental power is an effective one, i.e. if it is able to enforce its decisions inside the governed territory . . . only the effective occupation of a territory creates rights of the occupying State, i.e. the State must factually be able to govern the territory concerned.[62]

Control is the important consideration by which state territory has expanded in the past. Control was the measure, for example, by which territory extended into the sea when technologies created access to the sea and its 'resources'. Control (and state interests in retaining that control) is entirely bundled up into the importance of territory in international law. For example, the need to control airspace is largely why this space became part of the state's territory (if indeed it is part of state territory). Control over territory, the acts that constitute territory in the first place, is of continual importance not just a one-off establishment of the facts. This was already established above in connection to the idea of practices not being one off, given those practices are implementing the relation of control, it makes sense that those must also be continuous.[63] Moreover, the concept of control was key in the *Kasikili* case, but what Gathii shows is that it was only really the practices of control by Europeans that held weight for the bench, and not the 'use and

[60] Bílková in Kuijer and Werner (2017) at 41. See also discussion in relation to territorial control being invoked as a way to evaluate whether a state is sovereign 'from the mandate system of the League of Nations to . . . "unwilling or unable" arguments' (Kendall in Kuijer and Werner (2017) at 90).

[61] Orford in Crawford and Koskenniemi (2012) at 280.

[62] Bernhardt (1984) at 70.

[63] This was established above regarding the idea that practices constituting that space must be continual. See, in particular, *Island of Palmas Case* (n 25) 839; *The Government of the State of Eritrea and The Government of the Republic of Yemen, Award on Territorial Sovereignty and Scope of the Dispute* (n 547) para 239; *Legal Status of Eastern Greenland (Norway v Denmark)* (n 547) 45–6.

occupation' by the Masubia which were framed as 'primitive' (and thus not control in the 'civilised state' sense).[64]

This proposal is parallel with the definition of territory at its 'root' in geography. Territory within this discipline is often conceptualised as space that is 'claimed or occupied by a person or group of persons or by an institution'[65] where claiming or occupying territory is realised through practices and relations of control. McCarthy, for example, explicitly states that 'territoriality is the . . . exercise of power through control or influence over a bounded space [territory]'.[66] *The law* should be concerned with who has the right to exercise control over X, Y, or Z competences.

4.3.2 Who Controls?

Here I turn to the question of *who* does *what* controlling of territory. Control, it is understood here, must be exercised by *someone or some institution*; there must be an actor exercising some element of control or ability to influence or discipline a space and what happens within it. The narrow concept of territory present in international law understands only the state to be capable of exercising the relevant control necessary to produce territory. And as the *Kasikili* case and Gathii's interpretation of it shows, it is only the practices of certain actors that has far too often been deemed sufficient to qualify. But I have a more foundational question: why does this actor necessarily have to be the state? The actor could be a multi-national corporation (MNC), institution, or group of people. By thinking about the *who* in such a way, I suggest it helps us problematise and eliminate the normativity existing in the assumption that only states exercise relevant practices of control for the constitution of territory. It can also help diagnose patterns of thought that rely on ideas of European/North American superiority and Othered inferiority.

What contributes to the assumption that only state control matter is the unilinear historiography written of territory and the state; a unilinear

[64] Gathii (2002) at 583. This is why I also suggest below we need an expanded definition of control – as what counts as control continued to be determined by criteria that inform a 'civilised state'.

[65] Storey (2017).

[66] McCarthy (2007). This may appear at first glance to be circular reasoning. However, it would be circular reasoning to say '"territoriality is the . . . exercise of power through control or influence over a bounded space [which we call territory]" and territory exists because of territoriality', but McCarthy does not 'complete the circle' so to speak.

history that carries within it a grand narrative of progress, leaving the impression that the state and territory was a progressive development from what came before. This 'one way' narrative cannot convey the backwards and forwards between competing organising structures and ideologies, nor the competing political and legal arrangements that challenged or worked against state authority and control. The narrative helped ensure the entrenchment and success of the state from the fifteenth century onwards, but it also hides the many competing authorities both then and in contemporary international affairs. This unilinear narrative relating to the state and territory, which 'in its purest form assumes necessity in evolution',[67] is common in the discourse. A typical example can be seen in Khan's unilinear narrative account of the rise of territoriality and the 'upgrading' of territory as 'an important installment in the ongoing and century-long transitional process from medieval to modern statehood'.[68] This framing strongly suggests a final or single 'destination' (modern statehood) for the historical evolution of the relationship between state and territory. It falls into the progress narrative trap – the most extreme example of which is the End of History thesis, positing the liberal, democratic, *territorial* nation state as the 'final' model for political authority.[69] In a sense then, much of orthodox international legal theory understands the world as having been 'split up in separate territorial units'[70] – that is, states – *because* states succeeded in the ideological battle against papal and other authorities. As a result, the discipline of international law operates with a spatial imaginary dominated by the spaces of states.

Contrary to this unilinear narrative, Ford argues the relationship between the state and territory is not one of 'empirical fact but one of positive design'.[71] Ford observes:

> the first year student of property law learns that a subterranean gas reservoir "belongs" to a given piece of property only due to a set of contingent legal rules. The resources can be severed from ownership of the land on the surface and its status as property may depend on factors other than the status of the land immediately above it.[72]

[67] Sack (2009) at 20.
[68] Khan (2012) at 234.
[69] Dalby (1993) at 87.
[70] Bílková in Kuijer and Werner (2017) at 21.
[71] Ford (1999) at 843, 904.
[72] ibid.

As Ford points out, the relationship between territory and state in international law is often 'a natural or necessary correspondence'.[73] Why in domestic law is the relationship understood to arise as a result of contingent legal rules, but in international law there is an essentialisation of state and territory? The cartographical representation of the earth as state space dominating international law's spatial imaginary has much to answer for.

Rather than understanding territory as 'comprehensible only through its relation to the state and processes of statecraft',[74] I propose understanding territory in relation to additional authority and societal structures. The result untangles the state and territory such that they no longer 'reciprocally impl[y] the other'.[75] Instead, in adopting the proposed understanding of control, when and where any actors are capable of disciplining people, activities, processes, etc., it might be thought of as having a territory.

4.3.3 *Defining Control*

Thus far, the terms 'control', 'discipline', and 'influence' – and even 'use'– have been used interchangeably and this is relevant. None of these terms are ideal. The concepts of 'control', 'influence', 'discipline', and 'use' each have their own connotations. All are also spatialised, many of them are imagined as being top down. Control is a concept that fits the model of the notions of authority and actorhood that are familiar to international law today. Yet, terms, such as disciplining, can help diagnose those non-state actors that exercise influence on activities and discipline life in their spaces. This includes the World Bank, the International Seabed Authority, IMF, GAVI, the Vaccine Alliance, etc. This is a model of governance that is political in the broadest sense of the word. 'Use' or 'occupation' are also related concepts that can and have been used in international law discourse to understand the relation of people to space. Gathii discussed the priority of the geographical and scientific over the 'Masubia's use and occupation of the contested island as a basis for establishing historic title over the island to the Masubia' in the *Kasikili* case.[76] I, however, do not like the word 'use' as it easily slides into the

[73] ibid.
[74] Brenner and Elden (2009) at 353, 363.
[75] ibid at 364.
[76] Gathii (2002) at 582.

idea of using land productively and usefully in order to justify colonial expansion. Locke, Schmitt, Blackstone, etc. were all concerned about the correct and full 'use' of nature in order to have stronger title.[77] Given the struggle for finding the perfect or even just an appropriate word, I am going to retain 'control' for the purpose of this analysis as it does the job of signifying the main idea that I am trying to communicate.

However, this adoption is with a caveat: I do not propose adopting a high test of control – such as the idea that the only relevant control is the ability to enforce the will of the state militarily ('effective control') within the territory – but, in line with much of the governmentality discourse, I develop a looser test; namely, that the actor has the ability (often is legally empowered) to influence and discipline activity and people in some way.[78] This is because the way control is exercised, how relations of power are formed, how power is practised, will differ from one situation to another. As such, 'effective control' would be far too high a test for determining when a territory is constituted. Instead, it is a concept that reflects the implementation of an ideology about 'legitimate sovereigns', of sovereignty as an indivisible concept, and of territory understood in a geographically totalising sense. Once what is at stake in 'having' a territory is reduced, there is no need to retain any notion of effective control for the purposes of establishing that a territory exists.[79]

The important idea here is that this control is a spatial strategy and operates with a particular spatial logic, it does not always take the forms that international law has traditionally recognised, which have an imperialist legacy. Sack has observed that the notion of control is not 'precise or rich enough' to understand territoriality, or in other words, to understand the exercise of power necessary to constitute territory.[80] He develops a comparable notion, defining territoriality as a 'spatial strategy' to 'affect, influence, or control people, phenomena, and relationships, by delimiting and asserting control over a geographic area. This area will be called territory.'[81] The execution of such a strategy does not need to be the product of a single design. As others have considered

[77] Prost (2023).

[78] I am not referring here to the specific Foucauldian categories of control – juridical, disciplinary, and biopolitical – but rather to the idea that control can be exercised through many different means and in many different forms.

[79] States, I am sure, will still want to retain this test for attribution in the law of state responsibility.

[80] Sack (2009) at 19.

[81] ibid.

before me, any thinking about the form of control that constitutes territoriality should pay attention to all the various 'conscious and unconscious engagements and interrelations between individual and collective social actors and space'.[82] This understanding of the more subtle 'conscious and unconscious' modes of influence is similar to Foucauldian conceptions of power and power's relationality. Foucault observed that 'territory is no doubt a geographical notion, but it's first of all a juridico-political one: the area controlled by a certain kind of power'.[83] The strength of this approach lies in its emphasis on understanding the activities, processes, and relationships constituting territory as opposed to the usual physical geographic-referent definition of territory. It understands the more subtle practices that constitute territories and the relations of a far wider array of actors are relevant.

Territory, on this reading of things then, is a space produced by activities, processes, and relationships. Territory is not an object (natural or otherwise) but a space created by 'the social processes and relationships that produce it'.[84] Those social processes may comprise practices to influence those seeking to access the space, including the repelling of possible migrants by physically 'moving' borders[85] as well as various strategies to discourage movement in the first place (with policies aimed at 'helping refugees as close to the source of the problem as possible').[86] It may also comprise placing restrictions on people and activities such as the exclusion of refugees from jobs and social life. The explanatory power of this approach is great; many policies of social exclusion are not viewed as direct activities of control as international lawyers know the concept; the UK government does not force Syrians to stay in Syria or in refugee camps by any physical means but on procedural grounds and the chance of making an asylum application. Thus, bordering processes may 'be experienced wherever admission is being negotiated'.[87] While there are sometimes explicit legal arrangements, an important part is also played by communications and cultural messaging. Therefore, having a wider understanding of how influence over territories is practised today seems all the more pressing and essential given the gravity of the issues it interacts with.

[82] Klauser (2008) at 33.
[83] Foucault in Elden (2013) at 5, 7.
[84] Klauser (2008) at 36.
[85] Arbel (2013) at 65, 65.
[86] Teubner and Fischer-Lescano at (2016).
[87] Kesby (2007) at 101, 103.

4.3.4 Control over What?

The next consideration is control over *what*?[88] There are two key points here. First, it should be highlighted that *control over territory* is often used as a shorthand for control over the activities and people taking place in relation to the institution's space but all too quickly it stops being a shorthand and is then conflated with *control of the physical geography*. Besides, the spatiality often assumed with the preposition 'over' can be just as problematic in this regard. It would therefore be more accurate going forward to say that it is *control over functions* within or in relation to a particular territory rather than the shorthand. For it is too easy when adopting the shorthand to conceptually slip into saying 'control *over* territory' as opposed to 'control over functions' and to slip into the spatialised hierarchy of state over or above the physical geography. This gaze stems from and is enabled by a 'bird's eye'[89] or 'god's eye'[90] view of territory, which also tends to aid in the conceptual flattening of the concept. This is also reproduced by the cartographically disciplined imagining of territory addressed in the previous chapter.

Second, control need not be over *all aspects of social life* taking place in the same physical geographical space, only over some aspects. The centralisation of functions in the state bureaucracy[91] appears to have ruined us for understanding decentralised governance.[92] So while most accounts pick up on the idea that functions have been decentralised and distributed (away from the state), where those spaces of decentralisation exist are as yet unfamiliar and unknown. What is important to decentralised governance is there no single actor which exercises control over all

88 The *where* does not really need to be examined separately. The *where* is the territory; it is what is produced when actors exercise control.

89 Pickles (2004) at 80.

90 Rorty (1991) at 156. See also for a relevant critique, the 'god trick' by Haraway (1988) 575.

91 Sassen (2008) undertakes a thorough mapping of the centralisation of functions in the state, and also traces the decentralisation of the assemblages associated with the 'Global Digital Age', specifically the internet and financial markets. Julie Cohen also addresses new architectures of control in Cohen (2012).

92 Decentralisation is now less enfolded with associations of the 'primitive' pre-state models (i.e., feudalism and *lex mercatoria*) and is now very much in vogue with associations of being 'somehow more organic, more closely tied to communities, more encouraging of participation, more connected to desire, need and decision making, and so forth.' This is mapped by John Haskell in relation to crypto currency in Haskell (2022). See also Parkin who refers to 'algorithmic decentralisation' and notes that it is part of the 'hype' surrounding blockchain, helping the political project of dismantling centralised state power through software: Parkin (2020) at xiii.

functions traditionally assumed (itself quite an idealised assumption) to be within the control of the state. As such, there are now many new 'fresh'[93] spaces that have been formed upon the assumption of control by this array of actors. This point is related to my critique of exclusivity in the following chapter, where I argue there is a misconception of exclusivity present in the notion of 'control over territory'. Exclusivity often assumes there is comprehensive control over all activities and peoples in that particular physical geography. As I argue there, it is instead *rights* that are exclusive. In Chapter 5, I expand on this as it is key to offering a legal theoretical account of how, in relation to any one particular physical geography, numerous territories may exist with different actors controlling or influencing elements of social, political, legal, and economic life.

4.3.5 Legitimacy of the Exercise of Control

Finally, a word about the legitimacy of the control being exercised. I am not here outlining a theory of what is legitimate control, determining or judging what is legitimate control, or whether that control is legal or not according to international law. International law could decide that the exercise of control is illegal but still understand that an actor is exercising control in relation to its space. *Territory is itself not a question of being either illegal or illegal.* It is the relations that produce that territory that can be legitimate/illegitimate or legal/illegal according to some legal or moral system. In fact, this shows how unhelpful a physical understanding of territory is – its symbolic presence looms large. It could also be noted in this regard that international law already contains the categories of 'state territory' and 'occupied territory' in international law. This is an indication that the legal regime is capable of determining the legitimacy of different practices undertaken within the different territories of different actors. It is already possible to establish which actors have responsibility for exercising control. However, it is a category of space that is currently limited to states.

So, there is no misinterpretation, as what I am definitively not saying is that brute force is 'good' and ought to be 'recognised'. What I am trying to show is the factual exercise of power and how this is understood as constituting space. A future step would be, as a result, to take a turn in that normative direction, after determining the factual exercise of power,

93 Poulantzas (2000) at 104.

to understand who wields control, whether it is legitimate, and who ought to be held accountable.[94]

***

Having addressed the characteristic of control, the rest of this chapter turns to other individual characteristics of the concept of territory, each contributing to how any particular instance of territory is practised. If the practices constituting control may change, then so perhaps may many of the characteristics discussed in the previous chapter be reconfigured by the different territorial practices of various actors. For example, while all territory is bounded in some way, how these boundaries are practised, where they exist physically, how they function, and how they are represented are constantly being reconfigured.[95] It is to these other characteristics that I now turn.

4.4 The Times of Territories

Agnew's territorial trap, for all its highlighting of a trap, was itself still trapped.[96] It contained many prenotions, and one of those was the understanding that 'a state is a fixed territorial entity'.[97] This fixity and static quality, as discussed in Chapter 3, is common in international law discourse. This static temporality associated with territory is reproduced in much of the globalisation and global governance discourse. Soja illustrates this underlying assumption: '[t]here seems little doubt that global economic integration has been increasing, but this world of intensified economic flows remains constrained by more static political boundaries, older forms of political territorialisation and regulation that were constructed, for the most part, to meet very different demands.'[98] And yet, there is something that just didn't seem right to me about the supposed temporal dichotomies between traditional state territory and other spaces: instead, perhaps 'there is no static and stabilised space,

[94] This is for sure an area for future study, but not for this text. I am not considering these moral, ethical, or political questions here. Nor am I entirely comfortable with the idea of predetermining what is moral, ethical, or just. The object of this book is to outline the analytical and conceptual framework that is important to understanding the relation between space–power–law in international law and global governance.

[95] See more below on bordering territory.

[96] This has been very well explored and critiqued in Shah (2012) at 57.

[97] Agnew (1994) at 55.

[98] Soja in Houtum (2004) at 37.

though there are plenty of attempts to make space static and stable'.[99] I want to unpick this thinking. In Elden, I recognised a similar call in his recognition that 'the continual remaking and reshaping of spatial relations may take on, indeed must take on, different forms in different times and places'.[100] Our vision should not be limited to that 'of a static world of fixed territories suddenly thrown into flux, as it is in much of the literature on deterritorialisation'.[101]

Before going further in re-imagining the time of territories, the temporality of territory should be distinguished from the temporality of physical geography. Thinking back to the relationship between the physical and the social worlds, it is arguably a flattening of the physical and the social and the time of the physical imposed upon the time of the social that creates this problem. Physical geography is often thought of as 'permanent'. But it is, it should be noted, just a different perception of time and change. There are long-term transformations: ice melts, continents drift, islands 'drown', tides change, and land is 'reclaimed' (perhaps 'artificially' through human endeavour). Physical geography is hardly timeless. Massey is influential to my thinking here, with her reflections that all rocks are 'immigrant rocks'.[102] Using the example of Skiddaw in the English Lake Distract, she muses that '*when* the rocks of Skiddaw were laid down, about 500 million years ago, they were not "here" [Skiddaw] at all'.[103] These rocks were physically in a different location on the surface of the earth. They were, according to geologists, 'formed as black muds and sands settling on the seabed about 500 million years ago. They have since been raised up and crumpled and squeezed.'[104] So not only is the time of physical geography wrongly assumed to be more or less static, where territory and physical geography are conflated analytically, territory gains that static quality too. Closely associating the concept of territory with physical geography has repercussions limiting our understanding of the potential temporalities of territory.

[99] Helmig and Kessler (2007) at 241.

[100] Elden (2006) at 51.

[101] ibid.

[102] Massey (2005) at 137. I especially love her weaving of the story of the rock found in the river Elbe at Hamburg in autumn 1999 ('Hamburgs ältester Einwanderer!') and the change in German citizenship laws in January 2000 where 'Some established immigrants were to be granted citizenship, to be accepted – like the rock – as "of the place"' (at 149–50).

[103] Massey (2005) at 133.

[104] 'Landscape and Geology' (2006).

If we take seriously the idea that territory is 'produced by social practices over time and, hence, [are] lived and alive rather than an empty and static substance';[105] if we take seriously the idea that it is increasingly the case that 'spaces within the terrain of international law are not static, linear and ordered, but rather complex, fluid and uncertain, evolving continuously along with the interactions of the different actors present';[106] then, 'territory and borders should be viewed as fluid, adaptable practices rather than as static and immutable structures'.[107] It makes sense that if the practices take place in different times, the spaces these practices produce should also have their temporalities understood as more dynamic, multiple, and open ended.

However, the implication of the hegemonic assumption regarding the static time of territory present in international law discourse and theory is that it excludes spaces operating with a different temporal logic from being recognised as territories. If the time of territories could instead be recognised as impermanent, temporary, and dependent on particular times or activities, many more possibilities for recognising different practices of territoriality open up.

Understanding the temporal contingency of territories creates the potential to recognise more spaces as territories meeting the requirements of being governed and regularly controlled, that are legally created and established (such as financial centres) (and which do not 'belong' to states). This aids the comprehension of territories as simultaneous and as spaces of flow, as opposed to static and fixed to homogeneous geographic places.[108] If going forward, we can understand the temporality of territory as malleable, it becomes possible to perceive the formation of a particular territory as a one-off arrangement, or as regularised. This

105 Strandsbjerg (2010) at 56.

106 Pearson (2008) at 489, 497.

107 Lambach (2020) at 483.

108 There is often an opposability between territories and places (assumed to be more closed and less changeable, often associated with spaces of modernity) and 'new' spaces of flow. However, Massey, thinking with Derrida, has been influential in challenging this understanding 'neither imagination in its pure form is possible (neither a space hermetically closed into territories nor a space composed solely of flows)', Massey (2005) at 86. But even while challenging this, she seems to assume that territories are the opposite of flows, as here: 'Envisioning space as always-already territorialised, just as much as envisioning it as purely a sphere of flows, misunderstands the ever-changing ways in which flows and territories are conditions of each other', ibid at 99. However, I increasingly wonder aloud: if territories are understood as produced as a result of social practices exercising control, does that control need to be so constant/static? I think not.

insight is in part inspired by Sack who argues: 'a place can be used as a territory at one time and not at another'.[109] However, Sack refers to the state delineating a particular area for use by the manufacturing industry or for special financial assistance.[110] There is an element of longevity and stability even in so designating an area for manufacturing industry use – whether for five years or several decades. Instead, I propose understanding territory as being constituted and reconstituted on an even more regular basis. This could be, say, every Tuesday of the week or every second Saturday of a calendar month, or even only for a few seconds at a time when particular actions are undertaken (e.g., when an offshore accounting book is used).[111] Territory is dependent on certain actors performing a role or activities being performed and if these are temporally limited, why not the territory produced by it? Could territories exist, for example, whenever an email inbox or app is opened, or when a financial transaction is undertaken? If we 'conceived of territory as a process rather than an outcome' it would allow this insightful understanding of territory 'as something dynamic'.[112]

This is legally (and socially) possible. There are numerous historical examples, including the practice of granting markets jurisdictional rights and the creation of local tribunals administering market law.[113] It is the time of the state that has homogenised static time-space. In the example of town and village markets, the territorial and spatial scope of the jurisdictional rights and administration of law were limited and bounded by the market's extent (also note in connection to the following characteristic, that it is unlikely these were firm and fixed boundaries; authority would have petered out and dissolved gradually). The Courts of Piepowder or 'piepoudres' only had jurisdiction over actions arising in the fair or market.[114] Courts sat every market day.[115] Evidence shows they sometimes operated in connection with local borough courts but in other instances, borough courts were excluded from jurisdiction. Interesting for present purposes is evidence that '[b]y the Statute 17 Edward IV., c. 2, its jurisdiction was limited to things happening or

109 Sack (2009) at 19.
110 ibid.
111 I develop this idea much further in Lythgoe (2022) at 1.
112 'Dynamic Territories (S. Elden)' (2014).
113 Another example of non-state time is *lex mercatoria*. There is a temporality inherent to the idea of this being a spontaneous legal order. For more on this see Elcin (2012).
114 Gross (1906) at 231, 235. See also Hurst (1925) at 61, 61.
115 Gross (1906) at 236.

actions *arising within the precinct* of the fair and *during the continuance* of the particular fair at which the court was held'.[116] The temporal and spatial jurisdiction of the court was limited, but so too was the territoriality and temporality of the market. The court would stop sitting at the end of the market and wait until the next one to reconvene. Judgment could be 'deferred until the time of another fair or market'.[117] Notably, this was not a guaranteed or specified time. Interestingly, these courts also applied *lex mercatoria* and their procedure is said to have resembled that of 'the international law merchant as it was administered in all European tribunals'.[118]

This approach to the time of territories can be applied to help make sense of cloud computing and intangible data – allowing territorialisation of particular access points and logins which move geographically, but it is the same territory being 'switched on' with each access. This approach also aids our understanding of 'time-space compression' by technology. It helps us see that it is really the overcoming of distance as opposed to the 'annihilation of place by time' that is occurring: place, space, and territory *still matter* and have not been annihilated; it is distance that has been overcome and more easily traversed. Rather it is the homogeneity of the time of territory that enables the misleading conclusion that time has overcome space. Massey, too, argues that 'space cannot be annihilated by time' because the two are always 'mutually implicated'.[119] Instead, what is taking place are multiple relations constructed by new kinds of spatial configurations.[120]

Although this book concerns how territory can be conceptualised differently, and is thus seemingly about space, space should not be prioritised over time; nor should time be prioritised over space, which is often the case in historical accounts. Space and time are not 'abstract and separate entities, Newton-fashion'.[121] Time and space are not separable; all spaces have a time and all time takes place in space; they are mutually implicated.[122] If we think in this way, it is possible to

[116] ibid at 241, emphasis added.
[117] ibid.
[118] ibid at 245.
[119] Massey (2005) at 91.
[120] Massey is especially instructive on rethinking the once-assumed binary between space and time. I recommend, in particular, Part Three of *For Space*.
[121] Valverde (2015) at 31.
[122] Massey has been particularly influential in my thinking about time and space not as opposable but mutually implicated; Massey (2005) Part 2.

understand territory anew – as something not permanently present or switched 'on' but as contingent and dependent on particular activities, individuals being present, or functions being performed. And it is law that is often the means by which spaces are triggered and switched off again, making it crucial for lawyers to understand the time of territory in this sense.

4.5 Rebounding/Debordering

While the concept of territory is primarily of interest in this book – because the construction of space is fundamental to borders and to a legal system existing in the first place – logically, boundaries are second-order but necessary ideas.[123] As Lindahl puts it, 'no legal order is imaginable that does not close itself into an inside vis-à-vis an outside'.[124] Therefore, it is necessary to expound upon boundaries in at least some detail. Not least, because how orthodox international law currently conceptualises territory and its boundedness, invisibilises the territories of non-state actors that may be differently bounded.

Borders are overly essentialised concepts.[125] Given this, it is useful to give an overview of different historical practices of boundedness as it, firstly, shows that different practices of bordering can exist and have existed and, secondly, it helps makes sense of and throws into sharper relief the practices of bordering today. The realisation of this overly essentialised understanding of borders prompted much of the literature on the proliferation and heterogeneity of borders, finding that bordering practices are more varied than the hegemonic understanding of border accounts for.[126] Yet, international law in practice continues to operate predominantly with an essentialised notion. Moreover, its hegemonic understanding of borders results from prioritising the state as the essential political authority in international law with a territory, meaning that

[123] Elden (2011).

[124] Lindahl (2013) at 4.

[125] Balibar (2002) chapter 4. 'To the question, "What is a border?" . . . it is not possible to give a simple answer . . . because we cannot attribute to the border an essence which would be valid in all places and at all times, for all physical scales and time periods, and which would be included in the same way in all individual and collective experience. Without going back as far as the Roman *limes*, it is clear that the border of a European monarchy in the eighteenth century . . . has little in common with those borders the Schengen Convention is so keen to strengthen today' (p 75).

[126] Kesby (2007) at 101; Mezzadra and Neilson (2013); Arbel (2013); Topping (2014).

state territory and state borders tend to dominate the intellectual landscape.

The limits to the authority of different political institutions have historically been practised, and understood, in a myriad of ways. Elden's historiography of territory offers a different perspective on how boundedness has been practised by historical political authority structures, giving a plausible narrative as to how 'the idea of a territory as a bounded space ... with fixed boundaries'[127] was historically produced. He gives many persuasive accounts of the boundaries of empires, tribes, city-states, city-leagues, and towns, each having different forms and functions for their boundaries. For example, evidence shows empires stopped for practical reasons at physical barriers such as deserts or oceans, but given their ultimate aim was universality this 'border' was conceived of differently compared to those of today. Indeed, as a result of this universal aim, any boundary to authority was unthinkable. Where territory 'ended' was less a boundary and more a 'temporary stopping place where the potentially unlimited expansion of the *Pax Romana* had come to a halt'[128] or a 'floating zone'.[129] The Roman Empire is well known for having internal 'boundaries' but these were not defined and communicated lines representing an absolute limit. Rather, activities continued beyond walls or alternatively stayed inside them at considerable distances.[130] The public domain 'ended somewhere, but this end was not specifiable by means of a legally relevant line'.[131]

As for the demarcation between empires: the 'boundary' between the Holy Roman and Ottoman Empires was fluid and unstable. Where one empire ended and another began oscillated for many centuries and there were many overlaps.[132] While there were pressing reasons to delimit the boundaries between these two empires, it did not occur to either ruler to agree a boundary as neither recognised nor imagined the other as equal to themselves. Both thought they were only limited by what was feasible and economically desirable as opposed boundaries per se.[133] For example, Hadrian's Wall was a frontline of defence against barbarians,

[127] Elden (2013) at 31.
[128] ibid at 35.
[129] Kratochwil (1986) at 36.
[130] Elden (2013) at 35.
[131] Kratochwil (1986) at 35.
[132] Gottmann (1973) at 28.
[133] Spruyt (1994) at 16.

not a limit of the empire.[134] The functions of the boundaries were, therefore, different to our current understanding. There was no presupposition that space and power were equally understood by either empire, in contrast to assumptions underpinning today's geography of states. That our understanding of territory has 'descended' from either ancient Rome or Greece is a myth perpetuated in the history of territory and Elden roundly dismantles the assumption that these empires adopted the same sense of boundedness as today.[135] In contrast to empires in terms of spatial control, and also unlike today where 'just about all territory is encased in ... mutually exclusive states', city-states, towns, and city-leagues were not an 'exhaustive organizational grid'.[136] The territories of city-leagues could be considered as 'scattered territorialities'.[137] Empty space existed between the towns not subject to a league's control – the opposite of an exhaustive spatial expanse – with most of the physical geography remaining outside the control of leagues. City-states had authority within their city walls but for some functions their authority extended beyond the walls and this relationship was in continual flux. No clear lines demarcated where any particular authority ended – authority simply petered out.[138] Clearly, the imaging of boundaries and their practices have varied significantly.

Scholars have debated why and where the delimitation of boundaries first became important. Gottman has argued that the increase in the number of towns brought about the delimitation of their boundaries.[139] The idea here being that as towns grew and spread, they had to develop a means to delineate their spatial authority from others. This practice, according to Gottmann, served as a model for the formation of states. However, I am unconvinced by this causation narrative and more persuaded by the historical accounts of Elden, Kratochwil, and Sassen who, without reading contemporary understandings of boundaries into history, argue that towns and their increasing size and number did not create the borders understood today. Before mapping allowed for the visualising and agreeing of sharply demarcated limits, these would have been impossible. I am more persuaded by the evidence that it was the

[134] Elden (2013) at 89.
[135] ibid at 62–70, 96.
[136] Sassen (2006) at 54.
[137] ibid.
[138] Branch (2014) at 27.
[139] Gottmann (1973) at 36.

emergence of the state – a *competitor* to towns, city-states, and leagues[140] – assisted by its widespread adoption of cartography, that produced the boundaries recognised today:[141] 'mapping technology allowed rulers to have a spatial view of their possessions; thus, what were originally borderland or border regions progressively became boundaries or frontiers.'[142] And it was states that appear to have won the assumption of power over mapping (and data) in order to shift power from cities and leagues to states, and with the technology of mapping giving these actors the bird's-eye view necessary to lasso towns within their power.

None of this happened quickly. It is said that the Treaty of the Pyrenees in 1659 was 'the first official boundary in the modern sense'.[143] Yet this practice was not adopted everywhere immediately; it steadily grew. Early boundaries did not perform the same functions, nor did they have the same characteristics, as borders today. It was not until the twentieth century that boundaries were fully entrenched in spatial thinking across most of the world. Further, we should note that such conceptions of space were not and are not universal and most certainly were a European practice initially (often formed in confrontation with 'the Other'). Sack, for example, details the Chippewa tribe's alternative understanding of space confronting Europeans during the seventeenth century. The Chippewa occupied a vast area that was never clearly bounded, and which fluctuated from year to year.[144] Similarly contrasting accounts of space and boundaries have existed and continue to exist today.[145]

These accounts show that it is possible to rethink the boundedness of territories. Borders differ in purpose, time, form, and place. They may exist in many different locations and forms *in addition to* the cartographically depicted border. Borders serve different purposes at different times and in different places. The flow of capital into a state, for example, does not flow across cartographic borders but rather 'enters a state' as a result of a financial transaction. Thus, the location of a border for some purposes is a point of transaction – perhaps a bank or a mobile

140 Spruyt (1994).
141 Branch (2014).
142 Brunet-Jailly (2009) at 1.
143 Elden (2013) at 325.
144 Sack (2009) at 7. There are alternative conceptions of space in indigenous relations to physical geography, however, due to space, I am unable to expand further. For those interested in reading more, see for a start, Egan and Place (2013) at 129; Herman (2008) at 73; Larsen and Johnson (2012) 1; Prout and Howitt (2009) at 396; Roth (2009) at 207.
145 Yingzi Zhang and others (2018) at 304; Daugherty (2018); Hall (2018).

app – rather than a cartographic border. Moreover, it is often not the state in question's laws – laws that supposedly apply throughout the territory within the cartographic borders – governing the financial transaction. Goods entering a state via ground transportation will pass through the cartographically represented border and this border performs many functions in that location; however, many bordering practices may have preceded this physical border in the shape of regulations and customs arrangements.[146] For goods transported as air cargo, the geographic border matters for their *vehicle* in terms of entering airspace but their customs are not located at that cartographical border. Thus, there is a splitting up of functions often represented as assembling at the cartographic border. Instead, there are many differently located borders created for particular purposes.

These other borders are created by law just as much as cartographically located borders are, but these are not the borders international law traditionally refers to in 'defining' territory. Even where international lawyers pragmatically accept that these non-cartographic borders exist in practice, there is a disconnect by the referent underlying the concept of borders in international legal discourse and those in practice. By removing the underlying assumption that borders refer primarily to the cartographic border – that is, accepting borders are no longer only 'at the border'[147] – it can make visible the bordering practices in places such as: Heathrow airport;[148] along transit routes; Canadian borders inside US courtrooms;[149] and borders as 'separation walls, barriers, blockades, closures, road blocks, check points, sterile areas, special security zones, closed military areas and killing zones'.[150] A change of perspective also makes visible the borders inscribed on bodies, in workplaces,[151] universities[152] and public spaces.[153]

Bringing time into the when and where of borders, a key assumption made is that borders are always 'switched on', that they are always there; that borders are stable. Borders became increasingly stable during the twentieth century[154] as the modern (territorial) state became entrenched as the

146 Sassen (2013) at 31.
147 Mezzadra and Neilson (2013) at 29.
148 Painter (2010) at 1091.
149 Arbel (2013).
150 Mezzadra and Neilson (2013) at 8.
151 O'Carroll and Jones (2016).
152 Topping (2014).
153 Bauder (2014) at 76, 76.
154 Kuijer and Werner in Kuijer and Werner (2017) at 4.

primary institution and organising unit. While the location of borders may be subject to renegotiation, the negotiation takes place with permanency assumed – that is, once renegotiation or secession occurs, the borders resume this impulse towards stability. In other disciplines there has been a move away from understanding borders as 'frozen lines' towards perceiving the role and function of borders 'as institutions, symbols, and discourses that are spread *everywhere* in society'.[155] Boundaries are 'social constructs and processes rather than stable entities'.[156] Thus, a definition of territory that understands its limits as stable and frozen misses out important practices that make and remake its limits and the role of law in doing so. Chapter 2 gave an overview of the discourse that highlights the increasing porosity of borders. But this discourse continues to assume that (state) borders are always there, with simply more or less porosity for certain categories of people. This discourse tends to continue to treat the border as a black box concept. Thus, porosity fails to account for the diverse functions, spatialities, temporalities, and materialities of borders. So, while it is true the wealthy cosmopolitan 'denizens' of the world may find it easier to cross borders than refugees (a usual example of porosity), there are several factors influencing the physical crossing of a border. For example, research on the temporalities of border crossing challenges perceptions of 'border time'. Law and technology are mixed in order to speed up border crossing, for example through the use of biometric data and passport chips, while at the same time there are techniques to slow down border crossing, through detention and interception regimes, including preemptive *refoulment*.[157] State practices on a *regular* basis relocate the time and space of their borders, often to circumvent, for example, international refugee law obligations.[158]

Problematising the traditional understanding of the temporality of borders, helps make more visible the practices of bordering and question the functions, agents, and spaces of the border. Overcoming this assumption of rigidity and stability means borders are no longer 'symbols of the past'[159] or lines on the map, but current, dynamic, and as relevant as ever to international law discussions. Borders are not disappearing but appearing in more places and in different forms. Therefore, as with territory, borders

155 Houtum (2004) at 18.
156 ibid at 19.
157 Mezzadra and Neilson (2013) at 133.
158 Schloenhardt and Craig (2015) 536; Durieux (2016) at 637; Arbel (2013).
159 Houtum (2004) at 24–25.

or state borders are not vanishing. Instead borders and state borders are increasingly complex, proliferating, and heterogeneous. And because *borders often bound something*, that something – territory – may also be moving, proliferating, and becoming more heterogeneous.

Acknowledging this complexity helps in two ways: firstly, it makes visible the different, multiple, heterogeneous *state borders*, existing in new and unanticipated places, and which exist as boundaries between *states*; and secondly, this insight allows for and makes visible the territories of non-state actors which often have different characteristics informing their boundedness. I have found Lindahl helpful in diagnosing the boundaries of other actors, that might intersect with the same physical geography as state territory. In *Fault Lines of Globalization*, he gives an example of Lafayette as a legal space.[160] In three different scenarios, he shows actions across space, time, as well as the specific content of the action, which would be considered legal (buying the goods), illegal (stealing the goods), and a-legal (disrupting the usual system by protesting and negotiating with the manager). Alegality is the rupture and calling into question as to what is legal and illegal. Here I may be going further than Lindahl intended with his understanding of alegality. In his example, it was certainly a domestic legal order, and there is 'one' sovereign – the state – that is being challenged by the actions of the protesters; but what if we are talking about two institutions attempting to assert legality within their own legal orders. Here I think of alegality as an attempt to disrupt what is legal and illegal understood from the perspective of different (but overlapping the same legal geography) legal and politics orders. Imagine instead we are speaking of the powers of an international organisation, which a state contests are beyond the organisation's mandate or where an international organisation might be trying to assert a right or privilege against a state or another international organisation. Sometimes, questions such as these are settled by a court,[161] but far more often there will be a constant daily and

[160] Lindahl (2013) chapter 1.

[161] For example, *Reparation for Injuries Suffered in the Service of the United Nations, Advisory Opinion* [1949] ICJ Reports 1949, p 174 (International Court of Justice). *Reparation for Injuries Suffered in the Service of the United Nations, Advisory Opinion* [1949] ICJ Reports 1949, p 174 (International Court of Justice). The Opinion came about because states and the UN were trying to establish whether or not an international organisation could bring a claim against states for the death or injury of its agents. Eight UN personnel were killed or wounded in Palestine and the question became whether states could be held responsible for actions 'against' the UN. See also: *Appeal Relating to the Jurisdiction of the ICAO Council (India v Pakistan)*, ICJ Reports 1972, p 46

seemingly mundane negotiation of these boundaries between civil servants of international and domestic institutions.[162] For the avoidance of doubt, here we are talking about the boundaries between plural legal orders. But it is not the case that one is a spatial legal order and the other aspatial – *they are both spatialised legal orders*. There is thus a constant negotiation between actors as to what is legal and illegal, who is acting appropriately, and who is not. I also wonder aloud whether in the space-time content of alegality, we might find where power dynamics lie. This might again be taking Lindahl's concept of alegality further than he intended or misunderstanding it entirely. Yet, it seems to me that it is in this negotiated, liminal, and relational space that competences shift amongst actors, just as much as, if not more often than, in the entry into force of treaties endowing institutions with powers. It is in such practices, of treaty making, of decisions of courts and tribunals, of negotiating between institutions, that boundaries are established; that actors establish what is within and without their appropriate exercise of power.

Thus, boundaries and borders are more heterogeneous in location, function, representation, content, and practice than their cartographic representation; boundaries are complex relational social institutions. Understanding and accounting for this in international law's theory of territory is an integral part of rethinking territory and allows for a better spatial account of state and non-state actor bordering practices.

4.6 Representations of Territories: Mapping Dimensions

Before the advent of one-dimensional thought, humans could not comprehend direction, time, and patterns. This can be seen in the non-linear

(International Court of Justice); *Constitution of the Maritime Safety Committee of the Inter-Governmental Maritime Consultative Organization, Advisory Opinion of 8 June 1960*, ICJ Reports 1960, p 150 (International Court of Justice); *Certain expenses of the United Nations (Article 17, paragraph 2, of the Charter), Advisory Opinion of 20 July 1962*, ICJ Reports 1962, p 151 (International Court of Justice); *Jam v International Finance Corporation*, 139 US Supreme Court, 759 (2019); *ILO Judgment No. 245* (21 October 1974): *Meyer v International Atomic Energy Agency*; ILO Judgment No. 359 (13 November 1978) *Djoehana v Food and Agriculture Organization of the United Nations*; *Yassin Abdullah Kadi and Al Barakaat International Foundation v Council and Commission*, ECJ C-402/05 P and C-415/05, 3 September 2008; *Commission of the European Economic Community v Grand Duchy of Luxembourg and Kingdom of Belgium*; ECJ, 2/62 and 3/62, 14 December 1962.

162 Martin gives an excellent overview of this negotiation amongst states and international organisations during and after WW1 as it relates to competence over economic matters. See Martin (2022).

medieval understanding of time and space, where medieval Christians believed they were 'wedged somewhere' between the crucifixion and the second coming of Jesus; the personal experience of time and the end of time were seen side by side and simultaneously rather than as a sequential linear timeline.[163] The development of two-dimensional thinking enabled concepts to emerge that are flat as can be seen in the cartographical imagination of space. But this only allows us to partially understand space and time.[164] With new methods of mapping and representing space now available, can we go beyond a two-dimensional understanding of territory?

Ryngaert has briefly touched on this topic, arguing that 'digital technology may possibly enable us to depict nonlinear jurisdictional spaces.'[165] Digitally depicted nonlinear jurisdictional spaces create the potential to explore and understand better Lindahl's ideas on the spatiality of transnational authority[166] where 'non-state authority may not easily map onto a geometric grid-based map, but such authority still inhabits a space and has certain boundaries.'[167] This is the space of flows and networks often associated with globalisation that are assumed to be aterritorial.

Cartographical practices have directed international law's ontological imagination and structures its standard reasoning reflexes in ways that make it difficult (if not impossible) for the discipline to understand a number of important trends, processes, and phenomena not (yet) mapped and not mapped in the same way.[168] This includes, not least, the highly ambivalent role international law plays in enabling, entrenching, and reproducing a range of highly questionable political and economic practices such as tax evasion and secrecy jurisdictions. Most maps illustrate state space as a flat space (indeed, most depict state space in this dimension). This cartographical imagination of space has disciplined the legal imagination of territory. Consequently, territory exists only on a single plane in legal discourse. Fundamentally, because of this cartographic gaze, the exercise of political authority is directed to, and connected to, the physical geography thought to be 'occupied' by states, which are cartographically represented to the exclusion of other political

[163] White (2004) 125.
[164] TAB (2018).
[165] Ryngaert in Kuijer and Werner (2017) at 70.
[166] Lindahl (2010) at 33.
[167] Ryngaert in Kuijer and Werner (2017) at 70.
[168] See the idea of the 'cartographization of sovereign jurisdiction' in Kritsiotis (2009).

structures. States are assumed to not just 'look like' the depictions on maps but to actually be, or exist, in reality as represented.

Maps have produced the *assumed synchronicity of the spaces* of territory, jurisdiction, and sovereignty. In other words, territory and the territoriality of international law are based on a presumption of spatial divisions corresponding to the traditional cartographic representation of states, with jurisdiction and sovereignty synchronised over the same space. This also results, in the eyes of international law, for many purposes, a state's territory having the characteristic of homogeneous and uniform space.

Homogeneity serves several important purposes and has a lineage: 'we make our own history and geography, but not just as we please' but, Soja continues, in light of 'historical geographies produced in the past'.[169] Territories were not always understood as homogeneous; from Caesar's Ancient Rome, to the Roman Empire, Elden has given a *tour de force* of spaces dissimilar to territory today.[170] The reason for the development of this characteristic of homogeneity is explored by Poulantzas, who notes that there is a direct line between the ideological process marrying nationalism with territoriality and, as he puts it, 'that peculiarly modern phenomenon, totalitarianism: separation and division in order to unify; parcelling out in order to structure; atomization in order to encompass; segmentation in order to totalize; closure in order to homogenize.'[171] Leaving aside the question of totalitarianism, it bears noting the emphasis Poulantzas puts on the homogenising dynamics in the constitution of modern state space. The lineage between cultural homogenisation and the concept of national territory as 'continuous and homogen[e]ous space'[172] is central to the story of modern statehood and the ramifications of this lineage have disciplined the gaze of international law and its understanding of the concept of territory.

While, for many international law purposes, territory is represented as 'simple and uniform', critical geographers call for it to be understood 'as complex and highly differentiated'.[173] This would involve international law's gaze 'piercing the veil' of the otherwise flat, homogeneous, synchronised cartographical space to understand the historicity of the

169 Soja (2010) at 129.
170 Elden (2013) at chapters 2–4.
171 Poulantzas (2000) at 107.
172 ibid.
173 Klauser (2008) at 36.

quality of homogeneity and, more importantly, the different scales in which different spaces exist. But mapping new dimensions is required in order to realise that imagined space.

Debate turns on whether globalisation is viewed as operating over a flat (global) space as opposed to parcels of lands; or whether networks of space are created between cities, or other places, crisscrossing state territories. Perhaps, depending on the phenomena of globalisation being analysed, it is both. Ferguson argues that 'large scale capitalism' requires homogenisation, uniformity, grids and simplification in a similar manner to the state.[174] Much of the literature understands globalisation as homogenising global space, caused by and enabling integration and standardisation. Yet, it is also possible to understand globalisation processes as 'touching down' in specific places, then hopping to another, with 'empty' space in between these two points. In this vein, Ferguson also argues that the movement of capital could be understood as not 'covering' geographic space contiguously but jumping from point to point and 'bypassing' huge areas.[175] Understanding the particular process and its operating space is important, rather than attempting to describe and assess the broad and tangled mass of globalisation as one model. In other words, the territories of globalisation and global governance may in some instances rely on the same ideas of homogeneous, continuous space not dissimilar from state space, and others rely on heterogeneous space. Perhaps with new technologies time will become capable of being mapped in a way that captures the dynamism of spaces.

New technologies would also find a way to map overlapping territories. Viewing territory as a non-physical space allows for the overlaying and coexisting of different territories over the same physical geography. There is only one physical geography, but given territory is the socially constituted framework by which power is exercised, there can be more than one of these. As Müller-Mall observes: 'Law is not place, it is not a systematic order that makes it possible to define distinctly any place contained in it. Instead, law is space, it is constituted through practices, and these practices might be simultaneous and overlapping.'[176]

This overlap can be observed in circumstances where two or more states exercise power over the same physical space. I do not refer here to condominium. EU and Spanish territories overlap and AU and Egyptian

[174] Ferguson (2005) at 377, 377.
[175] ibid at 379.
[176] Müller-Mall (2013) at 90.

overlap; each has significant powers that they exercise in relation to their own territories regarding the same physical geography. We might also take as examples instances where sovereignty is thought to be 'in abeyance' or instances of leasing. This approach helps explain situations like Guantanamo Bay where Cuba is viewed as the sovereign that has 'leased' the territory somewhat indefinitely to the US.[177] As regards the physical geography identified as Guantanamo Bay, it is US territory for certain functions and competences, AND Cuban territory for other competences and legal rights. For example, the US does not have the right to mine and sell minerals. Another example is Sri-Lanka's leasing of the port of Hambantota to China for ninety-nine years.[178] Interestingly, it is not simply China but two state-controlled entities operating through China Merchants Port Holdings[179] that exercise 'sovereign like' governance and control in relation to this space. More broadly, the infrastructure space (ports, highways, railways, and pipelines) created by China's 'One Belt, One Road' policy created by free trade, investment or other agreements between China and other actors, can be better understood by conceptualising territory-as-space. Territory-as-space helps us to observe that in relation to any particular physical geographical space, there may be more than one actor exercising different powers, including so called sovereign powers, over different aspects of social life.

Adopting this framework could help reinterpret and re-imagine the relationships between state and non-state actors, including SEZs and international organisations (their headquarters and spaces of activity like refugee camps or the seabed). Ferguson and Gupta argued that an actor or organisation (international organisations, NGOs, etc.) '[does] not replace the older system of nation-states ... but overlays and coexists with it. In this optic, it might make sense to think of the new organizations ... not as challengers ... but as horizontal contemporaries ... operating on the same level, and in the same global space.'[180] And from the global space to the local, these actors may at any one time operate over the same physical geography. Each has its own territory in relation to which they influence and discipline activities. We can adopt two vantage points; we can focus on the geographical location and work out which actors are exercising power there at any

[177] See Raustiala (2004) at 2501.
[178] Abi-Habib (2018).
[179] Schultz (2018).
[180] Ferguson and Gupta (2002) at 994.

given moment of time, but we can also see this single location as part of a bigger territory associated with a particular actor. Above all, it allows proper scrutiny of actors and institutions, that currently remain somewhat fuzzy and obscured. Understanding territory as space helps achieve this.

Ferguson and Gupta advised 'it is necessary to treat state and nonstate governmentality within a common framework, without making unwarranted assumptions about their spatial reach, vertical height, or relation to the local.'[181] This is what I seek to do. Rather than assigning (or consigning) the framework of territory only to a state, which obscures the spatiality and spatial reach of non-state actors, it allows scrutiny of the territorialising practices adopted by non-state actors. A simple test is introduced: if the actor is exercising control of something territorially, it has a territory for those purposes. For it is the narrow concept of territory that gave rise to the idea that territory is no longer relevant to international law. Powers and competences are being reterritorialised but *where* they are being reterritorialised into is not just misunderstood but excluded, removing accountability for activities happening within those spheres.

This understanding of territory makes it possible to analyse the different spatial assumptions of diverse institutions, including the scope of operations, practices of agents, and their organising culture or logic. This conceptualisation allows us to ask new questions: do MNCs have a territorial logic, and can this be recognised by international law? Could globalisation itself be understood to have territorial assumptions? I believe 'yes'. Territory as a spatial framework explains the space created by customs and trade agreements more concretely. These agreements create territories only in respect of the functions and powers agreed; each agreement creates a different arrangement of the bundle of legal relations in different spaces and governance exercised by different actors, such as government ministers, experts, councils of ministers, committees, etc. Each agreement may create a different space and a different arrangement of the bundle – no two agreements will be the same. However, customs and trade territories will overlap with what is considered currently to be 'state space'.

Further, this rethinking permits more than simply the potential for overlapping territories. It creates *equality* between the actors and the

[181] ibid.

territories; it creates 'horizontal contemporaries ... operating on the same level, and in the same ... space'.[182] This removes the hierarchical sub- and supra-state spatial imaginary (demonstrated in Chapter 2 for example) that always starts and ends with state territory. Thus, state territory no longer dominates when it is viewed as one space among many. In short, this perspective allows us to see that different actors are exercising different powers in relation to their own territories that happen to share the physical geography as other territories.

4.7 The Politics of Territories: Why We Need a New Legal Geography

All this is well and good. I can propose a different understanding, and no one needs to listen to me. Why should we completely rethink everything we know about territory in international law? Well, I argue that there are specific insights about the *politics of territories* to be drawn out from the understanding of territory articulated in this chapter that are vital for international law discourse. By recognising territory as constituted and reconstituted by the relational and social, we can see territory structuring the spatial scope and application of international law, emphasising the strategic uses underlying and, at the same time, taking advantage of the spatial framework of international law.

Understanding territory as such a kind of socially produced space makes more visible the strategic uses to which the framework is applied. International law is not naturally organised via state territories. This has emerged from political struggle and entrenched through continual practice. This is also by now well known. Yet, many courts and tribunals, as established in Chapter 3, tend to rely on supposedly natural features to settle political disputes. This is problematic. Where territory is imagined as an object, there is a strong and continual risk of naturalising and neutralising the concept, obscuring its strategic appropriation and the underlying politics and ideologies. By understanding the concept of territory as contingent, that territory is 'socially constructed' and 'ideologically informed', 'then the forms of power which are inherently connected to territory may become more visible, and justifications, more clearly partial or partisan'.[183] But where territory is reduced to physical

[182] ibid.
[183] Delaney (2005) at 11.

geography and flattened, it allows an 'illusion of opaqueness'[184] such that it can make invisible what territory is being strategically used for and the political activities that create control over space. Territory is created by practices and, given it is often the legal system that gives effect to and actions of lawyers that make up these social practices, we should understand the role of law in making and unmaking territories.

Moreover, by only seeing state territories, it makes us blind to the non-state territorialising dynamics that compete and negotiate every day with state spatial logics. Tax havens here can illustrate what is at stake:[185] it is often assumed that states have a stable and static territory (Y state = Y territory (synchronised in relation to Y physical geography)) but if we look at the practices of tax havens this is not always the case. Instead, different actors – sub-state and supra-state – are differently active in relation to tax law and tax governance – hence, the territorial desynchronisation of sovereignty; each 'jurisdiction' exercises control over its own territory regarding tax as well as for non-tax sovereign powers. Yet these territories will overlap over the same physical geography. The UK provides an interesting illustration of these different overlapping spaces. For all intents and purposes, for example, when the UK signs an international treaty, it is expected to apply to the territories of Jersey and Guernsey. Yet this is not so for tax purposes. The territory of the UK desynchronises for these purposes. Jersey, for example, is often called a separate tax jurisdiction, and it is capable of entering into agreements with states to exchange information on tax-related matters.[186] For some international law purposes, Jersey is seen by some as a *sui generis* actor, but it is not a fully or formally independent state. By desynchronising sovereignty, territory, and physical geography, we can also 'see' the City of London and not just by piercing the sovereignty veil but also by understanding its strategic links with very separate physical spaces.[187] In doing so, this deconstruction process also allows us to 'see' other influences on the creation of tax havens and the offshore and better understand the power dynamic in these territories – perhaps calling it colonialism by other means[188] – operating currently by unclear overlapping jurisdictions,

[184] Soja (2010) at 7.
[185] See Lythgoe (2022) at 1.
[186] See, e.g., *Agreement between Jersey and New Zealand for the Exchange of Information Relating to Tax Matters*, 19 May 2009, online: <www.oecd.org/countries/jersey/43408818.pdf>.
[187] For a thorough understanding of this, see Ogle (2017) at 1431.
[188] ibid at 1439.

regimes, and arrangements that does not 'map' onto the orthodox understanding of the synchronicity of territory and sovereignty. By understanding the plurality of actors and spaces, it allows us as international lawyers to understand that the potential number of territories are relevant.

Moreover, these other spaces are currently invisible to the eyes of international law, we do not understand the different actors circulating within and constituting them. International law has an implicit geography that shapes an understanding of what is 'for' international lawyers to address and what is 'for' state actors to address. It may be plausibly argued that tax is one competence (indeed, *the* one competence) understood to still 'belong' to the state. Once visible, we can associate it with actors working within the governance regimes associating with these overlapping spaces, which may be joined – non-contiguously, of course – with spaces in other cities or state territories around the world, thus creating a recognition for a new framework for governance that has its own spatial logics that could be described as a territoriality. Thinking of the most well-known example of the offshore – the Euromarket – it is an obvious candidate for fitting into this description of supposed or false deterritorialisation. The Euromarket, 'which is a market unregulated by states'[189] and is thought of as 'a stateless offshore zone',[190] has been explored by many working in international politics and economics, but less so by international lawyers. States allowed, enabled, and participated in the creation of the offshore; the offshore was created through sovereign acts. Yet the 'offshore' is not simply an empty ungoverned political space, it is a highly legalised space, both in how it was constituted (the actions and decisions of sovereign states and a lot of help and pressure from private individuals and companies) and continually in its day-to-day activities. Not all activities in the offshore are the same, and, yet, when everything has gone 'offshore', we are unable to understand them, and it leads to an overly reductionist understanding of tax havens and the offshore. This process of pseudo-deterritorialisation has allowed for the invisibilising of activities that do actually take place on shore – the agents involved in creating and recreating spaces with every new activity and transaction 'offshore' are located in a physical geography – but they have also created a new territory, even if just for the exercise of these powers in order to control and discipline activities and people deemed to also be

[189] Palan (1998) at 632.
[190] Shaxson (2011) at 8.

within that territory, and with effects on other territories and actors. Law creates the space in the first place and, in some form, continues to determine the acts that continue to take place in this yet unfamiliar and unknowable offshore space.

More importantly, accepting multiple trajectories and the plurality of important spaces for international lawyers, 'future proofs' the discipline. Here again, Massey inspires much of this thinking. She argues that 'only if we conceive of the future as open can we seriously accept or engage in any genuine notion of politics. Only if the future is open is there any ground for a politics which can make a difference.'[191] If we imagine the question of territory and space of international law as a closed subject, we miss the politics of space. If space is 'closed it holds open no possibility for genuine change or intervention, for the radically new'.[192] If we embrace openness, there is room to challenge, disrupt, and understand different trajectories, trends, and actors. Massey's primary target is discourse around the spatiality of globalisation (including the annihilation of space by time), which is directly relevant to this inquiry. She argues:

> Globalisation is not a single all-embracing movement (nor should it be imagined as some outward spread from the West and other centres of economic power across a passive surface of 'space'). It is a making of space (s), an active reconfiguration and meeting-up through practices and relations of a multitude of trajectories, and it is there that lies the politics.[193]

Thus, lawyers need this new legal geography and to understand the multiple actors, spaces, and competences that otherwise elude us. It is vital for us to see space critically, for 'geography is . . . the art of war but can also be the art of resistance if there is a counter-map and a counter-strategy'.[194]

4.8 Conclusion

In this chapter, I have sought to reconceptualise our understanding of territory as a space – one intellectually realised, but quickly abandoned in

[191] Massey (2005) at 11. In this, Massey is specifically speaking about the assumptions of space made by structuralism – that it is static. Structuralists see the politics of time, but not of space.
[192] ibid at 44.
[193] ibid at 83.
[194] Said (1996) at 28–29.

practice and theory – and demonstrated how this space is realised and constituted. In addition to offering this look at how territory is produced and a different interpretation of the relationship of the concept of territory to the physical geography, I drew attention to two insights this paradigm offers; namely, the political and ideological strategies of these spatial frameworks, which are otherwise hidden if territory is based in natural and physical ideas, and that it also allows territories to overlap the same physical geography.

International law does not structure the exercise of states' or other actors' powers through *objects*, but through spatial strategies. This, then is a story of the relational and social constitution of territory. Yet, if territory is to be understood so dramatically differently, and in particular to now *exclude* any understanding of territory as an object, it poses a fundamental problem for many of international law's foundational theories, including territorial sovereignty, discussed in Chapter 3, or at least those theories that understand territory as an object or a physical essence for the state. As established, many of the accounts of territorial sovereignty, including the *Eigentumstheorie, Eigenschaftstheorie or Raumstheoriem*, and *Kompetenztheorie*, tend to assume exclusivity and contiguous territories that do not overlap. The orthodox operationalisation of concepts such as sovereignty and jurisdiction have been structured around the notion of (state-)territory, and yet in this chapter, I have been setting up the argument that a variety of actors are exercising different powers in relation to their own territories that happen to share the same physical geography as other territories. Further, for the story of reterritorialisation to be complete, the distribution of functions and competences once associated with the sovereignty of states is illegible without rethinking the divisibility of this bundle of powers between state and non-state actors – and providing a legal account of this. Therefore, given that these concepts and legal doctrines are often based on an understanding of territory as an object and primarily as something physical, the final step is to rethink the concepts of sovereignty and jurisdiction as a result of this different perspective on territory.

5

Reterritorialising International Law

> Territory does not cease to be important, rather it is no longer bound within a single state . . . if we are to make progress in understanding the geographies of globalization in relation to the territorial, deterritorialized and reterritorialized aspects, it behoves us to understand what their conditions of possibility are.
>
> Stuart Elden, 'Missing the Point'[1]

So far, I have demonstrated the problem of aterritoriality or post-territoriality,[2] and the associated loss of concreteness that comes with this, in much of the contemporary discourse about international law and global governance. I then demonstrated why this arises: it is in the way orthodox international law constructs the concept of territory that anything 'bypassing' or 'beyond' state territory is aterritorial, because that concept is imagined as physical, natural, flat, and associated only with, and often containing, the state. I then highlighted how we might rethink the concept of territory and addressed the qualities of this reconceptualisation and its relationship to society. Now comes the time to re-insert this concept back into the legal-theoretical framework.

In closing the previous chapter, I emphasised that international law does not structure the exercise of states' or other actors' powers through *objects*, but through spatial strategies. The present chapter weaves that story of the relationality and social constitution of territory through legal doctrine. I look at how this alterative concept can be realised in international law and how it might differently operationalise and spatialise concepts such as sovereignty and jurisdiction. For once we dereify territory, instead understanding it as social space, there are three key concepts to rethink: sovereignty, jurisdiction, and actorhood. Each of these three are continually connected in legal thought, doctrine, and discourse.

1 Elden (2005) at 16.
2 Van Staden and Vollaard (2002).

Therefore, I detail how these refreshed, spatially mediated concepts could be understood, for fundamental rethinking is required for each.

To that end, I first turn to the concepts of sovereignty and jurisdiction and show how they might be 'reinserted' into a 'spatially aware' theoretical conceptual framework. Given the concept of sovereignty, theories of the relationship between a sovereign and its territory, and the concept of jurisdiction are, at a fundamental level, often built around the assumption that territory is an object, if territory is, as I propose, no longer to be conceived of as such, the next step is to explore how this change mediates concepts like sovereignty. To rethink territory so radically, without rethinking the spatially structured concepts of sovereignty and jurisdiction, would leave the job unfinished. The reconceptualised concept of territory would be logically incoherent and problematic for international lawyers to apply. Taking the concept of sovereignty first, I operationalise it as a bundle of legal rights, duties, privileges, and immunities, informed by legal realist methods and social constructivism. To this legal realist sensibility, I continue to apply a spatial lens. Legal realists do not routinely undertake spatial analyses, so I combine the insights from this discipline with a spatial awareness of the territories relevant to international law and global governance. I then look at the operationalisation of jurisdiction as a result and question the 'boundaries' between jurisdiction and extraterritorial jurisdiction, exposing the normative project that underlies this discourse. As such, I reterritorialise extraterritorial jurisdiction.

Having demonstrated the reinterpreted relationship between territory and sovereignty and jurisdiction in turn, I can finally offer a legal-theoretical account of this concept of territory. I discuss the legal rights vis-à-vis this rethought concept, offering an alternative to the 'ownership' and 'exclusive' model of legal rights, which otherwise has at its core a reified and flat understanding of territory. This legal analysis of territory, and specifically a legal realist analysis, is, I hope, useful, for it helps to understand legal rights and duties vis-à-vis territory. I make clear what the distribution of power, sovereignty, authority, etc. in relation to territory is from a legal viewpoint.

The final part of this chapter visits the topic of actorhood. I demonstrate how the spaces of international organisations might also be understood as their territories. Inspired by those who 'see' like non-state institutions;[3] this final step fully realises and implements the

[3] Ferguson (2005); Valverde (2011) at 277; Broome and Seabrooke (2012) at 1. Of course, all this literature was inspired by Scott (1998). 'Seeing like' is an important move. But we need

foregoing conceptual discussion, demonstrating its usefulness in understanding what is occurring 'beyond the state'. To that end, I explore two organizations, the EU and International Seabed Authority (ISA) to demonstrate territories that 'overlap' state space (EU territory) and those which do not (the Area). I also look at one competence, data, which is being continually reterritorialised by different actors, to show it is also possible to 'follow the function' as well as 'follow the actor' to grasp the relevant legal and political spaces.

In the following, I specifically draw on insights and the 'intellectual mood' stemming from legal realism, legal geography and, more broadly, from social constructivism.[4] All three have relevant analytical frameworks that help to explain the reinterpreted international legal spatiality. First, the legal realist analytical framework posits that concepts like property, corporations, and sovereignty are bundles of legal relations. A vital part of this legal bundle is Hohfeld's analysis of rights as describing different legal relations and the subsequent analysis of these legal relations as a bundle. I apply these ideas in a similar way to Schlag, who has argued that Hohfeld's work 'might best be read as a contribution about how to think, not what to think' and that 'Hohfeld does not offer a substantive theory of law or entitlements or property or contracts or anything of the sort. All he offers is an analytical method.'[5] This rethink as a result proposes analytically understanding sovereignty as a bundle of legal relations in a similar manner to how legal realists have understood the legal concept of, for instance, title. What emerges from this exercise is a disruption of the oft perceived and applied monolithic concept of sovereignty with its exclusive spatial application, to understand the spatial application of individual components of this, once thought to be whole, bundle.[6] In addition to legal realism, and the legal geography sensibility that has been present throughout, I adopt a broadly social

to be able to 'see like' multiple institutions and along multiple trajectories, otherwise, we will be blinded by seeing like simply one institution. The discipline of international law has long only seen like a state with a very particular imaginary of state space. The geographical imaginaries of alternative institutions are important to understand the 'multiplicity and interdependence' (Massey (2005) at 158).

4 Horwitz (1992) at 169.

5 Schlag (2015) at 185, 186–187.

6 Or perhaps it would be more accurate to say sovereignty was once idealised as whole. Plenty of scholars have written about this historical myth of a monolithic concept of sovereignty, most recently Martin (2022). Martin argues that the so-called heyday of statehood in the twentieth century was rather more mediated by governance by international institutions and outlines a history of global economic governance. But see also

constructivist informed approach to space and to law. This approach allows me to offer an account of how sovereignty is to be detached from the state, because not only do I argue that it might be understood that other actors 'have' a territory, but also that they can be understood as exercising powers once associated with states in relation to the same physical geography as states.

Taking as its starting point the possibilities outlined in the previous chapter, especially of territorial pluralism, multiplicity, and continuous (re)production, and a departure from the cartographically disciplined state-territory imaginary of international law, the chapter ends with an account of territories proliferating rather than diminishing, both ontologically in the 'real world' in terms of number and in terms of its relevance for the discipline. Taking the idea of reterritorialising seriously, I propose a legal account of the relationship between actors and their spaces and think through the implications of this argument for international law. In short, I propose a 'rebirth' of the concept of territory for international law and global governance.

5.1 Of Sovereignty

In order to explain the relationship between territory and sovereignty in international law as a result of conceptualising territory as *space*, not as an *object* – and crucially space constituted by relations and practices of control – I first need to address how sovereignty can be understood to operate, for much of international law's account of the concept operates assuming territory is an object, as established in Chapter 3. Here is where the useful metaphor of legal bundles helps convey how sovereignty can be better understood, not least because the metaphor is especially helpful with comprehending the redistribution of different powers and competences, associated with the concept of sovereignty, to non-state actors exercising those powers in relation to their own territories. In this view of things, sovereignty is a bundle of powers, competences, rights, duties, privileges, and immunities – it is a bundle of legal relations that make up what is currently associated with the concept of sovereignty – and that different actors can 'hold' elements of this bundle.

In the following section, I work through and apply two relevant legal realist insights in more detail. I first briefly summarise the approach to

Herzog (2020) who would possibly call this 'ideal' notion the 'classic theory of sovereignty', at xi.

legal rights in legal realism, before introducing the idea of legal bundles and its value to understanding sovereignty and demonstrate how we might think about the concept of sovereignty operating in light of this.

5.1.1 Legal Realistic Approach to Sovereignty

Legal Rights: According to a legal realist way of thinking, 'a "right" exists when its possessor has the aid of some organized governmental society in controlling the conduct of another person'.[7] What is important is that there is 'some organised governmental society' that is doing the controlling – and international society is still organised and governed even if it is (and always has been) more 'complex' than the state-made ordering assumed by public international law. This understanding accords with the expanded understanding of the actors that exercise control from Chapter 4 that is necessary to grasp the changes in international legal and political systems (and of course we could problematise the assumption that there ever was a time when states did so wholly and exclusively exercise power).

Corbin would add to this understanding of legal rights that 'we cannot say once a right always a right, or here a right everywhere a right' and continues by saying that what is considered a right 'all depends, and it depends wholly, on what the individuals of the organised communities will actually do'.[8] What it depends on, therefore, is the content of the actual existing positive legal order, by which Corbin understands whatever the 'organised community' normatively will lend its aid to when it comes to controlling the conduct of its members.[9] Rights then are contingent and dynamic; they are constructed by an organised community. Notably in this regard, Corbin does not reify nor deify one particular actor, referring to an 'organised community' which may imply different institutional arrangements. Nor does he suppose a uniform or static spatiality to the application of legal rights. By doing so, legal realism offers a socially constructivist understanding of legal rights and how to diagnose their existence in an organised community.

The purpose here is not to defend international law from criticisms advanced by Austinians, who contend that without hierarchical and centralised power, there is no law. This has been thoroughly countered elsewhere, including by Kelsen: the lack of vertically integrated political

[7] Corbin (1924) at 501, 502.
[8] ibid at 508.
[9] This has parallels with Kelsen's basic definition of positive law as a system that is both normative and coercive. See, in particular, Kelsen (1967) at 198–204, 214–17.

structures in the international arena does not deprive the international legal order of its legal character.[10] Although this theoretical framework is equally as useful for achieving this. Instead, the purpose is rather to understand the idea of a right in law and the idea of organised communities, in order to follow the rights to new rights holders 'beyond the state'. Relatedly, legal realist analysis has been equally applied to contract law, which is a more horizontal and, especially in common law systems, historically at least, a customary legal regime. ('But look at contract law' is also a useful international lawyer's response to those who have overdosed on Austin and think that international law is not law and consequently that international legal rights are not legal rights in a pure sense.[11])

Bundles of Legal Relations: To understand the usefulness of the idea of legal bundles that are central to this rethink, it is important to first understand what constitutes these bundles; in particular, insights regarding legal rights, duties, privileges, and immunities developed by Hohfeld, as it is these, combined, that form bundles. The idea is that there are distinct fundamental legal categories that make up the larger 'bundles of legal relations' which might be called the right to life, or the right to a fair trial, or 'territorial sovereignty' (more on territorial sovereignty later).

Singer describes the different varieties of legal entitlements, and their opposites, that can go into the making of a bundle as follows:

> Hohfeld identifies eight basic legal rights: four primary legal entitlements (rights, privileges, powers, and immunities) and their opposites (no-rights, duties, disabilities and liabilities). "Rights" are claims, enforceable by state power, that others act in a certain manner in relation to the rightholder. "Privileges" are permissions to act in a certain manner without being liable for damages to others and without others being able to summon state power to prevent those acts. "Powers" are state-enforced abilities to change legal entitlements held by oneself or others, and "immunities" are security from having one's legal entitlements changed by others.
>
> The four negations or opposites of the primary legal entitlements refer to the absence of such entitlements. One has "no-right" if one does not have the power to summon the aid of the state to alter or control the behaviour of others. "Duties" refer to the absence of permission to act in a certain manner. "Disabilities" are the absence of power to alter legal entitlements and "liabilities" refer to the absence of immunity from having one's own entitlements changed by others.[12]

[10] Kelsen (1950) at 706–8; Kelsen (1953).
[11] Rasulov (2016a).
[12] Singer (1982) at 975, 982.

Now of course, the description will change slightly in international law application: for example, 'state power' must be replaced by the horizontal legal mechanisms found in international law. Singer was referring primarily to a domestic legal system, but these insights are equally applicable to international law as already established above.

Hohfeld then spoke of these primary legal entitlements (and their opposites) as *aggregating* in many possible different ways,[13] developed into the idea of bundles by subsequent legal realists.[14] This arrangement might be called 'a bundle of legal relations – rights, powers, privileges and immunities'.[15] Thus, these eight categories are assembled into 'bundles' of legal relations to create, for example, the right to life. Rasulov observes 'the "regular" right to life is, in fact, a privilege; the accompanying right to due process in case of death while in custody, on the other hand, is a right'[16] and of course it is not a right actually held by the person whose life it is (or was) but often their next of kin. Thus, there may be a number of different legal relations contained in the right to life, including, for example: a privilege to live one's life; a right to humane treatment in police or state custody, and correlatively police have no right to treat prisoners inhumanely; no right to die, for example, within the Council of Europe territory due to *Pretty v UK*,[17] which is really a disability for the individual, and a liability on the part of the third party (e.g., Dignitas), and so on and so forth. Moreover, and crucially, the right to life may be differently aggregated in the future and is already so in various legal systems around the world; legal entitlements change in different times (past and future) and spaces (EU, India, US, Cuba, UNHCR), and their arrangement in the right to life bundle alterable.

This approach has two main insights informing how we might think about legal concepts such as sovereignty: those which are usually called rights are not always only rights per se (a legal entitlement to something), nor are they singular monolithic constructs. First, they may instead be privileges or immunities, or conversely duties may be liabilities or 'no rights'. Second, that which are commonly referred to as a 'right', are bundled and not singular legal constructs. In international law then, the 'right to life' in human rights treaties, the 'right of self-determination', the

[13] See discussion on this in Johnson (2007) at 247, 253–54.

[14] ibid at 247.

[15] Corbin (1922) at 429, 429.

[16] Rasulov (2016b).

[17] *Pretty v United Kingdom* [2002] European Court of Human Rights Application no. 2346/02.

'right to exercise sovereignty over territory', etc. refer to complex legal regimes and are not monolithic essences; they do not describe singular nor unidirectional legal relations. Rather, each represents a highly complex, composite arrangement of distinct legal relations.[18] As we have seen, the right to life is a bundle composed of many small separate legal categories; it is not one right. Similarly, the right to property 'consists of a number of disparate rights, a "bundle" of them: the right to possess, the right to use, the right to exclude, the right to transfer'.[19] Some scholars have understood sovereignty thus; not least, Kennedy who argues: 'juridically sovereignty . . . [is at once] a unified idea, and at the same time, a bundle of rights to be parcelled out in a whole bunch of different directions'.[20]

The second insight from this approach is that there exists no 'natural' or 'correct' way to assemble any given bundle: every bundle of legal relations can be arranged in many ways. Applied to the concept of property: 'the concept of the bundle of sticks, with different "owners" holding different sticks, meant that property ownership was a very flexible concept'.[21] Ownership can thus appear in 'an almost infinite variety of ways'.[22] Ownership will be understood differently in different legal regimes. A duty to inform, and more often than not a duty to apply for permission to, a local authority about changes to the external appearance of a house will be different were the legally recognised owner to find their house in a space with a specially designated heritage status compared to an owner with a house in a space not thus designated. The same also applies to sovereignty. Each state's exercise of sovereign rights shifts from space to space. The rights of states are different within the EEZ compared to within their capital city. This is well established. On a more granular level, one state's rights in relation to the space of their capital city will not be the same as another's: one state may have a bilateral investment treaty (BIT) protecting the rights of foreign investors in relation to particular sites in their capital city, whereas another state may not allow any foreign ownership of property in their capital city or specified areas.[23]

[18] Rasulov (2016) at 3.

[19] Dukeminier, Krier, and Alexander (2006) at 81.

[20] Der Derian and others (2007) at 187.

[21] Johnson (2007) at 254.

[22] ibid.

[23] Thinking here of the introduction of new laws by Canada as of 1 January 2023 (Prohibition on the Purchase of Residential Property by Non-Canadians Act). According to the New York Times, 'the prohibition applies only in "census metropolitan areas" and "census agglomerations" – basically, cities that meet certain population criteria – and not to vacation homes in "recreational areas"' (Kaminer (2022)). This

This analysis does not assume that the regimes related to property and sovereignty are equivalent. There is a great deal of scholarship showing how the practice of sovereignty is either similar or dissimilar to the regime of property law.[24] Thus, in the eyes of those who reject sovereignty as ownership, it might be contended that a legal realist analysis of property cannot be applied directly to sovereignty because the legal regimes are not similar. There are two reasons this is not the case. Firstly, an absolute analogy between property and territory is not required. It is, I think, futile to outline an absolute analogy between property and territory – the history of the ideas, how similar the concepts are in reality, etc – although many scholars have discussed this in insightful ways,[25] because, while certain elements or structures of legal thinking and reasoning might be somewhat similar between the two (and some elements might look more similar to domestic property law depending on one's legal training and influence), the regimes are not exactly the same. Instead, I focus on how the legal realist *analytical framework* can be helpful to understand *legal rights and duties* generally; sovereignty being a bundle of these. Secondly, the legal realist framework can and has been applied to analyse everything from contracts, the corporation, and trusts to the right to life. It is not limited to ownership regimes in the first place.[26]

It is invaluable as a way of thinking about legal relations, for it also helps convey the complexity and concreteness of these relations: '[j]ust as

move has been criticised for missing the point and blaming the foreigner for 'low interest rates and very low supply' ('Explained' (2023)). I think it is more complicated than either simple narrative. The issue is not 'foreigners', nor can it be addressed by creating a greater supply of housing. I have found Massey's explanation of the issues that arise because of global financial industries to be very helpful in this regard. See, specifically, Massey (2005) at 155–59, 166–69.

24 Starting with Jennings (1963); Shaw (1982), in particular 74. Elsewhere, it is assumed that: 'When it comes to acquisition and transfer of territory of states international law treats it not entirely unlike property' (in Raible (2018) 315, 8).

25 Others have examined to what extent sovereignty over territory and property in land resemble one another or originate from roman law concepts of *dominium* and *imperium*; some debate the usefulness of thinking like this or point out the logical differences between the two. This has been well covered and is an interesting point to research further, but it is outside the scope of this thesis. In some ways, it is neither here nor there; the contribution from legal realism does not require an absolute analogy between the two to prove useful – mostly because it is helpful to explain legal rights generally which territorial sovereignty is a bundle of. For a discussion of the former see: Jennings (1963) at 2–6; Lauterpacht (1970) at 219; Shaw (2014) at 363; Orford (2008) at 984; Bílková in Kuijer and Werner (2017) at 34; Larkins (2009) at 127–30.

26 See, e.g., Easterbrook (1989).

there is no right amount of paint on a car, there is no right relation among managers, investors, and other corporate participants. The relation must be worked out one firm at a time.'[27] Any given analysis is only ever providing a snapshot into the distribution of legal relations. Similarly, 'sovereignty' is not the same for every state. Each state has different rights, duties, privileges, immunities, etc. At one level more abstracted, the functional or sectoral areas of competences (tax, health, security, foreign relations, transport) are also different for each state. This is obvious if we consider that states are, for example, members of different international and regional organisations or, as another example, have signed different BITs with one another. The legal relations of a state in the EU will be very different from the legal relations of a state recently having left the EU, or a state that is instead a member of the AU. While the EU may have the most pervasive[28] 'reach' into the sovereignty powers originally thought to lie with states, the AU is increasingly competent in relation to its scope of powers. For example, it has a well-developed and different regional peace and security arrangement.[29] Obviously the legal rights, duties, privileges, and immunities remaining in the state are different for Greece than for Libya because they are members of different organisations, but they would also be different for Libya than for Somalia, when there was an AU peace operation deployed (African Union Mission in Somalia (AMISOM), replaced by the African Union Transition Mission in Somalia (ATMIS), with effect from 1 April 2022).[30]

There is no 'objectively correct' way to configure the bundle, but this is the very way that international legal positivists think, if they suggest that sovereignty only remains in the state despite evidence of legal relations being distributed amongst different actors. It is, in many ways, the same thing as believing in natural law: that there is a proper order of things. How the bundle of sovereignty is put together is a question of *policy*, that is, choice, rather than 'logic' or 'truth'. Here, Hohfeld's interest 'in having [acknowledged] that judges were making policy choices that reflected social values'[31] is important. When using and abusing the term sovereignty, what international legal positivists, political party slogans about 'taking back sovereignty', and state speeches before the UNSC about

[27] ibid at 1428.
[28] de Mars (2020) at 88–89; Berry and others (2022) at 58.
[29] Jeng (2012) at 10–11; AfriMAP (2007) at 10.
[30] UN Security Council Resolution 2670 (21 December 2022) S/RES/2670 (2022).
[31] Johnson (2007) at 252.

intervening in a situation or not have in common is that this is all a question of politics and policy. Schlag also emphasises the benefits of this approach in exposing the policy and political role in constituting the arrangement of legal relations.[32] By adopting this we expose the normativity in sovereignty as currently understood and arranged.

To bring time back into focus, we might understand that many of these powers and rights may be retained by state actors but not for all time. So, for example, the parts of the bundle relating to 'permanent sovereignty over natural resources' (PSNR), in the way the sovereignty bundle is normatively arranged (i.e., the content of the positive legal system) today, is not as simple as all states having equally temporally unlimited, broad-ranging legal powers. PSNR is generally considered to have been a great win by newly decolonised states to have their PSNR recognised.[33] Yet, when we break down the bundle of rights in relation to natural resources, there is a different story to be told. While PSNR is hoped to be a recognition of an 'inalienable right', it is to an abstract and 'woolly'[34] idea. There is an obligation that the PSNR right 'must be exercised in the interest of their national development and of the well-being of the people of the State concerned'.[35] This has been exposed by Usha Natarajan as problematic: 'establishing control over their own natural resources was understood by Third World international lawyers as fundamental to postcolonial states' sovereignty and independence. That is to say, along with sovereign statehood, postcolonial states also inherited Western understandings about nature, including the role of the sovereign in disciplining the natural environment through law and making it optimally productive.'[36] The 'sovereign' rights were assumed by newly independent states with certain pre-loaded content which involved taming nature being a central governance mission of a 'legitimate' state.[37] Moreover, the idea of permanency is problematic, as the general bundle that might be associated with PSNR has been subsequently, and is continually being, modified by different regimes, in

[32] Schlag (2015) at 190.
[33] UN General Assembly Resolution 1803 (XVII) of 14 December 1962, 'Permanent sovereignty over natural resources'.
[34] Brownlie (1979) at 262.
[35] Operative Paragraph 1, UNGA Res 1803 (XVII). Nico Schrijver also recognises a number of duties that are involved with this right (Schrijver (2015)).
[36] Usha Natarajan (2017) at 213.
[37] Yao (2022) at 10–11.

particular, by the international investment law regime with the continually shifting power balance between states and private parties. The devil is in the detail of each BIT, contract, and determination of appropriate compensation.[38]

Moreover, the geographical imaginary of PSNR is one of conceptual smoothness, with little variation or discontinuities. Yet, Ferguson in 'Seeing Like an Oil Company', highlights the issue of extractive enclaving with foreign investors, foreign workers, and private security firms 'walled off' from the local population and with an immense ability to 'by pass the nation-state frame altogether'.[39] Putting aside that this imaginary still appears to rely, even if for descriptive purposes, on the idea of the state-territory as enframed, Ferguson's account points to the redistribution of power and competences between states, international organisations, and private MNCs and these practices of control are employed differently in relation to different spaces. Indeed, the use of private security firms rather than local military or policing is an important control mechanism for these spaces; they are a 'new technology of spatial and social regulation'.[40] According to Ferguson, 'global capitalism has neither abandoned Africa nor swept it up in a grand process of global homogenization and standardization. Rather, capital "hops" over "unusable Africa," alighting only in mineral-rich enclaves that are starkly disconnected from their national societies.'[41] Arboleda too, in his account of the spatial practices of planetary extraction, shows that there is no 'internally determined "hegemon"' such as the state that 'autonomously articulates a geopolitical project', but instead a myriad of companies from different countries,

[38] Nicolás Perrone makes a persuasive argument that legal techniques to control and use resources, such as the particular framing and content of property rights and then the subsequent shift to a 'particular view' of contractual techniques makes economic sovereignty of states 'impossible'. See Perrone (2017). We might also think of the implications of Toni Marzal's work on compensation and damages in ISDS. He notes that 'there has been a growing disquiet at the sheer amounts that have been awarded, as these seem to be constantly increasing and reaching, in some notable cases, multi-billion dollar figures. Among such mega-awards, as they are sometimes labelled, we may cite *TCC v Pakistan* (USD 5.84 billion), *Occidental v Ecuador* (USD 2.3 billion), *Yukos v Russia* (USD 50 billion), or *ConocoPhillips v Venezuela* (USD 8.7 billion), all of which amount to the staggering fraction of around 2% of the GDP of the respective countries.' Marzal (2021) at 249, 251. The potential to be hit with such enormous costs, may prevent states from acting.

[39] Ferguson (2005) at 379.

[40] ibid at 380.

[41] ibid.

employing labour from different workforces often produced by transnational migration flows.[42]

Like PSNR, citizenship and taxation are also functions commonly associated with the state. They are still assumed to be matters which are essentially within their domestic jurisdiction. Yet, these categories are too broad: many tax powers are exercised by state and non-state actors alike.[43] I am not only talking of the offshore as 'beyond the state', but that the likes of the City of London is the playground for multiple actors exercising control over tax powers. These are not contiguous, homogeneous, nor synchronised territories which the concept of territory in international law imagines. In the case of citizenship, the AU and EU are increasingly exercising many of the functions and powers previously exercised by states. As citizenship in the EU shows, this is not homogeneous across the entire territory of the EU. The complexities of EU territory and legal rights show there are often multiple, differently configured, territorial frameworks existing at the same time even for the purposes of citizenship. This makes the temporality of territory variable and the quality of the space uneven rather than uniform. Prior to Brexit, EU citizens could study at Scottish universities for free, but the same was not true for citizens from the rest of the UK. As a result, some EU citizens had different rights in some parts of EU territory in comparison to others. The African Economic Community, for example, is developing an African passport, and with this is taking on an institutional function comparable to the EU. The AU Commission facilitates the issuing of the passport and provides technical support to member states.[44] The territory of EU or AU territory will not be representatable on a map as exactly the same space for all competences. In comparison, with the homogeneous spatial imaginary usually associated with territory, this is represented as smooth uniform space. I return to EU territory in more detail below.

Finally, it should be noted that clearly sovereignty is divisible in this understanding. As Bartelson observes:

> although indivisibility has long been regarded a necessary attribute of sovereignty, scholars have equally long argued that this requirement does not correspond to empirical facts and, therefore, ought to be abandoned in favor of conceptions that are more closely aligned to political reality. In modern times, sovereignty has almost invariably been internally

[42] Arboleda (2020) at 69.
[43] On this, I have written in some detail. See Lythgoe (2022) at 171.
[44] AEC Protocol (2018) Article 10.

> divided between different authorities, and externally it has been constantly compromised through contractual and other means.[45]

The prevailing and long-held opinion in international law is that sovereignty is divisible. Ever since at least 1912 there has, at least according to Oppenheim, been 'no doubt about the fact that there are semi-independent States in existence, it may well be maintained that sovereignty is divisible'.[46] We may problematise this notion of 'semi-independent states' and also whether there are 'fully' independent states today in the way Oppenheim imagined. Relatedly, and given such the globalisation of law and governance that is the *problematique* of this inquiry, where I might differ further is that I advance the idea that sovereignty is divisible, indeed has been divided and distributed, across wider categories of actors than just states.

This insight points to what is being refashioned by global governance and globalisation while at the same time diagnosing why the orthodox theory tends to produce the rise/decline or obsoletion narratives in relation to sovereignty. A monolithic concept of sovereignty makes it appear as if sovereignty is waning: '[s]ome jurists have proposed to abolish the notion of the sovereignty of States, considering it obsolete'.[47] Understanding sovereignty as exclusive and whole, leads to all or nothing determinations; if sovereignty is understood monolithically, it becomes 'nothing' or obsolete. This arises *because of* the overly essentialised and over-determined bundle. We are left with little option but to think of sovereignty as waning. Instead, now various actors are exercising powers traditionally exercised by the state in relation to their legal and political spaces. Therefore, the discipline urgently requires an understanding of territory and sovereignty accounting for the distribution (and redistribution) of competences, liberties, powers, and rights traditionally associated with states but now exercised by different actors.

5.1.2 A Rebirth for Sovereignty

Like the concept of territory, the concept of sovereignty could not be thought of as having a fixed, unchangeable content nor that the legal bundle only 'belongs' to one category of actors. The legal rights

[45] Bartelson (2011).

[46] Oppenheim (1912) para 70.

[47] Separate Opinion by Judge Alvarez, *Corfu Channel (United Kingdom of Great Britain and Northern Ireland v Albania)* [1949] ICJ Reports 1949 4 (International Court of Justice) at para 43.

associated with sovereignty do not *have to evolve* into a predetermined form. Like territory, the concept of sovereignty is understood generally to be a relatively static bundle of legal rights; it is frozen in one particular configuration, that in the sometimes-confused international law discourse, is both understood as *title for states* and the consequent *rights states have over their territories*. Insights from legal realism allows us to understand that these concepts are (often similar) bundles of legal relations, which instead could be understood as alterable, reconfigurable, combinable, and recombinable in an infinite number of times and ways. In this view of things, there is no one configuration that is predetermined and 'correct'.

Approaching our understanding of the concept of sovereignty in this way helps explain the dynamics of what is happening to the bundle of powers relating to sovereignty, considering the increasing importance of non-state actors in international law making, international relations, and governance. There are many who now argue that 'contemporary sovereignties are far more complex than notions of mutually exclusive territories can capture'.[48] Competences and powers traditionally assumed to be state-territorially delimited and organised have been 'increasingly emancipated ... and create their own reality'.[49] Regardless of whether 'their own realities' follow a similar spatial logic to state territory (homogeneous, contiguous, ordered space) or are differently spatially configured, non-state actors can be thought of as increasingly exercising elements of the sovereignty bundle historically deemed to lie wholly or mostly with the state.

So rather than these elements – legal rights, immunities, powers, competences, functions, etc. – of the sovereignty bundle, in being 'emancipated', floating free of territorial states, the bundle is being reconfigured and re-assigned to different actors each reterritorialising these powers in their own relevant spaces – those in which they exercise control, consequently their territories. Thus, several actors, both state and non-state, are exercising different elements of the bundle, controlling and influencing these elements in relation to their own territories. But this can only be understood once the concept of territory has been de-essentialised, dephysicalised, and denaturalised. It also requires understanding territories as frameworks overlapping the same physical

[48] Sassen (2013) at 32.
[49] Helmig and Kessler (2007) at 241.

geography, with no one actor 'owning' physical geography exclusively (more on this below).

We do not need then to 'bury' sovereignty à la Herzog.[50] Just as we do not need to abandon the concept of territory and turn to functionalism instead. Yet, the precise content of that bundle called sovereign power is most definitely up for negotiation. Are there some essential elements of the bundle of sovereignty that ought to be included? Given my railing against essentialising territory, I try not to essentialise other concepts. Here I find Mégret's work on whether there are inherently sovereign functions in international law instrumental to my thinking on this.[51] Although I am less convinced by his argument that there *should* be inherently sovereign functions 'if international legal arguments militate against its privatization or outsourcing by the state'.[52] These are not, to my mind, legal arguments but political arguments, and I am sympathetic to the politics that underlies these. Moreover, I would perhaps go a step further and problematise whether there has ever been a stable content for 'the public and the private sphere' for these spheres now to be blurred. My take on this for the purposes of this book is simply if the international law community, including but not limited to states, politicians, activists, practitioners, scholars, finds it useful discursively to call something sovereign powers, and the concept is still clearly in use and has some (blurry and sometimes ambiguous) content assigned to it, then it continues.[53]

5.2 Of Jurisdiction

Jurisdiction is another concept that has been closely intertwined with the traditional understanding of territory, so closely that the default position behind much of this discourse still assumes that state territory forms the normal base for jurisdiction and every other mode of exercising jurisdiction is regarded as *extra*ordinary. In this section, applying the concept of

[50] Herzog (2020).

[51] Mégret (2021). Even where I disagree with it, this article's clear and concise argument and synthesis of the discourse creates the circumstances for thought provocation and debate.

[52] Mégret (2021) at 452, 454.

[53] Although I sympathise with those who find sovereignty a troublesome concept. I also leave it here because otherwise the book would be at least twice as long and a lot less coherent. 'It is outwith the scope of this study' but there is definitely room for further legal theoretical development. The same goes for the supposed distinction between public/private binaries.

territory as socially produced space, I show how the proposed reconceptualisation disrupts the 'supposed' extraterritoriality of jurisdiction. We can, in its place, account for the spaces where states (and other actors) exercise any particular power at any one point in time, *wherever that may be*, not as extraordinary, but as ordinary.

That the concept of jurisdiction is mediated by, or indeed premised on, the concept of territory is something of a commonplace. According to Bethlehem, '[f]lowing from sovereignty comes also the principle of state jurisdiction, that is, the authority of a state to govern persons, conduct, and property by its municipal law. Jurisdiction, although it has non-territorial dimensions, is largely manifest in territorial terms.'[54] In this regard, we should note as well that for Bethlehem sovereignty too 'rests fundamentally on ... territory'. Akehurst writes, 'jurisdiction ... can have a large number of different meanings' but 'sometimes it simply means territory'.[55] Similarly, Fawcett observed that 'jurisdiction and territory are so closely linked that statements about the one are often equivalent to statements about the other'.[56] Evocatively, Ryngaert, quoting Baldus, notes, 'territory and jurisdiction go together "as a mist to a swamp"'.[57]

5.2.1 *There Is Nothing Extra about Extraterritoriality*

The centrality of territory to the operationalisation of jurisdiction *produces* the structure dividing the concept of jurisdiction into territorial and *extra*territorial jurisdiction. Thus, according to Mills, 'territoriality is *supplemented* by other bases of jurisdiction'.[58] The word 'supplements' indicates these other bases of jurisdiction are something additional to territoriality, the core. Ryngaert uses the language of the exceptional to demonstrate how international lawyers understand the other bases too, stating that '[o]ther grounds of jurisdiction than the territoriality principle ("extraterritorial jurisdiction") are not logically deduced from that principle. Instead,' according to Ryngaert, these other bases '*function as exceptions to the cornerstones of international law* – territoriality,

[54] Bethlehem (2014) at 14.
[55] Akehurst (1982) at 102. It survives to modern day renditions of Akehurst, including Malanczuk (1997) at 109.
[56] Fawcett (1971) at 427.
[57] Ryngaert in d'Aspremont and Singh (2019) at 578.
[58] Mills (2014) at 187, 197, emphasis added.

sovereign equality, and non-intervention'.[59] Wallace too adopts the language of exceptionality where she notes that 'jurisdiction is primarily exercised on a territorial basis, but there are exceptions . . . there will be occasions when a state may exercise jurisdiction outside its territory'.[60]

Extraterritoriality is not a real-world ontological phenomenon but a narrative to explain the extraordinary exercise of power not fitting the ordinary model. The extraordinary – extraterritoriality – explains the manifestation of state power beyond state territory. But, as Ryngaert has pointed out, the term is confusing, suggesting extraterritorial jurisdiction 'ought to imply that a state exercises its jurisdiction without any territorial link ("extra-territorial"), although the expression is typically used in a context of States asserting jurisdiction on the basis of some admittedly non-exclusive, territorial link'.[61] This narrative is created because territory (and crucially this territory is equated with the physical geography) is assumed to be a stable, static 'starting point' or container of *exclusive* state activities. There is territory and then all other bases of jurisdiction are extra, demonstrating the centrality of territory to understanding and conceptualising jurisdiction even if only as a point of reference, because of course, according to Ryngaert, 'the international law of jurisdiction does not seem to prioritise the bases of jurisdiction'.[62] Ryngaert has elsewhere reflected on a 'territorial/extraterritorial binary' which he says have come to be 'viewed as natural, reflecting the cartographic carving up of the world into distinct territorial entities (States)'.[63] In a recent debate, O'Keefe argues, in response to Krisch's argument that there is an urgent need to rethink jurisdiction acknowledging the move away from a once-vital territorial jurisdiction,[64] that international law has long provided for extraterritorial heads of jurisdiction – and there are sixty plus years of practice evidencing this.[65] While international law 'always has' provided an exceptional jurisdiction, the point is precisely that this reasoning is structured territorially; it is just this has for a protracted period of time no longer really been exceptional despite the name. The 'remains' of the exceptionalising structure of legal thought, being structured by a

[59] Ryngaert (2015) at 37, emphasis added.
[60] Wallace (1986) at 101.
[61] Ryngaert (2015) at 7.
[62] ibid at 143.
[63] Ryngaert in d'Aspremont and Singh (2019) at 578.
[64] Krisch (2022) at 481.
[65] O'Keefe (2008) at 520–22.

particular concept of territory, is still traceable.[66] Territory endures, fundamentally, even according to O'Keefe, as 'the analytical starting point'.[67] The international law of jurisdiction has, in other words, 'retained an essentially "territorial orientation"'.[68]

Applying the concept of territory advanced in this book helps explain many of the phenomena otherwise associated with extraterritoriality, at least in so far as these concerns states.[69] Even now, nothing actually *is* extraterritorial; extraterritoriality is a narrative explaining where states are exercising power. It acts as a justification for why and how a state exercises power in a physical geography beyond where it is 'supposed' to. Given that where powers are exercised is not, in reality, limited to a uniform and permanent unit of space, the reliance on an understanding of territory as an object and its equation with physical geography requires the creation of this ordinary and extraordinary distinction. But it is not the only way of thinking about it. We could instead imagine territory as spatially extending to cover the space where any state (or any other actor) is exercising a particular function or power.[70]

Territory as relational and produced through practices of control could instead drive a different narrative that does not adopt normative ordinary or extraordinary assumptions – or at least not 'ordinary starting references, because perhaps there are just different 'oughts', exceptions, 'supposeds'. Territory in this way of thinking accounts for the spaces in relation to which states (and other actors) exercise particular powers at any one point in time, wherever that may be. In that sense then, I am suggesting that the *extra*-ordinary element be removed such that the 'ordinary' has the capacity to explain the spatial strategy for the exercise

66 Given this structure of exceptionalism exists in jurisdiction and in subjecthood, it only serves to highlight there is an over-essentialisation and over-determination of the state and territory in international law. The general rule is that states exercise sovereignty and jurisdiction territorially and are the only actor to 'have' a territory, synchronising the exercise of sovereignty and jurisdiction in relation to that territory. It is also this state-centric orthodox concept of territory that makes it difficult to establish the space where competences and powers are reterritorialised.

67 O'Keefe (2022) at 520.

68 ibid, 517, citing Krisch.

69 This is simply because non-state actors are not thought to exercise jurisdiction. There are those who are working on the idea of the jurisdiction of international organisations. See Burton (2018).

70 I deconstructed the traditional assumption of territory as a unit with static temporality and how we might otherwise think of territory as existing in a more dynamic temporality explaining movement. See Sections 3.3.5 and 4.4.

of power regardless of where it is. This might seem radical, but conceptualising territory as proposed achieves this.

Let us take the example of EU measures (including the Fuel Quality Directive, the Timber Regulation, and the Maritime Emissions Regulation)[71] aimed at reducing the carbon footprint of imports of goods and services consumed by EU citizens. These measures have been framed by many as an extraterritorial exercise of power 'circumventing the territorial system'.[72] It is framed thus due to the underlying spatial assumptions about how territory ought to work, creating extraterritoriality. (Here we assume lawyers accept the EU has a territory, which is not uncontroversial, but is often adopted without reflection. This is explored further below.) Territory as relational, and produced through practices of control, explains that for the duration of these directives, the EU's territory, for the purpose of these powers, is more than the homogeneous unit of EU geographical space. We can see this territorial extension as a *strategy* and as *relational*: as 'using [the EU's] market power to extend the geographical reach of its [greenhouse gas] mitigation efforts'.[73]

This concept of territory also offers an alternative narrative to interpret instances of extraterritoriality that the ECtHR has so famously struggled with. In *Al-Skeini*[74] and *Jaloud*,[75] the ECtHR found extraterritorial jurisdictional justifications to ensure accountability for human rights abuses. The Court appeared to find personal jurisdiction too weak a ground to wholly rely on, preferring territorial jurisdiction and, as a result, created a 'back up',[76] namely the exercise of extraterritorial powers in Iraq at the likes of a checkpoint to find that the UK and Netherlands failed in their duties to promote and uphold human rights beyond the ordinary, aka 'their territory'. With the concept of territory outlined in this book, this extraterritorial narrative does not need to be constructed, because it can account for *wherever* the UK and Netherlands exercise control at a particular point in time and view it as part of their territory for that particular purpose or function. It is thus under their jurisdiction

[71] Directive 98/70/EC (October 1998); Regulation 995/2010 (October 2010); Regulation 2015/757 (April 2015).

[72] Dobson (2018) at 75, 75.

[73] Scott (2015) at 92, 93.

[74] *Al-Skeini and Others v The United Kingdom* [2011] Grand Chamber, European Court of Human Rights Application no. 55721/07.

[75] *Jaloud v The Netherlands* [2014] Grand Chamber, European Court of Human Rights Application no. 47708/08.

[76] Miltner (2012) at 693, 738.

for the purposes of Article 1 of the ECHR and they can be held accountable. According to Ryngaert, *Al-Skeini* and *Jaloud* demonstrate the 'non-exclusive, territorial link'[77] basis for jurisdiction, but according to the proposed approach, the jurisdiction is simply territorial. The use of exclusivity here is revealing and is explored, and reinterpreted, further below. Exclusivity, in the sense Ryngaert uses it, is a myth because no actor exercises control exclusively in relation to physical geography. This situation could, applying this spatial imaginary, be distinguished from instances of 'kidnapping' suspects and exercising power, not over cities or checkpoints, but over individuals (as in *Eichmann*) which is more personal jurisdiction (extra-territorial jurisdiction without any spatial link, or 'without any territorial link' in the sense Ryngaert advocates).[78]

The proposed concept of territory can also make sense of situations of colonial exercise of power that de Lapradelle articulated in connection with French and Tunisian territory (explored in the previous chapter). The distinction at times between (neo-)colonialism and the exercise of extraterritorial jurisdiction can be arbitrary and will be viewed differently by different people. The EU could be said to be exercising 'neo-imperialism' as well as extraterritoriality in requiring compliance with climate change directions by non-EU states. What I have described regarding reinterpreting extraterritoriality is similar to what de Lapradelle argued regarding Tunisian and French territories: he was not arguing France had extraterritorial powers in Tunisia but that the same geographical space was also part of the territory of France – whether that be right or wrong legally, morally or politically. This conceptualisation of territory means we can instead challenge such situations by asking *why* a state is exercising powers in any particular place, because now we understand the strategic use of territory to exercise control. Tunisian territory is not naturally and 'originally' Tunisian. No territory is natural, it is instead continually produced through practices.

5.3 A Legal Theory of Territory: The Legal Relationship

The final step is to offer an account of the legal relationship between actors and their territories. This is to expound how this alternative

[77] Ryngaert (2015) at 7.

[78] ibid. Although I would still argue it is a strategy based on relations, and if all relations take place in space, then there is a spatiality to this personal jurisdiction – it just may not be a territorial one.

conception of territory can be re-inserted and applied into the legal theoretical account of international law.[79] There are two main threads to this. The first insight corrects the understanding of the legal relationship that is most important: law is *not* describing a relationship between actors and space, for territory as we have established, is created as a result of the exercise of control, and thus we understand that relationship already, but instead law describes the relationship *between actors*. This reframes the word exclusivity that is often carelessly tossed around, as the right to act, to the exclusion of others, in relation to objects, over peoples, activities, processes, etc. The second thread, as a result of the first, but also as a result of the conceptualisation of territory as social space constituted by the exercise of power, is to drop the idea of title to territory from our legal theoretical accounts of territory. For both, insights from legal realism and social constructivism are key.

5.3.1 *Emending Exclusivity*

A major contribution of legal realism to legal thought was to understand that the relationship in property law is not between the individual and 'their' property but between the particular right holder and all others, that is, those against whom the rights can be enforced, those whom have duties to the right holder, etc. Property *consists of legal relationships between different actors* rather than 'ownership of things or relationships between owners and things'.[80]

This insight is as useful to understanding the relationship between the state, or whatever institution is exercising 'sovereign' powers, and territory in international law as it is for conceptualising 'property'. Thus, 'the right (Recht) is always directed against a person ... The territory is a moment in the existence of the state, a designation of its spatial impenetrability. Land indeed, as a thing, supports human beings ... but the state is in relationship to [human beings not to territory].'[81] A state is also understood primarily, for the purposes of international law, in relation to other states, international organisations, and private actors, not their territory.

This insight helps make sense of the broader move to dephysicalise the concept of territory for the purposes of international law. In a similar way

[79] This is a modest attempt. It will no doubt spark off further discussion and expounding, as there are many facets to this.

[80] Johnson (2007) at 249.

[81] Rovira (2017) at 319, 329.

that territory is primarily associated with the physical space, traditionally property too was associated primarily with land, then other physical material things, such as cars or boats. Consequently, there was a focus on a '"physicalist" definition' which struggled with 'new, abstract, and intangible forms of wealth such as business goodwill or copyright and patent rights'.[82] But legal realists reframed this debate fundamentally, understanding that 'property is an abstraction. It refers not to things, material or otherwise, but to rights or relationships among people.'[83] This approach acknowledges that property regimes consist of legal relations. It is therefore analytically insightful for understanding space as socially constructed through relations too.

While it might be easy to think of sovereignty, in its monolith form, as a legal relationship between states ('their equal rank to other sovereign States are consequences of their sovereignty'[84]), in practice rights are often seen as *rights to* the physical geography. International lawyers often lose sight of the actual legal relationship. 'Sovereignty over natural resources' may be framed as a relationship between the state and 'its' natural resources, as opposed to rights and relationships among states and other actors. 'Sovereignty over natural resources' ought to be broken down into its component parts, for example, the right to mine, the right to create licenses for others to mine, the duty to protect territorial waters, rights and duties in relation to freshwater management, duties and powers in relation to conservation of, for example, biological diversity. *Exclusivity is in relation to the rights or duties*, not that these resources 'belong' to the states for all purposes. In other words, the exclusivity of one right or set of rights does not entail the exclusivity of other rights in relation to the physical geography. Thus, state A might retain the exclusive right to mine without retaining exclusive right of passage, as in the cases of overflight or innocent passage in territorial waters.

This may be further demonstrated by considering the continental shelf and EEZ where there are sovereign rights; these spaces, however, have never been assumed to be 'exclusive' areas of the state. In these areas, states have the rights designated by UNCLOS[85] and

[82] Horwitz (1992) at 145.

[83] Dukeminier, Krier, and Alexander (2006) at 81.

[84] Besson (2011).

[85] Article 56 states that coastal states have 'sovereign rights for the purpose of exploring and exploiting, conserving and managing the natural resources' in relation to the EEZ and Article 77 that the coastal state 'exercises over the continental shelf sovereign rights for the purpose of exploring it and exploiting its natural resources'.

CIL.[86] It would also be incorrect to say that states exercise ALL powers of sovereignty, that they act 'exclusively', in relation to the physical geography coinciding with their territory anyway. The contrast between the EEZ and state territory offers another insight into an erroneous assumption often made about territory, sovereignty, and exclusivity: there is often thought to be exclusivity because the *entire bundle* of rights (the regime of sovereignty) is assumed to be exercisable by the state, that is, the state exercises *all the rights* included in the bundle to the exclusion of all other states and they exercise all the rights 'over' a synchronised, container-like, physical area. This is the implication behind the assertion that '"sovereign rights" beyond state territory' are '[r]ights which are "owned" and in this special sense "sovereign" involve a broader concept, not reducible to territorial sovereignty'[87] because territorial sovereignty is something different – it is a specific regime that is in mind. It implies there are no other rights left for another actor to exercise in relation to that physical geography. That is untrue and an unflattened and dephysicalised understanding of territory makes this easier to observe.

Yet this slippage, or conflation between physical geography and legal rights, easily occurs in discourses concerning the transfer of title. It is often imagined that what is being transferred is the physical geography. How then should this be understood in this rethink? States should not be understood to exercise exclusive power 'over' physical geography in an ownership sense; instead, they are understood as exercising potentially exclusive rights, powers, etc. in relation to their spatial exercise of control. Further, control 'over' that same physical geography may be exercised by more than one actor and each actor is exclusively exercising (different) powers in relation to *their* territory. It is only when the concept of territory is flattened – such that in relation to any one piece of physical geography there is only one territory – that is has created the assumption that exclusivity operates in relation to physical geography rather than to the legal relations. So, a flattened concept of territory *makes it appear as if* the physical geography is also exclusively the state's, in the sense of the physical geography belonging to the state only. This plays out as the idea of exclusivity vis-à-vis territory such as in the following: '[m]any of the

[86] For example, recently there was much debate about the 'historic rights' or customary rights in relation to the UK's EEZ. See Collins (2019); Harrison (2019).

[87] Crawford (2019) at 194.

most fundamental principles of international law are predicated upon the concept of the territorial exclusivity of the state, and are aimed at protecting it'.[88] One such fundamental principle is the inviolability of a state territory, the principle of territorial integrity, such that any 'incursion' into another state's physical geography automatically counts as a violation of territorial integrity. Territorial integrity is not nearly as simple as this. Clearly, many international organisations and foreign private actors 'penetrate' the same physical geography that is often equated with state territory. For example, territorial integrity is not undermined when a UN Charter Chapter VII-authorised military operation takes place. That is because the United Nations Security Council (UNSC) is legally empowered to act in relation to this space. Territorial integrity is also not undermined when the WTO determines that a particular measure is a barrier to trade. Instead, we might think of it as follows: these are not incursions into state territory because these same physical geographies are also territories of these organisations for this particular legal relation. What would be a violation of territorial integrity is when a state has no right in the legal relation to exercise control (often militarily) over X, Y, or Z competence in relation to a particular legal geography.

Thus, it is the rights that can be exclusive not the relationship to physical geography (also because territory is not physical geography in the first place). This helps us rethink key legal doctrine. Shaw, if we remember, observes that '[t]he principle whereby a state is deemed to exercise exclusive power over its territory can be seen as a fundamental axiom of classical international law'[89] and Ryngaert explains that the international legal order is 'a system of territorially delimited nation States that have full and exclusive sovereignty over their own territory, and no sovereignty over other States' territory'.[90] In these two passages, if territory refers to physical geography this idea of exclusivity creates an assumption that no actor other than the state can exercise sovereignty (also monolithically conceived) in relation to the same physical space. However, if we now understand that the territory of an actor is created as a result of practices of control and physical geography does not become the 'property' of states as a result of their control, the relationship otherwise described as title in international law is not ownership over

[88] Shaw (1982) at 67.
[89] ibid at 61.
[90] Ryngaert (2015) at 51.

the physical geography but the bundle of legal rights and duties, etc. constructed between actors. Thus, for example, it would be incorrect to say the state is in a direct relationship in terms of legal rights with its space, rather it is with other states and actors. The relationship a state has with its territory are the practices it continually undertakes constituting that space. We might then reinterpret what is said above by Shaw and Ryngaert as follows: states exercise sovereign powers – which they may hold exclusively – in relation to their territory, and other actors exercise sovereign powers – which they too may do so exclusively – in relation to their territory, and this may overlap the same physical geography.

5.3.2 *Dropping Territorial Sovereignty*

This analysis leads to the explicit proscription of the very idea of title from this legal-theoretical framework. Territorial sovereignty is redundant as a concept because it presumes an ownership relationship between territory (read: physical geography) and the state (alone). This way of thinking assumes as a fundamental building block a physical space, and in the previous chapter, it was established that all space, including territory, is socially produced and territory does not equal physical geography. Thus, the concept of title is superfluous to requirements. It is redundant as a legal concept concerning territory. For instead, territory is the space constituted by the exercise of control. Territory is created and practised, not owned.

And where sovereignty and territorial sovereignty have been used interchangeably, we only need to retain one of them. The discourse does not require both sovereignty and territorial sovereignty. To my mind, it seems more appropriate that it is the concept of sovereignty that is retained for two reasons, First, territorial sovereignty has more consistently been associated with the idea of title, and that is the very thing being 'buried'. Second, the discourse no longer needs the qualifier of territorial sovereignty. All sovereignty is, or parts of the bundle of sovereign powers are, exercised territorially – even in the EEZ, which is part of the territory of the state for that particular set of legal relations as a result of the practices and relations of control. Where, the concept of sovereignty still does a kind of job, I do not propose burying it entirely. It can be used to describe the exercise of some 'sovereign' powers if this is found useful, even just heuristically useful. Its actual content – the content of the bundle – is up for negotiation as outlined above.

5.3.3 *Illegal or Legal Exercise of Power*

Whether a particular fact of control being exercised is legal or illegal is precisely what international law is for. However, the way the concept of territory is currently used in legal reasoning, as it is currently conceptualised in international legal discourse, is unhelpful. In this section, I insert the reconceptualised concept of territory into situations where force is exercised to 'annex' or 'occupy', and perhaps then the powers of a sovereign are exercised, such as policing, education, or issues relating to culture, such as determining the language spoken for administrative purposes, etc. As shown below, not only will this exploration show how the new concept of territory works in practice, but I argue the current situation is unhelpful and counterproductive. It is therefore necessary to insert this new concept into practical examples, not least because territory is conceptualised as an object in this traditional discourse, but territory is also used in an all-or-nothing sense (because of the inappropriate physicalised and totalised understanding of the space and its supposed 'exclusivity' outlined above). It is a deeply symbolic object with highly charged normative content.

The recent Crimea awards and cases are an excellent display of the issues with conceptualising territory as an object and how we might alternatively understand the spaces of Russia, Ukraine, and Crimea. This example helps elaborate how we might understand the question of territory in situations where the force is used by states. I am not an apologist of brute force.[91] This argument is not to be confused with a Morgenthau-esque or realist argument, in the IR sense of realism, that successful actors are those who can maximise their power, often by force, to maintain international relations. By recognising their territory, I am not 'recognising' their legitimacy, subjecthood, or the changed circumstances. I am not saying that brute force is good or saying it should be recognised as such. This proposed reconceptualisation of territory cannot tell us who the 'legitimate' or morally correct actor is by looking solely at territory – or even who is acting lawfully – for that is a matter for international law to determine. However, it can help clarify the legal analysis without the pesky problem that presents itself in the current state of affairs: that recognising some space as the territory of a particular state automatically transforms the situation into one of legality and offers a

[91] I unashamedly support pacifism, having grown up around peace activists protesting the Iraq war and outside Faslane, the UK Naval Base home to submarines armed with Trident nuclear missiles.

cloak of legitimacy to that state's actions. In this framework, there can still be a finding of illegality, such that when Russia annexes 'Crimea', the act is either good or bad, moral or immoral, legal or illegal according to international legal argument. What is undeniable is that Russia, for example, is exercising control, whether a particular person likes it or not. *The spatial extent of* its exercise of control has changed. This is the very issue that many of the arbitral tribunals in many Crimean arbitrations had to contend with (or tried to avoid at times). It is also an issue that the European Court of Human Rights regularly has to contend with.

The issue at stake before the Annex 7 Arbitration Tribunal in the *Dispute Concerning Coastal State Rights in the Black Sea, Sea of Azov, and Kerch Strait* was which state, Russia or Ukraine, should be exercising the rights and duties of the coastal state. Ukraine, arguing that there was an illegal invasion and annexation, denied that there should be any legal effect or recognition of Russian actions and that it was the rightful actor to exclusively 'engage in, authorize, and regulate exploration and exploitation of natural resources' and to 'authorise and regulate fishing' and that Russia's actions were and continued to be internationally wrongful.[92] The two states got into a mess arguing about whether this is a dispute concerning land territory or rights relating to the sea (note the distinction between land territory and rights relating to the sea and seabed), important because Russia claimed that land territory needed to be settled in order to resolve the dispute over rights within the jurisdiction of the Tribunal.[93] The Tribunal stressed that the recognition of a dispute 'over the territorial status of Crimea in no way amounts to recognizing any alteration of the status of Crimea from the territory of one Party to the other … neither would it imply that the Russian Federation's actions toward and in Crimea were lawful'.[94] The Tribunal found it lacked jurisdiction 'to the extent that a

[92] Ukraine's Notification and Statement of Claim, para 50 in *Dispute Concerning Coastal State Rights in the Black Sea, Sea of Azov, and Kerch Strait, Ukraine and the Russian Federation* [2020] Annex VII Arbitral Tribunal PCA Case No. 2017-06.

[93] Russia argued that the 'objective of Ukraine's claim is to secure a favourable determination on the sovereignty of Crimea' (Russian Federation's Preliminary Objections, para 45) which Ukraine argued that 'it ha[d] not brought the "illegal occupation of Ukrainian territory" before the Arbitral Tribunal' (Ukraine's Written Observations, para 56 n 91) and 'that the "sole actual objective" of its claims is the interpretation and application of [UNCLOS] in relation to the Russian Federation's actions in the Black Sea, Sea of Azov, and the Kerch Strait. Ukraine notes that even an express ruling by this Arbitral Tribunal reaffirming Crimea's status as a part of Ukraine "would not materially improve Ukraine's legal position on that settled matter."' (Award, para 62 n 91).

[94] Award, para 178 n 91.

ruling of the Arbitral Tribunal on the merits of Ukraine's claims necessarily requires it to decide, expressly or implicitly, on the sovereignty of either Party over Crimea'.[95] Here we see 'Crimea' as 'territory' which is a totalised physical object. The first benefit of the proposed reconceptualising territory is that there is no need to distinguish between land and water territory – there is no primacy between land, sea, and air concerning territory nor appurtenances which, while beneath the surface of the argument, is entirely the logic of the argument being made by Russia and implicitly accepted by Ukraine. And second, there is no finding of legitimacy and legality by recognising the spatial extent of an actor's practices of control. Instead, it is always a question about the exercise of powers wherever they are exercised: Are they legal or illegal under international law? It leaves behind the totalising effects of reognising territory.

Another arbitral case, brought by Stabil LLB and others against the Russian Federation, concerned the rights of investors when Russia 'incorporated' Crimea. At the time the investments were made, the claimants were nationals of Ukraine, but control over Crimea had in the meantime, shall we say, changed. One of the questions became whether the investments made by the claimants, Ukrainian nationals, should be protected by the Russia–Ukraine BIT. In other words, was Crimea now part of Russian territory such that the claimants had essentially become 'foreign' investors. The Tribunal found that 'the term "territory" for purposes of the Treaty to include territory over which a State exercises *de facto* control and jurisdiction',[96] adopting a definition close to one proposed in this book.[97] They construed the term territory in what they framed as an 'open-ended manner' even if Russia held 'no lawful title under international law'.[98] They did this because it would 'go against the object and purpose of the Treaty to leave without protection foreign investments on a territory over which a State exercises exclusive control and claims sovereignty'.[99] This is a similar issue faced by human rights courts: how to establish that a state is acting beyond its 'own' territory in a way that can still hold them accountable; how to get away from the unhelpful, overly determined concepts of 'territory' and

[95] Award, para 197 n 91.

[96] *Stabil LLC and Others v Russian Federation*, UNCITRAL, PCA Case no. 2015-35, Award on Jurisdiction, 26 June 2017, para 175.

[97] Although this conceptualisation of territory is still physical, it is still flat, it is still totalising, it is still statocentric.

[98] *Stabil LLC and Others v Russian Federation*, (n 95) para 146.

[99] ibid, para 158.

'jurisdiction'. In an attempt to get away from that problematic conceptualisation of territory, the claimants emphasised that there is a difference between 'territory [Russia] illegally occupies' and 'sovereign territory'.[100] Ukraine wanted to avoid the absurd position that would see it denying its nationals their rights and any compensation or damages because it could not admit to Crimea/the space in question being 'owned' by Russia (the current effect of recognising territory) at the risk of 'recognising' Russian sovereignty, allowing the act of illegality to be sustained and transforming the situation into one of legality. This can all be avoided by adopting this proposed concept of territory. There is no 'recognition' problem. All are 'state territory'. Yet, different legal rights and duties are entailed by different 'categories' of territory, that is, whether it is deemed to be occupied or not. The reconceptualisation of territory makes this easier to understand and does away with the idea that there is some kind of 'core' 'sovereign' territory of a state.

Similarly, the ECtHR has increasingly adopted the 'fact of control' as the solution to establishing the human rights obligations of states.[101] As Milanovic has identified, there is a different concept of jurisdiction present in human rights regimes – jurisdiction as 'factual power, authority or control that a state has over a territory'.[102] This is because it would go against the objective and purpose of human rights instruments to deny human rights just because a state is not acting in the space that international law thinks it should. However, the ECtHR has managed to get itself into a mess by bringing in state responsibility tests ('effective control') to apply to the control that actors exercise for the purposes of constituting territory (in Chapter 4, I advocated a much lower threshold

[100] Submission of Ukraine, §§ 20–21. Quoted in n 95, para 212.

[101] *Legal Consequences of the Construction of a Wall in the Occupied Palestinian Territory*, Advisory Opinion, ICJ Reports 2004 (9 July 2004) (CLA-61) (International Court of Justice) in which the Court determined that Israel did have human rights obligations to uphold 'essentially territorial' rights in the ICESR in the occupied Palestinian territory because Israel has exercised control in relations to these territories for over 37 years (para 112). See also the case of *Cyprus v Turkey*, ECtHR, Application No. 25781/94, Judgment (10 May 2001) where the Court found that not finding that Turkey had human rights obligations 'would result in a regrettable vacuum in the system of human rights protection' (para 78). A similar finding regarding obligations of a 'humanitarian character' was found in *Legal Consequences for States of the Continued Presence of South Africa in Namibia (South West Africa)* notwithstanding Security Council Resolution 276, Advisory Opinion, ICJ Reports 1971 (21 June 1971) (International Court of Justice), para 122.

[102] Milanovic (2008) at 428.

of control that constitutes territory). In *Georgia v Russia (II)*, the Court asserted that ECHR 'jurisdiction' is 'closely linked to the notion of "control", whether it be "State agent authority and control" over individuals or "effective control" by a State over a territory'.[103] This is a completely unnecessarily high bar, especially in the (further getting itself into a mess) 'context of chaos'[104] that is armed conflict. While the Court is grappling seriously with *extra*territorial activities of states, it does not yet have the onto-theoretical tools and 'spatial awareness' to make sense of the relationship between actors–space–power. It would all be a lot simpler, as indicated earlier, if we got rid of the 'extra' and brought in the concept of territory as socially produced space proposed here.

In many ways, I am depoliticising certain associations with the term territory while repoliticising space more generally. As it stands, territory is often all-or-nothing in international law discourse, precisely because of the disciplinary assumptions that in relation to physical geography there is only one territory. This in many ways is what causes the mess arbitral tribunals and courts try to avoid in dealing with questions of territory while also trying to establish who has jurisdiction and therefore responsibility for particular acts. The question instead can become one of whether it is legal or illegal for a state to be exercising powers. This is a decision about the legality or illegality of the act (usually some use of brute force) as well as the continuing exercise of powers from the sovereignty bundle. But states will still be held accountable for illegal acts. This is not a question, and never should be, about 'whose territory it *really* is'. For that would be to treat territory as an object. And we know that it is not one.

5.4 Seeing Like an International Organisation

Finally, these legal realist insights can create room for the adoption of a socially constructivist understanding of law and governance, rather than fetishising a particular stato-centric structure that is found in the normatively informed international legal positivism. This international legal positivism places emphasis on the will of states with 'the state []as the source of sovereignty'.[105] I see this account of the state as a choice for ordering and justifying international law. Revisiting the concept of

[103] *Georgia v Russia (II)*, Application no. 38263/08, Judgment, Merits [2021] European Court of Human Rights, Grand Chamber 38263/08 [136].

[104] ibid at (137).

[105] Kingsbury (2002) at 401, 410.

sovereignty in the manner outlined above challenges the fundamental tenets of this normatively orientated positivist account of international law. This section thus also revisits the concept of actorhood in international law that has been structured on the basis of the orthodox concept of territory. As should be evident by now, the concept of territory I propose need not refer only to state space, but the space of any actor exercising control. The bundle of rights, duties, etc., once assumed to be wholly held by the state, sovereignty, can be, and crucially have been, dispersed between many different actors and their territories. Therefore, this final section addresses the problematic of international legal positivism which would otherwise challenge this account of reterritorialisation.

As to the legal realist insights: well, Holmes argued that in order to understand a legal system, we should think like someone who wants to know what activities they can undertake without being punished and whose rules they should obey: 'you test [who] ... has legal authority in the legal system by which of them maintains its positions and throws or jockeys the other out'.[106] This relates to Corbin's contention that 'a "right" exists when its possessor has the aid of some organized governmental society in controlling the conduct of another person'.[107] In other words, legal realism does not presume the normative source of authority that international legal positivism does. Given that many of these legal powers are increasingly exercised by non-state actors in relation to their own territories (states are at times 'jockeyed out' and are 'outgoverned' by international organisations), there is a need for a different conception of sovereignty in international law. This would radically change the theory of how and why international organisations – or any other actors – exercise competences. It is not because particular rights, duties, competences, powers, immunities, etc. have been delegated or implied by the 'ultimate source', that is, by states, but because they are in reality exercising these powers and rights. Each of these autonomous actors operate within their own spaces, controlling, disciplining, and influencing activities in relation to these spaces.

The final step, then, is to remove the assumption that only one category of actor exercises sovereign powers and rights. By doing so, those who are *in reality* exercising powers, competences, rights, and

106 Llewellyn (2011) at 59.
107 Corbin (1924) at 502.

duties – elements of the bundle traditionally assumed only to be exercised by states – in respect of their spaces are now made visible. Orthodox theory cannot explain the many powers and competences international organisations are exercising that were never delegated. Positivism and its proponents ask the wrong questions, as we shall see, because it starts from a normative premise.

This involves rethinking some of the assumptions of international legal positivism. In the eyes of what is associated as international legal positivism, all sovereignty is rooted in nation-states, meaning that when it comes to international organisations, it is the states' decisions as to when and how much of its competences to delegate to these institutions. It is a flawed argument however, not least because it starts with an untested presumption – and proceeds by deducing the rest of the argument from it – that the state is the source of these competences. The result is a 'view from nowhere' understanding of how things are. International legal positivism in doing this is not purely positivist but is normative positivism.

Legal realism and social constructivism start instead from the position of the concrete individual subject. So, taking as examples states like Malta (independent: 1964[108]) or Republic of Tajikistan (independent: 1991[109]), it is clear that from their perspective, many of the sovereign functions exercised today by international organisations were exercised by other actors, say the UK or Soviet Union, in respect of their territories before the legal persons we know today existed and hence never 'belonged' to them in the first place. Hence, from this perspective, the assumption that states are the source of all sovereignty is simply incorrect.

If Malta or Tajikistan were to say they were 'taking back' sovereignty by leaving international organisations, it would be political rhetoric only. Rather, it would be a rearrangement of the bundle, such that the rights and powers would instead by held by Malta or Tajikistan to exercise in their own territories. The same applies with the UK leaving the EU: the UK is not 'taking back' sovereignty. It is not a simple reversal of a process because rights, duties, etc. were created as a result of EU membership (for the UK, other member states, and the EU) and for the duration of the membership never 'belonged' to the UK. Many rights and duties, such as the right to have MEPs in the European Parliament, were extinguished as

[108] Independent 21 September 1964. Joined the UN 1 December 1964.
[109] Independent 9 September 1991. Joined the UN 2 March 1992.

opposed to a 'repatriation of a territorial competence'.[110] There has been a deterritorialisation process of *some* powers and legal relations from the EU and a reterritorialisation to the UK, but other powers and legal relations were extinguished (and many others created, just think of the palaver that was the Northern Ireland deal).[111]

Furthermore, many of the powers and legal rights exercised by international organisations cannot in reality be exercised by states independently. This includes, for example, specific rights and duties created in the UN with regards to sanctions, human rights, blacklisting of terrorist suspects, climate change, etc. or sourced in the UNC to maintain international peace and security and uphold international law through the UNSC. Many of the sovereign powers exercised today by some international organisations – for example, UNSC powers under Chapter VII – were never exercised before they were created and subsequently developed by the UN and then exercised by the UN in respect of its space. So, can we really say that these legal rights were transferred to the UN or were they created *ex nihilo*?

The question then becomes: if states are not the ultimate source of authority – if actors other than states can, so to say, 'come into the possession' of sovereign packages without taking them from states – what then is the ultimate source of sovereignty?

But, of course, this is the wrong question. The right question from the legal realist perspective (and from the constructivist perspective) is not where did this social construction come from normatively, but: objectively, does this social construction appear to exist (as exhibited by the practices of the respective social actors) and is it experienced as real? Do states no longer freely choose everything in relation to the physical geography they believe is their territory? Do other actors have the ability to discipline activities over that same physical geography?

If the answers are 'yes', that other actors do control and discipline particular activities, peoples, processes, etc., then that is enough; for legal realism, for social constructivism, this is where the inquiry stops. The validity of a social fact lies in its existence. It does not require normative justification. One does not ask what the ultimate justification for social

110 Burke, Hannesson, and Bangsund in Kuijer and Werner (2017).

111 The Protocol on Ireland and Northern Ireland 2020, UK at <https://assets.publishing.service.gov.uk/government/uploads/system/uploads/attachment_data/file/840230/Revised_Protocol_to_the_Withdrawal_Agreement.pdf>.

reality is. Why ask what is the justification for 'how sovereignty is distributed in the world today'? We start from the facts ascertainable on the basis of a rigorous method. In Holmesean realism outlined above, it is the observation of enforcement patterns (broadly conceived) that determine which laws should be obeyed and who has authority.

Regardless, once we have reconstructed the shape of social reality, we analyse what is happening. We do not ask: but is it normatively justified that things are this way? We only ask: is it certain – are we clear – that things are this way? Then we evidence our conclusions ('diagnosis') based on empirical study.

The outcome is that by applying legal bundles to the concept of sovereignty we can observe the distribution of sovereign powers among the different actors operating in their territories – irrespective of how these territories are configured. If this is how sovereign powers are distributed today, then so be it. The arrangement of the bundles can change; making an account of how the bundles of legal relations are arranged only ever a snapshot, valid for a limited period of time. These legal bundles are contingent on power, politics, and policies operating at a period in time and are subject to change. Sovereignty is not static. The bundle and its relative distribution are constantly being redistributed as relative power shifts. If this is how the social reality is – at any one moment – so be it in this understanding.

Ferguson and Gupta work with similar notions in *Spatialising the State*. They argue 'we need to view states as themselves composed of bundles of social practices' instead of the usual analysis which tends to oppose society (dynamic) and the state (static).[112] 'International society' – MNCs, individuals, international organisations – are not opposable to or different from the state; the state is just one actor among many that may be territorially organised. Ferguson and Gupta example Zambia and the MNC that 'conquered [and] "pacified" the territory' (the British South Africa Company) as well as the transnational organisations continuing to exercise control in Zambia, including the IMF, World Bank, and several western banks, that 'often directly impose policies on African states'.[113] In the proposed paradigm of sovereignty laid out above, we understand that the British South Africa Company, the IMF, and other banks were, and are, exercising elements of the sovereignty bundle in relation to territories subject to their influence and control.

[112] Ferguson and Gupta (2002) at 992.
[113] ibid.

Many organisations are performing functions traditionally associated with the state (and thus the same physical geography becomes part of their spheres of influence) because states are apparently 'unable', 'unwilling', or 'incapable'. Ferguson and Gupta highlight the role of organisations such as World Vision International, Oxfam, and Doctors Without Borders in 'organising local affairs and building and operating schools and clinics', performing 'state like functions all across Africa.'[114] From the perspective of these organisations, they plan their provision of the function across their space. Their territories are differently constructed to those ascribed to states; their territories may not be abstract, homogeneous, uniform space but might operate as 'point to point' networks, both 'local and global'[115] in the same way as the state could be thought of as both 'local and national'. The territories of these organisations, where they exercise their elements of the sovereignty bundle, *do not replace state territory*, but coexist over the same physical geography.

This analysis collapses the artificial distinction between public and private in terms of who *ought* to exercise elements of the bundle. Although it is traditionally assumed that sovereignty is exercised by a public actor, history is furnished with examples where a distinction between public and private is blurred: the East India Company was '*de facto* exercising sovereign powers in ... non-European territories'.[116] Rather than understanding this practice as *sui generis* 'accidents of history', and bearing in mind how widespread this practice of non-state actors '*de facto*' exercising sovereign powers is today, the conceptualisation proposed better explains, visibilises, and accounts for these practices because it does not essentialise the state as sovereign.

Sassen adopts a similar position in her scholarship. Her understanding is that 'sovereignty is being partly disassembled ... over the last 20–30 years, depending on the country. While much remains formally included in the national state and sites in national state territoriality, some of it has shifted to other institutional spaces.'[117] This insightful analysis, however, needs added to it a legal-theoretical account, to create the necessary legal reasoning to make this account work within the discipline of international law. That is, I think, the value of adopting legal realist accounts as they consider sovereignty to be a bundle of legal relations. Note

[114] ibid at 994.
[115] ibid.
[116] Arcuri and Violi in Kuijer and Werner (2017) at 186.
[117] Sassen (2013) at 30.

however, 'disassembling' should not be taken as indicating there was a correct or original assemblage in the first place. As Sassen indicates this disassembling is 'not new'.[118] Powers and competences have been assembled and reassembled, created and recreated, throughout history; the metaphor of bundling further enables a historical view of things.

Sassen also emphasises that the sovereignty bundle is not divided the same everywhere. The disassembling of the bundle (and reassembling) is fragmented both between different states AND in different fields of international law – and it is most often *power* that is the determinant for how this is arranged. As an example of the former, the IMF exercises different powers in relation to influencing and determining 'public infrastructure and oil-related projects' over the physical geography shared with, say, Uganda than the space it shares with the UK.[119] As an example of the latter, the sovereignty bundle from the perspective of international economic law is more dispersed than it is in relation to the rights associated with self-defence; regarding the bundle relating to self-defence, only the UN and states can, in certain circumstances, legally use force in self-defence.

I recognise that this entirely rethinks orthodox thinking, which would maintain that:

> the United Nations cannot, for example, hold sovereignty over land, as a State could. (That is why disputed areas such as Jerusalem cannot be put under 'UN sovereignty', though they could be administered by the United Nations—as East Timor was administered by UNTAET, the United Nations Transitional Administration for East Timor—or on its behalf by a State—as Australia was the Trustee for the UN Trust Territory of Papua New Guinea, prior to its independence.)[120]

Leaving aside the issue that territory is being conceptualised as land which has been thoroughly addressed already, let me demonstrate how the proposed conception of territory-as-social-space works in practice with reference to three examples: the EU, ISA, and data.

5.4.1 *The EU*

Of all international and regional organisations, the EU is perhaps the most obvious and likely-to-be-accepted organisation with a

118 ibid at 32.
119 'IMF Country Focus' (2019).
120 Lowe (2007) at 123.

territory.[121] The EU may be the institution most like a state, being a 'supra-statal' organisation. There is, of course, ongoing academic debate about the nature of the EU: whether it is an international organisation; whether the presence of 'constitutional features' make it more akin to a state than other international organisations; whether it is a *sui generis* organisation; or whether it is a *sui generis* creature altogether.[122] This debate is not central to this thesis. Indeed, understanding sovereignty as a bundle of powers and legal relations, and rethinking territory, contributes an answer to this debate, sidestepping many of these questions. The proposed account adopts a position on the EU such that it is no longer ambiguous in nature: instead, the EU is one possible institutional arrangement among many, including the state (which is after all an institution constituted by social practices). For my purposes, the EU might be thought of as a particularly well-endowed institution, holding many sticks from the sovereignty bundle.

After briefly discussing the nature of EU territory, I evidence the existence of its territory by examining the rights and duties of, and tasks performed by, Frontex, the EU agency in control of external borders, because the presence and functions of this agency highlight the territory and sovereignty of the EU. I conclude with evidence that the EU thinks of itself as having territory with a very strong geographic imaginary of itself.

5.4.2 *The Nature of EU Territory: Distinct and Separate*

As has already been highlighted, the EU is sometimes referred to as a *sui generis* territorial entity;[123] a category which this argument concerning the territories of non-state actors disrupts. This approach instead equalises and regularises the spaces of states and international organisations alike.[124] Despite EU space perhaps being more readily accepted as a territory, however, this territory is extremely undertheorised in international law discourse. My investigations suggest that no one has explicitly and convincingly argued that EU territory *is territory* in

[121] I chose the EU because it is often the example that receives the most attention in textbooks and from international law scholars. However, what applies to the EU example applies *mutatis mutandis* to other regional organisations such as ASEAN, the AU, and the OAS.

[122] Palchetti (2018) at 1409, 1414. See also: Casteleiro (2016); Castellarin (2017).

[123] Shaw (2014) at 175.

[124] There is no need for a *sui generis* category if all actors can have territory. For more on the *sui generis* as a category see: Lythgoe (2023).

international law discourse.[125] Yet the term territory is sometimes used to discuss the space of the EU. It must be surmised that some instances use the term territory not as a legal term but colloquially or informally. This is because, with one potential exception, no international law scholarship in its dealing with territory, includes EU territory within the definition of territory for international law purposes.[126] I submit this undertheorising of EU space as territory arises because, as conventional international legal theory stands, the EU's legal and political space is not and cannot be territory. The outcome is pragmatic: EU space is thought of like a territory; scholars use the terminology of territory on occasion, but the issue is not addressed systematically.

As to its nature, EU territory is separate to member states' territories, it is not an aggregate of member state spaces. For example, the free movement of citizens within the EU created a new legal space controlled by the EU legal personality, not member states in aggregate. Nor does the EU simply share the member states' territories as this would be a condominium of sorts and the EU is not this. The EU is not a case of shared sovereignty, which would materialise in decisions made jointly. The EU clearly has a separate will. Hence, we understand the EU as a territorially ordered and defined organisation with its territory overlapping, but not always identical to, the same physical geography as the territorial frameworks of its member states.

For many purposes EU territory coincides with and is often informed by member states' territories. This is best exampled should a member state decide to leave the EU. In such circumstances the sovereignty bundle would be re-arranged and EU territory would no longer include this physical space. Another instance meriting mention is if a member state were to transfer all its legal rights to a non-EU state. The closest example we have of this is French Algeria becoming independent in 1962. This instance is comparable to a territory leaving an international organisation. The situation will differ depending on the reasons for the territorial framework changing, as well as the agreement of the parties involved. It could be that, by agreement, all legal competences are reassembled in a bundle held by the non-EU state, but if the non-EU state desires to join the EU, the arrangement of the sovereign bundle may be different.

[125] Most likely because it is impossible. A bit like customs union territory, it can be used informally, but it does not accord with the international law discipline's concept of territory. Hence the production of the '*sui generis* territorial entity' category.

[126] The one exception is Shaw. However, the presence of a *sui generis* category only proves the general rule, and Shaw leaves this unresolved.

While member state territories often inform EU territory, this is not always the case. Tax practices provide examples of the sovereignty games taking place with regard to British Overseas Territories. EU territory does not currently include the Cayman Islands for the purposes of the direct effect of EU Directives after the ECJ dismissed a case brought by the Government of the Cayman Islands against the Commission.[127] The Court of First Instance, in dismissing the case, found:

> Consequently, although there is no doubt in this case as to the existence of a political agreement at intergovernmental level pursuant to which, in the case of the Cayman Islands, the United Kingdom has undertaken, if the proposed directive is adopted, to take the necessary domestic (municipal) measures to ensure that, once the directive is implemented in the United Kingdom, the same measures will be applied to the territory of the Cayman Islands, this consequence, if it comes to pass, will not flow legally from the directive itself.[128]

The Cayman Islands government interpreted this as follows: 'the EU cannot directly impose any obligation on the Cayman Islands to implement the EU savings tax directive'.[129] This interpretation of the Order was never challenged. Therefore, although the 'Cayman Islands' were part of British territory for some purposes, they were not part of EU territory for these purposes because of the lack of direct influence the EU had vis-à-vis that space. This shows that the territories of member states do not always inform EU territory and the EU's territory is distinct from member states' territories.

Having discussed some relevant implications of EU territory, and its nature, I give two examples evidencing EU territory. The first is the EU's border agency and the legal spaces created as a result. The second evidences the EU regarding itself as having a territory, demonstrated through EU treaties and policy framework.

5.4.3 *The EU Border Agency*

In the following study of the European Border and Coast Guard Agency (hereafter Frontex or 'the Agency'), I highlight the legal space created by EU lawmaking and the agency set up to monitor, undertake operations

[127] *Government of the Cayman Islands v Commission*, Case T-85/03 (Court of Justice of the European Union).
[128] ibid, para 67.
[129] Cayman Compass, 2003, as quoted by Vlcek in Adler-Nissen and Gad (2012). Adler-Nissen and Gad (2012) at 124.

at, and control its borders – functions typically thought to be within the remit of a state. This is a striking indication of EU territory. The EU itself refers to this space as its territory in the Frontex Regulation: 'European Council called for wider efforts in resolving unprecedented migratory flows towards *Union territory* in a comprehensive manner'.[130] A number of remarkable features of this Agency add to the sense of EU territory. First, the Agency's staff and officers are employed by the EU, not member states (Article 58)[131] although the Agency can ask that staff from member states are seconded as experts (Article 20(11)). In terms of the governance structure, a Management Board takes all strategic decisions and functions analogously to an executive body of a state government.

Agency functions indicating the sovereignty exercised by the EU can be categorised into two: first, are those that previously would have been undertaken by states and have been 'reterritorialised' into the EU; and the second are those created by the Regulations and are unique to the institution. Such new powers include: vulnerability assessments of the capacity of member states to deal with threats and challenges at the external borders; mandatory recommendations and assistance; sharing information between member states and Europol; launching rapid border interventions and maintaining a pool of rapid response teams and equipment; training specialists 'who have the skills and expertise required to carry out return-related activities'; training national border guards; managing 'research and innovation activities' for control and surveillance of external borders; cooperating with the European Fisheries Agency and European Maritime Safety Agency; and assisting the European Border Surveillance System (EUROSUR) (Article 8). These are not minor functions and powers but core to the operations taking place at Europe's borders.

Remarkably, Frontex 'may carry out operations on the territory of non-EU countries neighbouring at least one Member State, in case of migratory pressure at a non-EU country's border'.[132] This means that for certain purposes and specified tasks and functions, the territorial framework is flexible and is contingent on one purpose and time. The EU's territory is not a container or unit, nor always uniform; for certain

[130] Regulation (EU) 2016/1624 (September 2016) preamble, para 1 (ea).

[131] Unless otherwise stated, all Articles relate to Regulation (EU) 2016/1624 (September 2016).

[132] 'Frontex "Origin & Tasks"' (2019).

functions and limited periods of time, its territorial framework expands. The spatiality of the EU is an interesting but underexplored area, especially because of these agreements with a third state. Further study is required to understand how its territorial frameworks operate in practice but regrettably most agreements with third countries are not publicly available. However, what this insight tells us is that EU territory may at times differ from the member state territory that it will overlap in most instances.

This brief examination highlights that the EU has a territory essential to how the organisation organises its activities and governs. Frontex's tasks and functions demonstrate just how important it is to understand this issue, given the Frontex Regulation conferred major functions and powers on the organisation. The proposed reconceptualisation of territory allows us to make better sense of, and scrutinise, the legal arrangements and practices of the EU exercised in reference to its territorial framework.

5.4.4 *'Union Territory' in EU Treaties and Policy Frameworks*

There is evidence through legal texts, such as EU treaties and Regulations, and EU policy documents, that the EU thinks of itself as having territory; it has its own geographic imaginary of itself. Turning first to EU treaties: in the 1997 Treaty of Amsterdam, the European Council determines the 'conditions of employment for third-country nationals legally residing in *Community territory*'.[133] Clearly, there is a juridical notion of 'community territory' separate from member states' territories. Where reference to member states' territories was intended in the Treaty, the term 'member state territories' was used. Article 18 relates to a body of the European Community – a separate legal person – with responsibility to determine employment conditions. The space in relation to which the power was exercised was the territory of the European Community. This provision was retained in the Treaties of Nice 2001 and Lisbon 2007 and is currently Article 153 of the Consolidated version of the TFEU.[134] Given the term existed in the Treaty of

[133] Article 18 Treaty of Amsterdam amending the Treaty on European Union, the Treaties Establishing the European Communities and Certain Related Acts 1997 (OJ C340/1), emphasis added.

[134] Article 117 Consolidated versions of the Treaty on European Union and the Treaty on the Functioning of the European Union 2012 (2012/C 326/01).

Amsterdam, it shows this concept is not new. It is, therefore, unconnected to EU attempts to introduce a 'constitution'. This makes the point that a looser-formed organisation can have a territory, just as an organisation comparable to a 'supra-state' can.

Articles 52 TEU, and Articles 355, 349, 198–204 TFEU, relate to the treaties' territorial scope and can be considered the initial territorial framework creating EU territory. While TEU and TFEU are useful guides to what EU territory became upon creation of the organisation, to identify EU territory for a particular sovereign right, assessing the application of EU law is important. This is because territory varies by purpose, for example EU territory for VAT purpose differs from that for EU Directive implementation. Numerous references to 'Union territory' can be found in various decisions and resolutions, including, for example, Commission Decisions such as Commission Implementing Decision EU 2015/789 (18 May 2015). This determines EU activities preventing the spread within the Union of *Xylella Fastidiosa* (a bacterial disease found in France and Italy having a severe impact on plants), such as 'establish[ing] a surveillance zone', and creates duties for EU member states, for example, 'carry[ing] out annual surveys for the presence of the specified organism in their territories', 'carry[ing] out regular official checks', and prohibiting certain activities such as the movement of plants within EU territory.[135]

The EU itself refers to its space as its territory in the Frontex Regulation: 'European Council called for wider efforts in resolving unprecedented migratory flows towards *Union territory* in a comprehensive manner'.[136] It also makes reference in this preamble to European Council Conclusions which upon examination speak of 'the management of the Union's external borders'.[137] Here, we note that the EU sees itself as having internal and external borders (varying striated and smooth), further evidencing the presence of a spatial imaginary that it has of itself. Union territory includes the same physical geography as its member states' territories (i.e., including seas and air) – usually within what is referred to as the 'External Borders of the Member States of the European Union, the European Union' (preamble para 1) but with the exception of

[135] Commission Implementing Decision (EU) 2015/789 (May 2015) European Commission, preamble para 8, Articles 3, 9, and 11.

[136] Regulation (EU) 2016/1624 (September 2016) preamble para 1. Emphasis added.

[137] 'European Council Meeting (25 and 26 June 2015) – Conclusions, EUCO 22/15, CO EUR 8 CONCL 3', para 3.

Ireland which does not participate in Schengen (preamble paras 66 and 67). According to EU Regulation 2016/399, 'external borders' mean 'the Member States' land borders, including river and lake borders, sea borders and their airports, river ports, sea ports and lake ports, provided they are not internal borders'.[138] On the face of it, we can conclude that to comprehend the boundedness of Union territory for Frontex purposes, we should initially be guided by the location of member states' borders. Internal borders are defined in Regulation 2016/299 as 'the common land borders, including river and lake borders, of the Member States; the airports of the Member States for internal flights; sea, river and lake ports of the Member States for regular internal ferry connections'.[139]

The EU has over time developed detailed policy frameworks based on the implicit assumption that its space is its territory. These policy frameworks afford a more in-depth look at how the EU considers its territory to be configured. In 1999 the Informal Council of Ministers agreed the 'European Spatial Development Perspective: Towards Balanced and Sustainable Development of the Territory of the European Union'.[140] The policy framework is interesting for several reasons, but I focus on its conceptualisation of EU territory. In this Perspective, EU territory is considered separate to member state territories, and it engages an understanding of territory which does not see territory as a homogeneous unit of space. It serves as a policy framework for 'the Member States, their regions and local authorities and the European Commission in their own respective spheres of responsibility'.[141] Each of these spheres is spatially delimited, thus, EU territory is not always homogeneous space for all purposes. The policy asserts: 'The characteristic territorial feature of the European Union (EU) is its cultural variety.'[142] The nation-state spatial model, of course, was famously based on creating a culture to be homogeneous within its space. The Policy believes this cultural variety distinguishes it from 'other large economic zones of the world, such as the USA, Japan and MERCOSUR'.[143] It indicates that EU officials themselves see the territory of the EU as heterogeneous. This is also reflected in the principle of subsidiarity, one of the 'key pillars of the European Union's

138 Article 2, Regulation (EU) 2016/399 (March 2016) 52.
139 Regulation (EU) 2016/399 (March 2016) 399.
140 'ESDP – European Spatial Development Perspective' (1999).
141 ibid at 3.
142 ibid at 7.
143 ibid.

legal and political architecture'.[144] We can of course question just how internally homogeneous the USA, MERCOSUR, or Japan actually are, just as we could problematise how internally homogeneous any state is. Compare this to the EU being a homogeneous space for other purposes: EU member states cannot create different policies for the importation of bananas for example, which as a minimum standard must not have 'abnormal curvature'.[145] This minimum standard is the same throughout the territory.

The policy framework acknowledges different local authorities and nations within its territory. This illustrates the piercing of the 'smooth' veil often perceived at an international law level and not merely of the usual object of state territory; the EU is an international organisation that imagines its own territory as heterogeneously constructed. In this policy framework, EU territory is seen as consisting of special zones – global economy integration zones, 'the pentagon defined by the metropolises of London, Paris, Milan, Munich and Hamburg'[146] – and islands of significant growth 'e.g. Barcelona, Region of the Øresund'.[147] The policy framework states that 'regional and local authorities must work together in the future across national boundaries'[148] which further indicates EU territory is separate from the territories of member states in the way cities, local authorities, and regions are expected to work together.

In short, the EU has a territory that is entrenched in how the institution organises its activities and governs in reference to a particular space. Frontex tasks and functions demonstrate just how important it is to understand this issue, given the major functions and powers exercised by the organisation. The proposed reconceptualisation allows us to make better sense of, and scrutinise, the legal arrangements: elements of the sovereignty bundle now sit with the EU and are exercised in reference to its territory. These functions and powers have not deterritorialised from the state to nowhere but have reterritorialised in EU territory.

5.4.5 *International Seabed Authority*

The second illustration, the International Seabed Authority (ISA), was established by UNCLOS and the 1994 Implementing Agreement to

144 European Committee of the Regions, 'EU Regional Policy' (January 2018).
145 Commission Regulation (EC) No. 2257/94, September 1994.
146 'ESDP – European Spatial Development Perspective' (1999) para 68.
147 ibid.
148 ibid, excerpt from the final conclusions issued by the German Presidency, para 4.

'organize and control activities in the Area, particularly with a view to administering the resources of the Area'.[149] The ISA's territory, initially, may be less obvious than the likes of the EU's. However, the reconceptualisation of territory and sovereignty makes apparent the rights in the bundle of powers exercised by the ISA in relation to the Area, meaning the Area is its territory.

There is renewed interest in ISA and its activities. At the time of writing, the ISA appears to be moving from exploitation of the Area to resource extraction. The Mining Code, still being developed in its entirety, consists of a 'comprehensive set of rules, regulations and procedures issued by the International Seabed Authority to regulate prospecting, exploration and exploitation of marine minerals in the international seabed Area (defined as the seabed and subsoil beyond the limits of national jurisdiction)'.[150] This process has caused renewed interest also in the idea of CHM, given it raises questions such as whether the particular provisions for extraction fulfils the values associated with the Area CHM designation; ensuring activities are 'carried out for the benefit of mankind as a whole … provid[ing] for the equitable sharing of financial and other economic benefits'[151] and being used exclusively for peaceful purposes.[152]

There are two reasons the ISA adds to our understanding of territory and sovereignty under the proposed reconceptualisation. First, the territory of the ISA does not at all overlap with state territories over the same physical geography.[153] In contrast, the ISA's territory – the Area – does not overlap at all. None of the Area is part of any state's territory. It is defined as 'the seabed and ocean floor and subsoil thereof, *beyond the limits of national jurisdiction*'.[154] Note, the legal provisions flatten the Area into the physical geography – it *is* the seabed and ocean floor. Yet, we now know space *is more than* the physical geography; it is something socially constructed. This space – informed by the definition given to the Area – under the control and influence of the ISA, is its territory. Second, ISA territory allows further consideration of legal bundles, given it involves consideration of the legal bundle associated with the CHM.

[149] ISA, 'About the International Seabed Authority' <www.isa.org.jm/authority> accessed 22 October 2019.

[150] ISA, 'The Mining Code' <www.isa.org.jm/mining-code> accessed 22 October 2019.

[151] Article 140, UNCLOS.

[152] Article 141, UNCLOS.

[153] I have argued elsewhere about the EU's territory which is a much more obvious overlap with state space. See Lythgoe (2022).

[154] UNGAR 48/263 (1994), preamble, emphasis added.

This discussion differs from earlier discussions regarding the re-arrangement of competences and legal relations between states and international organisations. No state had the powers the ISA now has in relation to the particular physical geography and, further, the Area's CHM status expressly disallows the right to appropriation – usually a right associated with 'owning' territory in international law. The CHM and the legal relations provided for in UNCLOS and the law of the sea generally, require a different analysis of the legal realist bundle of rights.

5.4.6 *Concerning the Common Heritage of Mankind*

Before I go further, let me outline the legal provisions creating and informing the space designated as CHM.[155] Key to understanding this legal space and the rights associated with it is Article 137 of UNCLOS which provides:

1. *No State shall claim or exercise sovereignty or sovereign rights over any part of the Area or its resources, nor shall any State or natural or juridical person appropriate any part thereof.* No such claim or exercise of sovereignty or sovereign rights nor such appropriation shall be recognized.
2. *All rights* in the resources of the Area *are vested in mankind as a whole, on whose behalf the Authority shall act.* These resources are not subject to alienation. The minerals recovered from the Area, however, may only be alienated in accordance with this Part and the rules, regulations and procedures of the Authority.
3. No State or natural or juridical person shall claim, acquire or exercise rights with respect to the minerals recovered from the Area except in accordance with this Part. Otherwise, no such claim, acquisition or exercise of such rights shall be recognized. (emphasis added)

Article 137 explicitly provides that no state can exercise sovereign rights over the Area and its resources and that no natural or juridical person may appropriate the Area. This includes international organisations and individuals. How then can it be argued this space is the ISA's territory?

Let us look next at what the CHM is. Most scholarship focuses on the legal content of the CHM and the substantive rules arising from the

[155] Article 136, UNCLOS.

UNCLOS regime, rather than its nature.[156] However, Feichtner defines CHM as a jurisdictional principle, 'like permanent sovereignty over natural resources' and 'forms the basis for the allocation of exploitation rights'.[157] I instead suggest CHM is possibly more comparable to, or in the same analytical category as, the regimes Crawford and Shaw discuss[158] – 'territorial sovereignty' as one such regime – *with implications for jurisdiction* as opposed to it being a jurisdictional principle. CHM is the name given to the bundle of rights – a particular arrangement of the legal bundle of rights, duties, privileges, and no rights. It is thus equivalent to, having the same ontological status as, for example, 'territorial sovereignty'/'sovereignty' or *res communis*. These are just alternative ways to arrange rights for the Area.[159] Each are just names given to what are thought to be a relatively static arrangement of a legal bundle. Moreover, CHM is thought to come with certain assumptions or principles 'built in' to any spaces designated as such; the same too applies to *res communis*. So too was sovereignty as a bundle at one point, yet we have already established that it is not in fact constant and static.

Applying legal realist understandings of legal entitlements to the CHM, we see that the inability to claim and appropriate the Area in Article 137(1) means there is a 'no right' to appropriate as opposed to the absence of a right. Hence, an organisation or state has 'no right' to appropriate and a duty not to appropriate that are packaged together and, as a result, other actors, due to that duty, may protest if that organisation or state appropriates. It is *not* that the ISA 'owns' the Area to the exclusion of others. This arises due to the erroneous idea of exclusivity of states vis-à-vis their territory and the idea that it is possible to 'own' a space in the first place, as opposed to the territory arising as a result of the exercise of control. Applying this to the question of appropriation in CHM, it follows that the arrangement of the legal bundle includes a 'no right' for any actor to exclude others and that no actor may hold the 'complete' bundle of 'sovereign' rights to the exclusion of all others in the Area. It is instead the ISA which has the responsibility and right to supervise and control certain activities in the Area.

Based on Article 137, it might be tempting to argue this is not the territory of the ISA but the territory of mankind: '[a]ll *rights* in the

156 Brownlie (1979); Pinto (2013b).
157 Feichtner (2019) at 601, 604.
158 See discussion in Chapter 3. Also, Crawford (2012) at 203.
159 Feichtner (2019) at 606.

resources of the Area *are vested in mankind as a whole, on whose behalf the Authority shall act*'. Feichtner emphasises that the ISA 'has indeed been established to administer and allocate rights to explore the deep seabed and exploit its mineral deposits on behalf of mankind as a whole'.[160] How can this territory be the ISA's? Three things are notable in answer. First, 'mankind' is not a legal person and has no rights and duties in international law.[161] 'Mankind' does not have standing in courts nor representatives in organs of international organisations. Second, the conceptualisation of territory developed here rejects the idea that territory is 'owned' in the common expression of possession and ownership. Moreover, CHM is a particular configuration of a bundle of legal relations. Territory is a socially produced space for, and created by, the exercise of power, it is not 'owned'. Saying an actor has a territory does not equal ownership. In fact, possession and exclusion are not factors at all. Treating them as factors means we have fallen into the trap of misunderstanding the legal relationship between owner and physical territory and not as between actors. Starting to refer to territory to mean an object moves us back to the realm of physical geography and the exclusivity of the rights of owners. Yet, we know this is not possible with regard to the Area because of Article 137 and its designation at CHM. Instead, the territory where the ISA exercises power is signified by the Area. Third, in the same way the state is theorised as acting on behalf of its population, so could the ISA be thought of as exercising power on behalf of mankind. The state is the oldest recognised unit of international law and according to Crawford, is legally representative (but perhaps not politically so) of their population, exercising rights and duties in international law as the state *qua* a community of persons.[162] Could we think of an international organisation *qua* mankind in the same way? That an international organisation has been given the power by states to 'administer and allocate rights ... on behalf of mankind as a whole'?[163] It is

[160] Feichtner and Ranganathan (2019) at 6, 612.

[161] This was discussed but never solved during the early stages of negotiation. Pinto examined this issue in his Recueil des Cours lectures: 'a question discussed during the early stages ... concerned whether international law had recognised, or would be ready to recognise, "mankind" as a person or legal entity capable of exercising rights, and being required to comply with obligations under that law. Leaving the question unresolved, negotiation of the convention proceeded on the assumption that the concept of "mankind" had been accepted, and was some practical reference value ...' (Pinto (2013b) 58).

[162] Crawford (1992) at 55.

[163] Feichtner (2019) at 612.

therefore acting in trust and exercises control in relation to its territory for mankind, in the same way a state exercises control in relation to its territory for its population.[164] Regardless of the 'why' rationale, which may be interpreted in different ways, the key thing I want to emphasise is that the Area can be understood as the territory of the ISA.

5.4.7 *Identifying the Powers of the ISA and Its Territory*

In the case of the ISA, the various legal provisions and implied powers indicate the arrangement of the sovereignty legal bundle it exercises in relation to the Area. It is possible to argue that these powers and legal rights are similar to many we assume states hold in relation to their territories. Under UNCLOS those particular functions, powers, and legal rights include: the promotion of growth, efficiency and stability of markets for commodities produced from the minerals derived from the Area; participating in commodity conferences and undertaking agreements in its own name; issuing authorisation for the plan of work; exercising control over activities in the Area as necessary for securing compliance with UNCLOS; and the power to limit the level of production of minerals from the Area (UNCLOS, Articles 151 and 153). Prospecting cannot occur without ISA approval (Implementation Agreement (IA), Annex III, Article 2). The approved plan of work must describe the equipment and methods, non-proprietary technology and information, together with any changes to this (IA, Annex III, Article 5) with approvals being for fifteen years. Post approval, the ISA retains control over activities in the Area during the work and may impose monetary penalties for violations (IA, Annex III, Article 18).

Taking a closer look at institutional features, the ISA Assembly's powers include issuing general policies, deciding on the sharing of financial and economic benefits, and suspending the exercise of rights and privileges of membership (UNCLOS, Article 160). The ISA Council's mandate increased during the drafting of the IA from that envisaged by UNCLOS.[165] Whereas the Assembly consists of representatives from member states, the Council has thirty-six nominated representatives (UNCLOS, Article 161). The Council has the power to: issue general

[164] The term 'in trust' or thinking of the ISA as a 'trustee' for mankind in the Area, was prevalent in a lot of discussions and negotiations. Although not part of the legal text explicitly, it underlies a lot of the thinking. On this, see Pinto (2013b) at 24.

[165] Querci (2017a) at 289.

policies; supervise and coordinate implementation of UNCLOS; enter into agreements with other international organisations; issue directives;[166] institute proceedings; issue emergency orders, which may include orders to suspend or adjust operations; disapprove areas for exploitation; and, importantly, to approve the plans of work from operators and exercise control over activities in the Area to ensure compliance with UNCLOS (UNCLOS, Article 162). The Secretariat, which includes the Secretary General and staff, is considered to consist of international civil servants and 'shall not seek or receive instructions from any government or from any other source external to the Authority' (UNCLOS, Article 168). Thus, independence and autonomy of the ISA from its member states is achieved.

The ISA therefore has the power to grant operating licences. No work, not even prospecting, can take place without its permission. This has led some commentators to conclude that: '[t]he ISA's jurisdiction was also to be exclusive because no other entity can engage in activities in the Area without the ISA's approval'.[167] Therefore, for the purposes designated by UNCLOS and the implementation agreement, the legal entitlements in relation to the Area could be said to be 'exclusive' to the ISA (similar to a state's legal rights). No other actor has the legal right to interfere in these areas of power. Furthermore, this mandate might expand beyond that explicitly provided for in the Agreements. Moreover, UNGAR 48/263 determined that the functions are based on an 'evolutionary approach … in order that they may discharge effectively their respective responsibilities at various stages'.[168] This gives a wide-ranging and long-term outlook for the ISA's legal entitlements to increase depending on what is required to fulfil the duties imposed under international law. Further, Jones considers whether the Enterprise could be thought of as having 'primary responsibility for mining' and notes this exists only on paper at the moment.[169] Jones never ventures as far as calling this space territory in the articles, but it read to me as circling around naming this space as such. The exercise of sovereign powers by non-state actors and the spatial logics of the exercise of such functions and powers, etc. simply cannot be described adequately using orthodox concepts, however. There is no

[166] The Enterprise, once operational, will be an organ of the Authority which conducts exploration and exploitation activities, as well as the transporting, processing, and marketing of minerals recovered from the Area.

[167] Querci (2017b) at 216.

[168] UNGAR 48/263 (1994), Annex Section 1, para 4.

[169] Jones (2016) at 315.

reason why this space is not the ISA's territory adopting the proposed concepts.

The above discussion highlights these are major rights in relation to the Area for the ISA. Just as a state exercises control in relation to its territory, so too does the ISA in relation to its territory. Further, this control is exclusive – no other actor or subject in international law has such legal rights in the Area, but they may have rights against the ISA if it acts *ultra vires* or fails in its obligations owed – other than perhaps the abstract 'mankind' which might struggle to bring a case to any court or tribunal. The Area designates where the ISA's authority begins and ends (it is thus bounded), and the ISA retains control over activities in the Area even after granting a licence to explore or exploit. The ISA has a bundle of rights and duties, a bundle of relations exercised in relation to a territory. Adopting a monolithic perspective on sovereignty generates confusion regarding 'ownership' or 'title' in international law and the assumptions that only states exercise sovereign powers, territory means land primarily, and that territory is something only states 'have', would prevent an enriched analytical understanding of such space.

Finally, it can be observed that humans and states have impacted upon the space of the high seas and seabed even if we do not think of them as territories; zoning and rules are imposed on spaces not part of state territories. We can think of these as spaces influenced and disciplined by states together – akin to a communally agreed dispersing of the sovereignty bundle and determining to apply many 'no rights' in these spaces. But this certainly does not mean that these are spaces absent of authority structures. Since the ISA became operational, this position changed. Some legal relations and competences have (re)territorialised into the ISA's territory. There is an identifiable actor responsible for exercising certain rights in relation to its territory in addition to states making determinations regarding the rights in relation to this physical geography. Having applied the reconceptualisation of territory and sovereignty developed in this project, the arrangement of the ISA's legal bundle and the particular rights in the sovereignty bundle being exercised by the ISA are clearer. We have been able to make visible the territory of the ISA which is otherwise invisible in the orthodox account of territory.

5.4.8 *Following the Function: Data*

With this final example, I address the exercise of competences regarding data by international organisations in reference to their spaces and spatial logics. In this example, I focus on the element of the sovereignty bundle that has been reterritorialised as opposed to any one institution and its territory, demonstrating that we can account for the changes taking place from the perspective of both the actor and the function. What is said here about the use of data to govern applies equally to the IMF, World Bank, UN, WHO, EU, OECD, ITU, IAEA, UNFCCC, World Economic Forum, and many other institutions.

The exercise of power and legal rights concerning data is an overlooked function but, while subtle and given less attention until recently,[170] the power to gather and interpret data is a significant element of the 'once state held' bundle of sticks associated with sovereignty currently exercised by international organisations.[171] With a fundamental role in controlling and 'knowing' society, data have always been an important project of power: 'knowledge gives power, more power requires more knowledge, and so on in an increasingly profitable dialectic of information and control'.[172]

One of the first practices credited as having empowered states to triumph over their competitor authority systems (city leagues, empire, etc.) are the early censuses centralising the collection and use of data.[173] The first census of this kind is thought to have taken place in France. Vauban is recorded as creating the first 'list of the people' – an 'ancestor of modern censuses'.[174] This is one of the earliest of functions that, along with other 'little things',[175] such as cartography, were assembled together into the spatial logic of the first states. The importance of census data and knowledge about space garnered through mapping and its contribution to producing the territorial state is recognised by scholars and legal historians, including Ford, who concludes: '[t]he conception of a bounded territorial region itself . . . was in a sense a product of the national project of self knowledge accomplished through the census

[170] The main exception to this is Johns (2016); Johns (2017). Johns's work on data territories is a brilliant contribution, but one which, I think, still primarily associates territories with states alone. See also, Johns in Kuijer and Werner (2017).

[171] Others have argued that data is not as 'intrusive' of sovereignty as other functions. See, for example, 'less interventionist endeavors characteristic of pre-1914 forms of internationalism, such as collecting data, organizing conferences, or standardizing regulations' (Martin (2022) 25). I wholeheartedly disagreed. Data crucial to policy and lawmaking – indeed it has been understood by many as one of the core reasons power was consolidated in the state.

[172] Said (2003) at 44.

[173] Gottmann (1973) at 59.

[174] ibid at 59.

[175] Thrift (2000) at 381–82.

and the map'.[176] Mapping and census-taking were employed by colonial powers to 'know' colonial people and colonised spaces.[177] There is extensive scholarship stressing that data gathering for controlling and producing knowledge is one of the more important sovereign powers: '[a]s nation-states grew and bureaucratized, sovereign power was exercised in the form of census-taking, counting the population, gathering information and regulating citizenship'.[178] Deleuze and Guattari highlight this too:

> [a]rithmetic, the number, has always had a decisive role in the State apparatus: this is so even as early as the imperial bureaucracy, with the three conjoined operations of the census, taxation, and election ... the number has always served to gain mastery over matter, to control its variations and movements, in other words, to submit them to the spatio-temporal framework of the State—either the imperial *spatium*, or the modern *extensio*.[179]

Without censuses and mapmaking, on these arguments, the state we know today would simply not exist.

There has been a noticeable turn to using large scale and complex data to inform governance and the exercise of control by states, international organisations and corporations. This is not to deny data has been used to govern for centuries. Censuses and the use of data for economic planning (data on unemployment, recession data, inflation, exports, GDP, etc.), about income for tax purposes, about housing for planning purposes, etc., have colossally increased since Vauvan's first census. Yet, there is a noticeable turn to entrenched and more complex data governing made possible due to technological developments. Outputs from large datasets are used by public and private sector actors, re-orientating business and political practices towards making best use of 'big data'.

Importantly for this project, many of the powers associated with data have increasingly deterritorialised from state territory and reterritorialised into the spaces of the international organisations as well as other actors, including corporations and private industry bodies. Data then have been *reterritorialised into a space*; it is *not* floating free over global

176 Ford (1999) at 878. In addition to Gottmann, Ford, and Thrift, see Strandsbjerg (2010) at 44–46.

177 Wilson and Donnan (2012) at 581–82; Appadurai (1996) at 116; VanValkenburgh (2017a); VanValkenburgh (2017b) at 117.

178 Mountz in Gallaher and others (2009) at 208.

179 Deleuze and Guattari (1987) at 389.

space aimlessly. International organisations have spaces in relation to which they exercise powers regarding data. The legal rights and power associated with data are being re-assembled in complex relationships between non-state actors and states, determining policies and responses. This represents an unbundling from the state where formerly the state governed through access to such data; data centralised in one institution. This relocation of collecting, determining, and using data from states to international organisations reflects the now well-known general trend of the shift in function from states to international organisations throughout the twentieth century at the very least. The competences in question might include, but are not limited to,: data gathering – on, for example, the economy, incomes, population, education system, policing, etc.; deciding what data to collect, by whom, and how frequently; its analysis, reporting, and interpretation; its communication, that is, what story to tell from data; and using data to implement policies, discipline behaviour, raise revenue, create laws and norms, etc.

5.4.9 *Information-as-Control*[180]

One key example of international organisations using data to govern is the attachment of conditions to assistance made by organisations and banks to states. Data influences the IMF's treatment of, and advice to, states. The IMF has used data to categorise some states as 'Fragile States' and this categorisation was informed by data capturing a range of social, economic, and political factors, including conflict. Based on these determinations, the IMF and other international organisations and financial institutions made decisions, with an enormous capacity to influence 'development' policy, advice, and lending decisions.[181] These categorisations influenced IMF expectations regarding the direction of state policies – perhaps advising a policy of austerity, requiring a commitment to lower government spending by states. The IMF sees itself as 'helping to restore macroeconomic stability, build core macroeconomic policy institutions, and catalyze donor support' in countries 'deemed an international priority because of their own great needs and the dangerous implications of persistent fragility for regional and global stability'.[182]

[180] Cohen (2012) at 6–9.
[181] Taylor and Schroeder (2015) at 503, 506.
[182] International Monetary Fund (2018) at 1.

According to the IMF, fragile states have 'generally limited capacity, weak governance, and often unstable political and security environment'.[183]

This designation influences more than simply the IMF's activities, but also whether and how other states engage in development and national policies, thought to be within the domain of the state to determine. Thus, the application of conditionality to assistance is a process which subtly changes the balance of power but with serious consequences. Tellingly, the IMF itself has realised the application of conditionality – which includes the rather vague 'prior actions, quantitative performance criteria, structural performance criteria, and structural benchmarks'[184] and 'a well-tailored pace of macroeconomic adjustment'; and 'a strictly prioritised, gradual agenda of key structural reforms'[185] – is unsuitable for 'fragile states'.[186]

What this example demonstrates is the multiple uses of data for governing: determining what criteria inform classification of a fragile state; which states are so classified; collection of social, economic, and political data, its interpretation and determining what levels and kinds of adjustment and reform are required. A further striking example is the way data determined and influenced the reaction of the EU and other international organisations to the 2009 Greek economic crisis and the conditions attached to assistance. Notably the EU accused Greece of falsifying economic data,[187] begging the question of how the EU could argue this without first having determined what would be 'correct data'.

From the economic field to humanitarian intervention and the refugee crisis, data are increasingly central to governing. For example, data gathered by the UN in refugee camps determine the management of aid distribution. Johns recently drew attention to UNHRC programmes registering the biometric data of Afghan refugees and their role in allocating humanitarian assistance. During the Haitian cholera outbreak, data from the location of phones was used to extrapolate information about the movement of people and potential spread of cholera.[188] Recently, the UN Statistics Division and the World Bank launched a guide to help nations better manage geospatial data, especially in low-

[183] ibid.
[184] ibid at 19.
[185] ibid at 20.
[186] ibid at 39.
[187] Barber (2010).
[188] Taylor and Schroeder (2015) at 510.

and middle-income countries. The 'Integrated Geospatial Information Framework' 'makes concrete recommendations on establishing national geospatial information management processes and putting that information to use'.[189] In the World Bank representative's own words:

> all governments hold a considerable amount of geospatial information, including databases on who has access to education; communities most affected by poverty; areas at risk of disasters; as well as mobile data that can keep more people informed about disease outbreaks and weather patterns . . .
>
> . . . The Framework will help countries in building capacity for using geospatial technology to enhance informed government decision-making, facilitate private sector development, take practical actions to achieve a digital transformation, and bridge the geospatial-digital divide.[190]

Lastly, although there are many more examples that could be given, there is the UN 'Global Pulse' Initiative, which attempts to 'harness[] big data for development and humanitarian action.'[191] The projects are already numerous and include 'Using Big Data to Study Rescue Patterns in the Mediterranean', 'Estimating Socioeconomic Indicators from Mobile Phone Data in Vanuatu', 'Using Mobile Phone Data and Airtime Credit Purchases to Estimate Food Security', and 'Detecting Structures in Satellite Images with A.I. during Humanitarian Emergencies'.[192] These 'Informing Governance with Social Media Mining'[193] projects mean international organisations steer state and non-state responses on everything from protests to preventing terrorism. Numerous actors are actively involved including local Pulse Labs in New York, Jakarta, and Kampala, UN Innovation, UNHCR, and country teams, as well as partnerships with telecom operators, WFP, FAO, corporations like IBM and universities.

By following the relocation of data competences, we see that both state and non-state actors govern and discipline the activities and people in

[189] 'UN Launches Guide for Countries to Improve Location-Based Data Management to Better Inform Decision-Making' (2018).

[190] ibid.

[191] <www.unglobalpulse.org>.

[192] <www.unglobalpulse.org/projects>. The list goes on and on . . . 'Using Call Detail Records to Understand Refugee Integration in Turkey', 'Understanding Perceptions of Migrants and Refugees with Social Media', 'Exploring the Effects of Extremist Violence on Online Hate Speech', 'An Analysis Tool for Insights into the SDGs'. These are just a handful of big data projects underway by Global Pulse.

[193] <www.unglobalpulse.org/project/informing-governance-with-social-media-mining/>.

their spaces. The World Bank, the UN, the FAO, and countless organisations besides use their powers to exert influence and control activity. These organisations do not act through accidental means around the globe. They are not acting at random and moving 'through space like billiard balls'.[194] They follow their own territorial logic. This power does not float freely and unsystematically around the globe. Moreover, the territories of international organisations are not homogeneous but differently arranged depending on the particular arrangement of data powers between international organisations and states. The potential of this approach, of understanding spaces as territories of each actor, is that it highlights the differently balanced distribution of power between actors without prioritising and naturalising one space over others.

5.5 Conclusion

To recap and conclude this chapter: I have argued that title is no longer a useful operative legal category, not least because it objectifies territory, but also because there is no such thing as a uniform and consistent bundle of legal rights called title. The concept and social practice of title becomes, I am almost afraid to say anticipating a backlash, entirely redundant. I also argued that sovereignty understood as a bundle of legal relations more helpfully explains the practice of sovereignty today and creates the possibility of observing individual legal rights and power. This, in turn, makes it possible to observe where these rights and powers are moving to. I also clarified the idea of exclusivity in international law and indicated that the legal relationship is between actors, not between a state and the physical geography or its natural resources. Instead, I propose understanding circumstances where rights and competences transfer not as territory or property transfer, but of states and international organisations changing the spatial configuration of their exercise of power.

There is no reason why the legal bundle of sovereignty must always be kept whole – it may be thought of as consisting *of a number of rights and attributes*. Nor is there a reason why only states have sovereignty. Other than, that is, the underlying normative positivism present in international law doctrine. My approach suggests viewing sovereignty as a bundle of legal relations, spatialised within a particular framework. This

[194] Sack (2009) at 26.

impacts the orthodox understanding of sovereignty and territory in international law. But as Judge Alvarez observed, in relation to whether 'to abolish the notion of sovereignty of state', '[the notion of sovereignty] has evolved, and we must now adopt a conception of it which will be in harmony with the new conditions of social life'.[195] What is taking place is simply another 'passage *within* the notion of sovereignty'[196] and of territory. It is based on new conditions of social life that I have constructed an interpretation of territory jurisdiction, actorhood, and sovereignty that, I hope, offers an account that is more reflective of social reality.

The pervading assumption that only states can 'have' sovereignty and 'possess' territory contributes to the territorial trap identified by Agnew. Where these are assumed, the rise and fall, decline, or obsoletion narrative concerning territory is always going to be close to the surface. Clearly, other actors are exercising sovereignty powers and rights and they are doing so in relation to their legal and political spaces. But if international legal theory can only account for states doing so, it will only perpetuate such narratives. We can only ever resort to the fall/decline/obsoletion narrative because *where the powers are going and in who's legal space they exist are invisible* for the orthodox theory of territory and sovereignty. We will always only have deterritorialisation without reterritorialisation. Taking reterritorialisation seriously, we might think of neither territory or sovereignty in decline or becoming obsolete, but rather are being refashioned. Our understanding of the concepts can reflect our changing legal realities. This rethinking makes visible and explains the new territories, actors, and processes that have emerged.

[195] Separate Opinion by Judge Alvarez, *Corfu Channel Case* (n 47) 43.
[196] Hardt and Negri (2000) at 88.

6

A New Legal Geography for International Law

For generations . . . space was treated as the dead, the fixed, the undialectical, the immobile.

Michel Foucault, *Power/Knowledge* [1]

If traditional international law and its techniques have little or nothing very apposite to say about ecological calamity, tech-enabled weaponised abuse of humanity and dignity, skewed distribution, human cloning, gene editing, gene drives, artificial intelligence, robotics, or even big-tech corporations and newer space activities, the lawyers might have nothing to do but cast an anxious glance toward the natural scientists or plumbers or the geneticists or the data scientists and hope they can do more . . . With venerable concepts and refurbished concepts and some new concepts, we can employ them as we think anew, to see what we might contribute (as well as what we might not contribute).

Benedict Kingsbury, 'Infrastructure and InfraReg'[2]

Recent decades have seen an important shift take place in the general paradigm of social sciences. Many disciplines are questioning their assumptions and searching for alternative ways to understand international law and politics and global governance. The goal of this book has been to contribute to a vital debate and bring some of this critical rethinking to the discipline of international law, revisiting some of the most traditional and long-established legal concepts, doctrines, and narratives.

My aim has been to understand what has 'happened' to territory in light of the many developments associated with global governance and globalisation taking place, some slowly, some dramatically, over the course of the latter half of the twentieth and the first two decades of

[1] Foucault (1988) at 70.
[2] Kingsbury (2019) at 171, 185–86.

the twenty-first centuries. Having set out originally to explore international law's deterritorialisation, this project in the end arrived at the conclusion that the best way to understand what we are witnessing in the international legal arena today would be to think of it actually as a process of *reterritorialisation* – of the legal bundle of sovereignty and the related international legal regimes by which it is constituted. Far from being made irrelevant or displaced, as claimed by the deterritorialisation narrative, by 'functionalism' and the rise of international organisations, territory remains one of the most important structuring frameworks for ordering international law and politics. To recognise this fact, however, requires us to learn to think of territory not as a physicalised entity or an object of ownership, but, in a broader sense, as the exercise of control over space and as a certain type of political technology. This understanding leads to 'conceiving of territory as the bringing together of a range of different . . . phenomena – economic, strategic, legal, and technical'.[3] And while spaces thus produced occasionally 'might take on a strictly bordered form' of the kind usually associated with Westphalian sovereignty, 'looser, overlapping and multiple arrangements are also possible'.[4] Ultimately, it means 'we can then understand the plurality of different political-spatial arrangements that take place'.[5]

The idea of territory as the exercise of political control over space, however, only marks the beginning of the process of critical rethinking. As lawyers, we must also determine who is appropriately exercising which particular forms of control, in relation to which particular spaces, and how exactly this came to be the case. To achieve this task requires us, however, first to reconceptualise the traditional international law understanding of sovereignty. Rather than being seen as a single monolithic status, sovereignty is better redefined as a bundle of different processes and power relations. By tracing the redistribution of the various competences, privileges, rights, and duties associated with the sovereignty bundle, we can begin to understand the ongoing transformations in the structure of global law and governance as the (re)assembling of new territorial frameworks controlled by a variety of international subjects, including non-state actors.

Concepts do not exist in a vacuum. One of the main consequences of the theoretical exercise proposed in this book is to bring out the idea that

[3] Elden (2011).
[4] ibid.
[5] ibid.

every conception of territory, ultimately, is contingent on the particular historical circumstances surrounding its production – including this one.[6] The geographical imaginary of international law cannot and should not remain frozen. Political and economic realities surrounding the international legal system change, and therefore, so too should its conceptual apparatus. The concept of territory still represents a useful instrument that can help us 'grasp the changes that are taking place in the world today'.[7] Rather than being overtaken by functionality as the central explanatory category for theorising contemporary global governance, it continues alongside it.

6.1 Four Findings

There are four key findings in this book that can transform our disciplinary approach to conceptualising territory. The first is the insight that territory, in law, can be more helpfully understood as a space, not an object. From this stems two further ideas: that every territory is a construct, not a natural fact, and that what this construct represents, ultimately, is not just physical geography. The second key finding is the understanding that territory can have many different configurations and practices constituting it. The third is the conclusion that the traditional legal concept of title does not explain the role territory plays in international law, since territory cannot be owned but is created, and so should be set aside going forward. The fourth finding is that with deterritorialisation always comes reterritorialisation. The transformations that are commonly understood to result in the deterritorialisation of international law, in fact, only lead to respective territorial frameworks being reconfigured and becoming more heterogeneous: 'deterritorialisation, in spite of its name, does not mean the end of the importance of territory. Indeed, far from it, because territory is both its condition of possibility and, in some newly configured form, its necessary outcome.'[8]

Applying these four insights leads to the following conclusions: all spaces are constructed by practices and do not exist separately from these; territory is a particular species of space constituted by practices of control and the exercise of power; the specific building blocks by

[6] The production of this concept of territory is without doubt impossible without the very many thinkers before me.

[7] Elden (2011).

[8] Elden (2006) at 50.

which territories are constructed are reflections of the corresponding bundle of legal relations. The legal relations in question are always multifaceted: each territory is ultimately the result of the exercise of a whole complex of rights, privileges, disablements, etc. that are typically associated with the idea of sovereignty. There exists no single correct way to arrange this sovereign bundle vis-à-vis its spatial dimension. In relation to any one actor's particular territory, different elements of the sovereignty bundle can be exercised.

A fundamentally different understanding of the concept of territory begins to emerge at this point than that underlying most other accounts of global governance and globalisation. Why might such a reconceptualisation be necessary? Kuijer and Werner's analysis illustrates some of the reasons that justify the theoretical exercise proposed in this book project:

> international law underwent significant transformations due to the rise of cosmopolitan values and supranational institutions. The question remains, however, what these transformations imply for the role of territory in international law. On the one hand, they challenge the idea that the best way to make legal sense of the world is to split it up in separate territorial units. On the other hand, they are still in many ways bound up with the powers of the very same States they seek to transgress.[9]

International lawyers retheorised the *dramatis personae* of international law, taking account of the plurality of actors involved in the legal system, but without questioning the spatial imaginary of international law, instead continuing to operate with the spatial logic of only one of these categories of actors. There are many more territories present in the contemporary international legal order than the two-dimensional, flattened units that underlie the spatial imaginary behind Kuijer and Werner's analysis. Theirs is a view of the world which accords with Anderson's observation that '[i]n the modern conception, state sovereignty is fully, flatly and evenly operative over each square centimeter of legally demarcated territory'.[10] The alternative approach proposed in this book allows us to escape from the false dichotomy between the notion of territorially separate legal regimes and the transgression of state powers and state boundaries. State space is only one territorial framework among many in contemporary law and governance, and the bundle of competences and powers constituting it remains in a constant

[9] Kuijer and Werner (2017) at 8.
[10] Anderson (2006) at 19.

process of being readjusted and reassembled. There is no doubt that states continue to wield enormous power. But the practices of modern-day sovereignty are becoming increasingly complicated to disentangle, yet our job as scholars is to attempt it. As sovereign bundles continue to undergo simultaneous processes of deterritorialisation and reterritorialisation, states no longer remain the only actors exercising sovereign powers.

6.2 The Diagnosis: Deterritorialisation without Reterritorialisation

I began by outlining the main theories trying to make sense of the changing dynamics on the international plane in Chapter 2. In particular, I looked at arguments addressing the themes of functionality and porosity of contemporary global governance. I then critiqued these accounts, by demonstrating that they still relied on an implicit prioritisation of states and their spaces, which led them, ultimately, to reproduce rather than question the orthodox concept of territory. With this orthodox conception – one that is not only rooted in the indispensability of state control but is also flattened and physicalised – there was no option BUT to conclude that territory ceased to be an important structuring framework for organising the exercise of global governance. Even those accounts that suggested there had been a relocation of powers, rather than a full deterritorialisation, have been unable to explain fully where and how the powers in question were relocated to; an aterritorial and despatialised future for international law, that could never be critically insightful.

I then outlined what these traditional concepts of territory are, for I do not think there is only one, and defined their relationship with other heartland concepts of subjecthood, sovereignty, and territorial sovereignty. This excavation found that territory often tends to be understood in pseudo-naturalistic terms, that is, it is defined as an element of the natural world or physical geography, though sometimes it is also construed as an area or a space – each of which, of course, implies a rather different real world understanding of the concept of territory. On one level of analysis, there is also present in the discourse a number of different usages of the concept of territory: territory is sometimes an object, sometimes a framework, or sometimes a subject. I concluded that a lack of awareness of this enables conceptual slippages. I also presented the argument and evidence that the discipline of international law tends to presume a very particular spatial imaginary that 'produc[es] international law's map of the world as a jigsaw puzzle of solid colour pieces fitting neatly together'.[11] This puzzle is two-dimensional, and the legal order created by the assemblage of these spatially configured legal regimes can be analogised to a one-level-deep (flat) structure that lacks any 'vertical' dimension. The default assumption produced is that any given piece of physical geography can only be subsumed within one territorial regime and there can never be more than one subject of international law exercising 'territorial' control in respect of any given physical land.

Concerning the concept of sovereignty and territorial sovereignty, I made several observations. A lack of uniformity was found in the way the two concepts are typically understood and there are times where they are used interchangeably. I looked at how the concept of (state-)territory structured the concept and operationalisation of sovereignty in international law discourse. Concerning territorial sovereignty, of the four accounts of territorial sovereignty that are commonly used in international law, one understands territory to be an object of property (*Eigentumstheorie)*, another regards it as an essential (physical) element of the state (*Eigenshaftstheorie)*, a third refers to it as the space of jurisdiction (*Kompetenztheorie)*, and the fourth favours a composite approach which sometimes views territory as an object and sometimes as a space. The implications of this orthodox state-centric concept of territory include the tendency to view the territorial structure of the global legal space as essentially flat, that is, not allowing any 'territorial' overlaps, thus, both presumes and reinforces the tendency to physicalise the concept of territory, reducing the construct of territory to the respective physical geography. It is this understanding of territory which prioritises the spaces of states and makes invisible the territories of actors associated with globalisation and global governance.

My aim with this research project became one of proposing a new legal geography. Thinking against my initial assumptions that territories were less relevant, I wondered if it was possible to instead see the spaces of other actors as territories. But going on this journey meant I had to contend with my own spatial assumptions about territories, to de-physicalise, unflatten and make less state-centric a concept in a way that will allow us to make sense of the new legal spaces and actors entering the

[11] Knop in Crawford and Koskenniemi (2012) at 95.

international legal stage. What is needed for that, however, is a fundamental reconceptualisation of territory and the spatially mediated concepts of sovereignty and jurisdiction and actorhood, indeed the entire spatial imaginary of international law.

6.3 How to Use the 'New' Legal Geography

There are three major steps to this rethink that I outlined in Chapters 4 and 5. Chapter 4 examined the spatial qualities and characteristics of space, which at the same time in many ways also revealed further underlying assumptions and the cartographical disciplining of international law's concept of territory. The main purpose, however, was to rethink how territory is configured through different practices in order to serve as a guide to identify, and make visible, the spatial configuration and relationality of other territories. Other spaces may be contiguous, bounded, or homogeneous without being territories, but this gave us an insight as to how *territories* are constituted. As a result, I argued there is currently one core idea that separates out territory from other spaces, a characteristic that constitutes a space as territory rather than some other space, and that is the notion of territory as controlled and disciplined space. I proposed a reformulation of territory as a space created for and by the exercise of a certain kind of political power, and thereby *excluding* any understanding of territory as a natural or physical object. Territory manifests and becomes real in the practices and exercise of power, and the way these practices are spatially structured determines the basic character of the respective territorial framework. Drawing on Lefebvre, territory, I argued, should be 'understood not as a fixed container of political action and international relations, but rather as a dynamic and constitutive dimension and space of struggle, one that is currently being reconfigured rather than eroded'.[12]

The final step was to insert this new concept into international law's theoretical accounts, including, or especially, to think through how sovereignty might be thought of as operating in relation to these other territories, given the concept is otherwise informed by the 'old' spatial imaginary of international law. Applying insights from legal realism, I explored how we might reformulate the concept of sovereignty as a bundle of legal relations, more accurately representing and interpreting

[12] Lefebvre (2010) at 36.

the complex realities of contemporary global governance. This approach makes it possible to observe individual legal rights and power and where they are reterritorialising to. I explored the common claim that the idea of sovereignty in law conveys the notion of exclusive control vis-à-vis territory and argued that, from a legal point view, this exclusivity should instead focus not on space itself (the idea that the space is exclusive to the state) but with regard *to the corresponding legal rights*. Taking this insight to its logical conclusion, the analysis decouples the idea of sovereignty from that of statehood: sovereign rights in international law can be enjoyed and exercised by different categories of actors, not necessarily limited to states. An implication of this approach was the conclusion that the concept of title does not constitute a useful analytical tool and should therefore be discontinued as an operative legal category. From a legal realist perspective, title has no fixed or stable meaning; nor, in fact, can it really have one. Further, title also necessitates thinking about territory as an object, which is inimical to the proposed new theoretical framework; territory is not owned but created.

6.3.1 Avenues for Further Research

The implications of this rethink of territory for international legal theory and for practice are clear, and in some respects fairly fundamental. I therefore gave three illustrations of how it might be applied in Chapter 5, in which I showed how this theory can also account for and explain the phenomenon of international organisations having their own distinct territories.

The opportunities to study and research further sites of reterritorialisation are numerous. The theoretical approach outlined in this work could be applied to further our understanding of the role international law plays in the construction of global refugee flows and, in particular, the corresponding legal spaces such as refugee camps,[13] but also the spaces of movement and other experiences refugees face in their journeys. It can also be applied to the study of infrastructure spaces, special economic zones (SEZs), and customs unions,[14] used to better explain the role and exercise of power by international organisations in relation to warzones and places of humanitarian catastrophes, and help

[13] Slaughter and Crisp (2009).

[14] A place to start would be: Easterling (2014); Maurer (2001) at 467; Buckley and others (2015) at 103; Abbott and Hampton (1999).

expose more clearly the contours of international law's constantly shifting relationship with neo-colonialism, settler colonialism, extraterritoriality, and hegemony. The novel conception of international law's relationship with space proposed in these pages can also inform a new understanding of the legal and territorial character of drone warfare and influence how the law regulates this issue, and cyberspace. It can also help formulate a different model of human rights protection, one that follows a lot more closely the realities of sovereignty exercised in today's multilayered legal spaces.

Fundamentally, the theoretical account developed in this work makes more concrete both the spatial strategies of different categories of international actors and the specific spatial dynamics of their exercise of power. In doing this, as per de Lapradelle's argument, it allows us to obtain a renewed appreciation of the complex realities of global governance and imperial hegemony rather than dismissing the whole problematic this raises by putting it in the box of 'extraordinary' exercises of jurisdiction. Thinking of the Belt and Road Initiative as just one contemporary example, China does not exercise jurisdiction extraordinarily when it extends the operation of its laws outside the 'territory' cartographically depicted as China. It exercises elements of its sovereignty bundle within that territorial ambit in relation to which these powers have been established. This way of stating the issue has the advantage not only of dispensing with the unnecessary degree of sensationalism that any mention of 'extraordinary' powers tends to invoke. It also helps us appreciate more clearly the complex spatial dynamics of Chinese power, and at the same time creates the possibility to hold China accountable for its activities wherever it factually exercises power. The same example, of course, applies equally to US, British, Dutch, Russian, or EU attempts to assert and exercise power 'extra'-territorially.

Finally, this approach to territory makes more concrete the territories of international law and the exercise of power in relation to international economic and political systems and processes. 'Social reality' according to legal geographers 'is shaped by and understood in terms of space and place'.[15] Where their spaces are unfamiliar or invisible to us, we will always fail to understand these processes and systems as well as we might. For example, the spaces of capital appear to be less concrete, relatable, or real than state space. Capital flows seem to circumvent

[15] Blomley, Delaney, and Ford ('Boundaries and Borders' nd) xv.

international law's spaces; capital appears too fluid and too ephemeral to have any territorial foundation. The primary space that capital is associated with is the globe, which is an ambiguous and imprecise space. And yet, the economic and political processes that constitute the circuits of global capital certainly do not take place haphazardly and at random. Nor do they unfold in this smooth abstract space devoid of any concrete territorial expressions, but operate rather according to very specific and strictly determined territorial logics of different actors. Making these territories visible and making the pictures we develop of them concrete is an absolutely vital task.[16]

Territories can be understood as more complex and dynamic than the discipline of international law has hitherto imagined them to be, and, at the same time, are devastatingly simple if we adopt an understanding of territory as constituted by practices of control performed in relation to specific spaces, and people and activities within those spaces. Territories are formed by social practices and at the same time they inform and direct their course. They are 'full of power and symbolism, a complex web of relations of domination and subordination, of solidarity and cooperation'.[17] And the role that international law plays in this web of relations is only starting to be understood clearly. It starts with fundamentally rethinking international law's geographical imaginary.

[16] There is some excellent work being undertaken in this outside of international law. This includes: Alami (2018) 512; Corbridge, Martin, and Thrift (1994); Leyshon and Thrift (2005).

[17] Massey (1992) at 66.

BIBLIOGRAPHY

Abbott JP and Hampton MP (eds), *Offshore Finance Centres and Tax Havens: The Rise of Global Capital* (Palgrave Macmillan UK 1999)

Abi-Habib M, 'About the Non-Cooperative Countries and Territories (NCCT) Initiative' <www.fatf-gafi.org/publications/fatfgeneral/documents/aboutthenon-cooperativecountriesandterritoriesncctinitiative.html> accessed 4 March 2020

'How China Got Sri Lanka to Cough Up a Port' *The New York Times* (8 October 2018) <www.nytimes.com/2018/06/25/world/asia/china-sri-lanka-port.html> accessed 26 May 2019

Adler-Nissen R and Gad UP (eds), *European Integration and Postcolonial Sovereignty Games: The EU Overseas Countries and Territories* (1st edition, Routledge 2012)

AfriMAP, 'Towards a People-Driven African Union: Current Obstacles and New Opportunities', report written and researched by Ibrahima Kane and Nobuntu Mbelle (African Minds 2007) <www.africanminds.co.za/wp-content/uploads/2012/08/13458150562122113878.pdf> accessed 26 October 2023

Agnew J, 'The Territorial Trap: The Geographical Assumptions of International Relations Theory' (1994) 1 Review of International Political Economy 53

Akehurst M, 'Jurisdiction in International Law' (1972) 46 British Yearbook of International Law 145

A Modern Introduction to International Law (4th edition, George Allan & Unwin (Publishers) Ltd 1982)

Alami I, 'Money Power of Capital and Production of "New State Spaces": A View from the Global South' (2018) 23 New Political Economy 512

Anastasopoulos A and others, *Imperial Geographies in Byzantine and Ottoman Space* (Sahar Bazzaz, Yota Batsaki, and Dimiter Angelov (eds), Harvard University Press 2013)

Anderson B, *Imagined Communities: Reflections on the Origin and Spread of Nationalism* (Revised edition, Verso Books 2006)

Anderson J and O'Dowd L, 'Borders, Border Regions and Territoriality: Contradictory Meanings, Changing Significance' (1999) 33 Regional Studies 593

Aoki K, 'Space Invaders: Critical Geography, the Third World in International Law and Critical Race Theory' (2000) 45 Villanova Law Review 913

Appadurai A, *Modernity at Large: Cultural Dimensions of Globalization* (University of Minnesota Press 1996)

Arbel E, 'Shifting Borders and the Boundaries of Rights: Examining the Safe Third Country Agreement between Canada and the United States' (2013) 25 International Journal of Refugee Law 65

Arboleda M, *Planetary Mine: Territories of Extraction under Late Capitalism* (Verso Books 2020)

Arcuri A and Violi F, 'Reconfiguring Territoriality in International Economic Law' in Martin Kuijer and Wouter Werner (eds), *Netherlands Yearbook of International Law: The Changing Nature of Territoriality in International Law*, vol 47 (TMC Asser Press, Springer 2016)

Arendt H and McCaddon W, *Eichmann in Jerusalem: A Report on the Banality of Evil* (Unabridged edition, Tantor Media Inc 2011)

Baker PJ, 'The Doctrine of Legal Equality of State' (1923) 4 British Yearbook of International Law 21

Balibar É, *Politics and the Other Scene* (Verso 2002)

Barber T, 'Greece Condemned for Falsifying Data' *The Financial Times* (12 January 2010) <www.ft.com/content/33b0a48c-ff7e-11de-8f53-00144feabdc0> accessed 12 October 2019

Barry P, *Beginning Theory* (Manchester University Press 2002)

Bartelson J, 'The Social Construction of Globality' (2010) 4 International Political Sociology 219

'On the Indivisibility of Sovereignty' (2011) 2 Republics of Letters 85–94

Bauder H, 'The Possibilities of Open and No Borders' (2014) 39 Social Justice 76

Benvenisti E, *The Law of Global Governance*, vol 24 (Brill Nijhoff 2014)

Berman PS, 'The Globalization of Jurisdiction' (2002) 151 University of Pennsylvania Law Review 311

'Towards a Cosmopolitan Vision of Conflict of Laws: Redefining Governmental Interests in a Global Era' (2005) 153 University of Pennsylvania Law Review 1819

Bernhardt R (ed), *Encyclopedia of Public International Law* (Elsevier Science Publishers 1984)

Berry E and others, *Complete EU Law: Text, Cases, and Materials* (5th edition, Oxford University Press 2022)

Besson S, 'Sovereignty' in Anne Peters (ed), *Max Planck Encyclopedia of Public International Law* (Oxford University Press 2011)

Bethlehem D, 'The End of Geography: The Changing Nature of the International System and the Challenge to International Law' (2014) 25 European Journal of International Law 9

Biswas S, 'W(h)ither the Nation-State? National and State Identity in the Face of Fragmentation and Globalisation' (2002) 16 Global Society 175

Blomley N, Delaney D, and Ford RT, 'Boundaries and Borders: A Story Map' <www.arcgis.com/apps/MapJournal/index.html?appid=7e4ac025d2b54b2b90b1a597b31526a0> accessed 29 September 2019

The Legal Geographies Reader (Blackwell Publishers 2001)

Bourdieu P, *On the State: Lecture at the College de France, 1989–1992* (Polity Press 2014)

Branch J, *Cartographic State: Maps, Territory, and the Origins of Sovereignty* (Cambridge University Press 2014)

Braverman I and others (eds), *The Expanding Spaces of Law: A Timely Legal Geography* (1st edition, Stanford Law Books 2015)

Brenner N and Elden S, 'Henri Lefebvre on State, Space, Territory' (2009) 3 International Political Sociology 353

Brierly JL, *The Law of Nations: An Introduction to the International Law of Peace* (4th edition, Oxford University Press 1949)

Brölmann C, 'Deterritorialisation in International Law: Moving Away from the Divide between National and International Law' in Janne E Nijman and André Nollkaemper (eds), *New Perspectives on the Divide between National and International Law* (Oxford University Press 2007)

Broome A and Seabrooke L, 'Seeing Like an International Organisation' (2012) 17 New Political Economy 1

Brownlie I, 'Legal Status of Natural Resources in International Law (Some Aspects)' (1979) 162 Collected Courses of the Hague Academy of International Law 245–318

The Rule of Law in International Affairs: International Law at the Fiftieth Anniversary of the United Nations (Kluwer Law International 1998) 156–61

Principles of Public International Law (7th edition, Oxford University Press 2008)

Bruce Katz and Jennifer Bradley, *The Metropolitan Revolution: How Cities and Metros Are Fixing Our Broken Politics and Fragile Economy* (Brookings Institution Press 2014)

Brunet-Jailly E, 'The State of Borders and Borderlands Studies 2009: A Historical View and a View from the Journal of Borderlands Studies' (2010) 1 Eurasia Border Review 1–15

Buckley PJ and others, 'The Economic Geography of Offshore Incorporation in Tax Havens and Offshore Financial Centres: The Case of Chinese MNEs' (2015) 15 Journal of Economic Geography 103

Burghardt AF, 'The Bases of Territorial Claims' (1973) 63 Geographical Review 225

Burton P, *The Jurisdiction of International organisations*, PhD Thesis (University of Manchester 2018) <www.research.manchester.ac.uk/portal/files/70405473/FULL_TEXT.PDF> accessed 26 February 2020

Buzan B and Little R, 'Beyond Westphalia? Capitalism after the "Fall"' (1999) 25 Review of International Studies 89

Callamard A, 'Use of Armed Drones for Targeted Killings. Report of the Special Rapporteur on Extrajudicial, Summary or Arbitrary Executions' (UN Human Rights Council 2020) A/HRC/44/38

Casteleiro AD, *The International Responsibility of the European Union: From Competence to Normative Control* (Cambridge University Press 2016)

Castellarin E, *La Participation de l'Union Européenne Aux Institutions Économiques Internationales* (Editions A Pedone 2017)

Cavnar A, 'Accountability and the Commission on the Limits of the Continental Shelf: Deciding Who Owns the Ocean Floor' (2009) 42 Cornell International Law Journal 388–440

Chimni BS, 'A Just World Under Law: A View from the South' (2006) 100 Proceedings of the Annual Meeting (American Society of International Law) 17

Clapham A, *Brierly's Law of Nations: An Introduction to the Role of International Law in International Relations* (7th edition, Oxford University Press, 2012)

Cohen FS, 'Transcendental Nonsense and the Functional Approach' (1935) 35 Columbia Law Review 809

Cohen JE, *Configuring the Networked Self: Law, Code, and the Play of Everyday Practice* (Yale University Press 2012)

Collins R, 'Sovereignty Has "Rock-All" to Do with It . . . or Has It? What's at Stake in the Recent Diplomatic Spat between Scotland and Ireland?' (EJIL: Talk!, 8 July 2019) <www.ejiltalk.org/sovereignty-has-rock-all-to-do-with-it-or-has-it-whats-at-stake-in-the-recent-diplomatic-spat-between-scotland-and-ireland/> accessed 26 March 2020

Corbin A, 'Taxation of Seats on the Stock Exchange' [1922] Faculty Scholarship Series, Yale Law School Legal Scholarship Repository 429

Corbin AL, 'Rights and Duties' (1924) 33 Yale Law Journal 502

Corbridge S, Martin R, and Thrift N (eds), *Money, Power and Space* (Blackwell 1994)

Craven M and Parfitt R, '7. Statehood, Self-Determination, and Recognition' in Malcolm D Evans (ed), *International Law* (5th edition, Oxford University Press 2018)

Crawford J (ed), *The Rights of Peoples* (Oxford University Press 1992)

Creation of States in International Law – Oxford Scholarship (Oxford University Press 2006)

Brownlie's Principles of Public International Law (8th edition, Oxford University Press 2012)

Brownlie's Principles of Public International Law (9th edition, Oxford University Press 2019)

Crawford J and Koskenniemi M (eds), *The Cambridge Companion to International Law* (Cambridge University Press 2012)

Curtis S, 'Global Cities and the Transformation of the International System' (2011) 37 Review of International Studies 1923

Cutler, AC, 'Transformations in Statehood, the Investor-State Regime, and the New Constitutionalism' (2016) 23 Indiana Journal of Global Legal Studies 95

d'Aspremont J, *After Meaning: The Sovereignty of Forms in International Law* (Edward Elgar Publishing 2021)

d'Aspremont J and Singh S (eds), *Concepts for International Law: Contributions to Disciplinary Thought* (Edward Elgar Publishing 2019)

Dagron S, 'Lawrence O. Gostin. Global Health Law' (2014) 25 European Journal of International Law 949

Dalby S, 'IV. Reading Peet, (Re)Reading Fukuyama: Political Geography at "the End of History"' (1993) 12 Political Geography 87

Dalrymple T, 'Why Borders Matter' *The Spectator* (1 September 2012) <www.spectator.co.uk/article/why-borders-matter/> accessed 12 October 2023

Daugherty JS, 'A Reflection on the Phenomenology of Tibetan Space' (*JHI Blog*, 28 February 2018) <http://jhiblog.org/2018/02/28/a-reflection-on-the-phenomenology-of-tibetan-space/> accessed 27 January 2023

Davies A, 'Episode: Milton Santos. "For a New Geography" (U Minnesota Press, 2021)', *New Books in Critical Theory podcast* (8 June 2022) <https://newbooksnetwork.com/for-a-new-geography> accessed 16 October 2023

Davis B, 'Rise of Nationalism Frays Global Ties' *The Wall Street Journal* (28 April 2008) <www.wsj.com/articles/SB120934738145948747> accessed 12 October 2023

de Sousa Santos B, 'Law: A Map of Misreading. Toward a Postmodern Conception of Law' [1987] Journal of Law and Society 279

'Definition of Appurtenance' <www.merriam-webster.com/dictionary/appurtenance> accessed 3 December 2018

'Definition of Framework' <www.merriam-webster.com/dictionary/framework> accessed 20 August 2019

Delaney D, *Territory: A Short Introduction* (Blackwell Publishing 2005)

Deleuze G and Guattari F, *Anti-Oedipus: Capitalism and Schizophrenia* (University of Minnesota Press 1983)

A Thousand Plateaus: Capitalism and Schizophrenia (Brian Massumi tr, University of Minnesota Press 1987)

Der Derian J and others, 'How Should Sovereignty Be Defended? in Christopher Bickerton, Philip Cunliffe, and Alexander Gourevitch (eds), *Politics Without Sovereignty* (UCL Press 2007) 187

Derrida J, 'Letter to a Japanese Friend' in David Wood and Robert Bernasconi (eds), *Derrida and Différance* (Parousia Press 1985)

Of Grammatology (Johns Hopkins University Press 1998)

Dinwoodie GB, 'A New Copyright Order: Why National Courts Should Create Global Norms' (2000) 149 University of Pennsylvania Law Review 469

Distefano G, 'Theories on Territorial Sovereignty: A Reappraisal' (2010) 41 Journal of Sharia and Law 25–47

Dobson NL, 'The EU's Conditioning of the "Extraterritorial" Carbon Footprint: A Call for an Integrated Approach in Trade Law Discourse' (2018) 27 Review of European, Comparative & International Environmental Law 75

Douglas IR, 'Globalisation and the End of the State?' (1997) 2 New Political Economy 165

Dugard J and Reynolds J, 'Apartheid, International Law, and the Occupied Palestinian Territory' (2013) 24 European Journal of International Law 867

Dukeminier J, Krier JE, and Alexander GS, *Property* (6th edition, Aspen Publishers 2006)

Durieux J-F, 'The Duty to Rescue Refugees' (2016) 28 International Journal of Refugee Law 637

'Dynamic Territories (S. Elden)' (*ICE LAW Project*, 20 August 2014) <https://icelawproject.weebly.com/dynamic-territories-s-elden.html> accessed 26 October 2023

Eagleton T, *Against the Grain: Essays 1975–1985: Selected Essays* (Verso 1986)

Easterbrook F, 'The Corporate Contract' (1989) 89 Columbia Law Review 1416–48

Easterling K, *Extrastatecraft: The Power of Infrastructure Space* (Verso Books 2014)

Egan B and Place J, 'Minding the Gaps: Property, Geography, and Indigenous Peoples in Canada' (2013) 44 Geoforum 129

Elcin M, *'Lex Mercatoria in International Arbitration Theory and Practice, Volume 1'* (EUI 2012)

Elden S, 'Missing the Point: Globalization, Deterritorialization and the Space of the World' (2005) 30 Transactions of the Institute of British Geographers 8

'The State of Territory under Globalization: Empire and the Politics of Reterritorialization' (2006) 12 Thamyris/Intersecting: Place, Sex and Race 47

'Land, Terrain, Territory' (2010) 34 Progress in Human Geography 799

'Territory without Borders' 2011 *Harvard International Review*, 21 August <http://hir.harvard.edu/territory-without-borders/> accessed 14 March 2017

The Birth of Territory (University of Chicago Press 2013)

'How Should We Do the History of Territory?' (2013) 1 Territory, Politics, Governance 5

Elden S and Crampton JW (eds), *Space, Knowledge and Power: Foucault and Geography* (Routledge 2016)

Emmenegger S, 'Extraterritorial Economic Sanctions and Their Foundation in International Law' (2016) 33 Arizona Journal of International & Comparative Law 31, 632–60

Emmerson B, 'Statement by Ben Emmerson, UN Special Rapporteur on Counter Terrorism and Human Rights Concerning the Launch of an Inquiry into the Civilian Impact, and Human Rights Implications of the Use of Drones and Other Forms of Targeted Killing for the Purpose of Counter-Terrorism and Counter-Insurgency' (2012)

'ESDP – European Spatial Development Perspective: Towards Balanced and Sustainable Development of the Territory of the European Union' (Office for Official Publications of the European Communities 1999)

Evans M, *International Law* (1st edition, Oxford University Press 2003)

Evans MD (ed), *International Law* (4th edition, Oxford University Press 2014)

'Explained: Why Canada Has Banned Foreigners from Buying Houses for 2 Years' *Firstpost* (2 January 2023) <www.firstpost.com/explainers/canada-ban-foreigners-buying-houses-two-years-justin-trudeau-11910942.html> accessed 4 January 2023

Fassbender B and others, *The Oxford Handbook of the History of International Law* (Oxford University Press 2012)

Fawcett JES, 'General Course on Public International Law (Volume 132)' [1971] Collected Courses of the Hague Academy of International Law 363–575

Feichtner I, 'Sharing the Riches of the Sea: The Redistributive and Fiscal Dimension of Deep Seabed Exploitation' (2019) 30 European Journal of International Law 601

Feichtner I and Ranganathan S, 'International Law and Economic Exploitation in the Global Commons: Introduction' (2019) 30 European Journal of International Law 6

Ferguson J, 'Seeing like an Oil Company: Space, Security, and Global Capital in Neoliberal Africa' (2005) 107 American Anthropologist 377

Ferguson J and Gupta A, 'Spatializing States: Toward an Ethnography of Neoliberal Governmentality' (2002) 29 American Ethnologist 981

Fischer-Lescano A and Teubner G, 'Regime-Collisions: The Vain Search for Legal Unity in the Fragmentation of Global Law' (2004) 25 Michigan Journal of International Law 999–1046, 999

Ford RT, 'Law's Territory (A History of Jurisdiction)' (1999) 97 Michigan Law Review 843

Foucault M, 'Space, Knowledge and Power' in Paul Rabinow (ed), *The Foucault Reader* (Penguin 1984) 239–56

Power/Knowledge: Selected Interviews and Other Writings, 1972–1977 (1st American edition, Random House USA Inc 1988)

The Order of Things: Archaeology of the Human Sciences (Routledge 2002)

Security, Territory, Population: Lectures at the College de France 1977–1978 (Michel Senellart and others (eds), Graham Burchell tr, 1st edition, Picador USA 2009)

'Fragmentation of International Law: Difficulties Arising from the Diversification and Expansion of International Law. Report of the Study Group of the International Law Commission: Finalized by Martti Koskenniemi' (International Law Commission, UN General Assembly 2006) A/CN.4/L.682

'Frontex "Origin & Tasks' <www.frontex.europa.eu/about-frontex/who-we-are/tasks-mission/> accessed 26 October 2023

Gallaher C and others, *Key Concepts in Political Geography* (SAGE Publications Ltd 2009)

Gardiner CA, 'Our Right to Acquire and Hold Foreign Territory' (1899) 33 The American Law Review 161

Gathii JT, 'Geographical Hegelianism in Territorial Disputes Involving Non-European Land Relations: An Analysis of the Case Concerning *Kasikili/Sedudu Island* (Botswana/Namibia)' (2002) 15 Leiden Journal of International Law 581

'Burying Sovereignty All Over Again: A Brief Review of Don Herzog's Sovereignty RIP' *EJILTalk!* 7 July 2020 <www.ejiltalk.org/burying-sovereignty-all-over-again-a-brief-review-of-don-herzogs-sovereignty-rip/> accessed 12 October 2023

'Geography, n.' <www.oed.com/view/Entry/77757> accessed 21 February 2020

Gordon H, *Notes from Deep Time: A Journey through Our Past and Future Worlds* (Profile Books 2021)

Gorji M, 'Being Unsituated: Christina Rossetti's Prepositions' (2019) 41 Nineteenth-Century Contexts 9

Gottmann J, *The Significance of Territory* (The University Press of Virginia 1973)

'The Evolution of the Concept of Territory' (1975) 14 Social Science Information 29

Gregory D, *The Colonial Present* (Blackwell Publishing 2004)

Gross C, 'The Court of Piepowder' (1906) 20 The Quarterly Journal of Economics 231

Güzel MŞ, *The Chagos Archipelago Case in the International Court of Justice* (Lulu Press 2020)

Hagan J, 'Borders and Boundaries', *Oxford Bibliographies* (Oxford University Press 2018)

Hall D, 'Borders, Divisions and the Space Between: Three Writers on Borders' (2018) (Pantograph Punch) <https://pantograph-punch.com//posts/borders> accessed 27 January 2023

Hanson D, 'Op-Ed: Why Borders Matter and a Borderless World Is a Fantasy' *Los Angeles Times* (31 July 2016) <www.latimes.com/opinion/op-ed/la-oe-hanson-borders-20160731-snap-story.html> accessed 12 October 2023

Haraway D, 'Situated Knowledges: The Science Question in Feminism and the Privilege of Partial Perspective' (1988) 14 Feminist Studies 575

Hardt M and Negri A, *Empire* (Harvard University Press 2000)

Harrison J, 'Unpacking the Legal Disputes over Rockall' (*SPICe (Scottish Parliament Information Centre) Spotlight | Solas air SPICe*, 18 June 2019) <https://spice-spotlight.scot/2019/06/18/guest-blog-unpacking-the-legal-disputes-over-rockall/> accessed 26 March 2020

Haskell J, '3 Crypto Fallacies' (Crypto Law Review, 31 May 2022) <https://medium.com/cryptolawreview/3-crypto-fallacies-f808c58e5675> accessed 27 January 2023

'The Spatial Dimensions of Extraterritoriality' <www.academia.edu/31265232/The_Spatial_Dimensions_of_Extraterritoriality> accessed 7 February 2017

Held D, *A Globalizing World?* (Routledge in association with The Open University 2004)

Held D and McGrew A, *Globalization/Anti-Globalization: Beyond the Great Divide* (2nd edition, Polity 2007)

Helmig J and Kessler O, 'Space, Boundaries, and the Problem of Order: A View from Systems Theory' (2007) 1 International Political Sociology 240

Herman R, 'Reflections on the Importance of Indigenous Geography' (2008) 32 American Indian Culture and Research Journal 73

Herzog D, *Sovereignty, RIP* (Yale University Press 2020)

Hill G, 'The Map and International Law's Stifled Visual Discourse' (2021) 13 European Journal of Legal Studies 15

Hinojosa-Martínez LM, 'President's Message: Sovereignty and Globalization' (*ESIL Newsletter, European Society of International Law|Société européenne de droit international*, June 2019) <https://esil-sedi.eu/esil-newsletter-june-2019/> accessed 28 June 2019

Holland EW, 'Deterritorializing "Deterritorialization": From the "Anti-Oedipus" to "A Thousand Plateaus"' (1991) 20 SubStance 55

Horsman M and Marshall A, *After the Nation-State* (HarperCollins 1994)

Horwitz MJ, *The Transformation of American Law 1870–1960: The Crisis of Legal Orthodoxy* (Oxford University Press 1992)

Houtum H van, *B/Ordering Space* (Olivier Kramsch (ed), 1st edition, Routledge 2004)

Hudson A, 'Beyond the Borders: Globalisation, Sovereignty and Extra-Territoriality' (1998) 3 Geopolitics 89

Hurd I, *International Organisations: Politics, Law, Practice* (Cambridge University Press 2014)

Hurst CJB, 'Wanted: An International Court of Piepowder' (1925) 6 British Year Book of International Law 61

'ICAN Cities Appeal' <https://cities.icanw.org/> accessed 3 January 2020

The IGLP Law and Global Production Working Group, 'The Role of Law in Global Value Chains: A Research Manifesto' (2016) 4 London Review of International Law 57

'IMF Country Focus: Uganda's Economic Outlook in Six Charts' (*IMF*, 9 May 2019) <www.imf.org/en/News/Articles/2019/05/08/na-0508-ugandas-economic-outlook-in-six-charts> accessed 17 May 2019

'India and Bangladesh Seal Land Swaps' *BBC News* (6 June 2015) <www.bbc.com/news/world-asia-33033342> accessed 23 April 2019

International Court of Justice, 'Part II. Speeches Made and Documents Read Before the Court.' From *Nationality Decrees Issued in Tunis and Morocco (French Zone) on November 8th, 1921, Great Britain v France* (1923) no. 4 (1923) PCIJ Series B no 4 (Permanent Court of International Justice)

International Monetary Fund, 'The IMF and Fragile States: 2018 Evaluation Report.' (International Monetary Fund 2018)

'Iran Files Complaint against U.S. over Violating Its Airspace' *Tehran Times* (29 June 2019) <www.tehrantimes.com/news/437540/Iran-files-complaint-against-U-S-over-violating-its-airspace> accessed 11 August 2019

'The Island that Switches Countries Every Six Months' *BBC News* (28 January 2018) <www.bbc.com/news/stories-42817859> accessed 23 April 2019

Jackson RH and James A (eds), *States in a Changing World: A Contemporary Analysis* (Clarendon Press 1993)

Jeng A (ed), 'Towards an Introduction', *Peacebuilding in the African Union: Law, Philosophy and Practice* (Cambridge University Press 2012)

Jenkins K, *Re-Thinking History* (3rd edition, Routledge 2003)

Jennings RY, *The Acquisition of Territory in International Law* (Manchester University Press 1963)

Jensen ET, 'Cyber Sovereignty: The Way Ahead' (2015) 50 Texas International Law Journal 275

Jessup P, *Transnational Law* (Yale University Press 1956)

Johns F, 'Data Mining as Global Governance' in Roger Brownsword, Eloise Scotford, and Karen Yeung (eds), *The Oxford Handbook on the Law and Regulation of Technology*, vol 1 (Oxford University Press 2017)

Johns FE, 'Data Territories: Changing Architectures of Association in International Law' (Social Science Research Network 2016) SSRN Scholarly Paper ID 2810897 <https://papers.ssrn.com/abstract=2810897> accessed 8 February 2017

Johnson DR, 'Reflections on the Bundle of Rights' (2007) 32 Vermont Law Review 247

Jones H, 'Lines in the Ocean: Thinking with the Sea about Territory and International Law' (2016) 4 London Review of International Law 307

Jones R and others, 'Interventions on the State of Sovereignty at the Border' (2017) 59 Political Geography 1

Kaminer M, 'Do You Want to Buy a House in Canada? Not So Fast.' *The New York Times* (29 December 2022) <www.nytimes.com/2022/12/29/realestate/canada-bans-foreign-buyers.html> accessed 4 January 2023

Kapur R, 'The "Other" Side of Globalization: The Legal Regulation of Cross-Border Movements' (2003) 22 Canadian Women's Studies 6–15

Karayanni M, *Conflicts in a Conflict: A Conflict of Laws Case Study on Israel and the Palestinian Territories*, vol 5 (Oxford University Press 2014)

Katz B and Bradley J, *The Metropolitan Revolution: How Cities and Metros Are Fixing Our Broken Politics and Fragile Economy* (Brookings Institution Press 2014)

Kelsen H, *The Law of the United Nations* (Praeger 1950) 706–8

'Théorie du droit international public' (1953) 84 Collected Courses of the Hague Academy of International Law 13–32

Principles of International Law (2nd Revised edition, Holt, Rinehart and Winston, Inc 1966)

Pure Theory of Law (University of California Press 1967) 198–204, 214–17

Kennedy DW, 'New Approaches to Comparative Law: Comparativism and International Governance' [1997] Utah Law Review 545

'Tom Franck and the Manhattan School' (2002) 35 New York University Journal of International Law and Politics 397

'The Disenchantment of Logically Formal Legal Rationality, or Max Weber's Sociology in the Genealogy of the Contemporary Mode of Western Legal Thought' (2004) 55 Hastings Law Journal 1031

'The Mystery of Global Governance' (2008) 34 Ohio Northern University Law Review 827

Kennedy M, 'Overseas Territories in the WTO' (2016) 65 International and Comparative Law Quarterly 741

Kesby A, 'The Shifting and Multiple Border and International Law' (2007) 27 Oxford Journal of Legal Studies 101

Khalili L, *Sinews of War and Trade: Shipping and Capitalism in the Arabian Peninsula* (Verso Books 2020)

Khan D-E, 'Territory and Boundaries', *The Oxford Handbook of the History of International Law* (Oxford University Press 2012)

Kingsbury B, 'Legal Positivism as Normative Politics: International Society, Balance of Power and Lassa Oppenheim's Positive International Law' (2002) 13 European Journal of International Law 401

'Infrastructure and InfraReg: On Rousing the International Law "Wizards of Is"' (2019) 8 Cambridge International Law Journal 171

Kingsbury B, Krisch N, and Stewart RB, 'The Emergence of Global Administrative Law' (2005) 68 Law and Contemporary Problems 15

Klabbers J, *International Law* (2nd edition, Cambridge University Press 2017)

Klauser FR, 'Rethinking the Relationships between Society and Space: A Review of Claude Raffestin's Conceptualisation of Human Territoriality' (2008) WP 37, Social Sciences Research Centre, National University of Galway, Galway <www.academia.edu/7934642/Rethinking_the_Relationships_between_Society_and_Space_A_Review_of_Claude_Raffestins_Conceptualisation_of_Human_Territoriality> accessed 26 October 2023

Kohen M (ed), *Territoriality and International Law* (Edward Elgar Publishing 2016)

Koller DS, 'The End of Geography: The Changing Nature of the International System and the Challenge to International Law: A Reply to Daniel Bethlehem' (2014) 25 European Journal of International Law 25

Korhonen O, 'Within and Beyond Interdisciplinarity in International Law and Human Rights' (2017) 28 European Journal of International Law 625

Koskenniemi M, 'What Should International Lawyers Learn from Karl Marx?' (2004) 17 Leiden Journal of International Law 229

Koskenniemi M and Schult A, 'Sovereignty, Property, and the Locus of Power' (*JHIBlog*, 17 October 2018) <https://jhiblog.org/2018/10/17/sovereignty-property-and-the-locus-of-power-anne-schult-interviews-martti-koskenniemi-on-the-conceptual-history-of-international-law/> accessed 26 October 2023

Kranjec A and others, 'Prescribed Spatial Prepositions Influence How We Think about Time' (2010) 114 Cognition 111

Kratochwil F, 'Of Systems, Boundaries, and Territoriality: An Inquiry into the Formation of the State System' (1986) 39 World Politics 27

Krauthammer C, 'To War, Not to Court' *Washington Post* (12 September 2001) <www.washingtonpost.com/archive/opinions/2001/09/12/to-war-not-to-court/86d5f7a6-b901-4a70-93be-01e718471169/> accessed 11 March 2020

Krieger H and Nolte G, 'The International Rule of Law: Rise or Decline? – Points of Departure', *KFG Working Paper Series, No. 1. October 2016* (2016) <https://ssrn.com/abstract=2866940> accessed 21 February 2017

Krisch N (ed), *Entangled Legalities Beyond the State* (Cambridge University Press 2021)

'Jurisdiction Unbound: (Extra)Territorial Regulation as Global Governance' (2022) 33 European Journal of International Law 481

Kritsiotis D, 'Public International Law and Its Territorial Imperative' (2009) 30 Michigan Journal of International Law 21

Kuijer M and Werner W (eds), *Netherlands Yearbook of International Law 2016: The Changing Nature of Territoriality in International Law*, vol 47 (TMC Asser Press, Springer 2017)

Kwiatkowska B, 'Judge Shigeru Oda's Opinions in Law-of-the-Sea Cases: Equitable Maritime Boundary Delimitation' [1993] German Yearbook of International Law 225

Kwiecień R, 'Does the State Still Matter? Sovereignty, Legitimacy and International Law' [2012] Polish Yearbook of International Law 45

Lachs M, 'The Development and General Trends of International Law in Our Time', *Collected Courses of the Hague Academy of International Law*, vol 169 (Martinus Nijhoff Publishers 1984)

Lambach D, 'The Territorialization of Cyberspace' (2020) 22 International Studies Review 482

Landauer C, 'The Ever-Ending Geography of International Law: The Changing Nature of the International System and the Challenge to International Law: A Reply to Daniel Bethlehem' (2014) 25 European Journal of International Law 31

'Landscape and Geology' (*Lake District National Park*, 18 September 2006) <www.lakedistrict.gov.uk/learning/geology> accessed 27 January 2023

Larkins J, *From Hierarchy to Anarchy* (Palgrave Macmillan 2009) <www.palgraveconnect.com/doifinder/10.1057/9780230101555> accessed 3 March 2016

From Hierarchy to Anarchy: Territory and Politics before Westphalia (Palgrave Macmillan 2010)

Larsen SC and Johnson JT, 'In between Worlds: Place, Experience, and Research in Indigenous Geography' (2012) 29 Journal of Cultural Geography 1

Lauterpacht E, *International Law: Being the Collected Papers of Hersch Lauterpacht*, vol 1 (Cambridge University Press 1970)

Lauterpacht H, *International Law, a Treatise by L. Oppenheim, Volume 1. Peace.* (8th edition, Longmans, Green & Co 1955)

Lefebvre H, 'Reflections on the Politics of Space' (1976) 8 Antipode 30

The Production of Space (1st edition, Donald Nicholson-Smith tr, Wiley-Blackwell 1991)

State, Space, World: Selected Essays (Neil Brenner and Stuart Elden (eds), University of Minnesota Press 2010)

Leyshon A and Thrift N, *Money/Space: Geographies of Monetary Transformation* (Routledge 2005)

Lindahl H, 'A-Legality: Postnationalism and the Question of Legal Boundaries' (2010) 73 The Modern Law Review 30

Fault Lines of Globalization: Legal Order and the Politics of A-Legality (Oxford University Press 2013)

Liste P, 'Colliding Geographies: Space at Work in Global Governance' 19 Journal of International Relations and Development 199

Llewellyn KN, *The Theory of Rules* (Frederick Schauer (ed), University of Chicago Press 2011)

Lowe V, *International Law* (Oxford University Press 2007)

Luhmann N, 'Die Weltgesellschaft' (1971) Archiv für Rechts und Sozialphilosophie 21, reprinted in Soziologische Aufklärung (1986)

Politische Theorie im Wohlfahrtsstaat (Olzog 1981) 22

Lythgoe G, 'Distinct Persons; Distinct Territories: Rethinking the Spaces of International Organisations' (2022) 19 International Organisations Law Review 365–90

'The Changing "Landscape" of Sovereignty Viewed through the Lens of International Tax: Reterritorializing the Offshore' (2022) 59 Canadian Yearbook of International Law/Annuaire canadien de droit international 171

'The Spaces of the Universal and the Particular in International Law: Questioning Binaries and Uncovering Political Projects' in Işıl Aral and Jean d'Aspremont (eds), *Universality and International Law* (forthcoming Oxford University Press 2024)

Eradicating the exceptional: The role of territory in structuring international legal thought Leiden Journal of International Law, 2023, First View, pp. 1–18 DOI: https://doi.org/10.1017/S0922156523000675

Lythgoe G and Tams CJ, 'Multi-level Governance of Global Health: Lessons from Covid-19' (2020) 2 GCR Quarterly 3

MacCormick N, *Questioning Sovereignty: Law, State, and Nation in the European Commonwealth* (Oxford University Press 1999)

Malanczuk P, *Akehurst's Modern Introduction to International Law* (7th edition, Routledge 1997)

Mars S de, *EU Law in the UK* (Oxford University Press 2020)

Martin J, *The Meddlers: Sovereignty, Empire, and the Birth of Global Economic Governance* (Harvard University Press 2022)

Martin R (ed), *Money and the Space Economy* (John Wiley & Sons Ltd 1999)

Marx K and Engels F, *Manifesto of the Communist Party* (Marxists Internet Archive (marxists.org) 1987, 2000, 2010 P 1848)

Marzal T, 'Quantum (in)Justice: Rethinking the Calculation of Compensation and Damages in ISDS' (2021) 22 Journal of World Investment and Trade 249

Massey D, 'Politics and Space/Time' (1992) 196 New Left Review 65–84

For Space (SAGE Publications Ltd 2005)

Massumi B, *A User's Guide to Capitalism and Schizophrenia* (MIT Press 1992)

Maurer B, 'Islands in the Net: Rewiring Technological and Financial Circuits in the "Offshore" Caribbean' (2001) 43 Comparative Studies in Society and History 467

Mbengue, Makane Moïse, 'Non-Self-Governing Territories', *Oxford Public International Law (OPIL)* (Oxford University Press 2013)

McCarthy J, 'Territoriality' in Mark Bevir (ed), *Encyclopedia of Governance* (SAGE Publications, Inc 2007)

McDougal MS, 'International Law, Power, and Policy: A Contemporary Conception' (1953) 82 Recueil des Cours 137, 161.

Mégret F, 'Are There "Inherently Sovereign Functions" in International Law?' (2021) 115 American Journal of International Law 452

Menon PR, 'The Legal Personality of International Organisations' (1992) 4 Sri Lankan Journal of International Law 21

Mezzadra S and Neilson B, *Border as Method, or, the Multiplication of Labor* (Duke University Press 2013)

Milano E, 'The Deterritorialisation of International Law' (2013) 2 ESIL Reflections 6

Milanovic M, 'From Compromise to Principle: Clarifying the Concept of State Jurisdiction in Human Rights Treaties' (2008) 8 Human Rights Law Review 411

'The Spatial Dimension: Treaties and Territory' in Christian J Tams, Antonios Tzanakopoulos, and Andreas Zimmermann (eds), *Research Handbook on the Law of Treaties* (Edward Elgar Publishing 2014) Electronic copy available at: <http://ssrn.com/abstract=2180597>

Miller RA and Bratspies RM (eds), *Progress in International Law* (Martinus Nijhoff Publishers 2008)

Mills A, 'Rethinking Jurisdiction in International Law' (2014) 84 British Yearbook of International Law 187

Miltner B, 'Revisiting Extraterritoriality after Al-Skeini: The ECHR and Its Lessons' (2012) 33 Michigan Journal of International Law 693

Morrison F, 'Condominium and Coimperium', *Max Planck Encyclopedia of Public International Law* (Oxford University Press 2006)

Moss HE, Tyler LK, and Taylor KI, *Conceptual Structure* (Oxford University Press 2007)

Müller-Mall S, *Legal Spaces: Towards a Topological Thinking of Law* (Springer 2013)

Natarajan U, 'Third World Approaches to International Law (TWAIL) and the Environment' in Andreas Philippopoulos-Mihalopoulos and Victoria Brooks (eds), *Research Methods in Environmental Law* (Edward Elgar Publishing 2017)

'Natural' <www.oxfordlearnersdictionaries.com/definition/english/natural_1>

'New Government Proposals a Wrecking Ball to the Right to Claim Asylum in the UK' (*Refugee Action*, 24 March 2021) <www.refugee-action.org.uk/new-government-proposals-a-wrecking-ball-to-the-right-to-claim-asylum-in-the-uk/> accessed 17 June 2021

Newman D, *Boundaries, Territory and Postmodernity* (Routledge 2013)

Nicholas B, *An Introduction to Roman Law* (Clarendon Press 1962)

Nijman JE, 'Renaissance of the City as Global Actor' in Gunther Hellmann, Fahrmeir Andreas, and Milo Vec (eds), *The Role of Foreign Policy and International Law Practices in the Construction of Cities as Global Actors* (Oxford University Press 2016)

Novak G, 'Overseas Territories, Australia, France, Netherlands, New Zealand, United Kingdom, United States of America', *Oxford Public International Law (OPIL)* (Oxford University Press 2013)

O'Carroll L and Jones S, '"It Was a Fake Meeting": Byron Hamburgers Staff on Immigration Raid' *The Guardian* (Online, 28 July 2016) <www.theguardian.com/uk-news/2016/jul/28/it-was-a-fake-meeting-byron-hamburgers-staff-on-immigration-raid> accessed 1 May 2019

O'Connell DP, *International Law for Students* (Stevens & Sons 1971)

Ogle V, 'Archipelago Capitalism: Tax Havens, Offshore Money, and the State, 1950s–1970s' (2017) 122 The American Historical Review 1431

O'Keefe R, 'The Doctrine of Incorporation Revisited' (2008) 79 British Yearbook of International Law

'Cooperative National Regulation to Secure Transnational Public Goods: A Reply to Nico Krisch' (2022) 33 European Journal of International Law 515

Oppenheim L, *International Law: A Treatise, Vol. 1 Peace* (2nd edition, Longmans, Green & Co 1912)

Orford A, 'Jurisdiction without Territory: From the Holy Roman Empire to the Responsibility to Protect' (2008) 30 Michigan Journal of International Law 981

Osiander A, 'Before Sovereignty: Society and Politics in Ancien Régime Europe' (2001a) 27 Review of International Studies 119

'Sovereignty, International Relations, and the Westphalian Myth' (2001b) 55 International Organization 251

Before the State: Systemic Political Change in the West from the Greeks to the French Revolution (Oxford University Press 2007)

Oude Elferink AG, 'The Outer Limits of the Continental Shelf beyond 200 Nautical Miles under the Framework of Article 76 of the United Nations Convention on the Law of the Sea (LOSC)', Presentation to the Seminar on the Establishment of the Outer Limits of the Continental Shelf beyond 200 Nautical Miles under UNCLOS: Its Implications for International Law (Tokyo, Japan, 27 February 2008) organised by the Ocean Policy Research Foundation

Paasivirta E, 'The European Union and the United Nations Convention on the Law of the Sea' (2015) 38 Fordham International Law Journal 1045–1071

Painter J, 'Rethinking Territory' (2010) 42 Antipode 1090

Palan R, 'Trying to Have Your Cake and Eating It: How and Why the State System Has Created Offshore' (1998) 42 International Studies Quarterly 625

Palchetti P, 'Unique, Special, or Simply a Primus Inter Pares? The European Union in International Law.' (2018) 29 European Journal of International Law 1409

Parkin J, *Money Code Space Hidden Power in Bitcoin, Blockchain, and Decentralisation* (Oxford University Press 2020)

Pearson Z, 'Spaces of International Law' (2008) 17 Griffith Law Review 489

Perrone NM, 'Neoliberalism and Economic Sovereignty: Property, Contracts, and Foreign Investment Relations' in Honor Brabazon (ed), *Neoliberal Legality: Understanding the Role of Law in the Neoliberal Project* (Routledge 2017)

Pickles J, *A History of Spaces: Cartographic Reason, Mapping, and the Geo-coded World* (Routledge 2004)

Pinto MCW, 'Article 76 of the UN Convention on the Law of the Sea and the Bay of Bengal Exception' (2013a) 3 Asian Journal of International Law 215

'The Common Heritage of Mankind: Then and Now' (2013b) 361 Collected Courses of the Hague Academy of International Law 9–128

Pistor K, 'From Territorial to Monetary Sovereignty' (2017) 18 Theoretical Inquiries in Law 491

The Code of Capital: How the Law Creates Wealth and Inequality (Princeton University Press 2019)

Poe M, 'Episode: Milton Santos. "For a New Geography" (U Minnesota Press, 2021)', *New Books in Critical Theory podcast* (8 June 2022) <https://podcastrepublic.net/podcast/593872749 > 26 October 2023

Popescu G, 'Borders and Boundaries' in Barney Warf (ed), *Encyclopedia of Geography* (SAGE Publications, Inc 2010) 293

'Deterritorialisation and Reterritorialisation' in Barney Warf (ed), *Encyclopedia of Geography* (SAGE Publications, Inc 2010)

Poulantzas N, *State, Power, Socialism* (Verso 2000)

Prost M, '"One Vast Gasoline Station for Human Exploitation": Sovereignty as Anthropocentric Extraction' in Vincent Chapaux, Frédéric Mégret, and

Usha Natarajan (eds), *The Routledge Handbook of International Law and Anthropocentrism* (Routledge 2023)

Prout S and Howitt R, 'Frontier Imaginings and Subversive Indigenous Spatialities' (2009) 25 Journal of Rural Studies 396

Querci I, 'Oxford International Organisations (OXIO) "Agreement Relating to the Implementation of Part XI of the United Nations Convention on the Law of the Sea of 10 December 1982 (UNCLOS)"' [2017a] OXIO 289

'Oxford International Organisations (OXIO) "Convention on the Law of the Sea, 10th December 1982 (1833 UNTS 3, UKTS 81 (1999), UN Doc A/Conf.62/122, UN Reg No I-31363)"' [2017b] OXIO 216

Raible L, 'Title to Territory and Jurisdiction in International Human Rights Law: Three Models for a Fraught Relationship' (2018) 31 Leiden Journal of International Law 315

Rajkovic NM, 'The Visual Conquest of International Law: Brute Boundaries, the Map, and the Legacy of Cartogenesis' (2018) 31 Leiden Journal of International Law 267

Rasulov A, 'Advanced International Law, Seminar 1, Class Handout "The Austinian Challenge"' (2016a)

'Advanced International Law, Seminar 3 Handout: Legal Realism' (2016b)

Raustiala K, 'The Geography of Justice' (2004) 73 Fordham Law Review 2501

Reynolds S and Muggeridge H, 'Remote Controls: How UK Border Controls Are Endangering the Lives of Refugees' (Refugee Council 2008)

Rodenhauser T, 'Another Brick in the Wall: Carrier Sanctions and the Privatization of Immigration Control' (2014) 26 International Journal of Refugee Law 223

Rorty R, *Objectivity, Relativism and Truth* (Cambridge University Press 1991)

Rosenne S, *The Perplexities of Modern International Law, General Course on Public International Law*, vol 291 (2001) (Martinus Nijhoff Publishers 2002)

Roth R, 'The Challenges of Mapping Complex Indigenous Spatiality: From Abstract Space to Dwelling Space' (2009) 16 Cultural Geographies 207

Rovira MG-S, 'Karl Viktor Fricker, On State Territory (1867)' (2017) 5 London Review of International Law 319

Ryngaert C, *Jurisdiction in International Law* (2nd edition, Oxford University Press 2015)

'The Concept of Jurisdiction in International Law' in Alexander Orakhelashvili (ed), *Research Handbook on Jurisdiction and Immunities in International Law* (Edward Elgar Publishing 2015)

Ryngaert C and Zoetekouw M, 'The End of Territory? The Re-Emergence of Community as a Principle of Jurisdictional Order in the Internet Era' (Social Science Research Network 2014) SSRN Scholarly Paper ID 2523354 <https://papers.ssrn.com/abstract=2523354> accessed 5 March 2020

Sack R, *Human Territoriality: Its Theory and History* (Cambridge University Press 2009)

Said EW, *Peace and Its Discontents: Essays on Palestine in the Middle East Peace Process* (Vintage Books 1996) 28–29

Orientalism (Penguin Books 2003)

Santos M, *The Nature of Space* (Brenda Baletti tr, Duke University Press 2021)

Sassen S, 'The State and Economic Globalization: Any Implications for International Law?' (2000) 1 Chicago Journal of International Law 109

Territory, Authority, Rights: From Medieval to Global Assemblages, vol 4 (Cambridge University Press 2006)

Territory, Authority, Rights: From Medieval to Global Assemblages (Updated edition, Princeton University Press 2008)

'When Territory Deborders Territoriality' (2013) 1 Territory, Politics, Governance 21

Schachter O, 'The Decline of the Nation-State and Its Implications for International Law' (1997) 36 Columbia Journal of Transnational Law 7

Schlag P, 'The Brilliant, the Curious and the Wrong' (1986) 39 Stanford Law Review 917

The Enchantment of Reason (Duke University Press 1998)

'How to Do Things with Hohfeld' (2015) 78 Law and Contemporary Problems 185

Schloenhardt A and Craig C, '"Turning Back the Boats": Australia's Interdiction of Irregular Migrants at Sea' (2015) 27 International Journal of Refugee Law 536

Schmidt R, *Regulatory Integration across Borders: Public–Private Cooperation in Transnational Regulation* (Cambridge University Press 2018)

Schrijver NJ, 'Fifty Years Permanent Sovereignty over Natural Resources' in Mark Bungenberg and Stephan Hobe (eds), *Permanent Sovereignty over Natural Resources* (Springer 2015)

Schultz K, 'Sri Lanka, Struggling with Debt, Hands a Major Port to China' *The New York Times* (7 August 2018) <www.nytimes.com/2017/12/12/world/asia/sri-lanka-china-port.html> accessed 26 May 2019

Schwarzenberger G and Brown ED, *A Manual of International Law* (6th edition, Professional Books Limited 1976)

Scott J, 'The Geographical Scope of the EU's Climate Responsibilities' (2015) 17 Cambridge Yearbook of European Legal Studies 92

Scott JC, *Seeing Like a State: How Certain Schemes to Improve the Human Condition Have Failed* (Yale University Press 1998)

Searle J, *The Construction of Social Reality* (The Free Press 1995)

Setser BW, 'Borders Still Matter; "The World Isn't as Flat as It Used to Be"' *Council on Foreign Relations* (29 April 2008) <www.cfr.org/blog/borders-still-matter-world-isnt-flat-it-used-be access> accessed 12 October 2023

Shah N, 'The Territorial Trap of the Territorial Trap: Global Transformation and the Problem of the State's Two Territories' (2012) 6 International Political Sociology 57

Shaw M, *International Law* (7th edition, Cambridge University Press 2014)

International Law (8th edition, Cambridge University Press 2017)

Shaw MN, 'Territory in International Law' (1982) 13 Netherlands Yearbook of International Law 61

Shaxson N, *Treasure Islands: Tax Havens and the Men Who Stole the World* (The Bodley Head 2011)

Sheller M and Urry J, 'The New Mobilities Paradigm' (2006) 38 Environment and Planning A: Economy and Space 207

Sheppard E, 'Geography or Economics? Conceptions of Space, Time, Interdependence, and Agency' in Gordon L Clark and others (eds), *The Oxford Handbook of Economic Geography* (Oxford University Press 2003)

Simma B and others (eds), *The Charter of the United Nations: A Commentary* (3rd edition, Oxford University Press 2012)

Singer JW, 'The Legal Rights Debate in Analytical Jurisprudence from Bentham to Hohfeld' [1982] Wisconsin Law Review 975

Slaughter A and Crisp J, 'A Surrogate State? The Role of UNHCR in Protracted Refugee Situations' (2009) Research Paper No. 168 UNHCR Policy Development and Evaluation Service <www.unhcr.org/4981cb432.pdf> accessed 28 April 2017

Sloterdijk P, 'Geometry in the Colossal: The Project of Metaphysical Globalization' (2009) 27 Environment and Planning D: Society and Space 29

Soja EW, *Postmodern Geographies: The Reassertion of Space in Critical Social Theory* (Verso 2010)

Sokol M, *Economic Geographies of Globalisation* (Edward Elgar Publishing 2011)

Sørensen G, *Changes in Statehood: The Transformation of International Relations* (Palgrave Macmillan 2001)

'"Spaces beyond Sovereignty: International Law Outside of Territorial Jurisdiction" 28th Annual SLS/BIICL Workshop on Theory in International Law' (2019) <www.biicl.org/events/11298/28th-annual-slsbiicl-workshop-on-theory-in-international-law> accessed 26 October 2023

Spruyt H, *The Sovereign State and Its Competitors: An Analysis of Systems Change* (Princeton University Press 1994)

Staden AV and Vollaard H, *The Erosion of State Sovereignty: Towards a Post-Territorial World?* (Oxford University Press 2002)

Storey D, 'Territory and Territoriality', *Oxford Bibliographies* (Oxford University Press 2017)

Storr C, 'Denaturalising the Concept of Territory in International Law' in Julia Dehm and Usha Natarajan (eds), *Locating Nature: Making and Unmaking International Law* (Cambridge University Press 2022)

Strandsbjerg J, *Territory, Globalization and International Relations: The Cartographic Reality of Space* (Palgrave Macmillan 2010)

Suarez SV, *The Outer Limits of the Continental Shelf: Legal Aspects of Their Establishment* (Springer 2008)

Sur S, 'The State between Fragmentation and Globalization' (1997) 8 European Journal of International Law 421

Syal R, 'National Borders Are Becoming Irrelevant, Says John McDonnell' *The Guardian* (31 January 2016) <www.theguardian.com/world/2016/jan/31/john-mcdonnell-open-borders-irrelevant-yvette-cooper-bbc-sunday-politics> accessed 12 October 2023

Szigeti P, 'Territorial Bias in International Law: Attribution in State and Corporate Responsibility' (2009) 19 Journal of Transnational Law and Policy 311

TAB, 'The Relativity of Knowledge and 2D vs. 3D Thinking. . .' (Medium, June 2018) <https://allbungled.medium.com/the-relativity-of-knowledge-and-2d-vs-3d-thinking-9aaea1472931> accessed 28 October 2023

Tally R Jnr, *Spatiality* (1st edition, Routledge 2012)

Taylor L and Schroeder R, 'Is Bigger Better? The Emergence of Big Data as a Tool for International Development Policy' (2015) 80 GeoJournal 503

Teubner G and Fischer-Lescano A, 'Saving Refugee Lives: Syria's Displaced Are Best Helped as Close to Home as Possible' [6 August 2016] *The Spectator* < www.spectator.co.uk/article/saving-refugee-lives/> accessed 26 October 2023

Thirlway H, *Concepts, Principles, Rules and Analogies: International and Municipal Legal Reasoning*, vol 294 (Martinus Nijhoff Publishers 2002)

Thrift N, 'It's the Little Things' in David Atkinson and Klaus Dodds (eds), *Geopolitical Traditions. A Century of Geopolitical Thought* (Routledge 2000)

Tomuschat C, 'Obligations Arising for States without or against Their Will' (1994) 241 The Hague Academy of International Law 195

Topping A, 'Universities Being Used as Proxy Border Police, Say Academics' *The Guardian* (2 March 2014) <www.theguardian.com/education/2014/mar/02/universities-border-police-academics> accessed 1 May 2019

Turner C, 'Jacques Derrida: Deconstruction' (*Critical Legal Thinking*, 27 May 2016) <http://criticallegalthinking.com/2016/05/27/jacques-derrida-deconstruction/> accessed 3 July 2019

'UN Forum Spotlights Cities, Where Struggle for Sustainability "Will Be Won or Lost"' (*United Nations Sustainable Development*, 12 July 2018) <www.un.org/sustainabledevelopment/blog/2018/07/un-forum-spotlights-cities-where-struggle-for-sustainability-will-be-won-or-lost-2/>accessed 26 October July 2023

'UN Launches Guide for Countries to Improve Location-Based Data Management to Better Inform Decision-Making' (*UN News*, 1 August 2018) <https://news.un.org/en/story/2018/08/1016162> accessed 29 July 2019

Unger RM, *Social Theory: Its Situation and Its Task* (Cambridge University Press 1987)

'The United Nations and Decolonization: Non-Self-Governing Territories' (United Nations) <www.un.org/en/decolonization/nonselfgovterritories.shtml> accessed 10 April 2018

Valverde M, 'Seeing Like a City: The Dialectic of Modern and Premodern Ways of Seeing in Urban Governance' (2011) 45 Law & Society Review 277

Chronotopes of Law: Jurisdiction, Scale and Governance (1st edition, Routledge 2015)

Van Dyke JM, 'Legal Issues Related to Sovereignty over Dokdo and Its Maritime Boundary' (2007) 38 Ocean Development & International Law 157

van Kleffens EN, 'Sovereignty in International Law: Five Lectures (Volume 082)' (1953) 82 Collected Courses of the Hague Academy of International Law 1–131

Van Schendel W, 'Stateless in South Asia: The Making of the India–Bangladesh Enclaves' (2002) 61 The Journal of Asian Studies 115

Van Staden A and Vollaard H, *The Erosion of State Sovereignty: Towards a Post-Territorial World?* (Oxford University Press 2002)

VanValkenburgh P, '"Indigenous Agency, Infrastructure, and Place-Making" at did Forced Population Displacements and the Making of the Modern World' (Brown International Advanced Research Institutes (BIARI), Brown University, 5 June 2017a)

'Unsettling Time: Persistence and Memory in Spanish Colonial Peru' (2017b) 24 Journal of Archaeological Method and Theory 117

Vehlken S, 'Pervasive Intelligence: The Tempo-spatiality of Drone Swarms' (2018) 4 Digital Culture & Society 107

Verzijl JHW, Heere WP, and Offerhaus JPS, *International Law in Historical Perspective* (Sijthoff 1968)

Vradis A and others, *New Borders: Hotspots and the European Migration Regime* (Pluto Press 2019)

Walker N, *Sovereignty in Transition* (Hart 2003)

Walker RBJ, 'The Territorial State and the Theme of Gulliver' (1984) 39 International Journal 529

Wallace R, *International Law* (Sweet & Maxwell 1986)

White GW, *Nation, State and Territory. Vol. 1, Origins, Evolutions and Relationships* (Rowman & Littlefield Publishers 2004)

Wight M, *Systems of State* (Hedley Bull (ed), 1st edition, Continuum International Publishing 1977)

Williams A, 'Public Functions and Amenability: Recent Trends' (2017) 22 Judicial Review 15

Wilson TM and Donnan H (eds), *A Companion to Border Studies* (Wiley-Blackwell 2012)

Wonders NA, 'Globalization, Border Reconstruction Projects, and Transnational Crime' (2007) 34 Social Justice 33

Wong D, 'Sovereignty Sunk? The Position of "Sinking States" at International Law' (2013) 14 Melbourne Journal of International Law 346–91

Wordsworth D, 'Mind Your Language' (2008) 306 Spectator 62

Worster WT, 'The Role of the Map in International Law' [2017] SSRN Electronic Journal

'The Frailties of Maps as Evidence in International Law' (2018) 9 Journal of International Dispute Settlement 570

Yao J, *The Ideal River: How Control of Nature Shaped the International Order* (Manchester University Press 2022)

Zhang Y and others, 'Geometric Spatial Structure of Traditional Tibetan Settlements of Degger County, China: A Case Study of Four Villages' (2018) 7 Frontiers of Architectural Research 304

Zumbansen PC, 'Defining the Space of Transnational Law: Legal Theory, Global Governance & Legal Pluralism' (2011) <https://papers.ssrn.com/abstract=1934044> accessed 14 March 2021

The Oxford Handbook of Transnational Law (Peer Zumbansen (ed), Oxford University Press 2021a)

'Transnational Law: Theories and Applications' in Peer Zumbansen (ed), *The Oxford Handbook of Transnational Law* (Oxford University Press 2021b) 5

INDEX

CAMBRIDGE STUDIES IN INTERNATIONAL AND COMPARATIVE LAW

Books in the Series

186 *The Rebirth of Territory*
Gail Lythgoe

185 *Reimagining Sustainable Development in International Law: Perspectives from African Legal Cosmologies*
Godwin Eli Kwadzo Dzah

184 *Collective Self-Defence in International Law*
James A. Green

183 *Weaponising Evidence: A History of Tobacco Control in International Law*
Margherita Melillo

182 *The Justice Factory: Management Practices at the International Criminal Court*
Richard Clements

181 *A Communitarian Theory of WTO Law*
Chi Carmody

180 *Drones and International Law: A Techno-Legal Machinery*
Mignot-Mahdavi

179 *The Necessity of Nature: God, Science and Money in 17th Century English Law of Nature*
Mónica García-Salmones

178 *Making the World Safe for Investment: The Protection of Foreign Property 1922–1959*
Andrea Leiter

177 *National Governance and Investment Treaties*
Josef Ostřanský and Facundo Pérez Aznar

176 *Who Owns Outer Space? International Law, Astrophysics, and the Sustainable Development of Space*
Michael Byers and Aaron Boley

175 *Intervening in International Justice: Third States before Courts and Tribunals*
Brian McGarry

174 *Reciprocity in Public International Law*
Arianna Whelan

173 *When Environmental Protection and Human Rights Collide*
Marie-Catherine Petersmann

172 *The International Law of Sovereign Debt Dispute Settlement*
Kei Nakajima

171 *The Everyday Makers of International Law: From Great Halls to Back Rooms*
Tommaso Soave

170 *Virtue in Global Governance: Judgment and Discretion*
Jan Klabbers

169 *The Effects of Armed Conflict on Investment Treaties*
Tobias Ackermann

168 *Investment Law's Alibis: Colonialism, Imperialism, Debt and Development*
David Schneiderman

167 *Negative Comparative Law: A Strong Programme for Weak Thought*
Pierre Legrand

166 *Detention by Non-State Armed Groups under International Law*
Ezequiel Heffes

165 *Rebellions and Civil Wars: State Responsibility for the Conduct of Insurgents*
Patrick Dumberry

164 *The International Law of Energy*
Jorge Viñuales

163 *The Three Ages of International Commercial Arbitration*
Mikaël Schinazi

162 *Repetition and International Law*
Wouter Werner

161 *State Responsibility and Rebels: The History and Legacy of Protecting Investment Against Revolution*
Kathryn Greenman

160 *Rewriting Histories of the Use of Force: The Narrative of 'Indifference'*
Agatha Verdebout

159 *The League of Nations and the Protection of the Environment*
Omer Aloni

158 *International Investment Law and Legal Theory: Expropriation and the Fragmentation of Sources*
Jörg Kammerhofer

157 *Legal Barbarians: Identity, Modern Comparative Law and the Global South*
Daniel Bonilla Maldonado

156 *International Human Rights Law Beyond State Territorial Control*
Antal Berkes

155 *The Crime of Aggression under the Rome Statute of the International Criminal Court*
Carrie McDougall

154 *Minorities and the Making of Postcolonial States in International Law*
Mohammad Shahabuddin

153 *Preclassical Conflict of Laws*
Nikitas E. Hatzimihail

152 *International Law and History: Modern Interfaces*
Ignacio de la Rasilla

151 *Marketing Global Justice: The Political Economy of International Criminal Law*
Christine Schwöbel-Patel

150 *International Status in the Shadow of Empire*
Cait Storr

149 *Treaties in Motion: The Evolution of Treaties from Formation to Termination*
Edited by Malgosia Fitzmaurice, and Panos Merkouris

148 *Humanitarian Disarmament: An Historical Enquiry*
Treasa Dunworth

147 *Complementarity, Catalysts, Compliance: The International Criminal Court in Uganda, Kenya, and the Democratic Republic of Congo*
Christian M. De Vos

146 *Cyber Operations and International Law*
François Delerue

145 *Comparative Reasoning in International Courts and Tribunals*
Daniel Peat

144 *Maritime Delimitation as a Judicial Process*
Massimo Lando

143 *Prosecuting Sexual and Gender-Based Crimes at the International Criminal Court: Practice, Progress and Potential*
Rosemary Grey

142 *Capitalism As Civilisation: A History of International Law*
Ntina Tzouvala

141 *Sovereignty in China: A Genealogy of a Concept Since 1840*
Adele Carrai

140 *Narratives of Hunger in International Law: Feeding the World in Times of Climate Change*
Anne Saab

139 *Victim Reparation under the Ius Post Bellum: An Historical and Normative Perspective*
Shavana Musa

138 *The Analogy between States and International Organizations*
Fernando Lusa Bordin

137 *The Process of International Legal Reproduction: Inequality, Historiography, Resistance*
Rose Parfitt

136 *State Responsibility for Breaches of Investment Contracts*
Jean Ho

135 *Coalitions of the Willing and International Law: The Interplay between Formality and Informality*
Alejandro Rodiles

134 *Self-Determination in Disputed Colonial Territories*
Jamie Trinidad

133 *International Law as a Belief System*
Jean d'Aspremont

132 *Legal Consequences of Peremptory Norms in International Law*
Daniel Costelloe

131 *Third-Party Countermeasures in International Law*
Martin Dawidowicz

130 *Justification and Excuse in International Law: Concept and Theory of General Defences*
Federica Paddeu

129 *Exclusion from Public Space: A Comparative Constitutional Analysis*
Daniel Moeckli

128 *Provisional Measures before International Courts and Tribunals*
Cameron A. Miles

127 *Humanity at Sea: Maritime Migration and the Foundations of International Law*
Itamar Mann

126 *Beyond Human Rights: The Legal Status of the Individual in International Law*
Anne Peters

125 *The Doctrine of Odious Debt in International Law: A Restatement*
Jeff King

124 *Static and Evolutive Treaty Interpretation: A Functional Reconstruction*
Christian Djeffal

123 *Civil Liability in Europe for Terrorism-Related Risk*
Lucas Bergkamp, Michael Faure, Monika Hinteregger and Niels Philipsen

122 *Proportionality and Deference in Investor-State Arbitration: Balancing Investment Protection and Regulatory Autonomy*
Caroline Henckels

121 *International Law and Governance of Natural Resources in Conflict and Post-Conflict Situations*
Daniëlla Dam-de Jong

120 *Proof of Causation in Tort Law*
Sandy Steel

119 *The Formation and Identification of Rules of Customary International Law in International Investment Law*

118 *Religious Hatred and International Law: The Prohibition of Incitement to Violence or Discrimination*
Jeroen Temperman

117 *Taking Economic, Social and Cultural Rights Seriously in International Criminal Law*
Evelyne Schmid

116 *Climate Change Litigation: Regulatory Pathways to Cleaner Energy*
Jacqueline Peel and Hari M. Osofsky

115 *Mestizo International Law: A Global Intellectual History 1842–1933*
Arnulf Becker Lorca

114 *Sugar and the Making of International Trade Law*
Michael Fakhri

113 *Strategically Created Treaty Conflicts and the Politics of International Law*
Surabhi Ranganathan

112 *Investment Treaty Arbitration As Public International Law: Procedural Aspects and Implications*
Eric De Brabandere

111 *The New Entrants Problem in International Fisheries Law*
Andrew Serdy

110 *Substantive Protection under Investment Treaties: A Legal and Economic Analysis*
Jonathan Bonnitcha

109 *Popular Governance of Post-Conflict Reconstruction: The Role of International Law*
Matthew Saul

108 *Evolution of International Environmental Regimes: The Case of Climate Change*
Simone Schiele

107 *Judges, Law and War: The Judicial Development of International Humanitarian Law*
Shane Darcy

106 *Religious Offence and Human Rights: The Implications of Defamation of Religions*
Lorenz Langer

105 *Forum Shopping in International Adjudication: The Role of Preliminary Objections*
Luiz Eduardo Salles

104 *Domestic Politics and International Human Rights Tribunals: The Problem of Compliance*
Courtney Hillebrecht

103 *International Law and the Arctic*
Michael Byers

102 *Cooperation in the Law of Transboundary Water Resources*
Christina Leb

101 *Underwater Cultural Heritage and International Law*
Sarah Dromgoole

100 *State Responsibility: The General Part*
James Crawford

99 *The Origins of International Investment Law: Empire, Environment and the Safeguarding of Capital*
Kate Miles

98 *The Crime of Aggression under the Rome Statute of the International Criminal Court*
Carrie McDougall

97 *'Crimes against Peace' and International Law*
Kirsten Sellars

96 *Non-Legality in International Law: Unruly Law*
Fleur Johns

95 *Armed Conflict and Displacement: The Protection of Refugees and Displaced Persons under International Humanitarian Law*
Mélanie Jacques

94 *Foreign Investment and the Environment in International Law*
Jorge E. Viñuales

93 *The Human Rights Treaty Obligations of Peacekeepers*
Kjetil Mujezinović Larsen

92 *Cyber Warfare and the Laws of War*
Heather Harrison Dinniss

91 *The Right to Reparation in International Law for Victims of Armed Conflict*
Christine Evans

90 *Global Public Interest in International Investment Law*
Andreas Kulick

89 *State Immunity in International Law*
Xiaodong Yang

88 *Reparations and Victim Support in the International Criminal Court*
Conor McCarthy

87 *Reducing Genocide to Law: Definition, Meaning, and the Ultimate Crime*
Payam Akhavan

86 *Decolonising International Law: Development, Economic Growth and the Politics of Universality*
Sundhya Pahuja

85 *Complicity and the Law of State Responsibility*
Helmut Philipp Aust

84 *State Control over Private Military and Security Companies in Armed Conflict*
Hannah Tonkin

83 *'Fair and Equitable Treatment' in International Investment Law*
Roland Kläger

82 *The UN and Human Rights: Who Guards the Guardians?*
Guglielmo Verdirame

81 *Sovereign Defaults before International Courts and Tribunals*
Michael Waibel

80 *Making the Law of the Sea: A Study in the Development of International Law*
James Harrison

79 *Science and the Precautionary Principle in International Courts and Tribunals: Expert Evidence, Burden of Proof and Finality*
Caroline E. Foster

78 *Transition from Illegal Regimes under International Law*
Yaël Ronen

77 *Access to Asylum: International Refugee Law and the Globalisation of Migration Control*
Thomas Gammeltoft-Hansen

76 *Trading Fish, Saving Fish: The Interaction between Regimes in International Law*
Margaret A. Young

75 *The Individual in the International Legal System: Continuity and Change in International Law*
Kate Parlett

74 *'Armed Attack' and Article 51 of the UN Charter: Evolutions in Customary Law and Practice*
Tom Ruys

73 *Theatre of the Rule of Law: Transnational Legal Intervention in Theory and Practice*
Stephen Humphreys

72 *Science and Risk Regulation in International Law*
Jacqueline Peel

71 *The Participation of States in International Organisations: The Role of Human Rights and Democracy*
Alison Duxbury

70 *Legal Personality in International Law*
Roland Portmann

69 *Vicarious Liability in Tort: A Comparative Perspective*
Paula Giliker

68 *The Public International Law Theory of Hans Kelsen: Believing in Universal Law*
Jochen von Bernstorff

67 *Legitimacy and Legality in International Law: An Interactional Account*
Jutta Brunnée and Stephen J. Toope

66 *The Concept of Non-International Armed Conflict in International Humanitarian Law*
Anthony Cullen

65 *The Principle of Legality in International and Comparative Criminal Law*
Kenneth S. Gallant

64 *The Challenge of Child Labour in International Law*
Franziska Humbert

63 *Shipping Interdiction and the Law of the Sea*
Douglas Guilfoyle

62 *International Courts and Environmental Protection*
Tim Stephens

61 *Legal Principles in WTO Disputes*
Andrew D. Mitchell

60 *War Crimes in Internal Armed Conflicts*
Eve La Haye

59 *Humanitarian Occupation*
Gregory H. Fox

58 *The International Law of Environmental Impact Assessment: Process, Substance and Integration*
Neil Craik

57 *The Law and Practice of International Territorial Administration: Versailles to Iraq and Beyond*
Carsten Stahn

56 *United Nations Sanctions and the Rule of Law*
Jeremy Matam Farrall

55 *National Law in WTO Law: Effectiveness and Good Governance in the World Trading System*
Sharif Bhuiyan

54 *Cultural Products and the World Trade Organization*
Tania Voon

53 *The Threat of Force in International Law*
Nikolas Stürchler

52 *Indigenous Rights and United Nations Standards: Self-Determination, Culture and Land*
Alexandra Xanthaki

51 *International Refugee Law and Socio-Economic Rights: Refuge from Deprivation*
Michelle Foster

50 *The Protection of Cultural Property in Armed Conflict*
Roger O'Keefe

49 *Interpretation and Revision of International Boundary Decisions*
Kaiyan Homi Kaikobad

48 *Multinationals and Corporate Social Responsibility: Limitations and Opportunities in International Law*
Jennifer A. Zerk

47 *Judiciaries within Europe: A Comparative Review*
John Bell

46 *Law in Times of Crisis: Emergency Powers in Theory and Practice*
Oren Gross and Fionnuala Ní Aoláin

45 *Vessel-Source Marine Pollution: The Law and Politics of International Regulation*
Alan Khee-Jin Tan

44 *Enforcing Obligations Erga Omnes in International Law*
Christian J. Tams

43 *Non-Governmental Organisations in International Law*
Anna-Karin Lindblom

42 *Democracy, Minorities and International Law*
Steven Wheatley

41 *Prosecuting International Crimes: Selectivity and the International Criminal Law Regime*
Robert Cryer

40 *Compensation for Personal Injury in English, German and Italian Law: A Comparative Outline*
Basil Markesinis, Michael Coester, Guido Alpa and Augustus Ullstein

39 *Dispute Settlement in the UN Convention on the Law of the Sea*
Natalie Klein

38 *The International Protection of Internally Displaced Persons*
Catherine Phuong

37 *Imperialism, Sovereignty and the Making of International Law*
Antony Anghie

36 *Principles of the Institutional Law of International Organizations*
C. F. Amerasinghe

35 *Necessity, Proportionality and the Use of Force by States*
Judith Gardam

34 *International Legal Argument in the Permanent Court of International Justice: The Rise of the International Judiciary*
Ole Spiermann

33 -

32 *Great Powers and Outlaw States: Unequal Sovereigns in the International Legal Order*
Gerry Simpson

31 *Local Remedies in International Law (second edition)*
Chittharanjan Felix Amerasinghe

30 *Reading Humanitarian Intervention: Human Rights and the Use of Force in International Law*
Anne Orford

29 *Conflict of Norms in Public International Law: How WTO Law Relates to Other Rules of International Law*
Joost Pauwelyn

28 -

27 *Transboundary Damage in International Law*
Hanqin Xue

26 -

25 *European Criminal Procedures* Edited by
Mireille Delmas-Marty and J. R. Spencer

24 *Accountability of Armed Opposition Groups in International Law*
Liesbeth Zegveld

23 *Sharing Transboundary Resources: International Law and Optimal Resource Use*
Eyal Benvenisti

22 *International Human Rights and Humanitarian Law*
René Provost

21 *Remedies against International Organisations*
Karel Wellens

20 *Diversity and Self-Determination in International Law*
Karen Knop

19 *The Law of Internal Armed Conflict*
Lindsay Moir

18 *International Commercial Arbitration and African States: Practice, Participation and Institutional Development*
Amazu A. Asouzu

17 *The Enforceability of Promises in European Contract Law*
James Gordley

16 *International Law in Antiquity*
David J. Bederman

15 *Money Laundering: A New International Law Enforcement Model*
Guy Stessens

14 *Good Faith in European Contract Law*
Reinhard Zimmermann and Simon Whittaker

13 *On Civil Procedure*
J. A. Jolowicz

12 *Trusts: A Comparative Study*
Maurizio Lupoi and Simon Dix

11 *The Right to Property in Commonwealth Constitutions*
Tom Allen

10 *International Organizations before National Courts*
August Reinisch

9 *The Changing International Law of High Seas Fisheries*
Francisco Orrego Vicuña

8 *Trade and the Environment: A Comparative Study of EC and US Law*
Damien Geradin

7 *Unjust Enrichment: A Study of Private Law and Public Values*
Hanoch Dagan

6 *Religious Liberty and International Law in Europe*
Malcolm D. Evans

5 *Ethics and Authority in International Law*
Alfred P. Rubin

4 *Sovereignty over Natural Resources: Balancing Rights and Duties*
Nico Schrijver

3 *The Polar Regions and the Development of International Law*
Donald R. Rothwell

2 *Fragmentation and the International Relations of Micro-States: Self-Determination and Statehood*
Jorri C. Duursma

1 *Principles of the Institutional Law of International Organizations*
C. F. Amerasinghe

For EU product safety concerns, contact us at Calle de José Abascal, 56–1°, 28003 Madrid, Spain or eugpsr@cambridge.org.

www.ingramcontent.com/pod-product-compliance
Lightning Source LLC
LaVergne TN
LVHW011807200926
848484LV00005B/1097
* 9 7 8 1 0 0 9 3 7 7 9 1 1 *